Houston's Forgotten Heritage

Dorothy Knox Howe Houghton

Barrie M. Scardino

Sadie Gwin Blackburn

Katherine S. Howe

Houston's Forgotten Heritage

Landscape, Houses, Interiors, 1824–1914

A PROJECT OF THE JUNIOR LEAGUE OF HOUSTON, INC.

Rice University Press   Houston, Texas

Copyright 1991 by The Junior League of Houston, Inc.

Printed in U.S.A.

First Edition

Requests for permission to reproduce material

from this work should be addressed to:

Rice University Press, Rice University

Post Office Box 1892, Houston, Texas 77251

Library of Congress Cataloging-in-Publication Data

Houston's forgotten heritage : landscape, houses, interiors, 1824–1914 / by Dorothy Knox

   Howe Houghton . . . [et al.].

       p.   cm.

     "A project of the Junior League of Houston, Inc."

     Includes index.

     ISBN 0-89263-311-5 : (deluxe ed.) — ISBN 0-89263-310-7 : (regular ed.)

   1. Houston (Tex.)—Social life and customs. 2. Dwellings—Texas—Houston—History.

   3. Architecture, Domestic—Texas—Houston. 4. Interior decoration—Texas—Houston—

History. 5. Landscape—Texas—Houston—History. I. Houghton, Dorothy Knox Howe.

II. Blackburn, Sadie Gwin. III. Scardino, Barrie M. IV. Howe, Katherine S.

F394.H85H68 1991

976.4′1411—dc20   91-52944

                                                       CIP

Cover photograph courtesy of the Harris Masterson family

Contents

Foreword

William Scale

Houston was founded with exuberance and optimism by two New Yorkers in the summer of 1836. Perhaps it was hot coals of some sort, carried from their hometown to start the new city's fire, that made Houston different. If so, then the coals still glow. No other Texas city has ever quite matched it in civic pride yet happily remained so "Texan."

In terms of modern architecture the "new" Houston qualifies as one of the most exciting cities in the United States. To an outsider's eye, the highrise developments along the freeways expand downtown into many downtowns, each with its own character but unfolding into a magnificent cityscape that is nearly endless in its perspectives. The closer look is quite as remarkable, for the extravagant positioning of monumental commercial towers in wooded and landscaped parks has a wondrous effect that knows no rival anywhere.

What Houston does not share with some other Texas cities is a consistent visible past. Houston's has not been a mellow growing. The houses moved to Sam Houston Park were plucked from the path of an advancing city just in the nick of time, to survive as examples of architectural and decorative styles. That does not include the Key West–type Kellum-Noble house, which has always occupied that site. People like to have their pictures taken in Sam Houston Park, next to the quaint frame houses, with the monumental new city looming behind.

As our definition of old and historic broadens, forgotten neighborhoods emerge as places to preserve. But Houston has little of the feeling of a city that has grown through long years of layering. Very little has been left behind of the city as it was before World War I. With the recent demise of the Shamrock Hotel, even the beacon of new Houston is lost.

This book takes us to a time we can no longer see. It captures the visual past of houses and gardens and lives once lived in Houston. Embarking at the beginning, with the Allen brothers, the book carries us into twentieth-century waters, which are more familiar, if only because some of the houses remain. Rarely have reflections on a city produced so fascinating a text and comprehensive a collection of drawings and photographs. The five authors, all experts in their fields, have pursued their Houston subjects for some years. Few others have trod the same paths, and none so far as this. So the essays on history, architecture, gardening, domestic life, and interior decoration can stand singly as important contributions to American and Texas studies. As a collection within a single volume, they bring to us a particular interpretation along domestic lines, not of the admired Houston of modern times, but of the now invisible city that went before it.

Preface

Houston's Forgotten Heritage paints a broad picture of domestic life during the first ninety years of Harris County. Representative houses and their occupants illustrate patterns of settlement, architectural and landscape development, interior design, and the resulting lifestyles in a nineteenth-century southern city. Because pictorial and written records of early Harris County are fragmentary, documentation of many houses and families simply does not exist. Photographs for this book were chosen mostly from previously unpublished images found in private collections. In addition to availability, the criteria for choosing illustrations were the quality of the image, the architectural or historic significance of the structure, landscape, or interior decoration, and the picture's relevance to social or cultural matters discussed in the text. The prominence of homeowners socially or in the business community and connections of individuals to the Junior League were not considerations for inclusion in this book.

The idea of the book originated in 1970 with Dorothy Knox Howe Houghton and Francita Stuart Koelsch. Their own family collections, particularly images of houses, inspired them to search local libraries and the attics of other families with roots in nineteenth-century Harris County for more evidence of local houses and neighborhoods that had long since been demolished or altered beyond recognition.

By 1974 Francita was unable to continue with the project, but she encouraged Dorothy Knox to pursue their research, with the goal of eventual publication. Dorothy Knox consulted architectural historian Stephen Fox, who introduced her to his colleague, Barrie Myrick Scardino, at that time the architectural archivist of the Houston Metropolitan Research Center, Houston Public Library (HMRC).

After nearly two years of preparation by Dorothy Knox and Barrie the Junior League of Houston, Inc. voted to sponsor "Domestic Architecture in Harris County, 1824–1914" as one of its projects. Working under Dorothy Knox and Barrie, Junior League volunteers collected, processed, and cataloged private papers, photographs, and pertinent library holdings, creating the Junior League Component of the HMRC. This collection of more than 2000 photographs and 25 linear feet of research files from the papers of more than 200 families provided the basis for *Houston's Forgotten Heritage* and is now opened to the public.

As numerous photographs of early interiors and gardens were discovered, Katherine Howe and Sadie Gwin Blackburn were persuaded to write additional chapters. Although the book has four distinct voices, the final manuscript was a true collaboration.

The advice and perception of two other people were critical to the quality of the manuscript. Stephen Fox, Fellow of the Anchorage Foundation of Texas, was involved throughout the project. He initially suggested the format of the book, read and edited the manuscript, provided valuable insight and criticism, suggested new avenues of research, and proposed the title. Nancy Lynn Hadley, assistant archivist of HMRC and associate editor of *The Houston Review*, skillfully reorganized subject matter, shortened unwieldy manuscripts, and smoothed out complicated and sometimes ambiguous passages. Nancy also prepared the index. The authors are unanimous in their gratitude to both Stephen and Nancy.

Dr. Margaret Swett Henson, whose area of expertise includes Harris County history, was invited to set the historical background in an introduction. James Glass, an architect with vast knowledge of early Harris County, produced four historical maps for the book. Francita Koelsch remained as a valued adviser and liaison with sustaining members of the Junior League throughout the project. She has thoughtfully read the completed manuscript and provided helpful suggestions. Special credit belongs to the editors at Rice University Press, who not only molded the final manuscript into publishable form, but provided the authors years of free counseling. Their patience was unwavering, as was their belief that this book would indeed one day be finished. And so it has been. Thank you.

Through the cooperation and generosity of David Henington, director of the Houston Public Library, Ruby Weaver, chief of the central library, and Dr. Louis J. Marchiafava, archivist, this project was based in the archives of HMRC. Louis Marchiafava's support and advice have been particularly helpful during the last eight years. Under his direction and that of assistant archivist Thomas Krenek, library photographers Luciaan Blyaert (1982–89) and Charles R. Hamilton (1989–91) copied hundreds of photographs. Other members of the archives staff were always helpful, including Michael Wilson and Deborah Moore. Also cooperative were librarians in the Texas and Local History Department: Marian Brannan (1970–74), and her successor, Dorothy Glasser (1979–91), head librarians, Douglas Weiskopf, Carole Lee, Will Howard, Anne Douglas, and Ellen Hanlon. Muriel Mintz helped with administrative details.

The personnel of several other research centers and libraries also deserve thanks: Nancy Boothe, Woodson Research Center, Fondren Library, Rice University; Pat Bozeman and Stephen Bonario, Special Collections, and Margaret Culbertson, School of Architecture Library, University of Houston; Jane Ellen Cable, Jan Wyatt, and Brenda Jordan, Harris County Heritage Society; Casey Greene, Rosenberg Library, Galveston; Don Carleton, Barker Texas History Center, University of Texas, Austin; Darrell McDonald, University of Texas, Tyler; and Elaine Taylor Brown

Sullivan, Texas Memorial Museum, Austin. The University of St. Thomas, the Baytown Historical Museum, San Jacinto Museum of History and the M. D. Anderson Library, Texas Medical Center, also provided materials and information.

Members of our Advisory Committee were particularly supportive in the early years of the project: Nia Becnel, Pat Butler, Tuffly Ellis, Pat Fleming, Stephen Fox, Betsy Griffin, Margaret Henson, Francita Koelsch, Louis Marchiafava, J. C. Martin, Susie Morris, and Brooke Tucker.

In addition to those already mentioned, those cited in footnotes, donors, and Junior League volunteers, some of whom worked as research assistants for one author, each of us received specific help from professionals in our own areas. The authors would especially like to thank their families and others who through some oversight have escaped mention here.

Dorothy Knox Houghton would like to thank the members of other Junior Leagues that have published volumes on their communities who graciously shared their experiences and gave advice at the beginning of the project: Douglas Sprunt and Page Boteler, Washington, D.C.; Martha Nell Crow, San Francisco; Carol Johnson and Mary Collins, Tulsa; and Helen Hayes, Memphis. Dorothy Knox would also like to express appreciation to Francita's father, Robert C. Stuart, and to William A. Kirkland, Rosa Tod Hamner, and Charles B. Sanders, Jr.

Barrie Scardino would like to acknowledge several architects and planners who provided encouragement and made suggestions germane to her chapter: Howard Barnstone, Mike Davis, Peter Papademetriou, Bill Stern, and Drexel Turner.

Sadie Gwin Blackburn is particularly grateful for the help of the following individuals: Ellen Red; Carrington Weems; Antonia Day; Barbara Link; Beverly Turner McDonald; John Koros, director, Mercer Botanic Garden; James Buckler, director of the Office of Horticulture, Smithsonian Institution; Diane Kostel McGuire, Boston landscape architect; Denolm N. Jacobs, trustee of the Asticou Terrace Trust, Seal Harbor, Maine; Georgia Simmons Pierpoint; Nancy Volkman, professor of landscape architecture, Texas A & M; and her secretary, Joanne Wallace.

Katherine Howe wishes to thank Peter C. Marzio, David B. Warren, George T. Shakelford, Mary Brimberry, and Ann Wood of The Museum of Fine Arts, Houston; Kristin Moore and Karen Skaer, Rice University interns at the The Museum of Fine Arts; and Patrick Butler and Bradley Brooks for their contributions to her chapter.

The following individuals and families graciously donated materials, and some gave extensively of their time helping to document specific facts. Without their trust in lending valuable family papers this book would not have been possible: Alexander D. Adams, Louise Dickson Adams, Mary McAshan Adams, Henrietta Cargill Adkins family, Jacolyn Alexander, Mary Greenwood Anderson, W. Graham Arader III, Mrs. Charles L. Ashton, Deedo Bering Bailey, Mimi Ballanfant, Richard Burton Ballanfant, Harriet Bath, A. Linton Batjer, Mrs. Daniel Bayless, Audrey Jones Beck, August Charles Bering III, Frank Lee Berry, Jr., Katherine Hackney Bertelson, Bess Kirby Tooke Black, Gordon Black, Stuart Davis Blackshear, Mrs. Ben Blum, W. J. Bowen, Albert M. Bowles, Jr., Mira Virginia Thompson Braly, James Lanier Britton, Jr., Edwin Rice Brown, George Anna Lucas Burke, Janet C. Burroughs, Irene Miller Byrom, Betty Scott Cahill, Katharine Hume Seymour Calhoun, Ann Japhet Cantwell, Fannie Simpson

Carter, Mrs. William Thomas Carter III, Rosalie Sherman Cartwright, Grace Leavell Core, William Kendall Craig, Mary Cullinan Cravens, Gladys Crayton, Anne Heyck Cronin, Annie Lee Mitchell Cruse, Charlotte Williams Darby, Mrs. Alfred Neal Dargan, Dorothy Dunn Davis, Alma Detering, Charles Dillingham, Atha Marks Dimon, Mrs. Edmund McAshan Dupree, Charlene Lusk Dwyer, Eagle Lake Rod and Gun Club, Betty Lee Elgin, Mary Alice Elgin, Seger Ellis, Martha Vinson Emerson, Dorothy J. Evershade, Homoiselle Haden Fay, Tarrant Fendley, Genevieve Filson, Lucinda Stewart Fleming, Elizabeth Sinclair Flowers, Iris Coughlin Foote, John H. Freeman, Jr., Anne Cochran Frischkorn, Vernon Frost, Cynthia Maddox Crane Garbs, Helen H. Garrett, John Wanroy Garrow, Jr., James Glass, Glenwood Cemetery Association, Sallie Gordon, Bettye M. Green, James Greenwood, M. D., Mrs. Lloyd J. Gregory, Jr., Elizabeth Pearson Griffin, Mr. and Mrs. John Grimes, Ellen Ross Hail, Peggy Golding Hamill, Brooke Hamilton, Mrs. Harris Hammersmith, Rosa Tod Hamner, Eiko Arai Harper, Maybell Harris, Edith Howze Hartung, Shirley Dissen Haverlah, Gordon F. Hayslip, Mrs. Frederick W. Heitmann, Daisy Sturgis Hendrickson, Frances Heyck, Mary Taub Hibbert, Ray Watkin Hoagland, George F. Horton, Dorothy Knox Howe Houghton, Edward Mandell House II, Harris Milton Howe, Patricia Peckinpaugh Hubbard, Lennie Estelle Hunt, Edward Chappell Hutcheson, Joseph C. Hutcheson III, Palmer Hutcheson, Jr., Anne Hogan Irish, Juliana Williams Itz, Catherine Jackson, Mildred Shaw Jackson, Mr. & Mrs. John Jacobs, Helen Adele Murray Johnson, Dorothy E. Justman, Marion Frost Keenan, Virginia Meek Keenan, Margaret Wier Kelsey, Mrs. Sidney Sherman Kendall, William A. Kirkland, Mariann Adkins Kitchel, Nan and David Kleb, Thornwell Kleb, Francita Stuart Koelsch, Pauline Jackson Kunze, Tom H. Langham, Flora Streetman Lawhon, Lee Averill Lawrence, William H. Lawson, Louis Lechenger, Thomas Peter Lee, Marjorie Leskovjan, Earl L. Lester, Sr., Nella Neville Letzerich, Charlotte Goss Lindsey, Rosanne Stockdick Lopez, Helen Lorehn, Berthold Albert Lottman family, Elsa D. Lottman, Ursula Guseman Lusk, Mrs. Andrew M. MacMahon, Orline Dunn Maer, Hoyt T. Mattox, Nancy Nelms Maxwell, Pauline McCullough, Jeanne McElvouge, Sears McGee, Thomas D. McGown, Abbie Dell Drouet Meroney, Mr. and Mrs. Joseph F. Meyer III, Alice Baker Meyers, Charles Dow Milby, Marian Fowlkes Minniece, Gustave Antoine Mistrot III, Buddy and Kay Mitchell, Joan S. Moore, Lila Godwin Moore, Martha Scott Moore, Jane Philp Moreland, William H. Murray, Jeanne Boulet Nelson, Betty Bosworth Neuhaus, Louise Smith Neuhaus, Mary Claire Denman Newman, Richard C. Noble, Maud Gray Hester Norris, Mary M. O'Rourke, Carla Neff Ohls, Jane Blaffer Owen, Ruby Oates Owens, Edith Hamilton Pearson, Mary Bain Pearson, Jane Cochran Coleman Peck, Estelle Garrow Perlitz, Mary Louise Philp, Sue Pittman, Imogene Kennedy Plank, Bessie R. Powers, Peggy Dorrance Powers, Mary Frances Pugh, Evelyn Matzke Ramey, Ellen Robbins Red, Hattie Lel Red, W. Scott Red, Mary Carroll Reed, Lynne Beach Renaud, Robert Renn, Mrs. Roland Ring, Elaine Finrock Roberts, The Rockwell Fund, Inc., William Rubey, Ruth Arbuckle Russell, Roberta Wright Rylander, Peter L. Scardino, Pierre and Lesley Schlumberger, Jane Shudde Schoen, Henrietta Hutcheson Schwartz, Marie Coughlin Scott, Peggy Scrivner, Jo Ann Bering Sellingsloh, Glenn Emile Seureau, Betty Hall Sewell, Dudley C. Sharp, Elaine Brady Shelton, Howard F. Smith III, Lenora Guseman Smith, Cora Conner Spear, Mary Jane Price Sponsel, Florence Powars Stancliff, Blanche Heitmann Strange, Julia Hurd Strong, Micajah S. Stude, John F. Sullivan, Edna Earl Brazelton Taylor, Mrs. Tom Teas, James B. Tennant, Aurelia Hart Thacker, Elizabeth Waldo Thatcher, J. Bates Thomas, Jr., Chaille Cage Thompson, Charles H. Thomsen, Michelene Guseman Toomey, J. Kittredge Vinson, Mary Ann Walker, Diana Walzel, Rosemary Hamner Ward, Carrington Weems, Marjorie S. Werlein, Andrew H. White, Jr., Virginia Dunn Whitley, Mrs. Willoughby Williams, Bessie May Sternenberg Wright, Frances Boyles Davis Wyllie.

Presidents of the Junior League who reaffirmed the League's commitment from year to year were Sarah Jones Roady, Nancy Powell Moore, June Milton Gray, Leigh Flowers Bonner, Anne Peden Tucker, Mary Nell Jeffers Lovett, Marthanne Gregg Snyder, Allyson Priest Cook, Susan Penn French, and Frances Nelson Arnoult.

Many Junior Leaguers from the ranks of the administration were supportive, beginning with Patsy Speed, Mary Kay Kyger, Ann Kelsey, Linda Murphy, Martha Maer, Helen Allen, Jeanne Daniels, Margo Salmonsen, and Nancy Wells, who helped get the project approved in 1982. League secretaries Carolyn McCairns, Barbara Whitman, Sharron Kinnaird, and Mary Swift provided office assistance. Chairs and their assistants of the cultural projects who attended meetings, filed reports, and generally kept us going were Susan Light Lawhon, Carter Lee, Allyson Cook, Aline Wilson, Patsy Burrow, Renee Davis, Carol Hoppe, Frances Arnoult, Julianne Harris, Linda Bloss, Kacky Dunwoody, and Jennifer McClanahan.

Junior League members Ellie Lippincott, Gwynne Smith, Trish Freeman, Michelle Lowe, Sue Work, and Deannie Heppler compiled statistics from U. S. Census records, which Ellie and her husband, Charles Lippincott, used to create the population tables showing domestic and foreign immigration into Houston between 1850 and 1910. Although the level of commitment and the number of years involved varied among the many volunteers, ten made particularly outstanding contributions: Gaynor Beesley, Pamela Budzinsky, Dorothy Crocker, Peggy Dear, Karen Hanson Flowers, Julie Itz, Ann Kelsey, Lelia Rogers, Nancy Wells, and Laura Wilson. The work of all of our volunteers, others of whom are listed below, was greatly appreciated: Sarah Ballanfant, Minnette Boesel, Martha Bowen, Kristi Cassin, Madelyn DiCorcia, Ellen Donnelly, Susan Elsaesser, Anne Eppright, Ethel Fisher, Anne Frischkorn, Tiggy Garrett, Deirdre Glober, Cynthia Grace, Catherine Hustedt, Susan Keeton, Letty Knapp, Betty Lander, Mary Ann Layden, Sharon Lorenzo, Debra Mangini, Lorez McGinnis, Carla Ohls, Dodie Otey, Carolyn Payne, Louise Rauls, Lynn Rawson, Ruth Russell, Cora Spear, Carey Shuart, Ellen Simmons, Clare Smith, Nancy Wheless, Caroline Williams.

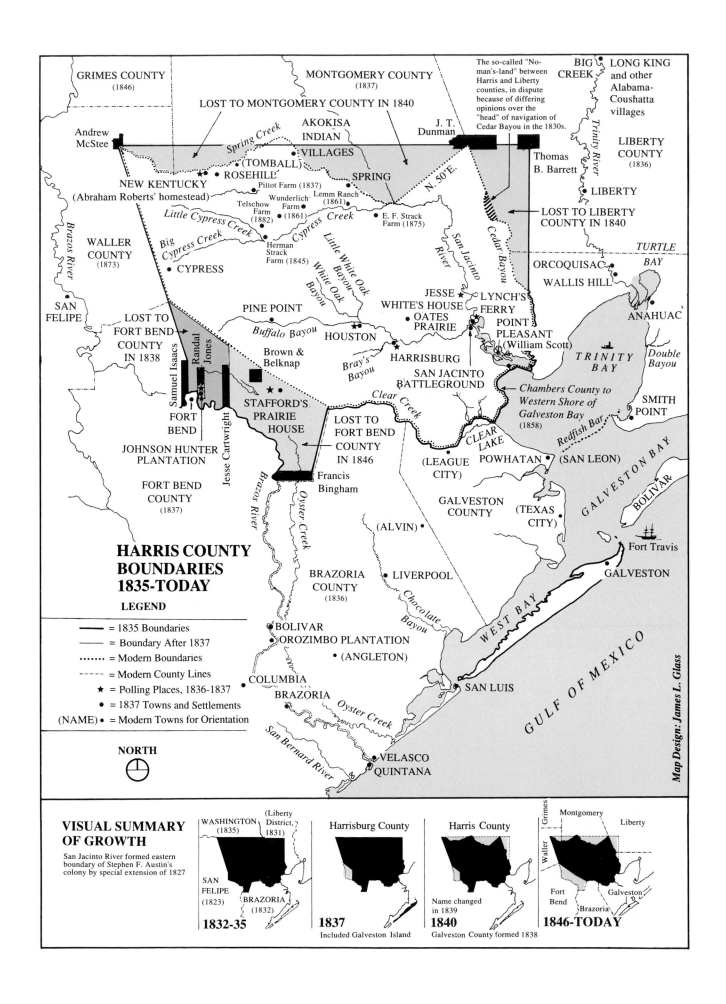

GRIMES COUNTY
(1846)

MONTGOMERY COUNTY
(1837)

LOST TO MONTGOMERY COUNTY IN 1840

AKOKISA
INDIAN
VILLAGES
(TOMBALL)

BIG
CREEK

LONG KING
and other
Alabama-
Coushatta
villages

The so-called "No-man's-land" between Harris and Liberty counties, in dispute because of differing opinions over the "head" of navigation of Cedar Bayou in the 1830s.

J. T.
Dunman

Andrew
McStee

Spring Creek

LIBERTY
COUNTY
(1836)

NEW KENTUCKY
(Abraham Roberts' homestead)

ROSEHILL

SPRING

N. 50°E.

Thomas
B. Barrett

Pillot Farm (1837)

Wunderlich
Farm
(1861)

Lemm Ranch
(1861)

LIBERTY

Brazos River

WALLER
COUNTY
(1873)

Telschow
Farm
(1882)

Little Cypress Creek

(1861)

Cypress Creek

E. F. Strack
Farm (1875)

LOST TO LIBERTY
COUNTY IN 1840

TURTLE
BAY

Big Cypress Creek

Herman
Strack
Farm (1845)

CYPRESS

Little White Oak Bayou

White Oak Bayou

San Jacinto River

Cedar Bayou

ORCOQUISAC

WALLIS HILL

ANAHUAC

SAN
FELIPE

LOST TO
FORT BEND
COUNTY
IN 1838

PINE POINT

Buffalo Bayou

HOUSTON

JESSE
WHITE'S HOUSE
OATES
PRAIRIE

LYNCH'S
FERRY

POINT
PLEASANT
(William Scott)

*TRINITY
BAY*

Double
Bayou

Randal
Jones

Samuel Isaacs

Brown &
Belknap

Bray's Bayou

HARRISBURG

SAN JACINTO
BATTLEGROUND

Chambers County to
Western Shore of
Galveston Bay
(1858)

SMITH
POINT

FORT
BEND

STAFFORD'S
PRAIRIE
HOUSE

Clear Creek

Redfish Bar

JOHNSON HUNTER
PLANTATION

Jesse Cartwright

LOST TO
FORT BEND
COUNTY
IN 1846

CLEAR
LAKE

POWHATAN

(SAN LEON)

GALVESTON BAY

BOLIVAR

FORT BEND
COUNTY
(1837)

Francis
Bingham

Brazos River

Oyster Creek

(LEAGUE
CITY)

GALVESTON
COUNTY

(TEXAS
CITY)

(ALVIN)

Fort Travis

**HARRIS COUNTY
BOUNDARIES
1835-TODAY**

LEGEND

BRAZORIA
COUNTY
(1836)

LIVERPOOL

Chocolate Bayou

GALVESTON

WEST BAY

———— = 1835 Boundaries
———— = Boundary After 1837
•••••• = Modern Boundaries
–·–·– = Modern County Lines
★ = Polling Places, 1836-1837
• = 1837 Towns and Settlements
(NAME) • = Modern Towns for Orientation

BOLIVAR
OROZIMBO PLANTATION
(ANGLETON)

GULF OF MEXICO

NORTH

COLUMBIA
BRAZORIA

Oyster Creek

SAN LUIS

VELASCO
QUINTANA

San Bernard River

Map Design: James L. Glass

**VISUAL SUMMARY
OF GROWTH**

San Jacinto River formed eastern
boundary of Stephen F. Austin's
colony by special extension of 1827

WASHINGTON
(1835)

(Liberty
District,
1831)

Harrisburg County

Harris County

Grimes

Montgomery

Liberty

SAN
FELIPE
(1823)

BRAZORIA
(1832)

Waller

Name changed
in 1839

Fort
Bend

Galveston

1832-35

1837

Included Galveston Island

1840

Galveston County formed 1838

Brazoria

1846-TODAY

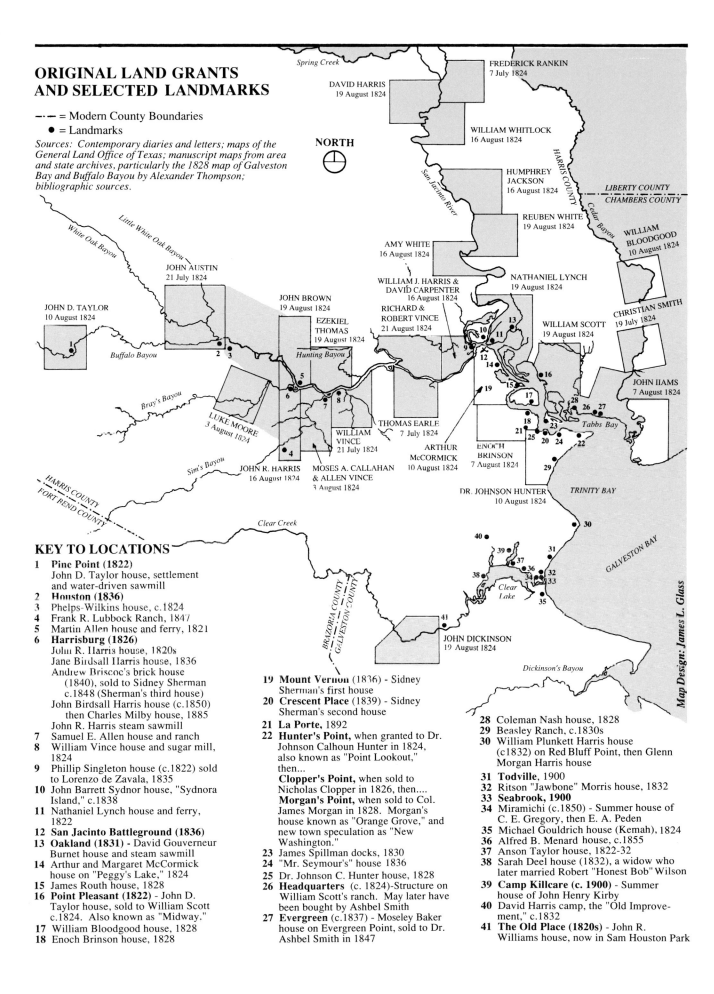

ORIGINAL LAND GRANTS AND SELECTED LANDMARKS

-··- = Modern County Boundaries
● = Landmarks

Sources: Contemporary diaries and letters; maps of the General Land Office of Texas; manuscript maps from area and state archives, particularly the 1828 map of Galveston Bay and Buffalo Bayou by Alexander Thompson; bibliographic sources.

NORTH

KEY TO LOCATIONS

1 **Pine Point (1822)**
John D. Taylor house, settlement and water-driven sawmill
2 **Houston (1836)**
3 Phelps-Wilkins house, c.1824
4 Frank R. Lubbock Ranch, 1847
5 Martin Allen house and ferry, 1821
6 **Harrisburg (1826)**
John R. Harris house, 1820s
Jane Birdsall Harris house, 1836
Andrew Briscoe's brick house (1840), sold to Sidney Sherman c.1848 (Sherman's third house)
John Birdsall Harris house (c.1850) then Charles Milby house, 1885
John R. Harris steam sawmill
7 Samuel E. Allen house and ranch
8 William Vince house and sugar mill, 1824
9 Phillip Singleton house (c.1822) sold to Lorenzo de Zavala, 1835
10 John Barrett Sydnor house, "Sydnora Island," c.1838
11 Nathaniel Lynch house and ferry, 1822
12 **San Jacinto Battleground (1836)**
13 **Oakland (1831)** - David Gouverneur Burnet house and steam sawmill
14 Arthur and Margaret McCormick house on "Peggy's Lake," 1824
15 James Routh house, 1828
16 **Point Pleasant (1822)** - John D. Taylor house, sold to William Scott c.1824. Also known as "Midway."
17 William Bloodgood house, 1828
18 Enoch Brinson house, 1828
19 **Mount Vernon** (1836) - Sidney Sherman's first house
20 **Crescent Place** (1839) - Sidney Sherman's second house
21 **La Porte,** 1892
22 **Hunter's Point,** when granted to Dr. Johnson Calhoun Hunter in 1824, also known as "Point Lookout," then...
Clopper's Point, when sold to Nicholas Clopper in 1826, then....
Morgan's Point, when sold to Col. James Morgan in 1828. Morgan's house known as "Orange Grove," and new town speculation as "New Washington."
23 James Spillman docks, 1830
24 "Mr. Seymour's" house 1836
25 Dr. Johnson C. Hunter house, 1828
26 **Headquarters** (c.1824)-Structure on William Scott's ranch. May later have been bought by Ashbel Smith
27 **Evergreen** (c.1837) - Moseley Baker house on Evergreen Point, sold to Dr. Ashbel Smith in 1847
28 Coleman Nash house, 1828
29 Beasley Ranch, c.1830s
30 William Plunkett Harris house (c1832) on Red Bluff Point, then Glenn Morgan Harris house
31 **Todville,** 1900
32 Ritson "Jawbone" Morris house, 1832
33 **Seabrook, 1900**
34 Miramichi (c.1850) - Summer house of C. E. Gregory, then E. A. Peden
35 Michael Gouldrich house (Kemah), 1824
36 Alfred B. Menard house, c.1855
37 Anson Taylor house, 1822-32
38 Sarah Deel house (1832), a widow who later married Robert "Honest Bob" Wilson
39 **Camp Killcare (c. 1900)** - Summer house of John Henry Kirby
40 David Harris camp, the "Old Improvement," c.1832
41 **The Old Place (1820s)** - John R. Williams house, now in Sam Houston Park

Map Design: James L. Glass

Key To Houses

Sources: City directories; contemporary newspapers and maps; maps of Key Maps, Inc.; private papers;

<u>Note</u>: *While the authors have taken every precaution to cross check the accuracy of locations cited, their research conclusions do not imply precedential documentation.*

★ = House built before 1875
■ = House built 1876 - 1899
● = House built after 1900

1 Charlotte Baldwin Allen - 718 Main
2 Samuel L. Allen - NSBB
3 John D. Andrews - 418 Austin
4 John J. Atkinson - 817 San Jacinto
5 James L. Autry (extant) - 5 Courtland Place
6 T. M. Bagby - S. E. Byers - 500 McKinney
7 Judge James A. Baker - 1104 San Jacinto
8 The Beaconsfield (extant) - 1700 Main
9 A. Bergamini - S. P. Coughlin - 1203 Milam
10 August C. Bering, Sr. - 3402 San Jacinto
11 J. C. Bering (1st house) - 1112 Milam
12 J. C. Bering (2nd house) - 1217 Holman
13 Frank Lee Berry - 3002 Austin
14 James H. Blake - 1517 Texas
15 J. Stuart Boyles - 1217 Fannin
16 Thomas J. Boyles - 1203 Rusk
17 John T. Brady - Milby at Harrisburg
18 Andrew Briscoe - 408 Main
19 Mary Jane Harris Briscoe - 620 Crawford
20 James L. Britton - 1010 Rosalie
21 Miss Browne's Young Ladies Seminary -
      McKinney at Crawford
22 Butler Flats - 1103 Rusk
23 J. I. Campbell - M. T. Jones - 2908 Main
24 James J. Carroll (extant) - 16 Courtlandt Place
25 James P. Carter - 2602 Main
26 Samuel F. Carter - 1804 Crawford
27 W. T. Carter, Jr. (extant) - 18 Courtlandt Place
28 William B. Chew - 1206 Fannin
29 Christ Church rectories - 1119 Texas
30 A. S. Cleveland (extant) - 8 Courtlandt Place
31 W. D. Cleveland - 806 San Jacinto
32 T. D. Cobb - B. F. Bonner - 1904 Main
33 William S. Cochran - 4004 Brandt
34 G. W. Collings - A. F. Amerman -
      35 Collings Place
35 Henry W. Cortes - 1118 Milam
36 James M. Cotton - 1018 Travis
37 B. J. Covington - 2219 Dowling
38 J. F. Crosby - James Bute - 1016 Main
39 Henry M. Curtin - 2111 Fannin
40 E. H. Cushing - Elgin at Holman
41 Nick D' Amico - 1219 Hamilton
42 Henry M. DeChaumes - 2203 San Jacinto
43 Michael DeGeorge - 918 Bagby
44 Charles L. Desel - 3518 Main
45 S. K. Dick - Capt. J. A. Baker - 1416 Main
46 Charles Dillingham - 1214 Rusk
47 John M. Dorrance (extant) - 9 Courtlandt Place
48 Robert C. Duff (extant) -
      803 McGowen (original site)
49 Robert M. Elgin - 1404 Texas
50 Cornelius Ennis - 1618 Congress
51 Presley K. Ewing - 1103 Clay
52 M. Floeck - C. S. Longcope - 109 Chenevert
53 Gustav A. Forsgard -
      Holman, Austin, Winbern, San Jacinto
54 Henry S. Fox - 1206 Main
55 J. M. Frost - 406 Gray
56 William Fulton - 1507 Rusk
57 John W. Garrow (extant) - 19 Courtlandt Place
58 Richard A. Giraud - 1718 Main
59 Herbert Godwin - 1112 Holman
60 William Fairfax Gray - 308 Fannin
61 T.L. Hackney - J.J. Sweeney - 2210 Main
62 William Hamblen - William E. Kendall - 315 Milby
63 F. W. Heitmann - 1116 Dallas
64 Louis Gray Hester - 1102 Elgin
65 Gustav G. Heyne (extant) - 4008 Austin
66 Charles S. House - 1806 Main
67 Thomas W. House, Sr. - 706 Smith
68 Thomas W. House, Jr. - 1010 Louisiana
69 Milton D. Howe - 918 Austin at McKinney
70 J. C. Hutcheson (1st house) - 818 Travis
71 J. C. Hutcheson (2nd house) - 1417 McKinney
72 William J. Hutchins - 1416 Franklin
73 Jehu Johnson - J.O. Ross - 710 Hadley
74 William E. Jones - 319 Robin
75 Levi M. Kaiser - 1404 Rusk
76 Margaret Kinkaid - San Jacinto at Elgin
77 Kellum - Noble (extant) - Sam Houston Park
78 John H. Kirby - 2006 Smith
79 L. J. Latham - 1318 Walker
80 W. H. Leavell - J. M. Howe - 1112 Elgin
81 Jemison E. Lester - 3112 Main
82 Abraham M. Levy - 2016 Main
83 J. W. Link - T. P. Lee (extant) - 3812 Montrose
84 Robert Lockart - 2915 Commerce

85 Cesar Lombardi - 806 Austin
86 I. C. Lord - 412 Tuam
87 Robert S. Lovett - 2017 Main
88 A. Thomas Lucas - 2017 Milam
89 James S. Lucas - 818 Chartres
90 Louis C. Luckel - 3019 Main
91 Harris Masterson (1st house) - 820 Crawford
92 Harris Masterson (2nd house) - 3702 Burlington
93 S. M. McAshan - 1315 Main
94 S. K. McIlhenny - 1314 McKinney
95 James V. Meek (extant) - 3704 Garrott
96 Lee B. Menefee - 2106 Crawford
97 August L. Metcalf - 402 Westmoreland
98 W. E. Miller - 310 Robin
99 Gustave A. Mistrot - 1504 Clay
100 Sterling Myer (extant) - 4 Courtlandt Place
101 William R. Nash (extant) - 217 Westmoreland
102 Charles L. Neuhaus (extant) - 6 Courtlandt Place
103 Edwin L. Neville (extant) - 11 Courtlandt Place
104 Nichols-Rice-Cherry (extant) -
      Courthouse Square (original site)
105 Edward A. Palmer - 1410 Rusk
106 William H. Palmer - 1116 Travis
107 E. B. Parker Cottage (extant) - 2204 Baldwin
108 E. B. Parker-Capt. J. A. Baker
      (The Oaks) 2310 Baldwin
109 E. A. Peden - 1017 Bell
110 Erastus S. Perkins - 1508 Texas
111 Eugene Pillot (extant) -
      1803 McKinney (original site)
112 Will Powars - 1206 Brazos
113 N. P. Pullum - 1319 Andrews
114 Emmanuel Raphael - 1820 Rusk
115 Samuel Clark Red - 817 Caroline
116 Jonas S. Rice - 2304 Crawford

117 E. R. Richardson (extant)
      1311 Holman (original site)
118 Henry F. Ring - 1510 Crawford
119 J. M. Rockwell - 2116 Crawford
120 A. P. Root - 1410 Clay
121 The Rossonian - 913-919 McKinney
122 H. Sampson / M. Urwitz - 1104 Preston
123 The Savoy (extant) - 1600 Main
124 T. H. Scanlan - 1917 Main
125 W. G. Sears - H. E. Detering - 1417 McGowen
126 W. J. Settegast - near 2310 Baldwin
127 Edward W. Sewall - 614 San Jacinto
128 Walter B. Sharp - 4301 Main
129 John Shearn - 1304 Main
130 B. A. Shepherd - Travis at Lamar
131 B. C. Simpson (1st house) - Youngs (Riesner)
132 B. C. Simpson (2nd house) - 804 Main
133 B. C. Simpson, Jr. - 3804 Fannin
134 Howard F. Smith - 2204 Main
135 William A. Smith - 3614 Travis
136 Henry T. Staiti (extant) -
      421 Westmoreland (original site)
137 J. H. S. Stanley-B. Repsdorph - 406 Capitol
138 John E. Sternenburg - 3018 Austin
139 Sam Streetman - 2616 Louisiana
140 David F. Stuart - 1116 Texas
141 Horace D. Taylor - Smith at Preston
142 A. A. VanAlstyne-J. F. Dickson - 1216 Main
143 Hugh Waddell - 2404 Caroline
144 J. P. Waldo (extant) - 1213 Rusk (original site)
145 William S. Wall - 3717 Main
146 T. W. Ward - I. Roberts - A. Sessums - 402 Main
147 B. F. Weems - 1616 Rusk
148 Prof. C. Welch - 2215 Caroline
149 M. L. Westheimer - 1612 Hadley
150 Alfred J. Whitaker - Main at Holman
151 James T. D. Wilson - 608 Rusk
152 Hosmer W. Wood - 409 McKinney
153 The Rev. Jack Yates - 1318 Andrews

STRUCTURES IN THE ORIGINAL 62-BLOCK AREA OF HOUSTON

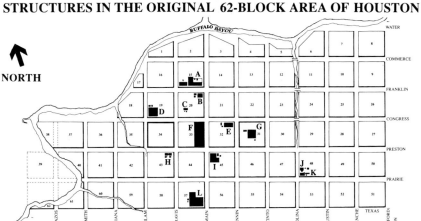

NORTH

A 1837 - CITY HOTEL, block 15, lots 1, 6, 7, 8 and 12. Lot 6 was the site of the Hutchins House in 1867.
B 1837 - HOUSTON HOUSE (hotel), block 20, lot 5.
C 1837 - JOHN KIRBY ALLEN HOUSE, Northeast half of lot 7, block 20.
D 1837 - MANSION HOUSE (hotel), block 19, lots 1, 4 and 5.
E 1840 - ALABAMA HOUSE, block 32, lot 5. Later known as the Pierce House which was razed for the construction of the Pillot Building in the 1850s.
F 1837 - LONG ROW or MERCANTILE ROW, block 33, lots 1 through 5.
G 1838 - COUNTY COURTHOUSE AND JAIL, block 31.

H 1837 - SAM HOUSTON HOUSE AND OFFICE (double log cabin), block 43, lots 9 and 10.
I 1838 - PRESIDENT'S HOUSE, block 45, lots 9 and 10.
J 1838 - SAM HOUSTON HOUSE (during construction of I), block 48, lot 7.
K 1837 - AUGUSTUS CHAPMAN AND CHARLOTTE ALLEN HOUSE (during construction of later home on Main Street), block 48, lot 6. John Kirby Allen was brought here to die in 1838.
L 1837 - CAPITOL OF THE REPUBLIC OF TEXAS, block 57, lots 1, 2 and 12.
      (Old Market Square)

<u>Sources</u>: Maps in the Texas and Local History Room of the Houston Public Library: Deed Records of Harris County: Records of the 11th Judicial District Court; letters and manuscripts; Sam Houston House sources.

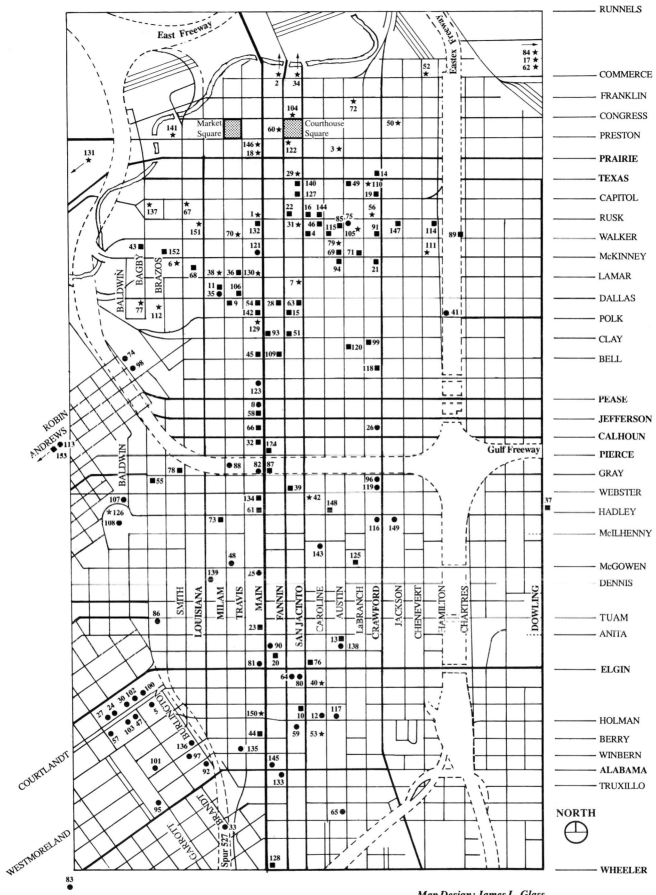

RUNNELS

COMMERCE

FRANKLIN

CONGRESS

PRESTON

PRAIRIE

TEXAS

CAPITOL

RUSK

WALKER

McKINNEY

LAMAR

DALLAS

POLK

CLAY

BELL

PEASE

JEFFERSON

CALHOUN

PIERCE

GRAY

WEBSTER

HADLEY

McILHENNY

McGOWEN

DENNIS

TUAM

ANITA

ELGIN

HOLMAN

BERRY

WINBERN

ALABAMA

TRUXILLO

WHEELER

NORTH

Map Design: James L. Glass

HOUSTON CITY LIMITS AND SUBDIVISIONS

Houston's original boundaries were first modified in 1839, and in 1840 a supplement to the city charter allowed for the delineation of four wards, each with two elected aldermen. The First Ward was north of Congress and east of Main; the Second Ward was north of Congress and west of Main; the Third Ward was south of Congress and east of Main; and the Fourth Ward was south of Congress and west of Main. Later the Fifth Ward was formed north of Buffalo Bayou and east of White Oak; and the Sixth Ward was north of Buffalo Bayou and west of White Oak Bayou. As early as 1848 residential additions were developed by private investors. Several additions north of Buffalo Bayou were developed in the 1860s primarily with rent houses for railroad and dock workers. However, in the late nineteenth century the most densely populated areas were south of the original townsite where land owners developed tracts as small as one block from the 1890s to the 1910s. Additions and

subdivisions noted on this map are by no means all of those developed before 1914 but are chosen because they are discussed in the essays, because they are particularly large or prominent, or because they represent similar tracts developed in the same areas at the same time. The dates noted are from official Harris County Plat Maps or published announcements of new additions that appeared in local newspapers. When the plat was filed in a later year than the planned development was announced, the earlier date is noted. This map is based on the 1917 Houston Title Guaranty Co. Map.

KEY TO LOCATIONS

1 A. C. Allen addition 1860
2 Avondale 1907
3 Beachamp Springs 1838
4 Brooke Smith 1905-06
5 Brunner 1890
6 Bute 1907
7 Castanie Addition 1848
8 Catholic Cemetery (Holy Cross)
9 Catholic Cemetery (Glenwood)
10 Central Park 1912
11 Chapmanville (Chapman's Third Addition) 1866
12 Cherryhurst 1908
13 Chew Addition 1898
14 Courtlandt Place 1906
15 Cushing Park Addition 1901
16 Denver**
17 Eastwood 1911
18 Empire Addition 1901
19 Engelke Addition 1866
20 Episcopal Cemetery (destroyed)
21 Factory Addition 1867

22 Fairgrounds Addition 1889***
23 Fairview 1893
24 Forest Hill 1910
25 Frost Town 1822
26 German Society (Washington) Cemetery
27 Glenwood Cemetery
28 Harrisburg 1826
29 Hebrew (Beth Israel), City (Founders) Cemeteries
30 Hermann Park 1914
31 Hollywood Cemetery
32 1st Houston Country Club 1903-04
33 2nd Houston Country Club 1908
34 Houston Harbor 1911**
35 Houston Heights 1892
36 Hyde Park 1905-06
37 Independence Heights 1910*
38 Kenilworth Grove
39 Lubbock's Grove
40 Magnolia Park 1893***
41 Montrose 1911
42 NSBB additions platted 1860s
43 Oak Lawn 1893
44 Old City Cemetery (destroyed)
45 Pless Addition 1861
46 Port Houston (NSBB) 1908
47 Port Houston (SSBB) 1908
48 Quality Hill 1850s
49 Rice University 1911
50 Sam Houston Park 1899
51 Seneschal Addition 1848
52 Settegast-Upham 1897
53 Shadyside 1916
54 "South End" additions platted 1890s-1910s
55 Southmore 1914
56 Sunset Heights 1910
57 W.A. Wilson Realty Co. Addition 1900
58 W. R. Baker Addition 1856
59 Westmoreland 1902
60 Woodland Heights 1907

* *Independence Heights was Houston's first neighborhood developed specifically for black citizens.*
** *Although a small subdivision called Denver Harbor was platted in 1952, the large area known today as Denver Harbor is made up of several early nineteenth century additions including Denver, Houston Harbor, Liberty Heights and Harbordale. Settlement began in this area in 1891.*
*** *The Fairgrounds addition was platted on the site of the old Fairgrounds, a recreational area where the last fair was held in 1873. The Magnolia Park addition was platted on the site of Magnolia Park.*

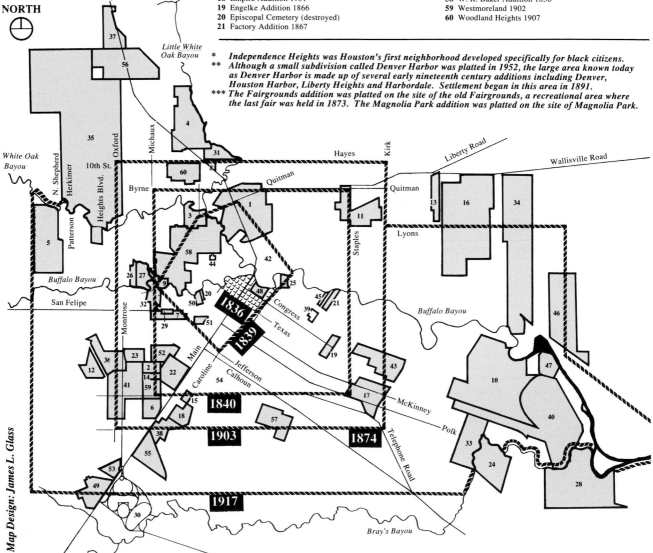

NORTH

Map Design: James L. Glass

Introduction

A Brief History of Harris County

Margaret Swett Henson

———————————

The first Anglo-Americans who settled in what was to become Harris County arrived by boat from Louisiana in early 1822, one year after Mexico achieved independence from Spain. Most chose homesites along the San Jacinto River estuary to take advantage of the convenient waterways that drained the prairies and forests surrounding upper Galveston Bay. Some of these pioneers had explored the area when residents of the United States joined Mexican republicans who used Galveston Island as a site for launching attacks against Spanish Mexico between 1816 and 1820. The Americans who joined or supplied food to the expeditions of Henry Perry, Xavier Mina, Jean Lafitte, and James Long immediately recognized the potential economic advantages of the Galveston Bay system.[1] They saw that farmers, ranchers, and merchants would have easy access to Louisiana markets by land and sea as soon as Mexico won independence from Spain.

Until that time Spain had virtually ignored the Texas coast. The first Spaniard to visit Galveston—Álvar Nuñez Cabeza de Vaca—had described the area as a wasteland of nomadic natives, thus postponing its development. Spain only took notice of Texas when Robert Cavelier, the Sieur de LaSalle, established a French fort on Matagorda Bay in 1685. Then, to show Spanish hegemony, Mexico City sent missionaries and a handful of soldiers to occupy strategic entrances to Texas, but all of them overlooked Galveston Bay.

Throughout its colonies, Spain restricted trade to Spanish ships and goods and forbade visits by foreign vessels. Nevertheless, French traders from New Orleans arrived in Galveston Bay in the 1720s intending to build a trading post for the Orcoquisacs, who lived in semi-permanent villages along the upper San Jacinto and lower Trinity rivers. No French structure was erected until 1754, when Joseph Blancpain built a small depot on the lower Trinity River just above present-day Interstate Highway 10. Indians informed the Spanish authorities, and the commandant sent troops to arrest the French intruders. Although this event clearly demonstrated a threat to Spanish control, the government in Mexico City failed to place a colony on Galveston Bay. After Spain acquired Louisiana in 1763, no effort was made to occupy the coast between La Bahia (Goliad) and St. Martinsville on the Bayou Teche. In 1786 José de Evía, who was mapping the entire Gulf Coast, named the bay and the island for his patron Bernardo de Gálvez, viceroy of Mexico and former governor of Louisiana.[2]

The Indians described by the Spanish and French in the sixteenth and eighteenth centuries were ancestors of the Karankawas and Attakapas. They visited Galveston Bay streams seasonally to procure seafood, particularly the rangia clams found in tidal waters. Over the centuries huge piles of clam shells accumulated at favored campsites along the San Jacinto estuary, Clear Lake, and Cedar Bayou. Later, Anglo settlers would use these convenient shell middens for walkways, streets, and foundations, and the stylized drawing of the Sarah Deel Wilson house (fig. 1) on an early map of southeast Harris County suggests that it might have been built atop such a pile.

The primitive Indians and even their descendants in the early nineteenth century lived very simply, with few possessions other than pottery, skin huts and clothing, bows and arrows, spears, primitive fish traps, and tools and ornaments made from shells and flotsam available along the coast. They traded shore items with inland tribes for forest products, and in spite of legend were not cannibals in the sense that they ate human flesh as food. That myth stemmed from a ritual common among various tribes of eating fingers, hands, and sometimes the hearts of captives taken in combat. By 1822, however, no Indians lived in Harris County, and those who occasionally visited the shore were survivors from various tribes diminished by attacks from American and European invaders.[3]

As a consequence, the pioneer settlers in Harris County could establish homes without fear of Indian raids, while their contemporaries along the lower Brazos and Colorado rivers still encountered active opposition through 1826. These Anglo-Americans came to Texas after learning about the cheap land available through Stephen F. Austin. His father, Moses, had received an empresario contract from the waning Spanish government in December 1820 (Mexican independence was achieved in 1821) to bring Roman Catholic families from formerly Spanish Missouri and Louisiana to develop the almost vacant Texas frontier. Upon Moses Austin's death in June 1821, the son assumed the responsibility of fulfilling the contract, which was expected to restore the family's finances. The Austins had suffered a severe setback from the banking panic of 1819 and hoped that the empresario grant, which cost nothing, might be profitable if colonists were charged 12½ cents per acre. This offer proved to be attractive to Americans, who had to pay a minimum of $1.25 per acre for vacant land at United States land offices.

Unfortunately for Austin, even though his Spanish grant was reconfirmed by the new Mexican government, he was forbidden to charge colonists even so modest a fee. His only reward was the 23,000 acres he would receive for the settlement of each group of one hundred families. Instead of paying Austin, each head of a family paid a total of about $60 to the state and its officials for one league and labor (lah-*bor*) of land. This was the equivalent of 4,605 acres for less than one penny per acre! Immigration to Austin's colony increased rapidly as word spread about this bargain. The newcomers, many suffering financial distress similar to the Austins', willingly took an oath to become Mexican citizens, uphold the Mexican constitution, and become Roman Catholics (the state religion), the requirements for receiving land.[4]

Between 1822 and 1835 there developed a strong expectation among Anglo-Texans that Texas, at least to the Brazos or Colorado rivers, would soon be annexed to the United States through diplomatic means. When this failed to happen, the disappointed Anglo-Texans, disturbed about recent political changes in the Mexican republic, took advantage of a civil war between factions to declare their independence in 1836. Annexation to the United States, which they had hoped would follow, did not occur, however, until December 29, 1845. Many of the pioneers had expected to become rich by selling their land to newcomers as soon as Texas joined the union. But the extensive acreage became a burden during the period of the Texas republic when the new government taxed land in order to raise revenue. Under Mexico, land was not taxed and revenue rested on tariffs and excise taxes.

At first Harris County was not part of Austin's colony, which encompassed only the lower Colorado and Brazos watersheds. But in 1824 the government gave Austin special permission to issue titles to those already settled along Buffalo Bayou, the San Jacinto River, and Cedar Bayou. The empresario, his secretary, and the state land commissioner traveled through the colony delivering deeds. Residents around the San Jacinto estuary met for the ceremony in August 1824 at the home of William Scott, whose large house was located on a bluff near the present-day Exxon refinery at Baytown. Altogether, the commissioner issued twenty-five titles to families within the present boundaries of Harris County under the terms of Austin's first contract for three hundred families. From the first, these settlers were called the "Old Three Hundred" and were viewed as a historic elite. Under subsequent contracts Austin issued twenty-two more patents in Harris County between 1828 and 1832, when the colonial phase ended. Each recipient had to live on the land for six years and make improvements in order to perfect the title. The land could be sold only to other Texas residents but might be willed to heirs in the United States if they agreed to move to Texas and become Mexican citizens. In other words, Mexico allowed no absentee landowners.[5]

Harris County's pioneer Old Three Hundred included John Austin, William Bloodgood, Enoch Brinson, Moses Callahan and Allen Vince (single men could join to form a family), John Brown, Thomas Earle, David Harris, John R. Harris, William Harris and D. Carpenter, Dr. Johnson Hunter, Humphrey Jackson, Nathaniel Lynch, John Iiams, Arthur McCormick, Luke Moore, Frederick Rankin, William Scott, Christian Smith, John D. Taylor, Ezekiel Thomas, Richard and Robert Vince, William Vince, Mrs. Amy White, Reuben White, and William Whitlock.

John R. Harris, for whom the modern county is named, was the first to plat a town in the area. The New York native chose his league on Buffalo Bayou at its confluence with Brays Bayou, and in 1826 he had the village of Harrisburg platted there. He built a home and a store and in 1829 began assembling a steam sawmill in partnership with others. He died of yellow fever that same year while in New Orleans on business, and his brothers, David and William P. Harris, carried on until 1833, when Harris's widow, Jane Birdsall Harris, and his eldest son, De Witt Clinton Harris, arrived. David Harris operated a coastal schooner and William P. Harris brought the *Cayuga* to Harrisburg in 1834, the first steamboat to serve Texas. This vessel played a vital role in supplying the Texas army during the struggle against Mexico.[6]

Harrisburg, absorbed by Houston in 1926, was just below the modern Port of Houston's turning basin. It served as a port of entry and trading center for the earliest settlers. The town was the seat of the local justice of the peace from 1826 to 1835, when it became a Mexican municipality entitled to two alcaldes: Hosea H. League and Nathaniel Lynch. Their jurisdiction stretched northeast from Clear Lake across the San Jacinto River estuary to Cedar Bayou, then up that stream and west to the settlements along Spring Creek, then southwest to the headwaters of Clear Creek in present-day Fort Bend County. The Harrisburg municipality sent three delegates, Andrew Briscoe, John W. Moore, and Lorenzo de Zavala, to the March 1836 convention at Washington-on-the-Brazos, where the Texas Declaration of Independence was adopted.

Briscoe had been a merchant at Anahuac in 1835 in partnership with De Witt Clinton Harris; he married his partner's sister, Mary Jane Harris, in 1837 when he became the first county judge of Harris County. Moore was a popular military leader and later served as sheriff. Zavala came to Texas in July 1835 and bought a house on Buffalo Bayou opposite present-day San Jacinto State Park. He intended to lead the opposition movement against his former friend, President Antonio Lopez de Santa Anna. A native of Yucatán, Zavala had been Mexican minister to France from 1833 to 1835 when he resigned in protest against Santa Anna's attacks on the Mexican constitution. Zavala's New York–born second wife and their three children joined him in Texas in December. The delegates to the convention named Zavala vice-president of the ad interim government of the new republic at the same time they chose David G. Burnet president. Burnet lived near Lynchburg and had come to Texas from New Jersey in 1831 with his bride and equipment to erect a steam sawmill on the San Jacinto River.[7]

Not only could the Harrisburg municipality boast of having both the president and the vice-president as residents, but for a brief three weeks Harrisburg functioned as the capital of the republic. The Washington convention adjourned hastily on March 17 when rumors indicated that the Mexican army was advancing. The five-member cabinet agreed to join Burnet and Zavala in Harrisburg for the sake of safety and easy access to the water route to New Orleans. The party reached Jane Harris's house on March 22, and after brief visits to their own homes, Burnet and Zavala convened the cabinet at the Harris residence two days later. The cabinet dwindled to two when the ill secretary of state went to the United States, the naval secretary left for Galveston to oversee the port, and the secretary of war joined Sam Houston's army encamped on the Brazos River near present-day Hempstead.[8]

Harrisburg also served as a funnel for Texas refugees streaming toward Louisiana in March and April of 1836 when Santa Anna's army started eastward. Participants in the Runaway Scrape, as it was called even then, followed Buffalo Bayou to Lynch's ferry on the San Jacinto River, where a road led northeast to Liberty and the trail to Opelousas. People with means preferred to take a boat from Lynchburg to Galveston Island in hopes of finding a ship going to New Orleans. On April 12 word reached Harrisburg that Santa Anna was crossing the Brazos, and Burnet and Zavala rushed to evacuate their families. Two days later, the same day that Houston's army started toward Harrisburg, Jane B. Harris and the remaining government clerks and officials abandoned Harrisburg for Galveston on board the *Cayuga*. When Santa Anna reached the deserted village on April 15, he allowed his soldiers to loot and burn the buildings, including the Harris house. The Zavalas and the Burnets barely escaped to the island on board other vessels before the Mexican cavalry reached Morgan's Point on April 16. The soldiers seized James Morgan's warehouse filled with supplies intended for the Texas army and also captured a number of people, including Morgan's housekeeper, Emily D. West, a free black woman who had come from New York City at the same time as Mrs. Zavala. Morgan was the agent of the New Washington Association, a group of New York speculators, who dispatched the housekeeper and other employees to Morgan's Point in October to build and maintain a hotel, a store, and a number of houses. Modern myth-makers have given Emily D. West the sobriquet of "the Yellow Rose of Texas" and suggest, unrealistically, that she intentionally delayed Santa Anna in dalliance on April 21, giving the Texans the chance to surprise and defeat the Mexican army at the battle of San Jacinto.[9]

Few Harris County men served at the battle, which took place on Mrs. Peggy McCormick's league on April 21, because a number were serving on vessels, engaged in building a fort on Galveston Island under the direction of Colonel James Morgan, or escorting their families to safety. Morgan learned about the damage to his property a few days after the battle, but the Runaway Scrape refugees did not discover their losses until May when most returned home. Objects not hidden had been stolen along with food and livestock. It was crucial to replace corn and cotton seed in order to produce a crop later in the season. Some of the residents arranged to take Mexican prisoners for use as laborers. For example, four prisoners helped to rebuild the Harris house (fig. 9), and other captives worked at Burnet's old steam mill that had been purchased by the Texas government to supply lumber for the Galveston fort. While Santa Anna was freed and sent home by way of Washington, D. C., in November 1836, the remaining forty officers and four hundred or so soldiers were not released until May 1837.[10]

The first election for president, vice-president, and members of Congress for the Republic of Texas took place in September 1836. Voters chose Sam Houston of Nacogdoches as president, and he assumed office in October. Congress convened in October at Columbia on the Brazos River, temporarily the capital, and in December created Harrisburg County and named Briscoe judge. The new county included the old municipality and also Galveston Island. For reasons of national security, Mexico had forbidden settlement along the Texas coast and thus most of present-day Galveston County remained uninhabited until Texas became a republic. The town of Houston, founded on August 30, 1836, by Augustus Chapman and John Kirby Allen, was named the new capital of the republic and also the county seat of Harrisburg County. The raw village lay fifteen miles up Buffalo Bayou from devastated Harrisburg. The two New York brothers capitalized on the popularity of the "Hero of San Jacinto" when they named their new town for their friend and neighbor.[11]

Houston remained the capital only until the summer of 1839, when the government moved to Austin. Congress abandoned Houston for two reasons: politics and the unpleasant climate on Buffalo Bayou. President Houston was limited to one term, and when his faction lost the presidential election in 1838, his victorious rivals, Mirabeau Buonaparte Lamar, also a hero at San Jacinto, and David G. Burnet, supported a move from the town that bore Houston's name. Elected to Congress in 1839, Sam Houston endured a frontier Austin that was still exposed to Indian attack, but when he became president again in 1841, he quickly found an excuse to return the capital to Houston. Congress met there from June 27 to July 23, 1842, but in September, President Houston agreed to move the government to Washington, where it remained until Texas was annexed to the United States in 1845.[12]

Even after the founding of Houston, Harrisburg continued to serve as a port for passengers and freight. Many vessels preferred Harrisburg as a more convenient port until after the Civil War, when Houston merchants deepened and straightened the bayou so that larger ships could unload farther upstream. The only east-west stream in the area deep enough for shipping, Buffalo Bayou remained the favored route to the interior settlements until late in the nineteenth century when rails reached the hinterlands.[13]

Although the loss of the government offices hurt Houston's economy at first, the town steadily grew as more businesses located along Buffalo Bayou. Immigrants from Europe and the United States moved through the area in the 1840s, and many remained in the new city. In 1844 a group of German noblemen, including Prince Carl von Solms-Braunfels, formed a society called the *Verein* to encourage immigration to Texas from the politically torn German states. Unfortunately their planning and financing were inadequate for the thousands of farming families who fled their homeland. Revolution in 1848 sent many German intellectuals to Texas, too, and many newcomers, hearing about the hardships of their compatriots in the area around New Braunfels, chose to stay near the ports of entry. Thus a number of German artisans and merchants remained in Houston while many farmers settled in northern Harris County, where vacant land was more plentiful because of heavier forestation. By the 1850s Germans had established thriving rural communities, among them Cypress, Rosehill, Big Cypress (now Klein), and Spring. A sprinkling of Irish, English, and French immigrants also arrived in the 1840s, and European immigration in smaller numbers continued until the end of the century.[14]

A large portion of those emigrating from the United States were from the South. Because cotton culture exhausted the land, planters (those with twenty or more slaves) and small farmers alike constantly moved west into virgin land where their first year's crop would pay the expenses of the move. During the Mexican period, slaves could be brought to Texas only as indentured servants because of Mexican laws against slavery. However, the 1836 constitution for the Republic of Texas, not surprisingly, guaranteed the rights of slaveholders. Free blacks were allowed to remain in Texas only if sponsored by reliable citizens. There were fewer slaves in Harris County than in adjoining Brazoria and Fort Bend counties, where the rich river bottoms were more suitable for plantation economy. During the Civil War, many southerners sent their chattels to Texas for protection, so the black population increased just before emancipation. After "Juneteenth" (June 19, 1865), when Maj. Gen. Gordon Granger declared Texas slaves free, a number of freed men and women drifted to Houston and formed enclaves such as Freedmen's Town in Houston's Fourth Ward.[15]

Harris County economy depended on agriculture. At first, newcomers, enchanted with the flat grassy plains without rocks, planted cotton wherever they lived. They soon discovered, however, that the soil was variable and within a few years it became clear that the prairies south of Buffalo Bayou were better suited to raising livestock. For a number of years Harris County led Texas in cattle production, in part because steamboat transportation to market was readily available along Buffalo Bayou. Before the Civil War most cattle were slaughtered along the bayou for their hides and tallow, with meat selling for pennies per pound or given away. But after 1865 the market for beef in the Northeast led to more scientific cattle raising, and animals were sent live to market by rail until mechanical refrigeration again changed the industry. The large Samuel Ezekiel Allen (not related to the city's founders) ranch (fig. 27) along Sims Bayou, for example, had its own boat landing and railway loading pens. Dairy farmers scattered herds over the county and found city dwellers a ready market at first, and later, with the advent of refrigeration, large companies built bottling plants for local distribution of dairy products.[16]

Cotton raising in Harris County gave way to cotton merchants, cotton compresses, and cotton seed mills. Soon after the city's founding, businesspeople in Houston profited by marketing produce grown in nearby counties. Likewise, Harris County sawmills exhausted local forests at an early date, and lumber companies moved farther into eastern Texas's dense woods. However, many firms had their offices in Houston for convenience. Rice growing in Harris County began near Baytown in the 1890s but did not become a major agricultural industry until after World War I. In other words, Harris County agrarian capitalists invested in produce usually grown elsewhere but sometimes processed locally before shipment to market. Merchants also profited by supplying the equipment and staples for the production needs of the farmers, ranchers, and lumber workers. Beyond the basic necessities, merchants found new demands for more deluxe items among the families with disposable income. The agrarian capitalists in turn stimulated the growth of new transportation systems.

Dreams of railroads to connect the inland agricultural areas with the bayou began to be realized in 1841, when Andrew Briscoe received a charter for the Harrisburg Railroad and Trading Company to bring produce from the Brazos River to Buffalo Bayou. A lack of capital forced him to sell his interest to Sidney Sherman, another hero of San Jacinto, who had settled in Harrisburg after the war. Sherman believed in the soundness of Briscoe's plan and in 1850 received a charter for the Buffalo Bayou, Brazos, and Colorado Railway Company (BBB & C). Although the line ended at the Harrisburg wharf, he interested Houston businessmen William Marsh Rice and William J. Hutchins in the scheme and with the aid of Massachusetts capital built the first railroad in Texas. The first BBB & C train reached Stafford in 1853, and seven years later the rails extended to the Colorado River. During the 1850s Galveston and Houston entrepreneurs fought each other to build railways to their ports; Houston gained an edge by building a connecting line to the BBB & C. By 1861 five railroads, none longer than one hundred miles, radiated from Houston.[17]

The Civil War interfered with rail building but proved the efficiency of rail transportation. The line from Houston to Galveston had just been completed when the war began and was used to move people and supplies to the island fortress. A Union naval blockade of the Texas coast from July 1861 through 1864 hampered normal water transportation. A number of Houston merchants, including Thomas W. House, Cornelius Ennis, and W. J. Hutchins, made fortunes sending blockade runners with cotton to Matamoros and Havana and returning with arms, medicine, clothing, and luxuries. William Marsh Rice operated his business from Matamoros after the death of his wife in August 1863, and he returned to Houston after the war even wealthier. Rail lines east did not yet connect Houston with Louisiana, but the Confederates used what portions were available to send troops and supplies to the front. Some Harris County men volunteered for service in the more elite units organized by local leaders, while others were recruited for the regular army. One company of horsemen was accepted into the colorful ranger unit organized by Fort Bend County's Frank Terry and in September 1861 rode "the cars" to the end of the line near Beaumont on their way to Kentucky.[18]

The federal fleet captured Galveston in October 1862 and refugees crowded Houston. John Bankhead Magruder, who assumed Confederate military command of Texas about that time, made his headquarters in the home of William R. Baker (originally built by Edward Albert Palmer, fig. 16) in Houston while planning his daring and successful New Year's Eve raid to recapture Galveston. The island remained under control of the Confederate forces from January 1, 1863, until the end of the war although the Union blockade continued. The July 1863 defeats at Gettysburg and Vicksburg foretold the end of the Confederacy. But Texans were heartened when a Houston resident, Irish bar owner Lt. Richard W. Dowling, disobeyed Magruder's order to spike the six cannon at Sabine Pass and, with his forty young men, prevented a federal invasion force of 5000 troops from landing on September 8, 1863. The only medals awarded by the Confederacy went to the men of the Davis Guards for this heroic action.[19]

When the war ended in 1865, the Houston business community resumed its struggle with Galveston for supremacy in transportation. The resumption of railroad building transformed Houston into a hub for railways in southeastern Texas by the 1880s. But so long as large ships had to unload cargo at Galveston and transship goods to Houston on smaller steamers, Houston could not dominate transportation. Houston entrepreneurs joined forces with shipping magnate Charles Morgan of New York and Louisiana, who had his own disagreements with the monopolistic Galveston Wharf Company and wanted to bypass the island, to straighten and deepen the channel to Houston. A nine-foot-deep channel was dredged through the upper bay and Buffalo Bayou while a cut of the same depth through Morgan's Point eliminated a shoal hairpin turn.

Completed in 1875, the new channel allowed most ocean-going vessels of the day to deliver goods directly to Houston, fifty miles inland, more quickly and economically than through Galveston. Houston's victory was not permanent, however; as vessels continued to increase in size, Houston would have to fight again and again for channel improvements.[20]

Harris County's economic development continued to depend on agrarian capitalism. Commission merchants were not only storekeepers and traders; they also acted as bankers because of widespread Jacksonian suspicion of banks and their paper money before the Civil War. The Texas state constitution of 1845 prohibited chartering banks that issued paper money, but in 1863 the national Congress made government paper money legal tender for all debts and also chartered national banks. Federal requirements and controls resulted in safer banks. The earliest national bank in Houston was the First National Bank, which opened in 1866, but it immediately encountered financial difficulty during the hard times following the war. The next year, respected commission merchant-banker B. A. Shepherd assumed control of the First National. Private banks such as that of T. W. House continued to be important until the end of the century, although state-chartered banks, briefly allowed from 1869 to 1875, were not permitted until 1905.[21]

Houston and Harris County endured the epidemics and disasters that afflicted the Gulf Coast such as yellow fever, fires, floods, and tropical storms. Two hurricanes, one in 1875 and the other in 1900, profoundly affected Houston's future when they proved that the inland city withstood strong wind and high water with less damage than nearby Lynchburg or Galveston Island. The 1875 storm destroyed Lynchburg, which had become a modest shipbuilding center and depot for transferring goods from large ships that did not want to travel up Buffalo Bayou. While the more affluent residents of the river port lived on a bluff twenty feet above the bank, most of the working class resided near the docks and shipyards along the San Jacinto River. An unprecedented storm surge of fifteen to twenty feet filled with debris churned up the estuary driven by hurricane-force winds from the south. The wall of water swept away wharves, buildings, and shipways. Lynchburg never recovered. The same storm-driven high tide caused Buffalo Bayou to cover the railroad tracks at Harrisburg and ruined its wharf. In contrast, Houston's docks and bridges remained intact, and business leaders were relieved to learn that the newly dredged cut through Morgan's Point actually improved with the scouring tide.[22]

The hurricane that struck Galveston on September 8, 1900, brought storm tides that filled city streets fifteen feet deep, washing flimsy structures off their pilings and severely damaging the buildings that survived. Debris made the high water dangerous; a shoreline railway trestle with rails still attached piled high with wreckage became a two-hundred-foot-long instrument of destruction, upsetting a raft with twenty-five people clinging to its perimeter before plowing into homes. The last recorded wind velocity at the United States weather bureau on the island was 84 miles per hour, but experts guessed that it reached perhaps 120 miles per hour. An estimated 6,000 people died during the storm. All communication with the mainland was cut off when telegraph and telephone poles went down and railroad and wagon bridges were severed. Within a week heroic measures restored the railroad bridge, allowing relief workers and supplies to reach the victims and permitting some survivors to leave. Cautious investors, however, deserted the island and relocated to Houston, where maximum winds had reached only sixty miles per hour. While roofs, trees, and power lines were damaged in the Bayou City, no lives were lost.[23]

By 1910 Houston had a population of more than 78,000, twice as many as the city of Galveston; Harris County counted 115,693 persons, two and one-half times larger than Galveston County. Yet Houston was not Texas's largest city, trailing San Antonio (with Fort Sam Houston) and Dallas. Not until 1930 did Houston become the largest city in the state. One reason for this growth was that Houston's economy expanded significantly around the turn of the century. Railroads had become not only a source of individual wealth, but by 1910 were Houston's most important industry. The freight yards, repair shops, and related manufactories such as the Dickson Car Wheel Company all provided numerous jobs.[24]

Another reason for Houston's growth was the oil gusher that blew in at Spindletop near Beaumont on January 10, 1901. Although oil had been found elsewhere in Texas before this time, no wells had produced such quantities, and none had been found so near a growing metropolis like Houston with its excellent land and water transportation. The Humble field just north of Houston began producing in 1904, and Houstonians worried that a proposed pipeline from Humble to the refineries at Port Arthur that served the Spindletop field would divert revenue away from Harris County. Almost immediately the Texas Company and the Gulf Oil Company built pipelines and storage facilities from the new field to Houston's rail lines and then to Buffalo Bayou. In 1908 the Texas Company moved its headquarters from Beaumont to Houston, and other companies followed when the Goose Creek field at Baytown began producing oil and gas. Joseph S. Cullinan, the founder of the Texas Company, was the first to visualize the potential for refineries along Buffalo Bayou, and between 1916 and 1930 eight companies built refineries in the area and moved corporate offices to Houston. Moreover, the petroleum industry spawned allied businesses like oil-tool companies and pipe manufacturers.[25]

Shipping continued to be a mainstay of the Houston economy, but vessels had grown since the opening of the nine-foot-deep channel in 1875. In 1896 the U. S. Army Corps of Engineers completed a twenty-five-foot-deep channel at the entrance to Galveston Bay, protected by four-mile-long jetties on either side. This "deep-water" channel extended to the Galveston wharves, allowing the largest vessels to dock at the island, and Houstonians immediately sought congressional approval for a similar channel to Houston. After the 1900 hurricane an eighteen-foot-deep ship channel and turning basin for the large vessels just above Harrisburg was completed in August 1908. But Houstonians were not satisfied, and they created a navigation district to control the watercourse and issue bonds for financing the deeper channel by offering to match federal funds, setting a precedent for cost-sharing. With the approval of Congress and local voters, Houston bankers under the leadership of Jesse H. Jones bought the bonds, and construction on the deep-water project began in June 1912. The twenty-five-foot-deep Houston Ship Channel opened amid great ceremony on November 10, 1914, when President Woodrow Wilson pushed a button in Washington, D. C., that fired a cannon located at the Turning Basin.[26]

The various economic successes generated skyrocketing growth in Houston and Harris

County. The Houston elite had traditionally sent its youth to well-known eastern schools. After the opening of Texas A & M in 1876 and the University of Texas at Austin in 1883, however, many attended those colleges. William Marsh Rice conceived the idea of local higher education and in 1891 incorporated the William Marsh Rice Institute for the advancement of literature, science, and art, giving it a small endowment. After his death in 1900 and lengthy litigation over his will, the bulk of his large estate went to the long-planned school, which opened in 1912. Under the guidance of its first president, Dr. Edgar Odell Lovett, a mathematician from Princeton, the school emerged as a leader in academic excellence and a source of civic pride.[27]

Thus, by 1914 ninety years of development had changed the Harris County area from an untapped wilderness into the third most heavily populated area in Texas, with the potential to become a major business and population center in the United States. Houston's growth, initially based on water transport, had been spurred by its network of railroads in the late nineteenth century, the devastation of its primary rival Galveston in 1900, and the improvement of Galveston Bay and Buffalo Bayou. The first settlers were attracted to Harris County for its access to convenient transportation and natural resources—which, almost one century later, proved to be a wise choice.

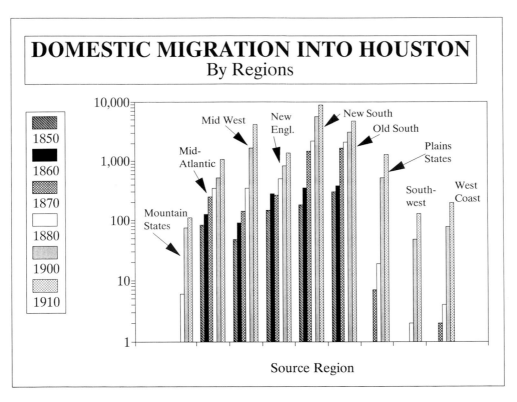

DOMESTIC MIGRATION INTO HOUSTON
By Regions

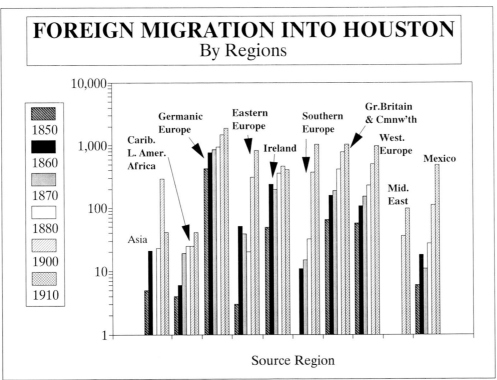

FOREIGN MIGRATION INTO HOUSTON
By Regions

The data for both tables from 1870–1910 was compiled from the United States Census. The Eleventh Census (1890) information is not available for Texas because most of the records were destroyed in a fire in the Commerce Department Building in 1921.

Information on 1850 and 1860 migration trends came from a doctoral thesis submitted by Mary Susan Jackson to the Graduate Department of History at Indiana University in 1974 and entitled *The People of Houston in the 1850's*, pp. 59–62, 245–248.

1 The Evolution of the Houston Landscape

Sadie Gwin Blackburn

Coastal Texas was viewed as a veritable natural paradise by early travelers to the area. The Austin Colony, which included present-day Harris County, was situated on the great prairie lying along the Gulf Coast of Texas between the Trinity River and the Lavaca River. Four rivers and numerous bayous running across these plains drained into the Gulf of Mexico from northwest to southeast. Only Buffalo Bayou flowed from west to east into the expanse of Galveston Bay and thence to the gulf. Joseph Clopper has left the best description of Buffalo Bayou in its pristine state, as he saw it in 1828:

> We enter the mouth of Buffalo Bayou—this is the most remarkable stream I have ever seen—at its junction with the San Jacinto [it] is about 150 yards in breadth having about three fathoms water with little variation in depth as high as Harrisburg— 20 miles—the ebbing and flowing of the tides observable about 12 miles close up to each stream [giving it] the appearance of an artificial canal in the design and course of which nature has lent her masterly hand; for its meanderings and beautiful curvatures seem to have been directed by a taste far too exquisite for human attainment. Most of its course is bound in by timber and flowering shrubbery which overhang its grassy banks and dip and reflect their variegated hues in its unruffled waters. Those impending shrubs are in places overtopped by the evergreen magnolia rising in the grandeur of its excellence to the reach of deserved pre-eminence where it unfolds its far-scented magnificence; softening to the eye of admiration the dazzling lustre of its expansive bloom by agreeable blending with the deep sea-green of its umbrageous foliage—the banks of this stream are secured from the lavings of the water by [protruding roots], which are here termed 'cypress knees'—these are apparently exuberances of cypress roots and shoot up along the margin of the waters to the heights of three and four feet and from three to ten inches in diameter without leaf or branch; and so closely and

regularly are they often found standing in lines as to resemble piles driven in purposely as security against the innovation of the tides.[1]

On the south side of the bayou between Harrisburg and the future site of Houston was a fine stand of *Magnolia grandiflora*, tall evergreen trees with shiny deep green leaves and large white blossoms that filled the air with fragrance in May and June. The banks of the bayou were lined with a tangled magnificence of native growth: several varieties of oak trees draped with Spanish moss, river birch, bay, sweetgum, sycamore, hickory, and walnut trees, the evergreen American holly and yaupon, both covered with red berries in the winter months, and the tall feathery-leaved cypress trees with their roots projecting above the water along the banks. Grapevines grew thickly up into some trees, and the undergrowth was equally luxuriant: small-leaved evergreen cherry laurel, different varieties of hawthorne and viburnum, low-growing palmetto, and native dogwood with its white blossoms shining out of the shade of taller trees[2] (fig. 2).

North of the bayou was the tip of the great forest of mixed evergreens and hardwood trees that swept across the southern United States from the Carolinas to Texas; its southwestern edge stopped just at Buffalo Bayou. On the other side of the bayou the grasslands began, a vast plain stretching south to the warm tropical climate of the Mexican coast and also west to the Texas Hill Country. This change, which followed exactly the line of the bayou, had resulted from two separate episodes of deposition of soil on the ancient Brazos River delta and from differences in rainfall. North of the bayou, the moderately permeable Montgomery formation supported forest growth in the rainy east and graded into grasslands in drier western Harris County. South of the bayou the heavy clay soil of the geologically younger Beaumont formation was a natural prairie that supported the lighter growth of grasses. It was a classic tallgrass prairie with a lush growth which included switchgrass, eastern grammagrass, and big and little bluestem.[3] This vast grassland was broken only by the tree-lined watercourses of rivers and bayous or by scattered clumps of trees in areas near the coast. At the northwestern extremity of this sparsely populated region lay a wide belt of blackland prairie, which was to become one of the richest agricultural hinterlands of the future city of Houston.[4]

The vast prairies were impressive but sometimes dangerous to newcomers. The enormous expanse of waving grass stretched off into seemingly illimitable distance without a single landmark; a traveler could walk in circles for days without realizing it and possibly perish. The same thing could happen to those who ventured without a compass into one of the canebrakes that grew on the prairie near waterways. In these forests of cane, the stalks could grow to a height of twenty or twenty-five feet, "rising so high as to shut out the view of the sky as well as every terrestrial object."[5] When green, these canebrakes provided a natural fodder for cattle and horses, but they were for the same reason favorite haunts for the black bear, which could be dangerous to unwary human intruders.[6]

Canebrakes were often cleared for farmland after it was observed that the crop yield from such land was usually quite good. Mary Austin Holley explained in her book, *Texas*, published in 1836: "The undergrowth of the best land . . . is cane and a species of laurel, the leaves of which taste like the kernel of a peach-stone. . . . The leaves of the laurel resemble those of the peach tree. Hence it is called by the colonists the wild peach. This tree is an evergreen, and grows to the height of twenty or thirty feet though usually not exceeding ten. It is regarded as a certain indication of the best soil. Hence, when a colonist wishes to describe his land as first rate, he says it is all *peach and cane land*."[7]

The "bottoms" were another characteristic of the coastal plains of Texas. These were the bottoms of the canyons cut into the flat prairie during glacial periods hundreds of thousands of years ago and refilled by the periodic flooding of rivers and streams; alluvial layers of rich silt were deposited for miles along the lower reaches of these watercourses by the floods that followed heavy rains. "The 'bottoms' of the rivers are of various breadths on different streams, and at different places, from a few rods, to ten or even twenty miles, and often form a feature in the landscape, while they comprise in great measure, the country's resources in timber. . . ."[8]

An anonymous visitor came to Texas in 1831 to validate a land grant from the Galveston Bay and Texas Land Company, a New York real estate promotion located just east of the Austin grant, with an office near Anahuac on Trinity Bay. He traveled from the Brazos River around the head of Galveston Bay to his destination; this route covered much of the area later to be known as Harris County. His descriptions contain valuable information about early homes and their surroundings. The first houses on these plains were log cabins built at the edge of a grove of trees, with fruit or "china trees" planted in a yard surrounded by a fence. There was also usually an enclosed field of several hundred acres that included a vegetable garden along with a crop of cotton or corn. The landscape was the sweep of the prairie, broken only by scattered "islands" of trees, extending as far as the eye could see.[9] Nature had done the landscaping in this vast parkland. The taste of the era was for picturesque nature. The English landscape garden, which was developed in the eighteenth century and widely imitated all over Europe, was carefully designed to achieve an informal, natural look. Thus, both European and American travelers found the Texas landscape in harmony with their existing landscape ideals.

The visitor, proceeding from Anahuac back to Brazoria, witnessed one of the most spectacular natural phenomena Texas had to offer—the spring eruption of wildflowers.

> I had never been at all prepared for the indescribable beauty of a Texas Prairie at this season of the year. . . . The wild flowers . . . spread around us in the utmost profusion, and in wonderful variety. Some of those which are most cultivated in our northern gardens were here in full bloom and perfection, intermingled with many I had never before seen, of different forms and colors . . . these fields of flowers were . . . extensive almost beyond limitation. . . . After looking on their rich and ever varying display, I thought I could almost give my mustang his liberty, throw myself on the ground, and spend the whole season among them.[10]

Davy Crockett wrote to his children from the Alamo: "Everyone knows that Texas is the wild-flower garden of the world," and Ashbel Smith wrote in an article included in Henry Stuart Foote's *Texas and Texans* about "prairies clothed with a most luxuriant growth of grasses gorgeously enameled with flowers."[11]

There were negative aspects to this paradise, however: "wet northers" could sweep down from the northwest, dropping the temperature suddenly, with violent winds accompanied by torrents of rain that flooded watercourses and inundated prairies. Slow drainage produced quagmires of mud, which were impassable by man or beast. When travel at last became possible, travelers were surrounded and attacked by great clouds of mosquitoes; even worse, dreaded diseases such as malaria, yellow fever, and cholera followed these overflows.

Thomas Drummond, a botanist from Scotland, came in 1833 on a plant-collecting expedition for Sir William Jackson Hooker, Regius Professor of Botany at the University of Glasgow and later director of the Royal Gardens at Kew. The specimens that Drummond sent back included those collected in the Houston-Galveston area in the winter and spring of 1833–34. He experienced almost all of the natural disasters Texas could offer: he arrived during the Great Overflow of 1833 and was forced to go by boat over the prairie, which stood nine to fifteen feet deep in water; he contracted cholera in Velasco and was the only victim to survive there; the quality of his botanical drying paper was compromised by the constant humidity, and he had to pay a large sum for an oxcart to carry his scientific equipment from place to place. Despite these hardships, he thought of settling his family in Texas and conducting a plant inventory for the Mexican government. Unfortunately, however, he died on a collecting trip to Cuba shortly after leaving Texas.[12] Among the seeds Drummond sent back to Europe were new species of wild phlox, which Hooker named *Phlox drummondi*. The lavender flower from this area became an immediate favorite in European gardens and was thence transmitted to the United States. Mary Austin Holley wrote: "Mr. Thomas Drummond of Glasgow has done more than any other man toward exploring the botany of Texas. He sent home many plants and seeds which have been successfully cultivated there, and drawings of them have been given in late numbers of Curtis's Botanical Magazine."[13]

The natural beauty of the Texas coastal prairie was radically altered by development over the years. The process began when the early settlers pushed back the native vegetation to make room for planted gardens and fields. Until the last quarter of the nineteenth century, botany, horticulture and agriculture were regarded as one integrated area of knowledge and practice, with various areas of special concern, such as plants for food, plants for medicine, and plants for building materials. This utilitarian emphasis was especially true on the frontier. Information on the culture of garden vegetables was printed in the newspapers along with information about growing crops. Fruit orchards and vegetable gardens were sometimes planted in the enclosed field with staple crops, although fruit trees were often also planted decoratively within the yard around the house. Large vegetable gardens were needed to feed a household, including the slaves as well as the families of the settlers. Herb gardens were planted near the kitchen door or along with the vegetable garden.

Settlers of the Austin Colony, established in 1822, hastened to plant their vegetables, fruits, herbs, and crops as soon as possible after their arrival. They imported a wide variety of plants.

An early manifest of garden seeds that arrived in Brazoria for the Austin Colony in 1832 listed beet, onion, "raddish," turnip, cabbage, okra, white mustard, parsley, spinach, parsnip, peas, and beans; several varieties of each vegetable were included.[14] J. J. Crawford, living six miles above Houston in 1844 on the north bank of the bayou, listed "herbs, sage, rhue, thime, horsh radish, wormwood, balm, feney, hops, &c, &c,."[15] Almost all fruit trees except apple, pear, and cherry were easily grown; peach, orange, and fig were mentioned often, as were all kinds of berries. The native grapes, Mustang and muscadine, were much appreciated and cultivated both for eating and for making wine. Wheat did not thrive in south Texas. The principal staple crops were corn and cotton. Corn was used mostly for consumption by the family, and cotton was the cash crop. The soil and climate of the area grew cotton that was the equal of the famous Sea Island variety, and the demand was enormous. Cotton culture, however, was a labor-intensive endeavor, and slavery, which had been forbidden but not prevented by the Mexican government, became integral to the life of the republic. On the coast and in east Texas, rice and sugarcane were also grown as income-producing crops.

Most of the early plantations were in the Brazos River valley, but there were some in the more sparsely settled area near Galveston Bay and inland along the bayous. Probably the best documented of these was Orange Grove, situated on a peninsula of land between Galveston Bay and the mouth of the San Jacinto River (fig. 5). The tract was originally deeded to Dr. Johnson Hunter as his league of land in the Austin Colony; in 1826, however, it was purchased by Nicholas Clopper, a merchant from Baltimore and Cincinnati. Nicholas Clopper was the chief supplier of merchandise to the Austin Colony; in 1822 he was deeded a league of land and opened a store in San Felipe, which he supplied by the tortuous route up the Brazos River. After the Harris County area became part of the Austin Colony in 1824, it was possible to use the waterway through Galveston Bay and up Buffalo Bayou for a short overland trip to San Felipe. This soon became the principal trade route into the interior. In 1826 Clopper formed the Texas Trading Association with his three sons and several friends, opened a store in Harrisburg, and bought Hunter's peninsula, which then became known as Clopper's Point. The first view of it by his sons is recorded by Joseph Clopper on January 1, 1828: "[We] . . . go ashore on father's league known by the name of Hunter's Point—a lovely spot of land surrounded by a beautifully picturesque scenery decorated with groves of cedar, pine, magnolia, etc., presenting a perpetual view of evergreen scenery and considered one of the handsomest situations in all the Colony. The bay on one side—the meandering San Jacinto or sacred hyacinth on another—the back of it prairie and timber standing in bodies and clusters like small islands of green upon the broad waste of ocean."[16]

The Clopper family's experience offers a good example of the importance of gardens to the early settlers. Edward Clopper's journal notes on January 3: "Went ashore this morning and planted some orange and Lemon seeds. . . . "[17] This planting may well have been the genesis of the orange orchard that later provided the name of the plantation on the peninsula. The Cloppers planted an acre of sugarcane adjoining a vegetable garden at their store in Harrisburg, "which if it grows well will produce seed sufficient for ten acres." On the peninsula next to their warehouse residence, they planted "a vegetable garden along with corn and potatoes."[18] The Texas Trading

Association ceased to exist in 1830, possibly because of the interdiction of the Mexican government against further immigration from the United States, which nullified Nicholas Clopper's plans for his family to join him in Texas. He put his plantation up for sale. Among the potential purchasers were Augustus C. Allen and John K. Allen, who were already looking for a place to build a city in Texas, but they considered the price of two dollars an acre too high.[19]

A New York company headed by James Swartwout, who had also been a principal stockholder in the Galveston Bay and Texas Land Company, persuaded James Morgan, owner of the general merchandise store in Anahuac, to act as agent to buy Clopper's Point. On December 22, 1834, the peninsula became the possession of their New Washington Association. This group planned to build a city there by that name and made sure that all the maps of the day noted the location. It was one of many "cities on paper," but James Morgan waxed enthusiastic about its potential: "I never saw such oranges growing anywhere . . . the fruit [will serve to] bring N. W. more into notice. It is the only bearing grove in all Texas."[20]

Orange Grove became a popular stopping place for important government visitors and travelers between 1834 and 1866, the year of James Morgan's death. In 1837 John James Audubon visited the plantation and described it: "This spot, possessing a fine extent of woodland, surrounded by vast prairies, ornamented with numerous detached groves, reminded us of some of the beautiful parks of England."[21] Ferdinand Roemer, a German geologist, stopped at the plantation ten years later and described the house situated on an elevation twenty feet above the bay surrounded by a lawn with scattered red cedar trees. Behind the house was a virgin forest, whose tall trees were so covered with Spanish moss that they seemed to be covered with a gray curtain. The orange trees had been killed by a severe freeze but were apparently still standing. Roemer wrote: "[Morgan] also carried on agriculture with his fifteen slaves and raised, principally corn in such quantities, that after he had supplied the needs of his family, of his slaves, and of his cattle, he still had some for sale. During the past few years he had also experimented with raising sugar cane and the results were very gratifying. . . ."[22] Morgan's Orange Grove exemplified the Arcadian nature of the Texas settlement. It was only necessary to build the house; the landscaping was already in place. Native grasses could feed the cattle, and the mild climate allowed them to survive without winter shelter. The same climate and fertile soil guaranteed good crops for household use and agricultural commerce.

Roemer also visited the nearby plantation of Dr. Ashbel Smith, who was a leading citizen of Texas and who called his plantation Headquarters. Dr. Smith served as surgeon general of the army of the Republic of Texas and later was appointed minister to both France and Great Britain, where he participated in the crucial negotiations that preceded Texas's admission to the United States in 1845. Dr. Smith's visitors were astonished at the austerity of the household of such a distinguished individual. His library and his gardens, however, were extensive. There were two beds of strawberries each a hundred feet long, and immediately in front of the house was a thirty-acre cultivated field, enclosed with the customary rail fence.[23] The field was planted in corn and cotton, with peach trees growing between the rows of corn. The manner of planting in this garden was widely used all over the South and is believed to be derived from Indian custom.[24] In 1848

Ashbel Smith bought from Moseley Baker's estate the adjoining plantation known as Evergreen; he moved from Headquarters into an equally modest house and hired an overseer to operate the combined properties under the name of Evergreen (fig. 6). It was there that he conducted numerous scientific experiments with various crops such as wheat, sugarcane, and Sea Island cotton in order to prove the practicality of crop diversification after the Civil War.[25]

Francis R. Lubbock owned both a home in Houston and an outlying plantation. Lubbock, who was born in South Carolina, married Adele Baron of New Orleans in 1835 and brought her with him to Texas in 1837. He bought four hundred acres on Sims Bayou from the John R. Harris estate and used it primarily as a cattle ranch (fig. 7). Lubbock owned another piece of property in Houston, known as Lubbock's Grove because of a fine stand of trees there, which was often the setting for picnics and outdoor gatherings of a number of early organizations in Houston. In 1847 the Lubbocks sold their home in Houston and moved to their ranch. Mrs. Andrew Briscoe had given Mrs. Lubbock some plants from her garden in Harrisburg before they sold their brick house there to General Sidney Sherman: Mrs. Briscoe's letters to her husband mention fruit trees, ornamental shrubs, and trees, specifically "Bodark" trees, grapevines, and altheas.[26] It was believed at this time that the prairie, which supported only grasses, would not grow crops. Lubbock found otherwise:

> It was black hog-wallow, or heavy black waxy prairie, and its need was drainage, and I had it well ditched and drained. . . . My land was laid off in beds of twelve feet wide, thrown well up, and the corn planted on those beds in rows of three or four feet apart. This gave admirable drainage. The next year I would plant them with a subsoil plow, and I invariably made good corn. While I did not plant cotton for a crop, the land would produce it well, as I found by my experiments . . . it yielded very fine oats and peas and sweet and Irish potatoes of the best quality; in fact vegetables of all kinds grew well. I also had a good peach and plum orchard and very many fine fig trees. Blackberries and dewberries, indigenous to the sandy soil, grew in great profusion upon the waxy land after it was plowed; sorghum made luxuriant crops.[27]

Texas plantations in the Harris County area yielded abundant returns to knowledgeable early settlers.

While plantations grew up mostly in the east and south of the Harris County area, the north and west sections were gradually occupied by widely scattered farms of immigrants from northern Germany who began coming in the early 1830s. Farms on Buffalo Bayou approximately ten miles above Harrisburg were situated close together in a vicinity known as Germantown. Just west of this area, at the confluence of White Oak and Buffalo bayous, the Allen brothers founded the city of Houston in 1836.

It is important to an understanding of the development of the Houston landscape to recognize that the city was laid out in an orderly fashion from the beginning. Despite its appearance as a tent city with stumps in the streets and the rapid influx of inhabitants that resulted from its designation as the capital of the new Republic of Texas, building proceeded according to a plan.

A. C. and John K. Allen instructed the surveyor to lay out the city in a grid pattern with wide streets commensurate with the great city they envisioned. It was oriented not to the compass but to the bayou, that watery highway that was to carry the commerce that would ensure its future greatness. As the center of government, the city needed food and water for large numbers of people, and arrangements for provisions from nearby farmers quickly brought the surrounding areas into close contact with the infant city. Market Square alleviated the urgency for making individual gardens, although most new residents lost no time in planting a garden and fruit trees as soon as possible after their arrival.

Some early gardens that provided supplies for pioneer Houstonians were recorded in books and newspapers. Henry Kessler operated a saloon in a round tent, which was an early landmark in Houston. He had a garden "about ten miles from Houston, where Mulberry trees and unusually high corn were raised and which the owners planned to make accessible for the public."[28] A man who was undoubtedly Kessler's supplier and customer owned a racecourse and a plantation three miles out of town where he grew garden fruits and vegetables that were sold in Market Square. Gustav Dresel reported that this man had realized a thousand dollars one year by his sale of mint alone. "This plant, like woodruff with us, is used for a drink which Americans appreciate greatly and which is known as mint julep throughout America."[29] It is not known when Phineas Jenks Mahan put in his garden in a bend of Buffalo Bayou near the later site of Jefferson Davis Hospital, but it was at least some time before December 4, 1841. On that date an advertisement offered fresh garden seeds "warranted the growth of 1841." The seeds were for sale in the Market House, during market hours and at all times at Mr. Wm. Dankewerth's store opposite the market. Mahan sold produce and seeds to Houstonians for thirty years.[30]

One of the topographical attributes of early Houston, not discernible today, was a series of ravines cutting through the town site, which had been formed by water draining from the prairie into Buffalo Bayou after periodic floods. A painting by Thomas Flintoff of St. Vincent's Church, built on Franklin Street in 1841–42, is valuable for its depiction of one of the best known of these natural landmarks. Dr. S. O. Young described the gully appearing in Flintoff's painting: "In the early days Houston was remarkable for its numerous large gullies. There was one great one that took up rather more than the lower end of Caroline Street. It was narrower after reaching Congress Avenue and gradually narrowed until it completely disappeared between Prairie and Texas avenues. There were two big bridges crossing the gully, one on Franklin and the other on Congress Avenue."[31] Another gully began on Milam and ran between Texas and Prairie avenues to the bayou; at the point where the gully passed Smith, there was a very large spring, which had minnows swimming in it and a large oak tree hanging over it.

Gardens around houses in the new city were of the simplest sort. Andrew Briscoe, recently appointed chief justice of Harrisburg County, came to Houston and bought a house under construction by Thomas William Ward[32] (fig. 10). The garden, as it appears in an early painting, was typical in design but rather elaborate in its execution. As with all residences, a fence was the first necessity; horses, cattle, and pigs roamed freely in the streets, and gardens had to be protected from their ravages. Picket fences were most commonly used. Native trees in the painting include flowering magnolia, oak, and possibly hackberry. Smaller trees, probably planted by the Briscoes, included fruit trees, a flowering crape myrtle by the front walk, and a few rose bushes planted at the side of the house.

One large house built in Houston in the earliest years was the John D. Andrews house (later numbered 418 Austin Street). John Andrews brought his family to Houston from Virginia, along with all the materials for the house, to make a life for them that would uphold the traditions from which they came. The house was "encircled by 35 large fig trees, enclosing an orchard containing peach, pear and plum trees and six large grapevines, all of which provided preserves, jellies and wines for the household."[33] On a corner lot across the street between Prairie and Preston was a vegetable garden around a large pond. The pond would have been convenient for watering the garden, since in the early years water had to be hauled from Buffalo Bayou or purchased by the barrel. A grandson remembered crawfishing in the pond and watching quail compete for grain with the chickens in the chicken yard.[34] The practice of using adjacent land for vegetable gardens and other utility purposes was quite common throughout this period.

Some early writers maintain that German settlers introduced vegetables to Texas and that the Anglo settlers did not have vegetable gardens. Early travelers, principally Germans, complained about the monotonous diet of Texans: cornbread, bacon, sweet potatoes, and coffee, three times a day. Apparently this was the standard meal offered to travelers for one dollar, no matter what time of day they arrived. Correspondence of the time indicates that this was the practice of certain settlers both to accommodate newcomers and to make money in the process; better food and a more balanced diet were available from plantation households without charge. Terry Jordan, of German descent himself, states that research indicates that Anglo-Americans and all other ethnic groups, except the blacks, grew and served vegetables as soon as they could plant a garden after settling.[35]

The year 1839 was a turning point in Houston history. A devastating yellow fever epidemic in 1838 had claimed many lives, including that of John Kirby Allen, and was one of the reasons for the removal of the capital to Austin the following year. The loss of population meant that the people remaining would have to redefine the character of the city. Editorials in the newspapers urged city improvements, specifically that the city council build sidewalks in the downtown area and that residents plant street trees.[36] In the early 1840s the economic depression in the United States reached Texas, but the editor of the *Morning Star* did not relent in his campaign for civic beautification:

The present season is most favorable for the transplanting of trees and we trust our citizens will improve it to advantage. The small water oaks that are found in great numbers in the woods near the city can be transplanted, probably at less cost than any other trees and they will grow very thriftily in the prairie soil. If the persons owning property on the principal streets of the city would transplant a few of these trees to the sidewalks, they would thus not only enhance the value of their property but contribute to secure the health of the city. If rows of these trees should be set one on each side of Main Street from the bayou to the "Old Capitol" it could soon be rendered one of the most beautiful streets of the South.[37]

Successful transplanting techniques had been developed in England in the 1830s; the instructions printed in the Houston newspaper in 1843 for transplanting evergreens was a transmission of this new information.[38] The time between discovery in England and practice in Houston was remarkably short.

Information about native Texas plants was sent from Texas to several botanical gardens in these early years. Ferdinand Jacob Lindheimer was one of the German intellectuals who fell afoul of the German authorities and came to America seeking freedom. Living first in the Mississippi valley German communities, he came to Texas as a member of a volunteer company raised to help Sam Houston fight the Mexicans. After the Revolution, he tried farming around Houston but found it unsatisfactory, either because he did not like it or because he discovered a "weakness in the lungs" that forced him to a less arduous way of life. On an earlier occasion he had collected plants in Mexico for Dr. Georg Engelmann, who had become established as a botanist in St. Louis; Engelmann now wrote Asa Gray at the Arnold Arboretum in Boston and convinced the Harvard botanist that Texas specimens could be used in Gray's research and then sold for Lindheimer's benefit. Lindheimer began by collecting extensively in the Houston-Galveston area in 1843, ten years after Drummond's collection.[39] Many of the plants were new to the botanical world and named for Lindheimer. One of the most familiar is the *Gaura lindheimeri*, or false honeysuckle. While little noted at the time, this scientific recording of native Texas plants was important to future understanding of plant resources and habitat.

As Houston grew, gardens became more varied and reflected the gardening traditions of the individuals who made them. The Allens came from upstate New York and Sarah Chapman (Mrs. Roland) Allen, mother of the founders, grew up in Westchester County near New York City; many of the other early settlers came from that state as well. Gardening traditions were strong in that area; the earliest nurseries in the United States had been established in New York. Andrew Jackson Downing, a member of a family that owned a nursery in Newburgh on the Hudson, became nationally prominent for his book *A Treatise on the Theory and Practice of Landscape Gardening*, and his influence on horticulture was further extended through his magazine, *The Horticulturist*, the first of its kind in the United States.

In 1844 architect F. Jacob Rothhaas came to Houston, probably from New York, at the instigation of two immigrants from New York, Erastus S. Perkins and George Allen, a brother of the founders. Judge Perkins' orchard was reported to be a gorgeous sight in spring, with "the delicate colors of all the fruit trees in bloom," and equally in the fall when, through his skill in gardening, apple and quince trees bore fruit.[40] On January 27, 1844, the *Telegraph and Texas Register* carried an advertisement of European and American grape cuttings for sale by Jacob Rothhaas, with orders to be addressed to E. S. Perkins.[41] On July 31, 1844, the *Telegraph* reprinted an article from the Cincinnati newspaper which read: "Texas is said to be one of the finest grape growing countries in the world . . . a gentleman of Cincinnati received lately 500 cuttings . . . of Post Oak Grapes of Texas—a purple grape of fair size free from pulp, and of an excellent flavor, either as fruit or making wine. They came from Mr. Perkins, at Houston who has a vineyard containing 10,000 rooted vines."[42] It seems that Mr. Rothhaas had brought and planted at least some of Judge Perkins's 10,000 grapevines (fig. 12).

Rothhaas is known to have been the architect and possibly the landscape designer of the plantation of George Allen. George Allen was given land outside the city, perhaps on Sloop Point,[43] and built a plantation home for his family. Rothhaas painted a watercolor rendering of this house and garden in 1845 (fig. 13). In the painting the house is surrounded by a sturdily built picket fence. Native trees and grass provided the basic design of the property. Near the front gate a fairly large magnolia was blooming, and other plantings had been added to enhance the beauty of the entrance: three blooming white crape myrtles, three white altheas with rose pink centers (this was a popular althea of the day called Rose of Sharon), and immediately to the right of the path at the gate were pomegranate bushes. Several kinds of wildflowers, ferns, and palmettos seemed to be springing up through the grass-covered lawn, while the owners standing in the driveway surveyed the scene.

Other gardening traditions came with immigrants from Europe. Germans arrived in great numbers beginning with the *Verein* settlement efforts in the 1840s. So many Germans had remained in Houston rather than continuing inland that Houston's population was 40 percent German in 1850. Victims of the potato famine in Ireland arrived in Houston during these years also. The new residents clustered together in a pleasant area on the bayou known as Frost Town. "Small homes were surrounded by kitchen and flower gardens and the addition of a cow, goats, and chickens made each household a self-contained domestic unit."[44]

The English love of horticulture and the Scottish gift for gardening were evident in the gardens of several families in Houston, including those of T. W. House, James Bute, and Charles Shearn. T. W. House, originally from England, built one of Houston's early large residences at 706 Smith Street at the corner of Capitol, probably soon after his marriage at the beginning of the 1840s to the daughter of Charles Shearn, an earlier arrival from England[45] (fig. 14). The vegetable garden was located on a separate block where a log cabin had been built for the gardener. Reputedly, one of the sights to be seen in Houston in the springtime was a wide flower bed filled with blooming white narcissi running just inside the whole front length of the picket fence.[46] Such a flower bed was a new thing for Houston gardens. Although landscape of native grass and trees would continue for some time in Houston's gardening history, new traditions were in the making; flower beds were finding a place in the urban landscape.

The activities of two brothers illustrate the general development of the Houston landscape by 1850. Born in New England but moving to Charleston, South Carolina, and then to Texas in pursuit of business opportunities, Edward and Horace Taylor became cotton commission merchants in Houston. Edward bought a large acreage on the bayou at the edge of town with a house and garden for his family; Horace lived in bachelor quarters in their warehouse downtown on the bayou. Edward became involved in other business ventures, including railroad building, and eventually built a large house and garden in the newly fashionable residential district facing Courthouse Square. Horace married in 1852 and bought his brother's property on the bayou, a six-acre triangular tract bounded by Smith Street, Preston Avenue, and Buffalo Bayou. He had always admired the spot and loved the woods that grew there along the bayou. There were sycamore, prickly ash, bois d'arc, sweet gum, and holly with undergrowth of box-elder and mustang grapes, but the most spectacular trees were the magnolias. Some of them were nearly a hundred feet tall and could be seen from afar by travelers approaching on Washington Road across the bayou.[47] A long bridge had been built across the bayou from Washington Road to Preston to accommodate trade with the farming population north and west of Houston, and H. D. Taylor set up a campground on his property at the foot of the bridge where farmers could stay overnight when they came to market.[48] The description of Houston at this time is best given in his own words:

> The main street runs from the wharf on Buffalo Bayou out some three quarters of a mile to the prairie on which street are most of the stores. Most of the dwelling houses are built on prairie lots and have large Gardens attached. The dwelling houses are all built of wood, very few of them being more than one story high but with commodious Piazzas which are absolutely necessary in this almost tropical climate. What renders them more pleasant to the eye is their neat exteriors all being painted white. Such houses when surrounded by foliage are truly delightful.[49]

The town that had been cut out of the Texas landscape on Buffalo Bayou was creating its own planted environment in private gardens and street trees. New plants, including Chinaberry, crape myrtle, and many varieties of fruit trees, joined the earlier introductions of peach, orange, and fig trees. Roses, bulbs, and a great variety of other garden flowers were brought in by the early settlers. Two new plants arrived on ships from the West Indies: the oleander via Jamaica and the banana tree from Cuba.[50]

Vigorous development in railroad building by Houstonians during the decade of the 1850s made Houston a market and distribution center for the agricultural population of Harris County. Five railroads radiating out in all directions provided a local transportation network, regardless of weather, and gave the smaller communities a more dependable early access to distant markets and new products than was usual for most rural towns in frontier areas. This early initiative placed Houston in a favorable position for leadership not only in agricultural services but in general trade and commerce.

Frederick Law Olmsted came to Texas in 1854 to write a series of journalistic reports on life in the South. An abolitionist, he found much to criticize in antebellum Texas, but he approved of the Germans, admired the magnolia trees of Houston, and described the city: "It shows many agreeable signs of the wealth accumulated, in homelike, retired residences, its large and good hotel, its well-supplied shops, and its shaded streets. The principal thoroughfare, opening from the steamboat landing, is the busiest we saw in Texas."[51] This was Houston on the eve of the Civil War (fig. 18).

During the Civil War, gardens reverted to the earlier priority of food production—not only for those at home but also for the soldiers of the Confederacy. In his *Tri-Weekly Telegraph* E. H. Cushing wrote in April 1862: "As this is the time for gardening, we suggest that an extra crop of tomatoes be planted, with a view of preserving them in the summer in air-tight cans. No vegetable is so conducive to health as this, and if enough can be preserved to furnish our armies with rations two or three times a week, it will be a most excellent thing."[52] Because of the Union blockade, seeds had to be obtained from Mexico; James Burke advertised El Paso onion seed.[53] There was a drought in 1862 and prices went up, so home gardens were necessary for that reason also.

The suburban home of Robert Lockart was one of the centers of activity in Houston during the Civil War (fig. 19). The Confederate headquarters for Texas was in Houston, and Francis R. Lubbock was the state's wartime governor. Mrs. Lockart was Lubbock's sister, and since his house was out on Sims Bayou, the Lockart household became a meeting place for the governor when he was in town.[54] Robert Lockart came to Houston from Pennsylvania in 1843 and in December of that year married Anna Blythewood Lubbock. He bought the property, which was later designated as 2915 Commerce Avenue, on the eastern edge of Houston from James T. D. Wilson in 1847 and planted his fields with cotton.[55] A painting of the house and grounds in 1872 by an itinerant artist, Walter Sies Finnil, indicates that the planting around the house was in the natural landscape tradition of native grass and trees. The rail fence enclosure was usual for property in the country, and horse grazing was one practical method of keeping the grass cut; the hot, heavy work of scything was the alternative. Robert Lockart planted a number of pecan trees around the homestead during the Civil War, possibly for food since there was much hunger toward the end of the war. Pecans were native but grew principally along the waterways. The few gardens planted during the Reconstruction years generally followed this simple but effective landscape design tradition.

One of the houses in the prestigious Quality Hill neighborhood became the home of Cornelius Ennis and his family in 1871 (fig. 20). The garden at 1618 Congress Avenue was enclosed with a taller than usual picket fence, and evergreens planted at equidistant intervals across the front of the property provided a green accent in the winter landscape. The general design of the area was typical of most Houston gardens of this period. A six-foot fence divided the front yard from the back yard, where there was a vegetable garden. A row of pecan trees stood along the fence, which was covered with honeysuckle. Lantanas, moss roses, and coral bush honeysuckle bloomed in warm months. "Quantities of four o'clocks, adding their brilliant hues as well as their permeating fragrance, daily furnished a bit of entertainment to all the neighborhood children, who delighted in watching the blossoms open."[56] It is significant that all of the flowers were native plants and would have required a minimum of care.

The Raphael family garden was planted around the house built in 1868. Samuel Raphael arrived in Houston from Birmingham, England, in the 1850s and served as Houston's rabbi until his death shortly after the Civil War. His two sons, who were working as telegraph operators, built a cottage for their mother and sisters on the corner of Rusk Avenue and Hamilton Street on the prairie outskirts of Houston. In 1871 they built a two-story addition to the front of the cottage[57] (fig. 21). They soon arranged for Charles Albrecht to plant trees of several varieties around the prairie home. The Raphael garden was later described in the *Houston Daily Post* as standing on a fourth of a block of ground, with spacious lawns, shrubbery, and flower beds on all sides of the house. "Stately oaks and elms surround the place and their grateful shade is a lasting credit to the arboricultural skill of the late Mr. Albrecht."[58] The fact that the Raphael house and garden were created at all was an exception to the general rule in the years between 1860 and 1880.

Although Houstonians seldom had time or money to spare for creating elaborate gardens in the aftermath of the Civil War, the study of agriculture and horticulture remained an important concern. Three men, Thomas Affleck, Edward Hopkins Cushing, and Ashbel Smith, were the principal experts on agriculture, horticulture, and gardening in the Houston area during this period.

Thomas Affleck was nationally known when he moved to Brenham in Washington County in 1858. Born in Scotland, he came to America as a young man. He worked as a nurseryman in New York, Indiana, and Ohio, eventually becoming editor of the Cincinnati *Western Farmer and Gardener* in 1840.[59] With B. N. Norman, he wrote the first scientific agricultural almanac in 1842 and continued this annual publication on his own after 1852, under the title of *Affleck's Southern Rural Almanac and Plantation and Garden Calendar*. Working to relieve debts on his wife's family plantation in Mississippi, Affleck reorganized the business and wrote the *Affleck Plantation Journal and Account Book* for cotton and sugar growers to accompany his almanac. He established the Southern Nurseries at the plantation and became widely respected for the plants he produced and the horticultural practices he advocated.[60] In 1854 the Afflecks built a plantation home near Brenham, Texas, named Glenblyth, to which they moved in 1858.[61]

In Houston, Affleck engaged J. H. S. Stanley as agent for his Central Nurseries in Brenham and planted a whole grove of ornamental trees around Stanley's house at 406 Capitol Avenue. Stanley was an early daguerreotype artist in Houston, but he also kept a supply of Affleck's greenhouse plants and shrubbery for sale.[62] He advertised that, as agent for Mr. Thos. Affleck, he had received "a collection of plants . . . [which] are in the most perfect condition and comprise varieties that have hitherto been unknown in the state."[63] As agricultural editor for the *Telegraph and Texas Register*, Affleck gave horticultural and agricultural advice on a wide range of subjects, including kitchen gardens. He acclimatized plants and identified varieties that would grow well in warmer climates; he advocated manuring and rotation of crops to avoid a one-crop economy;

and he "taught to thousands" the art of budding and grafting to extend the range of plants available to southern planters. The first successful cultivation of fine pears in the far South was attributed to him. Affleck died suddenly of pneumonia on December 30, 1868. In the newspaper obituary, E. H. Cushing described him as a man ahead of his time,[64] and, indeed, the 1860 edition of his almanac provided the basic information on which Texas and southern agriculture was reestablished after the Civil War[65] (fig. 29).

The editor of the *Telegraph*, Edward Hopkins Cushing, regarded his paper as an instrument for public education, and he used it well. He was a native of Vermont, a Dartmouth graduate of 1850 who had come to Texas as a teacher. While teaching in Columbia, he wrote articles and also became editor of the paper *Democrat and Planter*. In 1856 he came to Houston as editor and later owner of the *Telegraph and Texas Register*. His avocation was horticulture, and so deeply did he study and practice this discipline that he was recognized and respected by many trained botanists of the time.[66] He built a house on ten acres south of town and called it Bohemia (fig. 30).

> Several acres were set aside for flowers and shrubs. The rarest and most beautiful flowers were propagated and raised. He delighted in massing collections of rare plants, arranged to give beautiful effects when in bloom. . . . A staff correspondent of a northern newspaper stated that the flowers of "Bohemia" were one of the most complete collections in the United States, she having counted more than three hundred varieties on one visit. . . . What were rare vegetables in this country, such as artichokes, asparagus, celery, cauliflower, etc., etc., were first grown in his gardens.[67]

It was said that "his garden and stables were the nearest approach to an agricultural station then in Texas."[68] Cushing was also aware of new developments in landscape design. The structure of his rose garden was described as "an innovation . . . in the shape of a great wheel with a shrub in the center of the circle with half a dozen radiating paths marking off small beds . . . edged with violets."[69] When his critical attitude toward Reconstruction military forces necessitated the sale of his newspaper, he opened a book and printing store and continued to exert a wide influence in the city and surrounding area.

E. H. Cushing and Ashbel Smith were close friends. While Cushing was active locally through teaching and publishing about gardening and horticulture, Smith's sphere of influence was larger because he served several terms in the Texas legislature and maintained his contacts through travel to meetings and exhibitions in the United States and Europe. He was interested in many things, including agriculture. He strongly advised farmers to practice crop diversification in order to increase their income. Through his own experimentation with Egyptian and Sea Island cotton, sugarcane, and grapes, Ashbel Smith set an example for his contemporaries. Service in the legislature and as a trustee of numerous educational institutions provided opportunities for expressing his ideas and extending his influence. One of the most significant educational posts he held was commissioner of the board to help organize the "Texas Agricultural and Mechanical College for the benefit of Colored Youths" in Prairie View, northwest of Houston.[70] This school educated many black people in successful agricultural practices as well as providing them with a general education. Its influence was second only to the churches in the African American communities of Houston and Harris County.

Along with the recovery of agriculture and advances in agricultural and horticultural education, a new interest in public planting appeared in Houston during the Reconstruction years. This interest was one aspect of the awareness of a general need to plan for the public welfare and provide urban amenities as Houstonians rebuilt their city. Houston did not suffer the terrible destruction of southern cities east of the Mississippi, but the Union blockade had prevented most trade, which was the source of the city's wealth. In general, Houston citizens were left with their homes but little else, and their city was in sad repair. Buffalo Bayou had silted up and was filled with snags, the few streets that had been paved with shell were again deep with mud, and houses and gardens had not received normal upkeep during the war years.[71] Repairing the neglected infrastructure and providing basic utilities to the community were the most pressing problems facing the populace and the Reconstruction city government. Improvements , however, were limited to the downtown business area in order to give the appearance of a thriving city in which northern concerns might be willing to invest. The needs of residential districts were ignored, and homes and gardens remained in a frontier condition.[72]

Public landscaping for parks as a civic amenity had been advocated as early as 1866, when the first *Houston City Directory* was published. It suggested:

> our City Fathers should not forget that mere utility is not the standard which should govern their actions for the public good. Our city needs adornment; our people to be treated not merely as money-making machines, but as social, moral, and intellectual creatures. Now is the time for suitable locations for public squares, places of resort for the people, when the business and labor of the day is over, where something can be seen to relieve the monotony of brick walls and crowded business highways. Provisions for the cultivation of a taste for the beautiful in city improvements have entered largely into the municipal legislation of all of the large cities of the world.[73]

The first action that might be considered a response to this call was the new City Market House, completed at considerable cost in 1871, financed by municipal bonds. This three-story building was erected downtown in the middle of a full city block and "the grounds landscaped into a well-manicured park." In 1876 this civic symbol burned to the ground, leaving the city with its huge debt and removing one of the major sources of municipal revenue.[74] Lack of water pressure in water mains from the bayou was blamed for the disaster. Reconstruction mayor T. H. Scanlan had traveled to other cities to observe the technology necessary for public utilities, invested heavily in the Houston Waterworks, and became its president. After the Market House fire, the city council corresponded with other city governments about their systems, and in 1878 commissioned James M. Lowerie of New York to install a complete system, including a reservoir, a pumping station, and four miles of distributor mains.[75]

A national desire for public parks had followed the completion of New York's Central Park, designed by Frederick Law Olmsted in the 1860s. Such an undertaking not only demonstrated civic responsibility in providing public recreation but also expressed a profound belief in the moral healing power of the beauty of Nature. Not many cities could afford such a grand public park, however, and the cemetery park provided a viable alternative. Traditionally located within city churchyards, cemeteries were now placed in scenic rural settings and landscaped as public parks with curving walks and drives to conform to natural topography. The practice became widespread in the United States.

Alfred J. Whitaker became the spokesperson in the effort to provide Houston with a rural cemetery park. Whitaker was a trained botanist who came to Houston from England in 1859.[76] In 1871 he and his subscribers successfully petitioned the Texas legislature in the name of the Houston Cemetery Association for a charter to buy land and use it for cemetery purposes. A beautiful piece of wooded property lying along the north side of Buffalo Bayou on Washington Road was chosen for the purchase.[77] An article from the *Daily Telegraph* of October 26, 1871, contains the information that the new cemetery covered sixty acres and was being enclosed by a picket fence five or six feet high, the whole circumference being over a mile. The sides were to be hedged with bois d'arc and the front with arbor vitae. "Passing through the entrance, 30 feet wide, you come to a deep ravine with precipitate banks, thickly grown with the 'short leaf' pine, the 'sweet gum', the wild peach, cottonwood, oak, an occasional magnolia, and other trees, over whose branches the wild vine clambers in attractive profusion. The ravine is now having a bridge built across it, over which a graded avenue, now being constructed is to pass. . . ." The newspaper account compares Glenwood to other well-known cemetery parks: Laurel Hill of Philadelphia and Greenwood in Brooklyn.[78]

Glenwood Cemetery was, at least during the nineteenth century, a cemetery park. The families whose loved ones were buried there came every Sunday after church to put flowers on the graves. These offerings added to the quiet beauty already present in the natural surroundings and the landscaping. Many other families brought picnic lunches to enjoy on the bank of the bayou. Thus, only eight years after the completion of Central Park, Houston became one of the American cities with a cemetery park where its citizens could enjoy Nature in respite from the city environment.

Whitaker's own home was pictured on the Wood map of 1869 (fig. 31). The house was situated at the edge of a wooded area against which it was silhouetted. The garden was enclosed by a wire fence, and the relatively small size of the plants indicates Whitaker's short term of residence in Houston. The liberal use of evergreens in the landscape was one of Whitaker's strong recommendations for landscape design in Houston.

Alfred Whitaker was probably chosen to lead the movement for establishment of a rural cemetery because of his highly successful participation in the Texas State Fair in 1870. The Texas

State Fair was held in Houston from 1870 through 1873.[79] In 1866 a group of Houston men headed by John T. Brady formed the Agricultural, Mechanical, and Blood Stock Association, which had conceived the idea of holding a state fair in Houston. Incorporated by the legislature, the association opened the first Grand State Fair of Texas in May 1870 at the Magnolia Warehouses and adjoining grounds in downtown Houston.[80] Whitaker was given space for plant exhibits where he created a Temple of Flora with "a fountain, filling the foliage and growing flowers with rain drops . . . columns of evergreens entwined with blossoms and buds, artistic groupings of rare flowers . . . cages of singing birds and hanging baskets."[81] The women of Houston were invited to enter a competition of flower arranging and participate in a horticulture competition of roses and herbaceous plants from their gardens. Most of the entries were from Whitaker himself, but some entries did come from the public. Houston had just participated in its first flower show. Even the official committee from the legislature that came to view the fair was impressed. "Texas is entitled to receive her pro-rata share of exotics from the National Gardens at Washington through her Federal representatives and we would respectfully suggest the transmission of this pro-rata to the most successful florist of the Southwest, Mr. Whitaker of Houston, for reproduction, propagation and state dissemination."[82]

In 1871 the Fairgrounds were set up south of town on Main Street at the edge of the prairie.[83] The buildings, which were finished barely in time for use that year, included a main hall, an amphitheater around a stock ring, and an octagonal floral hall with two entrances and three tiers of seats for spectators.[84] J. T. Brady extended the tracks of his transit company out Main Street to the Fairgrounds so that regular transportation was available by horse-drawn trolley. Alfred Whitaker was in charge of the grounds but no money was made available for landscaping that year.

In 1872 there was great excitement over the addition of a race track to the installations at the Fairgrounds. Upon the discovery that some gentlemen from Austin had engaged Whitaker to do some special planting around the track, Houstonians felt it necessary to come forward with the financing for landscaping. Competition between the Texas cities was keen. Houstonians did not relish the idea of any part of the fair being identified with another city through landscaping by their own Alfred Whitaker. It was decided to make the Fairgrounds into a park just as the Cemetery Company was doing with Glenwood north of the bayou.[85] An article in the April 1872 newspaper was headlined "Fair Park—a Beautiful Scene—A Drive through the Hyde Park of Houston," with a report that all flowers planted around the buildings were growing splendidly.[86]

Repeated reference to the Bermuda grass sown on the grounds by Whitaker indicates that it might have been new to Houston at this time. "That peculiarly green grass—the Bermuda—is to be planted over the [race] course, as it has been over the 'main drive' leading from the chief entrance with the effect of consolidating and hardening the dirt, and preventing slipping and other accidents in sloppy weather."[87] Bermuda grass was not immediately used in Houston gardens, however. The grass took hold and spread so rapidly that scything could not control it. When the lawnmower, which was an English invention of 1843, became available in Houston about 1890, Bermuda grass lawns in Houston gardens rapidly became the norm (fig. 251).

At the 1873 fair the flower show enjoyed increased participation because a special prize was offered "for the most beautiful bouquet of flowers made by a lady of Houston."[88] Whereas in earlier times agriculture and horticulture were two aspects of one area of concern, industrialization in America after the Civil War was changing that perception. The presence at this fair of many national companies exhibiting agricultural machinery testified to the mechanization of agriculture, its emergence as a business, and its consequent differentiation from horticulture. Nevertheless, the state fairs were a focal point for horticultural education and display and a stimulus to the growing interest in flower gardens.

The stock market crash in 1873 spread over the whole nation. Depression set in everywhere, including Houston. The fair of 1874 was canceled. An abortive attempt to revive the fair in 1878 met with a lack of interest. The prevailing economic climate discouraged the business leaders, and the horticulturists were not interested because the formation of the Texas Horticultural Society in 1875 provided a forum and exhibition opportunities for those seriously interested in horticulture.[89] The Fairgrounds, however, remained for a time as a landscaped park south of Houston as Glenwood was on the north.

When the Fairgrounds were opened, an acre was made available to the Germans for their Volkfest, which they had been celebrating since 1869. "A Parade featuring floats and King Gambrinus, the German Bacchus, usually led the way to the Fairgrounds. Here on an acre of land decorated with flags and evergreens would be swings, dancing circles, seats, benches, and booths for the sale of lemonade, ice cream, sherbet, venison, beer, pies and perhaps 'solid shot' for older people."[90] The Germans continued to hold their Volkfest at the Fairgrounds as late as 1883.

The Volkfest and the trolley to the area undoubtedly influenced the Settegast brothers to buy land adjacent to the Fairgrounds and build a house large enough for two families. (fig. 33).[91] The Settegasts' garden nicely illustrated the European traditions maintained by Germans in Houston at that time. The method of pruning the trees, pollarding, is the European practice of removing all small branches and cutting the main limbs back fairly close to the trunk. This produced many-branched growth the following spring and promoted a pleasantly shaped tree. The severe simplicity of the garden landscape was softened by the charming arched arbor placed at the front entrance. The move away from specifically German neighborhoods was evidence of the progressive assimilation of the Germans into the general population and the merging of their horticultural expertise into the general body of gardening knowledge.

Women were gaining prominence in the gardening world through books published in both England and America. A knowledge of botany was considered essential to the education of a young lady. A dedicated teacher in Miss Brown's Young Ladies' Seminary in Houston, Mrs. M. J. Young, wrote a book for her pupils entitled *Lessons in Botany*, which was published by E. H. Cushing. She planted the school grounds with plants to illustrate her instruction and took her charges on field trips during the spring wildflower season. She also brought back plants from her travels, which included "two Mexican vines, the foxbergia and the coral vine which grows so luxuriantly in Houston. . . . Her curious night-blooming cereus was the inspiration of many evening parties."[92]

Horticulture of this period reflected a special preference for the rose. A favorite of pioneers because it traveled and transplanted well, and a favorite of households at all times for its beauty and fragrance, the rose held a preeminent place in Houston gardens, especially the climbers. During this period, varieties most often mentioned were Niphetos, La Marque, Marechal Neil, Cloth of Gold, Fene d'Or, Reine, and Marie Henrietta.[93] The Lady Banksia rose planted at the home of T. M. Bagby and trained across the whole length of the front porch was famous for the profusion of its bloom.[94]

Another well-known rose garden was at the Christ Church rectory, 1119 Texas Avenue (fig. 34). The rectory was built on the corner east of the church in 1857, but the garden received its greatest attention during the tenure of an Englishman, the Rev. John Julyan Clemens, from 1874 to 1885. He energetically repaired the church, enlarged the rectory, and "landscaped the mud puddle between the rectory and the church creating a lovely English rose garden."[95] The rose garden was intersected by white shell paths, and the whole block of church property was surrounded by a picket fence. The plantings at the rectory were simple: a few shrubs across the left front of the house, and a thickly growing vine trained on wires in front of the front porch to provide privacy and shade from the hot summer sun. The vine might have been a cutting from the ivy growing on the church, which is said to have been brought from Westminster Abbey.

The difference between gardens with or without an ample water supply is so great in degree that it becomes a difference in kind. The two B. C. Simpson gardens are a case in point. Benjamin Charles Simpson came to Houston in 1859 from Rochester, New York, and opened a foundry; shortly afterward he became a Confederate soldier in Hood's Texas Brigade. In 1873 he married Rebecca Wheeler, daughter of Daniel G. Wheeler, an owner of the Phoenix Iron Works. The garden at their home at 24 Youngs Avenue (later Riesner) was enclosed with a well-built "Gothic" fence, a familiar type in New York State[96] (fig. 35). Street trees had been planted, but planks had to be placed across the open gutter for access from the street. An interest in horticulture is evident in a wooden trellis with climbing roses planted at the base and a number of plants in buckets on simple stands. All of the plantings were done in a fashion that required a minimum of watering. Soon after 1880, the Simpsons built a house at 804 Main Street on a block where Mr. Wheeler had once had his homestead. The garden at 804 Main (fig. 36) was quite a contrast to that on Youngs Avenue. The well-tended flower bed between the house and an encircling sidewalk held rosebushes and violets growing luxuriantly. Climbing roses covered an arbor framing a rear side door. In the closely cropped lawn a water hydrant was visible indication that some utilities were finally being provided to residential areas. The horticultural variety in this garden was impressive:

An unusual fig orchard was the delight of B. C. Simpson, whose large home was at Main and Rusk Avenue. Every known variety was included in this orchard and all of them proved adaptable. Crape myrtles in several shades of pink brightened the side yards, and under these, small flower beds edged with violets offered an abundance of gay spring blossoms. Two roses, a white La Marque and a red Henrietta, climbed over the front porch, yielding a profusion of mixed color and fragrance, while conspicuous in the front yard was an immense round bed of red Amaryllis lilies, whose cheerful brilliance was constantly acclaimed by the many pedestrians along the way.[97]

The handsome cast-iron fence, made by Phoenix Iron Works, allowed a view of the garden and was probably one of the earliest of its kind in Houston.

After the Civil War the layout of the grounds around houses in Houston gradually changed to accommodate the shift from "natural landscape" to ornamental urban gardens. Whereas previously, property around houses had been simply encircled by a fence without further division, now the enclosed space around the house was subdivided into a decorative front yard presented to public view and a utilitarian back yard where the more private functions of the household took place. The earlier picket fence was replaced by a decorative wire or iron fence. A walk led from the entrance gate to the steps of the front porch, and narrower walks branched away at the front steps on one or both sides of the house, making narrow beds between the walks and the foundation of the house. A fence of vertical boards or latticework extended from each side of the house to the outer side fence, screening the back yard utility area. The back yard held various outbuildings, such as a chicken house, an outhouse, a carriage house, a well or a cistern for rainwater, a vegetable garden in which a few flowers might be grown, and play equipment for the children. The back yard was usually bare ground except for the garden space. The front yard was a simple tree-shaded lawn of grass as in earlier gardens, but now the narrow bed at the foundation of the house was planted with vines strung on wires, climbing roses on a trellis, or a few low shrubs widely spaced. Trees were usually planted outside the fence along the streets, responding to the sustained campaign to make Houston a "city of trees." Containers with plants were often placed on the side rails of front steps or on the front porch.

It is possible that the new division of front and back yards evolved from the German custom of laying out the household landscape in quarters, with house and flower garden equally dividing the front of the lot, and vegetable garden and utility area dividing the back. Whether the Germans were the source for the Houston yard division or not, it is interesting to observe how many houses were built to the corner of the lot. On the other hand, the new front yard–back yard arrangement could have evolved for purely practical reasons. As lots filled up, it was necessary to contain all activities within the boundaries of one's own property and the utility area needed to be screened from public view.

The bare ground of the Houston back yard was known as a "swept yard." The origin of the swept yard is ambiguous. It may have been a legacy from African slaves who were responsible for utility areas on plantations. In Africa a swept area around the dwelling was a matter of cleanliness and safety. Grass could hide dangerous insects, rodents, and snakes; bare ground was safer, cleaner, and gave evidence that someone was keeping the wilderness away. African American homes in Houston had swept yards (fig. 37), and back yards of the homes of many Anglo-American families were swept yards also (fig. 38). On the other hand, the swept yard may have come from the German "raked yard"; it was a German custom to build flower beds divided by raked dirt paths or a whole raked yard with flowers but no grass within the fence.

Among the many gardens in Houston reflecting the new division of front and back garden areas was the S. M. McAshan garden.[98] Located at 1315 Main at Clay it was planted about 1880 (fig. 39). The property was surrounded by a decorative wrought-iron fence. Street trees lined the sidewalk; the paved entrance walk led to the front steps and a narrower walk circled around the house to the right. On the left, a board fence with a gate next to the house screened the back yard. Gardenias flanked the front walk at the porch steps, and larger cape jasmine bushes followed the outer edge of the walk circling the house. These shrubs grew seven or eight feet high and "necessitated a stepladder whenever the blooms were cut. . . ."[99] The screening of the back yard utility area in this garden was accomplished by both fencing and planting.

A book published in 1870 anticipated a change in attitude toward planting urban gardens. Frank J. Scott, in *The Art of Beautifying Suburban Home Grounds*, said that "landscape gardening" in this country was restricted to public parks and cemeteries, but that "home-grounds" might be decorated to good effect if certain principles of taste were used in planting. He proceeded to give specific advice, encouraging cooperation between neighbors to create a general design effect for the neighborhood. He advised the use of iron fences when possible to allow the public to see and share the beauty of the individual landscaping; not to share one's garden was not only unneighborly and undemocratic, it was "unchristian." Scott also wanted to liberate American thinking from English preconceptions. He felt that the word "park," derived from the deer park of the English manor houses, should be removed from the American vocabulary of garden design so that people would begin to think of their own yards as proper subjects for artistic planting and their neighborhood as a park: " . . . the ambition of private wealth in our republic should be to make gems of home beauty on a small scale. . . . A township of land, with streets, and roads, and streams, dotted with a thousand suburban homes peeping from their groves; with school-house towers and gleaming spires among them; with farm fields, pastures, woodlands, and bounding hills or boundless prairies stretched around—these altogether, form our suburban parks, which all of us may ride in, and walk in, and enjoy. . . . "[100] His book encouraged the landscaping of home gardens by professionals, though they were few, and certainly he laid a foundation for the idea of urban planning. By the last quarter of the nineteenth century, many Houstonians were ambitiously involved in ornamental gardening in both private and public arenas, but only at the end of the century would Scott's vision of urban landscape come to the forefront.

Victorian gardens flourished in Houston between 1880 and 1900. The changes in landscape design clearly reflected the fact that this was an age that celebrated horticulture, especially the cultivation of flowers. Flowers, in fact, became a medium for the expression of emotions, which Victorians considered unseemly. *The Language of Flowers* offered information about the assigned meanings of floral tributes between men and women, family, and friends.

The new "exotica," plants from foreign countries, were the great preoccupation of Victorian gardeners. A transportation revolution effectively unified the whole world for the first time, and it was a mark of prestige to import foreign plants for the garden. Steamships and growing railroad connections made delivery swift and widespread, and the Wardian case made the transportation of plants over long distances practical. Made of glass sections and air-tight, the case could hold a rooted plant, and the water that evaporated during the day condensed on the glass at night and was returned to the plant. Plants that would have been lost during long voyages now arrived at their destinations in prime condition.[101]

The garden flower bed designs that became popular were created to display the characteristics of individual plants, and juxtapositions of these plants were planned to dramatize differences in color, form, and texture. Advances in technology, mostly in England, eventually enabled even those of the middle class to own a greenhouse and indulge in "bedding-out."

Bedding-out was the name given to that process of growing enough plants indoors or in a greenhouse to make it possible to set them out all at once in arranged patterns of color in the flower bed. As knowledge of exotic plants from around the world increased, different shapes of flower beds evolved in order to display the new plants more effectively. Beds were mounded into domes and berms of various shapes. "Ribbon bedding" created successive bands of bright contrasting color, one variety in each band, planted to conform to the shape of the bed. To spotlight the form and color of newly introduced plants, the well-planted flower bed separated each plant clearly from the other, like the tufts of a carpet, hence the term "carpet bedding." The same idea of separation, the principle of "scatter," was applied to trees and shrubs planted in the lawn: they were to be placed singly so as to arrive at their own peak of perfection and be viewed from all sides like pieces of sculpture.

Color was a prime ingredient in Victorian planting and design. Contrast was needed to emphasize pattern, and the bright tropicals coming from Africa and the Americas encouraged the use of strong color. Color became more subdued at the end of the period, however. Ribbon bedding used graduated shades of one color, and as the olive greens of new varieties of cacti and succulents became popular, color became somewhat muted. Echeveria ("hens-and-chickens") was a particular favorite for use as a jewel-like edging band for flower beds. Along with flowers, Victorian gardeners used an endless variety of materials in these patterned plantings: gravel, foliage, and grasses all played a part.

The formal parterre, which had once served as a transition between the dwelling and the natural landscape, moved out into the lawn in a variety of geometric shapes filled with pattern and color. Houston gardeners became enthusiastic about the new style of gardening. "Fancy shaped flower beds in crescents, stars, ovals, squares and octagons sprang prolifically

[sic] . . . outlined with bricks laid criss-cross, conch shells, bottles turned up-side-down. . . . A book, 'Geometrical Flower Beds' was much quoted and handed about for its pleasing ideas on bedding-out."[102]

Thomas W. House, Jr., was one of the first to use Victorian garden design in Houston. In 1869 House married Ruth Nicholson, the daughter of English parents, from Bastrop, Texas. In 1872 Ruth and T. W. House, Jr., built a house at 1010 Louisiana on the block of property that had formerly served as a vegetable garden for House's parents.[103] The gardener James Gaughan worked for the T. W. House, Jr., family for forty years. He left a handwritten diary in which he described the vegetable garden: "the blk. Was a farm and Garden Combined. Sorgum for the Cows Corn for the chickens and turkeys and Vegetable Garden Complete Aspargus Beds lasting for years Cut Fresh daily for the table One of Mr. Houses favorite dish. Cauliflower small and tender toothsome as It is called. garden contained Every Vegetable Known to Man. Fig Orchard pecan grove."[104] The property was encircled with forty live oak trees on the four sides of the block; flower beds along the front and side of the house were lined with different colored upside-down bottles. Gaughan's diary described the garden. "In the Center of Lawn a 15 foot Star Made with Coleus Also Half Moon Raised in Red and yellow Coleus . . . Two Immense Oak trees graced the Lawn"[105] (fig. 41). These trees were fifty feet tall when they were blown down in the 1900 hurricane.

The garden of the brothers Harvey T. D. and Hubert S. H. Wilson was one of Houston's most carefully designed and planted. The house, built by their father James T. D. Wilson, stood in the middle of a whole block bounded by Rusk, Walker, Louisiana, and Smith streets (fig. 42). Later additions made to the house included dormers, so the dormers in the photograph indicate that this garden was in place after 1873; the two sons became the owners after their father's death. Harvey T. D. Wilson, financial and insurance agent, also owned the Forestdale Nurseries and was aware of the latest developments in garden design.[106] The geometric round and star-shaped beds and the gazebo were typical fashions of the Victorian era (fig. 43).

Cement paving appeared in Houston during the 1870s. Owners of homes with gravel or shell paths hastened to avail themselves of this new material, which made it possible to avoid the Houston mud during rainy spells. Such paving accented the basic pattern of Houston gardens with the white ribbon of cement going in from the street and separating into neat white strands circling the house. The homes of Howard F. Smith (fig. 46), G. A. Mistrot (fig. 58), and Levi M. Kaiser (fig. 83) illustrated this pattern well. At the houses of E. A. Peden (fig. 47), Milton Howe (fig. 48), and Samuel K. Dick, the cement posts and base of iron fences became a decorative element in the garden design. Cement was too expensive for street paving, however, and Houston streets received witty notoriety from Alexander Sweet, a columnist for the *Galveston Daily News*. "Houston is celebrated for the luxuriant beauty of her private gardens and for the fluent muddiness of her streets. The main thoroughfares have not been improved by the labor of man since their foundations emerged out of the profundity of chaos on the date of creation."[107] In the early 1890s, the city council seriously addressed the muddy street problem. Although shell and woodblock paving had been used on earlier major streets, an intensive study of drainage methods and paving materials used in other cities resulted in the first brick paving being laid in 1894 and the first asphalt paving in 1897.[108]

Utilities provided by city franchises eventually made possible the elimination of "back yards" in the old sense, allowing Houstonians to surround their houses with expansive lawns, garden ornament, exotic shrubs, and trees. Many functions that previously necessitated outbuildings and fenced back yards were incorporated into the house itself: kitchen faucets instead of wells, bathrooms instead of privies, gas heating instead of firewood. Instead of a functional utilitarian area, the back garden became an outdoor gathering place for family and friends or disappeared altogether as a separate entity. Garden ornament to create a romantic atmosphere became an important element in planning. Garden furniture, whether rustic natural bark, painted wood, or metal, played a significant role in garden design. Benches, tables and chairs, gazebos, and arbors gave evidence of the desire to sit outside and enjoy the sight and fragrance of all the varieties of flowers that had become the major concern of Victorian gardeners. Four Houston gardens illustrate various ways in which this development took place.

The Alexander Porter Root house built in 1894 at 1410 Clay stood on a whole city block. A. P. Root grew up in Galveston and married the eldest daughter of Houstonian B. A. Shepherd. Root moved to Houston in 1874 and eventually became an officer in the First National Bank. The favorite haunt of family members was a back garden enclosed by a hedge (fig. 49). Brick paths made a bed near the house that was planted with Shasta daisies and violets. A small arched bridge was built at one end of the garden in front of a clump of banana trees, and a bench with a high rounded back beside the hedge was a place to read or daydream.[109] The garden conveyed a sense of simplicity and serenity since all garden structures were painted white.

The Joseph Chappell Hutcheson garden at 1417 McKinney at La Branch had no dividing fences. There was a lattice-enclosed gazebo in the back garden for outdoor seating (fig. 50). A descendant remembers enjoying the view in springtime of a long flower bed that was filled with dahlias every year. Beds filled with a single variety of flower became a popular practice during the Victorian period. A later photograph of the garden revealed that a tall lattice structure was built to screen the stables where riding horses were kept. Latticework was widely used in Victorian gardens in Houston not only as decorative structures but for screening purposes in fences, back porches, and other utility areas. From 1892 to 1897 Hutcheson served as a representative in Congress and campaigned for federal funding for a deep-water port in Houston. A congressional committee came to Houston in 1896 to investigate the feasibility of such a port, and the Hutcheson home and garden were the scene of a reception during their stay.[110] The city's provision of utilities by this time allowed the garden to become an area suitable for entertaining guests.

The Jedidiah Porter Waldo house at Caroline and Rusk on the northwest corner of the block was built in 1884–85 (fig. 51). Waldo was a leader in railroad circles and had a family of five children. The garden around this Houston home had Victorian elements, specifically the sidewalk circling the house and the sparse foundation planting. The lawn was left open inside a low iron fence, however, a harbinger of a new trend in garden design. Sidewalk trees were planted opposite each other in formal straight lines, giving the property an air of elegant simplicity.

One of the most formal gardens in Houston during these years was that of Mr. and Mrs. James O. Ross at 710 Hadley (fig. 54). Deep red sweet peas were planted on the fence from the side of the servants' quarters to Louisiana Street every spring. The greenhouse was attached to the house on the side toward the servants' quarters; it was here that the Italian gardener Tony Martino grew the plants that were later set out in the garden. The round bed in the circle of the driveway was planted in roses. The long walk running to a gate at the corner of the property was lined with a single variety of blooming flowers according to the season; poppies were always planted there as a part of the spring bloom. Crape myrtles with watermelon red blossoms were spaced around the circumference of the property inside the fence and live oaks lined the streets outside. Camphor trees were featured in the tree plantings, along with sycamores and magnolias. Mr. and Mrs. Ross entertained for his brother's wedding by welcoming guests to a garden party with tents entirely covered with white Cherokee roses.[111] Gardens were being used frequently as the setting for the most important celebrations in private homes in Houston.

During the last decade of the nineteenth century, South Main Street became the premier residential section in Houston. Houses were built, usually on a block or a half block, and were surrounded with highly decorative gardens (fig. 52). Stretching out Main Street beyond the business section, "beautiful gardens continued to Calhoun, where the Calhoun ditch and 'Calhoun river' at times carried the storm waters off into Bray's bayou."[112] Among the much-admired gardens were those of Henry S. Fox at 1206 Main (fig. 91), Albert A. Van Alstyne next door at 1216 Main at Texas (fig. 53), and T. H. Scanlan a few blocks away at 1917 Main (fig. 55). A carriage drive out Main Street beyond the residential district was a refreshing experience often enjoyed by Houstonians: "the beauties of South Main Street centered on Hill block, where giant oak trees, planted from giant acorns from Columbia, were located. This was the prettiest spot in Texas at the time . . . farther south was the George Hermann wood and sawmill site, now the Hermann Park. Another large strip of woods was at Bray's Bayou making three distinct and dense woods on Main."[113]

The Victorian emphasis on elaborate horticulture required professional growers to supply the plants and advise on planting and care. There was little differentiation between nurserymen and florists during this period. The training of the most prominent growers in Houston varied widely. Alfred Whitaker was a trained horticulturist; M. A. Wright was an experienced nurseryman when he arrived in Houston; Mrs. S. E. Byers and Nancy Ellen Westgate may or may not have had some training, but they were successful growers, knowledgeable, and trusted sources for plants and advice for Houstonians. There were other growers who sold plants for gardens but eventually used their plants chiefly for decoration for special events or for sale as cut flowers. Growers in the latter category eventually became the founders of the Houston Floricultural Society in 1889. Many of them specialized in some particular plant or plants. Charles Albrecht, for instance, provided and planted only trees; Wright eventually specialized in cape jasmine; Nancy Ellen Westgate was known for her orchids. Mrs. Byers planted different varieties of crape myrtle around her house so buyers could choose before ordering. A greenhouse was erected on the property of Glenwood Cemetery in 1889 for Whitaker to grow plants specifically for landscaping the cemetery. Several growers produced plants of such quality and quantity that an export trade in flowers arose. Mrs. Byers shipped tuberoses and gardenias to northern markets, and an 1894 publication stated that M. V. Wright shipped "quantities of jasmins to as many as seven or eight states, and he has even sent shipments of these beautiful flowers as far as Paris, France."[114] The Kutschback florists participated in this national trade as well, shipping jasmine flowers in $1.00 baskets, a hundred plants to a basket.

When M. V. Wright moved from St. Louis to Houston in 1882, he leased property, which he later bought, just to the west of the entrance to Glenwood Cemetery for a nursery. This energetic grower quickly made a name for himself by obtaining seeds of varieties of plants not then grown in Houston and propagating these new plants for his customers. New varieties of coleus, so popular for Victorian bedding out, were among his earliest successful introductions.[115] By 1894 Wright was well established in business with an office and greenhouse on Main Street in addition to his garden near Glenwood. In Alvin he had eighteen acres under cultivation, eight of which were planted in cape jasmine.[116] Although he maintained a large retail trade, it is obvious that Wright's wholesale trade in plants and flowers became increasingly important as Houston grew.

The Kutschbach Florists were located on the east side of the entrance to Glenwood Cemetery on property that had belonged to Mrs. Kutschbach's family, the Proctzels, one of the first German families to settle in Houston. Their block of property was surrounded by a picket fence. The back yard was a raked yard beyond which was the greenhouse; the front yard had raised flower beds with gravel walks. There were trees, including pear, persimmon, and fig trees among others, around which ferns were planted. There was no grass. The Kutschbach business began rather casually with the sale of flowers from the garden to families that came to visit loved ones' graves at Glenwood on Sunday after church. These occasional sales developed into a business of providing plants and floral decorations for all kinds of special occasions. The business was a family operation. Mrs. Kutschbach supervised the production and care of shrubs and flowers, while her son August and his cousin Henry Blecker made the deliveries and did the decorating. Mr. Kutschbach went on frequent plant-collecting expeditions to Mexico and on one occasion brought back the first poinsettias Houstonians had seen. Great quantities of flowers were grown for seasonal demand, such as lilies for Easter, geraniums for summer, chrysanthemums for fall, and poinsettias for Christmas. Bedding plants were also propagated and either sold or set out to grow in fields for use in floral decorating (fig. 63). Holland bulbs were available through German representatives who appeared in Houston every year to take orders.[117] By the turn of the century, the Kutschbachs had established one of the largest florist enterprises in Houston.

Another nurseryman, active around the turn of the century, made a significant contribution to academic knowledge. Frederick W. Thurow, a native of Germany, migrated to Hockley, Texas, and then to Houston Heights, where he owned a small nursery at 601 West 13th Street. In addition to merely selling plants, he devoted every spare moment to a research project to collect and identify all native plants and the hardy introductions to the Houston area. His herbaria now repose in the Thurow Collection at Sam Houston State College, the Smithsonian Institution, and the Houston Museum of Natural Science. His work went largely unappreciated in an age that was fascinated with exotic flowers, but the record he left is now a priceless resource for a dependable listing of the native flora of this area.[118]

Houstonians obtained plants and learned horticulture from the growers, but knowledge also came from periodicals and from experience in growing for exhibitions. Thomas Meehan's *The Gardener's Monthly*, published in Philadelphia, had absorbed Downing's *Horticulturist* in 1870, and a number of letters printed in that magazine about exhibitions at the Texas Horticulture Society meetings testify to a respectable readership from the Houston-Galveston area. Peter Henderson's book *Gardening for Pleasure* (1875) was widely read, and his information on Victorian flower beds provided a source of instruction to gardeners all over the United States. The Philadelphia Centennial exposition in 1875 gave visual expression to Victorian garden fashions in design and horticulture.

The last decade of the nineteenth century in Houston was a time of growing for competition and display. The garden of Mrs. J. J. Atkinson was planted primarily to produce cut flowers for arrangements (figs. 64, 257). She delighted in providing flowers for the altar of Christ Church and for decorating on special occasions for her friends. In 1893 women on the board of the newly created Faith Home for Orphans staged a flower show competition to benefit the new institution. Held at the home of Mrs. S. E. Byers, it featured chrysanthemums, and after prizes were awarded, the flowers were sold in the evening at the Market House.[119] In the following year, another group held a larger flower show in Bryan Hall, also to raise money for Faith Home. Whereas there were only two competitive classes in the previous year, the 1894 show had twelve, ten for chrysanthemums and two for other varieties of cut flowers. In addition, the room was decorated with chrysanthemums "on the stalk, cut and put in boxes, arranged in baskets, worked into crosses, monuments, ladders, birds, crescents, umbrellas and every other form and manner of thing into which flowers could be wrought."[120] Such competitions stimulated more people to garden and increased their knowledge and skills in the process.

Observing the public interest in the flower shows, the businessmen of Houston organized the Fruit, Flower and Vegetable Festival in 1895 to celebrate and encourage economic and agricultural recovery from the depression of the mid-1890s.[121] All of Harris County participated annually in a wide range of events over several days, which included a parade, exhibits of produce from farmers countywide, social gatherings, and visits to some of Houston's most beautiful gardens. Two of those gardens were fine examples of late Victorian design.

T. W. House, Jr., remodeled his house extensively in 1890 and also transformed his garden (fig. 65). The expanse of lawn was broken only by large trees. Hibiscus provided a mass of bloom in summer, and his flower beds were filled with many species, both annual and perennial. His rose collection included two hundred varieties. In his greenhouse were many horticultural treasures; the gardener Gaughan mentions palms, ferns, primroses, gloxinias, pandanus, fuschias, asters, cactus, and night blooming cereus.[122] House was particularly interested in succulents, and he is credited with introducing palms into Houston gardens. He planted two large date palms to replace the oaks lost in the 1900 storm and was rewarded fifteen years later during the 1915 storm when the palms bent but did not break in the high wind. "He brought vast numbers of rare and gorgeous plants to the city and was ever alert for new developments of every kind."[123] A photograph taken during the festival of 1898 shows a driveway centered by a round bed of alternanthera and lined on the outer edge by a border of blooming flowers (fig. 66). The gardener recorded that the driveway border contained plumbago, roses, verbenas, phlox, zinnias, petunias, lantanas, and sweet alyssum. House was a dedicated horticulturist, and it was natural that his garden would be one of those chosen for display at the festival.

Another of the gardens on the tour was that of James Bute. Bute's father, John, was a Scot who had come to Houston from Canada and established a company that imported paint supplies. His son James inherited the business but also became deeply involved in horticultural activities in Houston and served as the first treasurer of the Texas Horticultural Society. He was active in that society for many years and participated in exhibitions held in connection with the meetings. According to a descendant, Bute did not have a gardener but tended his garden himself, engaging help only for his more ambitious projects.[124] The banana trees and geraniums spaced across the entrance area and the ribbon-bedded mound in the driveway were typical Victorian plantings (fig. 67). Bute's wife, Sarah, was a sister of T. W. House, Jr., and the two brothers-in-law seem to have been friendly rivals in the prestigious world of Houston horticulture. The Fruit, Flower and Vegetable Festival was absorbed into the No-Tsu-Oh celebration in 1899. The earlier festival, however, provided a great stimulus to the spread of horticultural knowledge in Houston and Harris County.

During the final decade of the nineteenth century, a major event relating to urban planning was the development of Houston Heights, a complete, planned community north of Buffalo Bayou in Harris County several miles northwest of Houston. The undertaking involved a major investment of northern capital. A consortium headed by Oscar Martin Carter, president of the First National Bank of Ashland, Nebraska, formed the Omaha and South Texas Land Company and purchased 1,765 acres of land in the upper league of the John Austin grant. This naturally wooded area on a high bluff north of White Oak Bayou was well above the low-lying plain that was the site of the city of Houston; this elevation gave the town its name.[125]

Subdivisions and industrial residential areas linked to factories had been built earlier in the northeastern and midwestern United States, but the concept of building a complete preplanned town was new. Engineers or landscape architects, such as Frederick Law Olmsted, were essential to the planning and installation of utilities and civic amenities for an entire community. A town plat for the Houston Heights, 1890, seems to be the work of a professional, but unfortunately the name of the designer is not known[126] (fig. 74). The long rectangular grid of sixty-two blocks is bisected on the north-south axis by an esplanaded boulevard, running almost the whole length of the town. A formally landscaped park was indicated just northwest of the north end of the boulevard; a streetcar railway ran along the boulevard, turned past the park area and back down the boulevard on across the bayou to the city of Houston some three miles distant. A plat circa 1893 indicated a more naturalistic plan for the park with curving drives.[127] Apparently the park was never built. The depression of 1893 curtailed further developments, and the subsequent creation of Coombs Park on sixty-four acres between Second and Fourth streets on White Oak Bayou fulfilled the need of Heights residents for public outdoor recreation.[128]

Some of the principal investors in the land company moved to homes in the new town, among them Daniel Denton Cooley, John Milroy, N. L. Mills, and C. A. McKinney. Other members of the consortium invested in businesses and erected houses for sale. Large houses went up on the Boulevard and more modest ones on side streets. "The southwestern and northwestern sections of the Heights . . . [contained] the industrial and heavy commercial elements. . . . To supply the factories with workers, several small, frame cottages and shotgun houses were built along the tracks and in the northern and southwestern sections of the Heights. In those areas, blocks had been planned with smaller lots for just such a purpose. Because of their proximity to industry, much of these areas was made available to black families, who were otherwise excluded from owning property in the new, carefully planned suburb."[129]

L. D. Folse installed the esplanade planting on the boulevard, the first of its kind in Harris County and one of the earliest in Texas (fig. 75). Trees were cut to make way for streets but were left standing on residential lots to enhance the landscaping around future homes. The D. D. Cooley house at 18th and Boulevard (fig. 76) and the John Milroy house at 11th and Boulevard had an immediate well-established look as a result of the large trees in their gardens. W. B. Hamblen, at 605 Boulevard, and N. L. Mills (fig. 77), on the other hand, chose to remove the trees to create a large expanse of lawn, a design feature that became important at the turn of the century.

O. M. Carter bought the Houston City Street Railway and converted it to an electric system; he used the profits from the transit company to develop the new community and added a railroad spur to serve industries on the west side of the town. Unfortunately, the development of Houston Heights was so costly that Carter's Omaha and South Texas Land Company was forced into bankruptcy after the nationwide depression in 1893. A lawyer new to Houston, John Henry Kirby, managed the receivership so that within a year the bondholders realized less interest but were also the owners of the property.[130] Houston Heights maintained its separate identity until 1918, when it became part of the city of Houston. The wooded character of the development, the spacious boulevard, and the public transportation system connecting the Heights to the city of Houston and to Houston's industrial district north of the bayou were all advantages that argued convincingly for comprehensive town planning.

In the latter part of the nineteenth century, more and more people came to believe that time spent outdoors in natural surroundings was essential for good health, both mental and physical. Public parks were perceived as the best way to provide this for the whole city population: parks were the gardens of the people. John Thomas Brady was responsible for the first large public park open for Houstonians. He began with an idea for a business venture but ended by creating a popular recreation place for a whole generation of Houston residents. Brady owned the tract of land on the south side of Buffalo Bayou where the magnificent stand of magnolia trees had attracted the attention of early Texas travelers. He had participated in the effort to provide a deep-water channel to Houston and believed that a channel to his land with a railroad into Houston would best accomplish this trade advantage for the city. The idea did not materialize, however. The shipping company of Charles Morgan chose to place its docks and railroad on the north side of the bayou after dredging a canal through Clopper's Point, now known as Morgan's Point. Brady, therefore, decided to develop his property into a park. He built a pavilion where boats could dock and constructed winding roads through the beautiful area (fig. 93). "In 1890 . . . Brady proudly showed off his property (where 3,750 magnolia trees were then in bloom) to prominent business leaders returning to Houston by boat from Galveston."[131] Although Brady's Houston Belt and Magnolia Park Railway was originally built to promote his ship channel ideas, it was principally used by the Houston public, who flocked to Magnolia Park for picnics and other outdoor events. His own home was out in the country nearby and landscaped in the fashion of southern plantations (fig. 94).

The fact that Houston had been rejected as a deep-water port by Congress because of the pollution of Buffalo Bayou by its residents was one reason that Samuel Brashear was elected mayor of Houston in 1898. A tug-of-war had developed over the best method of financing city improvements: one faction favored private franchises and the other favored municipal ownership of public facilities. Brashear was a strong advocate of public ownership, and he promptly engaged a civil engineer from New York, Alexander Potter, to produce a comprehensive plan that included an electric power plant, a waterworks, a sewage treatment plant, and a garbage incinerator.[132] He believed not only that the city should own and operate municipal utilities but that it should own and operate city parks for the people. In 1899 he implemented this conviction by purchasing property for the construction of the first city park. The acreage included the old Samuel Young brickyard on the north side of Buffalo Bayou and the Noble and Byers property on the south side. City engineer John W. Maxcey drew plans for the park, in which the Kellum-Noble house became a park shelter, and "new improvements included a small lake with a conservatory nearby, a bandstand in the center of the park, a pavilion and an arbor"[133] (fig. 95). A wooden bridge was to connect the drive through the park to the north bank of the bayou and Youngs Avenue. A number of monuments were erected in the park, and Sam Houston City Park became a popular gathering place in downtown Houston. Both the municipal government and private citizens were developing broader conceptions about public welfare and urban planning.

By the turn of the century, ornamental landscaping in Houston reflected styles in other parts of the United States. Houses were surrounded by decorative gardens in the prevailing Victorian tradition. The interest in horticulture, moreover, was not limited to the few: school curricula, public flower shows, and festivals extended this interest to the whole population. On a broader community scale, the principle of municipal responsibility for the public welfare, which originated in the 1870s, had resulted in public services to neighborhoods and the creation of a public park. National and international thinking influenced developing attitudes toward the city landscape and the choices Houstonians made in designing and planting their gardens.

The Chicago World's Columbian Exposition in 1893 was a watershed event. Under the leadership of architect Daniel H. Burnham of Chicago, a collaborative effort by architects, landscape architect Frederick Law Olmsted, artists, and sculptors produced the famous White City on the shores of Lake Michigan. Olmsted's magnificent use of space itself as a major element in landscape design, specifically in the Court of Honor, demonstrated a structural relationship between architecture and landscape that made the possibilities of urban design abundantly obvious. A groundswell of interest in the total landscape of cities ensued, and the new discipline of landscape architecture became a focus of attention. The Columbian Exposition recognized landscape architecture as a fine art, and in 1899 the American Association of Landscape Architects formally sought its recognition as a profession.[134]

At the turn of the century, three major trends of thought began to influence the design of residential gardens in the United States and in Houston: the idea of the integration of house and garden into a unit for domestic living; the idea of using a particular historical style as a point of departure in architecture and landscape design; and the idea of the superior value of country living over life in the city.

Charles Platt provided the initial impetus to the idea of regarding house and garden as a single unit. His tour of Italy in 1893 resulted in a book, *Italian Gardens*, illustrated by photographs he had taken of Italian Renaissance villas and their gardens.

> The evident harmony of arrangement between the house and surrounding landscape is what first strikes one in Italian landscape architecture—the design as a whole, including gardens, terraces, groves . . . no one of these component parts was ever considered independently, the architect of the house being also the architect of the garden . . . the architect proceeded with the idea that not only was the house to be lived in, but that one still wished to be at home while out-of-doors; so the garden was designed as another apartment . . . where one might walk about and find a place suitable to the hour of the day and feeling of the moment, and still be in that sacred portion of the globe dedicated to one's Self.[135]

Platt's book and his later activity as a landscape designer and architect initiated a considerable vogue for the "Italian garden" during the early part of the twentieth century and contributed to the idea that house and garden were equally important in domestic life.

The historical influence in garden design had its inception in a controversy that arose in the latter years of the nineteenth century. Landscape designers in England and the United States reacted sharply to the contrived flower bed designs and garish colors of the Victorian garden. A strong difference of opinion existed, however, as to whether landscaping should be primarily architectural or horticultural, that is, whether it should relate primarily to the architecture of the house or to the world of Nature from which the plants came. In England, William Robinson advocated a return to the natural landscape garden of the eighteenth century, using native and hardy plants to recapture the simplicity and fidelity to Nature of that period. As it had been in that century, the landscape designer should be a horticultural artist who produced a pictorial landscape, using plants instead of paint, to create mass and line, color and texture simulating Nature. Robinson's contemporary, Reginald Blomfield, felt that the Renaissance and baroque formal gardens provided better examples for landscape design because they complemented and reinforced the architecture.[136] This dichotomy existed also in America; landscape architects and architects designing gardens tended to use formal, historical design, and the landscape gardeners advocated the horticultural, natural approach.

At the end of the nineteenth century, a new awareness of Nature in America greatly influenced landscape design ideas. Although the urban population of the United States did not exceed the rural population until 1920, urban Americans were seized by a great nostalgia for rural living about 1890. By this time the American countryside had been made accessible by a network of railroads, and the wilderness, which had once been an adversary, was now perceived to be one of the nation's greatest assets. Between 1890 and 1915 government action created eleven national parks in addition to Yellowstone, which had been set aside in 1872; these were chosen for their scenic, scientific, or historical values and were to remain public property in perpetuity.[137] About the same time, many men whose great wealth stemmed from industry and commerce bought properties that exemplified these newfound values in the beauties of Nature. They built houses and gardens in the country to escape both the pressure of business and the ugliness of unplanned urban development. Middle and lower classes joined in the general movement according to their economic capacity, but it was the country places of the wealthy that created a style of architecture and garden design that became known as "Country Place Era" design. Gardening and other outdoor activities played a large role in the leisure hours of American households during the period from about 1890 to 1940.

The earliest Country Place houses were based on European historical prototypes but were quickly superseded by country places reflecting the simpler architecture of colonial America: Tudor Colonial, Southern Colonial, New England farmhouse. Architecture should mirror the history of the country of its origin, and gardens were to follow the design traditions of the historic period of the architecture. This formal, historical, house-and-garden design principle has been described by the general term "creative eclectic." Houses and gardens of the Country Place era were not necessarily isolated properties far from the city. They might be a cluster of homes in an enclave in a small community or around a country club, or even a home on a spacious lot in a planned suburb. "[Urban] Americans insisted on defining 'country living' as the highest expression of cultural society. . . . "[138] From this perspective, garden design and gardening became more important than ever in America because gardens symbolically expressed the new ideal of Nature and outdoor living in a context of the established ideals of home and family.

In Houston the first evidence of the Country Place trend was the Bay Ridge Park Association. About 1890 a group of friends formed this organization to build cottages on a strip of property on the north shore of Galveston Bay.[139] A gazebo was erected on shore at the foot of a long fishing and boating pier, owned by the association and available to all families who built bay houses along the high bluff above the water's edge (fig. 96). Gardens at the bay houses of R. D. Gribble (fig. 248), J. T. Scott (fig. 97), and H. S. Filson (fig. 98) were examples of the kind of landscaping done at the bay in the early part of the twentieth century.

Meanwhile, the city of Houston was growing at an unprecedented rate. The devastation of Galveston by the hurricane of 1900 and the discovery of oil at Spindletop near Beaumont four months later ensured Houston's future as a major trading and business center. Houston's population almost doubled between 1890 and 1900, and doubled again between 1900 and 1910. The business district was expanding into the residential district encircling the downtown area. This growth was both rapid and haphazard, cutting into even the wealthiest neighborhoods. New residential areas were needed, and the character of these developments would reflect the landscaping ideals of the country place. Houston Heights was instructive regarding the value of comprehensive planning, but Houstonians were also in touch with suburban developments in other cities, most notably St. Louis.

The St. Louis private places were relatively small, one or two streets a few blocks long, conforming to the city grid pattern but owned and maintained by the property owners; ornamental gates marked the entrances. The layout used landscaping to create a parklike setting within the area and often included a protective strip of green around the outer perimeter. Deed restrictions established high minimum standards in the places, which were intended as enclaves for the civic mercantile elite in outlying suburban areas. Two of the most prestigious of the St. Louis places were Westmoreland Place and Portland Place, laid out by the German-born engineer Julius Pitzman.[140]

The first of Houston's new, planned residential areas was Westmoreland, organized in 1902, south of the city; it was included, however, in a large area that was annexed by the city in 1903.[141] In August 1906, A. L. Hamilton, T. A. Cargill, and Sterling Myer incorporated the Courtlandt Improvement Company, bought 15.47 acres along the northern boundary of Westmoreland, and named it Courtlandt Place.[142] In 1907, Avondale was laid out north of Courtlandt, and the Bute Addition south of Westmoreland. Some distance to the northwest, the Hyde Park and Cherryhurst additions were established in 1906 and 1908, respectively. In 1911, J. W. Link organized Montrose, including all of the large area west of the Bute-Westmoreland-Courtlandt-Avondale tracts and south of the Hyde Park–Cherryhurst property (see map 4). Three of these developments, Westmoreland, Courtlandt, and Montrose, were modeled after the St. Louis private places.

The ties between St. Louis and Houston were strong because of their shared status as railroad centers and because of the personal connections among leaders in the railroad business. A member of the Waldo family was instrumental in using the St. Louis private places as a model for Westmoreland. The Waldos were highly respected members of the national railroad community, wherein personal relationships played an important role. Houstonian Jedidiah Waldo had moved his family to St. Louis when he became vice-president of the Missouri-Kansas-Texas Railroad. When his younger son, Wilmer, who was a Princeton graduate in civil engineering, returned to Houston after his father's death, he was engaged as the supervising engineer for a planned residential area being developed by W. W. Baldwin of Chicago, assistant to the president of the Chicago, Burlington, and Quincy Railroad. The South End Land Company, organized by Baldwin, developed Westmoreland on forty-four acres south of Houston and west of Main Street at the end of the trolley line. The property had been used for florists' gardens, so it was known that plants would grow well in that soil. Pitzman himself was hired to lay out the development, and it was named after one of the private place he had designed in St. Louis. The Houston developers intended their Westmoreland to be equally prestigious.[143] Blocks were divided into spacious lots with building restrictions that provided for unfenced houses set well back on the lot in order to create an unbroken green space down the streets. Ornamental stone pillars with wrought-iron gates and fence delineated the boundary of the development, and sidewalks invited walking in the neighborhood "park." Westmoreland was the first "improved" residential area where business and civic leaders could erect houses and gardens without fear of industrial-business intrusion on the sylvan environment being created.

Courtlandt Place was the classic example in Houston of a residential area that was truly private. The Courtlandt Improvement Company engaged civil engineer A. J. Wise to plat the fifteen acres of its land into twenty-six lots on either side of a one-block-long street with a wide esplanade. The original plat indicated that the street was closed at the west end, and a crescent-shaped entrance with gates was constructed at the east end of the street opening on Brazos Street (fig. 99). Although the street in Courtlandt Place had been closed to through traffic, it became the only paved street by which residents of Montrose could gain access to the downtown area. The city sued, and the property owners deeded the street to the city in exchange for municipal maintenance of the esplanade, which would preserve the parklike environment of the neighborhood.[144] In 1912 the property owners joined the company in establishing deed restrictions in perpetuity. Deed restrictions were a voluntary agreement by the property owners, binding on all future property owners, which controlled land use and building standards within the subdivision. "The neighborhood's urban-country origins are still evident in the stables behind many of the big houses and by the hitching posts in the front yards."[145] About 1907 Arthur James Seiders, then a partner and landscape designer in the Hyde Park Floral Company in Austin, was employed to landscape the entrance and the esplanade and a few years later was invited to landscape some of the houses on Courtlandt Place. Seiders was unusually well qualified. Early in his career he had landscaped the extensive grounds of the Hospital for the Insane in Austin and Landa Park in New Braunfels, and later he was engaged to teach landscape design and horticulture at the College for the Industrial Arts in Denton. Intermittent attacks of tuberculosis interrupted his career in later years, and in 1909 he began to devote full time to landscape design.[146] Other than architects, such talented and experienced nurserymen were the usual advisers on landscaping to Houstonians.

As the developer of Montrose, J. W. Link built an imposing house and garden at 3812 Montrose Boulevard[147] (figs. 100, 242). Montrose was much larger and less exclusive than Courtlandt Place; nevertheless, it was considered a choice residential neighborhood by virtue of its esplanaded boulevard and building restrictions. The St. Louis influence was not confined to the South

End, however. For instance, Woodland Heights, developed north of Buffalo Bayou in 1907–1908, had comparable deed restrictions as well as impressive entrance gates and a lake for the recreation of its inhabitants.

The idea of residential areas created with appealing landscape spread from the elite to the working-class subdivisions. Magnolia Park was subdivided to become the Magnolia Park Addition in 1909 (fig. 101), followed in 1912 by the Central Park Addition on the bayou westward toward Houston. Magnolia Park was between Harrisburg and the Turning Basin, which was under construction at the time; its location made this a particularly attractive area for homes of workers in the nearby industries, and transportation was provided into the city on the Houston Belt and Magnolia Park Railway line. The native magnolias in the area described by Joseph Clopper so many years before were still appreciated by twentieth-century Houstonians, but most were removed in the development of subdivisions. Easy installment-purchase options with a life insurance policy to cover the debt in case of death apparently attracted many buyers,[148] but industrial development along the ship channel eventually dampened enthusiasm for residential living in that area. Park Place, situated on the Interurban Rail Line between Sims Bayou and Plum Creek about six miles east of Houston, was platted in 1911 with a "central park, shade trees along all boulevards and avenues, parkways adorned with flowers and ornamental shrubs" which would also "adorn all parkings" (fig. 102). Utilities were available, and there was to be a "handsome interurban station."[149] The concept of the unifying effect of a sequence of green front lawns, first used in Westmoreland, was becoming an accepted ideal for all neighborhoods (fig. 103).

African American neighborhoods had grown up in Houston in islands scattered about the city. These neighborhoods were similar to earlier areas where German and Irish families clustered together. Black Houstonians had taken full advantage of the limited educational and land-ownership opportunities offered them. Their numbers had been augmented by the arrival of well-educated blacks from other parts of the South, and a multiplicity of social and public service organizations operated within the African American community.[150] The advent of public transportation and voting controversies at the turn of the century led to segregated public facilities, Jim Crow laws, and the poll tax. There was, nevertheless, pride in the achievements of their community, and some of their members were able to prosper from economic opportunities in the growing city of Houston. The gardens in these neighborhoods were often filled with bright blooms and sometimes were designed along the lines of gardens in the more affluent parts of town. The Reverend N. P. Pullum house at 1319 Andrews Street in the Fourth Ward had foundation planting around the raised cottage, which included jasmine, climbing roses, and evergreens. A potted palm was placed on the railing of the front steps, and hanging baskets hung between the porch columns. The Reverend Mr. Pullum had his own brickyard and owned property in addition to his pastoral work at the Friendship Baptist Church. Another attractive garden at 310 Robin Street in the Fourth Ward belonged to Professor W. E. Miller (fig. 104). A native of Belton, Texas, he came to Houston in 1892. His house was surrounded by a decorative picket fence partially covered by luxuriant vines. Hanging baskets of fern across the front railing of the porch were a beautiful restrained decoration. Dr. B. J. Covington was born in Marlin, educated at Hearne College, and began practicing medicine in Houston in 1903. His house and garden at 2219 Dowling Street in the Third Ward were not only attractive but stylish (fig. 105). Potted plants gave balance to the entrance steps, vines grew over the porch railing, a planted urn was placed at the corner of the railing, and a fountain with a classic figure adorned the side yard. These gardens, like those in other neighborhoods, expressed the status and the leadership of the owners.

The idea that residences were incomplete without gardens was so prevalent that residential hotels and early apartment buildings in Houston included roof gardens. The Rossonian, built by J. O. Ross in 1910, was an apartment building eight stories high with roof gardens bordered by pergolas at the front and back (fig. 106). The Fox Apartments were more modest, only three stories high with the garden on the roof at the second level enclosed in the U shape of the surrounding apartments.[151] In most kinds of residential dwellings gardens were an integral part of the plan for everyday living.

The increased interest in landscape design brought about a growing sophistication in residential gardens. The John Henry Kirby garden at 2006 Smith Street, installed in 1901 or 1902, must surely have been one of the first in Houston to contain features of the newly fashionable Italian garden. The house, bought from J. S. Price in 1896, had been remodeled and featured a conservatory (figs. 118, 119). The enthusiasm for conservatories during this period reflected the increasing appreciation of gardening as a part of domestic life (see also fig. 107). In 1901 a natatorium facing Smith Street was constructed southwest of the house as the final stage of remodeling (fig. 123). Kirby wrote to Joseph Henry Curtis, a landscape gardener in Boston, asking for landscape plans for the whole property, which covered an entire city block and had been christened "Inglenook." Curtis responded to Kirby's letter regarding landscape plans in 1901 with a preliminary plan for their approval. He sent also "parts of numbers of 'Country Life,' which contained suggestions for pergolas, fountains and sun-dials," from which they could choose garden ornaments.[152] Receiving approval of his plan, Curtis wrote: "As the plan is drawn on a scale your local surveyor will be able to stake it out on the grounds. With regard to the detail of planting, I should like to have sufficient time to familiarize myself as far as possible, with regard to the growth best adapted to the climate. I received an answer to my letter to Professor Bray in reference to the sources of information in regard to this subject. In order to get the most satisfactory result, whatever is to be planted should be adapted to the soil and climate."[153] W. A. McMillen was the architect for the natatorium, which was under construction at the time, and he probably arranged for the building of the structural landscape features chosen for the garden. Major areas in the Kirby garden were the baroque water parterres with the large fountain bearing the figure of Flora, northeast of the house at the driveway and porte-cochere (fig. 120); the conservatory; the pergola (fig. 121) curving from the house to the natatorium, which also screened the utility area with the greenhouse (fig. 122) from the expanse of the front lawn; the rose garden, surrounded with dense planting in front of the natatorium (fig. 123); a circular grass-terraced garden at the west end of the natatorium; and, in the southwestern corner, a lake surrounded by trees and overarched by a rustic bridge (fig. 124).

Joseph Henry Curtis was a landscape designer who insisted on the title "landscape gardener" because he was an early advocate of the use of native plants in landscape design.[154] After consulting Professor Bray, a botanist at the University of Texas, Curtis's plan included native palmettos, altheas, yuccas, and such well-adapted plants as willows, violets, and roses, along with the semitropical palms, hibiscus, and Mexican cup-of-gold. While classical garden structures derived from the Italian were employed in the several different areas, the garden itself was not organized into clearly defined outdoor rooms; the areas flowed one into the other and were characterized more by the mood evoked by the method of planting than by the traditionally Italian structural organization. The designation "Italianate" is most appropriate. This garden is notable as the first garden in Houston known to be planned by a professional landscape designer.

The Robert Crews Duff garden at 803 McGowen (fig. 125) illustrates a quite different approach to landscape design. The designer of the Duff garden is not known, but the careful integration of landscape and architecture would point to the architect of the house, George Freuhling. The Italian Renaissance garden was obviously designed to complement the architecture of the house. Every part of the garden reflects the classicism of the whole in the best tradition of creative eclectic design. The house was situated on the southwest corner of the property, which covered a whole block. The land fell away toward the back, which gave the opportunity to use terracing, one of the cardinal characteristics of the Italian garden. Three shallow terraces running the whole distance across the front lawn gave an illusion of greater height (fig. 126). The stone terraces with a classic Renaissance balustrade made a strong transition between house and landscape; the same balustrade was used to divide the front lawn from the back garden, which was a half story lower than the front. Stairways led from the upper to the lower garden and continued down another level to the back street. Plantings of trees and shrubbery in the front lawn were symmetrical and emphasized the straight horizontal lines of the balustrade, terraces, retaining wall, and sidewalks. Classical sculptures in the lower garden (fig. 127), urns on the terrace, and crouching lions flanking the entrance walk were carved from Texas stone by the Austrian-born sculptor and stone contractor, Oswald J. Lassig.[155] The plants in the garden were reported to have been imported from Italy, but this assertion cannot be documented. It is known, however, that the planting was installed by the Sellers and Dorlund nurseries of Houston.[156] This garden was universally admired and was the scene of many meetings, teas, and garden parties; it was the gathering place for honoring World War I soldiers and the background scene for an early motion picture. The Duff garden was a superb example of the integration of landscape and architecture as well as a beautiful adaptation of the Italian garden.

The historical architectural style of garden design was predominately used in the new, planned neighborhoods of the city. One fine example was the Harris Masterson house and garden at 3702 Burlington. Finished in 1907, the Masterson house was one of the earliest in Westmoreland. R. D. Steele was the architect. The garden around this Colonial Revival house was probably the result of the architect's suggestion of a design that would be historically appropriate to the architecture.[157] In the Mastersons' garden nothing was allowed to disturb the tranquillity of the front lawn, of course, which was an obligatory part of the neighborhood area park, but the maze at the side of the house formed a decorative area that was also a joy to the Mastersons' grandchildren (fig. 128). The clipped hedges were evergreen native yaupon, and the repeated use of this motif in different geometric shapes for other childhood play areas was a beguiling feature in the back garden (fig. 129). On the opposite side of the house was an arbor with climbing roses over a walk edged with violets and a bench where one might sit and enjoy the fragrance and view of the garden. One of the Masterson grandchildren remembers pansies, geraniums, and amaryllis growing in the garden and moon vines on the trellis near the back door. "Everyone had satsuma trees and mulberry trees, and there were camphor trees planted between the sidewalk and the street."[158]

The Masterson garden is an excellent example of the creative eclectic house and garden of the Country Place era. The premise that the garden should harmonize with the architecture is evident, though the architect probably left the choice of horticulture up to the owners. The Colonial Revival architecture reflected the southern heritage of the Masterson family; the maze was a garden design affiliated with the historical period of the architectural design but completely personalized in the way it was adapted as a play area for the grandchildren. This kind of overt representation of the personal attributes of the family who occupied the house became a hallmark of early twentieth-century gardens.

The E. L. Neville garden at 11 Courtlandt Place, installed in 1914, was probably designed by the architect of the house, Birdsall P. Briscoe (fig. 130). The straight lines and symmetry of the house are echoed and reinforced by the planting close around the edge of the front terrace and covered side porches. A narrow earth terrace extending beyond the built terrace was a structural tie between house and lawn. A low clipped hedge provided an edging for the terrace and was carried down each side of the steps to border the front sidewalk. Vines placed on trellises formed an inner border for the brick porch columns. Evergreens in planters were placed against the house at equidistant intervals across the front terrace. The pyramidal shape of two magnolia trees planted on both sides of the front steps repeated the shape of the gables and added a vertical dimension to the predominately horizontal lines of the planting. This garden was less dependent than others on historical derivations but was a thorough integration of house and garden, in that plants themselves were used primarily to emphasize architectural lines. Briscoe used the same principle in landscaping the Garrow garden, using tall vertical shrubs at corners and low growing horizontal ones in between (fig. 133). The practice of architects acting as landscape designers continued in Houston at least until World War II.

During this period the nursery and florist businesses became differentiated and well established. In the nursery business, Alfred Whitaker disappeared from the scene in the early years of the century, but M. V. Wright's Garden and H. T. D. Wilson's Forestdale Nurseries were joined by others, such as Sellers and Dorlund, Edward Teas, and the Japanese Nursery.

Edward Teas arrived in Houston in 1906. A nurseryman from Joplin, Missouri, he was particularly interested in fruit trees and had heard of a remarkable fruit-growing area at La Porte in Harris County.[159] Teas was impressed with what he saw, bought several tracts of land, and planted a citrus orchard. Edward Teas came from a family of nurserymen. His grandfather and great uncle began a small nursery in Indiana and in 1860 became charter members of the Indiana Pomological Society. His father moved to Missouri and established one of the largest nursery businesses in the country; Edward helped start a branch business in Joplin and participated in the development of new hybrids, including the Weeping Mulberry, the white redbud, and several varieties of the catalpa tree.[160]

Edward Teas met W. W. Baldwin of Chicago in 1906 when on a business trip to Houston, and eventually Baldwin persuaded him to move to Houston and landscape his newest suburban development, which had been laid out by the Kansas City landscape architect Sid T. Hare. The property had been the W. M. Rice ranch, which Baldwin purchased and developed as Westmoreland Farms and the town of Bellaire. Using his training in landscape engineering, Teas started a nursery business in Houston in 1910. He maintained his contact with the United States Department of Agriculture and through this connection received plants from foreign countries. Chinese tallow trees were introduced to Houston in this way.[161] Teas Nursery did the original planting at the Rice Institute in 1911, the planting along Bellaire Boulevard, and many other civic projects. Innumerable residences were landscaped by Teas; the name became a household word in Houston when planting was contemplated.

Another nursery that provided plants for Houstonians during this period was the Japanese Nursery. Saburo Arai came to Alvin, Texas, in the early years of the twentieth century as president of the Alvin Japanese Nursery Company. The Mitsui Bussan Company, Ltd., of Japan, set up the corporation, bought one hundred acres of land, and planted a Satsuma orange orchard.[162] All the orange trees were killed in a severe freeze several years later, and the company went bankrupt. Nevertheless, Arai decided to stay in the United States and secured financial backing from C. E. Schaff of St. Louis, who was president of the Missouri, Kansas and Texas Railroad and who maintained a second home in the Houston area. Arai opened the Japanese Nursery in Genoa, Texas; the business became so successful that offices were opened in Galveston on Broadway and in Houston at 7200 Lawndale.[163] The Japanese Nursery catalog presented a wide spectrum of native and imported plants, and the nursery developed into a major source of plants for Houston, particularly Oriental varieties such as azaleas and camellias. One particular plant became almost as popular in Houston gardens as Bermuda grass: the waxleaf ligustrum was introduced by the Japanese Nursery in 1912, and it became the plant of choice for hedges in Houston gardens.[164]

By the second decade of the twentieth century, at least one landscape architect was active in Houston. Edward Dewson was educated at the Massachusetts Institute of Technology as an engineer and worked in the Boston area for a time after his graduation. He came to Houston in 1910, where he served as editor of the short-lived *Southern Architectural Review*; subsequently, he conducted a private practice in Houston until 1919.[165] One of his earliest commissions in the Houston area was to landscape E. A. Peden's country place, Miramichi, on Clear Lake. The Miramichi guest book is a good source of information about the landscaping because Peden occasionally made extensive diary entries regarding activities at the lake house. On February 11, 1912, Dewson brought Edward Teas for a visit with E. A. Peden to choose plants for landscaping Miramichi, and the list of plants from Teas Nursery later included in the guest book makes it clear that the landscaping was extensive.[166] The design of the garden in front of the remodeled house was left very simple with grass and trees (fig. 134); in the back area where the driveway circled and the house sheltered plants from the salt breezes, more varied planting was done (fig. 135). On February 1, 1914, the family was able to enjoy some of the results of the landscaping: "An ideal day. Inside the fire is comfortable but outside the warm sunshine reminds one of early spring. This morning, as an harbinger of sunny spring, we found a few blossoms of the sweet yellow jasmine and beneath the large cedar on the lawn a profusion of wild violets."[167] The Pedens spent so much time at Miramichi—three or four months in the summer and numerous weekends at other times of the year—that it truly could be called a second home.

Only one garden in Houston can be definitely ascribed to Edward Dewson. The Henry Staiti house at 421 Westmoreland Avenue (fig. 136) was built in 1905, but the landscaping was completed in 1917, after the house was remodeled by Alfred C. Finn following the 1915 hurricane.[168] Contemporary photographs reveal that the garden was installed almost exactly as drawn in Dewson's landscape plan (fig. 137). The front of the property was left as an open lawn. Palm trees, spaced across the front between the sidewalk and the street, were encircled with beds of mixed flowers at the base. The garden was placed on a lot next to the house, in front of a fenced utility area, the greenhouse, and the garage area. It featured a pergola leading to a treillage tea house painted white. Behind the pergola was an open parterre of roses edged in violets and several larger rectangular beds with cape jasmine planted within the violet edging (fig. 138). A path led around the back of the tea house to a flower border, where a garden bench was set against the vine-covered fence screening the utility yard. The whole garden area was sited so that it might be seen from the dining room windows and might at the same time be enjoyed by passersby.

It is instructive to consider Dewson's landscaping approach in terms of historian Norman Newton's analysis of the principles of Country Place Era design. Newton enumerates meticulous care for detail, proportion, and scale; space treated as a plastic material; clarity of circulation; relation between form and material to emphasize geometric form; and understatement and reserve rather than exaggeration.[169] The Peden landscaping at Clear Lake is difficult to evaluate, though nothing seems to violate these principles. An examination of the Staiti garden, however, reveals an adherence to every one of these principles. Indeed, it is the clarity of the engineering eye that underlies the beauty of the planting. The siting of the garden area to be visible from the dining room and easily accessible from the private rooms of the house gives evidence of Dewson's concern for an interrelationship of indoors and outdoors.[170] He divided the outside area according to function: garage area, utility area, greenhouse-garden-teahouse, and public lawn with flower borders. He was true to one of the guiding principles of twentieth-century garden design in his obvious adaptation of outdoor areas to the family life and interests, and his skillful inclusion of so many garden elements added to the prestige of the property. There seem to be no echoes of historic landscape styles either in the garden or in its relation to the house; the relationship is pure design. To quote Newton once more: "the power of simple geometry . . . is independent of 'historic' styles."[171]

The principles evident in Edward Dewson's work reflect an influence from new developments in architectural theory. The formal geometric style of garden design had been used principally for houses built in the historical creative eclectic tradition. The use of historical styles in building and garden design was challenged, however, by midwestern progressives such as Louis H. Sullivan, Frank Lloyd Wright, and George W. Maher. This school believed that house and landscape should be based on function and celebrate the artistic characteristics of the geographical region in which it was to be built. The horizontal, spare, flowing lines of the prairie were the dominant feature of the Midwest; therefore, its architecture and landscaping should express that spirit. The historical American Colonial connotations should be left to the eastern seaboard. This independent regional attitude appealed to all areas of the United States that had been part of the westward movement. In landscape design, Jens Jensen was the foremost proponent of these principles. He felt that their application to the landscape necessitated the use of the native plants of the region, although he did allow an intermixture of plants that proved hardy in the area. He often used wildflowers in his landscapes. He was the artistic heir of Frederick Law Olmsted in his love of Nature and his desire to recreate its presence in the city environment. He considered not only color, texture, mass, and space, but also the artistic effects of light and shadow in the landscapes he designed.[172] Two Houston houses gave evidence of the influence of these progressive ideas: The Oaks, built by Edwin B. Parker, and The Country Place, owned by Walter B. Sharp.

Edwin B. Parker was a partner in the law firm of Baker, Botts, Parker and Garwood. In addition to his law practice, he was general counsel for the Southern Pacific Railroad, president of the Houston Lighting and Power Company, and chairman of the Houston Board of Park Commissioners.[173] Horticulture and gardening were Parker's principal avocation. He accumulated a fan-shaped piece of property of ten acres on Bagby and Baldwin, which included a fine stand of magnificent oaks, about half of which "dated back to primitive times in the history of Houston and Texas."[174] Parker named his home The Oaks. Sanguinet & Staats of Fort Worth designed the house in the style of Frank Lloyd Wright, with "absolutely plain lines governing everything . . . [and the color scheme chosen] for modesty."[175] A *Houston Daily Post* article of 1912 states: "the builder, guided by the owner's suggestions, has modified many of the characteristic features of this established style, making the home as it stands perfect in its adaptation to the special exigencies of our Southern climate."[176] In 1909, even before the house was built, there was great interest in this new departure from established practice in Houston:

> Mr. Parker . . . lays not so much stress on the house itself as he does on his scheme for beautifying the surroundings . . . the work of beautifying the grounds will be the all important consideration. In this Mr. Parker will be in his element. . . . In the front there will be nothing but the giant trees that are now standing there. The lawn will be sodded and carefully kept

always. But in the rear of the house and to the Baldwin street side is where the most beautiful profusion of plants and flowers are planned. It is contemplated that all sorts of shrubbery will be planted here, with due consideration being given always to its hardihood and its beautifying attributes. Walks will wind about through a veritable Eden and if there are those who fail to find the home itself a pleasing sight they will certainly be able to lose their criticism in the gardens[177] (fig. 139).

Parker engaged Arthur James Seiders from Austin to obtain and install the plants in the garden. The work was so extensive that Seiders lived at the Parker home during the project. Seiders made a trip to California "to study the landscaped homes and parks there" and to secure plants that would do well in Houston; he returned with a whole railroad car of plants to be used at The Oaks.[178] There was greenery in planter boxes under the casement windows and there were "sunken flower beds, [the plants] growing flush with the floor" of the porch (fig. 140). Inside there was a large "floral conservatory" with walls that could be thrown open toward the music room to enlarge the capacity for guests. A pergola extended from the rear entrance into the back flower garden with raised beds and gravel paths between the house and the honeysuckle-covered garage (fig. 141). A rustic arbor grown over with vines led perpendicularly off to the tea house, "a quaintly roofed summer house, in style suggestive of Japan." Beyond this area were groves of sweet gum trees and "regularly laid out flower gardens, chicken yards and vegetable beds."[179] Mr. Parker designed his garden in the manner recommended by Wright: a natural landscape approach with unobtrusive plantings around the front porch and in boxes under the windows to emphasize architectural lines; flower garden, teahouse, garage, vegetable garden, chicken yard each in its own compartment according to function. The loveliness of this garden arose from its simplicity and the rich horticultural diversity in shrubbery and flowers selected by a knowledgeable plant lover and an experienced nurseryman.

The W. B. Sharp house at 4301 Main Street was known as The Country Place (fig. 142). It truly was in the country at the time; the Sharps acquired the property when Main Street was still a gravel road near their house. In 1896 Walter Benona Sharp married Estelle Broughton, who had moved with her family to Dallas from Flint, Michigan. The Sharps moved to Houston in 1905 and bought the property south of town on Main Street in 1907. The property included thirty five acres and the residence of Gustav F. Sauter, who was said to have operated a beer garden under the beautiful trees around his home.[180] The extensive property lent itself to a natural landscape design. The Sharps added a tennis court, a barn, a stable for Mrs. Sharp's horses, and a gardener's cottage. The Victorian house was surrounded by tall trees and shrubs but with a wide lawn opening toward the wooded area near the side of the house (fig. 143). Specimen plants introduced among the natives in the area around the house included a date palm and a large pittisporum (fig. 144). Mixed flowers were planted around the base of some trees and in front of some of the shrubs edging the lawn. This informal landscape garden intruded very little on the surrounding country landscape yet made a strong statement with its magnificent horticultural specimens of trees and shrubs. It seems possible that Mrs. Sharp was familiar with the work of Jens Jensen, who had landscaped a number of country estates in Michigan, and that she was influenced by his ideas of garden design. The natural disposition of the major plants added near the house, the choice of plants hardy to the region, the careful attention to patterns of sun and shade, the garden room (fig. 145), obviously built to view the beauties of Nature while indoors, all indicate the values that Jensen emphasized in his garden designs.

The concern with private gardening and landscaping in the first two decades of the twentieth century was accompanied by a new conceptual sophistication in terms of city beautification and urban planning. Civic and business leaders were firmly committed to making Houston a progressive modern city, a "Greater Houston." The Houston Business League, organized in 1898 by Rienzi Johnson, editor of the *Houston Post,* provided a contact point for the business leaders concerned about the city's future development during rapid growth. In 1904, under Mayor H. Baldwin Rice, "Houston became the first city in the United States to institute a commission form of government in the absence of extraordinary exigencies."[181] A monthly publication entitled *Progressive Houston* was issued by the city from 1909 to 1912 to inform and influence the public regarding the activities and goals of the administration.

In 1902 Charles Mulford Robinson's book *Modern Civic Art or the City Made Beautiful* appeared, and major cities all over the nation became involved in city planning. The modern city was the City Beautiful. Public planning in Houston was spurred by large gifts of property from William M. Rice and George H. Hermann, and the vision of a planned and beautified Houston became a reality in the South Main Street area. This was the height of civic development in Houston, and the resultant unity of architectural and landscaped beauty has never since been equaled.

Rice, who had no children, set up a fund to establish the William M. Rice Institute for the Advancement of Literature, Science and Art in 1891 and willed his estate to the projected school. In 1907 six tracts of property totaling 227 acres were purchased one and a half miles from downtown Houston on a gravel road extension of Main Street.[182] Edgar Odell Lovett was invited to become the president of the new institution, and the Boston firm of Cram, Goodhue and Ferguson was selected to draw up architectural plans. These architects were leading exponents of the formal, historical, architectural landscape theories. Cram felt that the architecture should be derived from the Mediterranean environment, which most closely approximated the Houston climate: "it must *look* like a college, and one built in a warm climate. . . . Here was a plane-like area with no cultural traditions except the flimsiest with Mexico. Racially it was New England, culturally it was Middle West. . . . "[183] Cram's amalgam of Mediterranean styles into a new style was finally agreed upon by all parties; in the final form, it was the Byzantine element that prevailed over others. As in all creative eclectic productions, the landscape was an integral part of the planning process. The landscaping plan was probably done by Cram's partner, Bertram G. Goodhue; the Persian gardens that were to be the feature of the three great courts of the Institute were similar to landscaping he had designed in the Mediterranean style in California.[184] Lawns, tree-shaded drives, groves, and gardens were arranged in a careful array of widening vistas along the main axis of the campus. All of the pools originally drawn by the architects were removed from the plan, however, because of Houston's mosquito problem.

Edward Teas installed the planting on the campus and advised on horticultural choices. The existing trees were incorporated into the design. Oaks, magnolias, and many other plantings were used to create a formal effect. Buildings defined the space of the Academic Court; within this architectonic space, close-clipped yaupon hedges in horizontal parallel lines combined with the upward vertical thrust of rows of cypress to make the landscaping a strong companion to the architecture (fig. 146). Local leaders watching this process developed a deeper sense of regional identity and an increased awareness of what they wanted to express in urban design.

In 1910 Mayor H. Baldwin Rice created a Board of Park Commissioners with Edwin B. Parker as chairman and William A. Wilson and George H. Hermann as the other members. An editorial in *Progressive Houston* praised the gift of land made in the will of William Cameron to the city of Waco for a municipal park and further commented: "nor do we doubt that in nearly every city and considerable town in Texas there is at least one wealthy man who would like to leave some testimony of his appreciation of the prosperity he has enjoyed in his own town and partly as the result of the labors of his neighbors . . . what better way is there than to leave his town a park? . . . Of all the tendencies that our time discloses none is more marked than the eagerness of urban people to soften and beautify their environment."[105] In January 1911, Mayor Rice stated that the objective of the park board was to establish "a 'park circle' around Houston, to be accomplished by joining Houston's parks with landscaped parkway boulevards."[186]

In 1912 the Board of Park Commissioners engaged Arthur Coleman Comey, a landscape architect from Cambridge, Massachusetts, to make a comprehensive survey of Houston's park status and requirements. His report, *Houston, Tentative Plans for Its Development*, indicated that Houston was quite deficient in providing park and recreational space for its citizens. He recommended that a park system be planned that would ensure ample park space for years to come, saying: "the backbone of a park system for Houston will naturally be its bayou or creek valleys, which readily lend themselves to parking and cannot so advantageously be used for any other purpose. These valleys intersect the city in such a way as to furnish opportunity for parks of unusual value within a comparatively short distance of most of the residential areas. . . ."[187]

Comey also advised the purchase of property for a park on the east side of Main Street across from the newly opened Rice Institute. In 1914 George H. Hermann donated to the city a 285-acre tract of land in this area along Brays Bayou. After his death a few months later, the city purchased an additional 122 acres from his estate and named the new park for the benefactor.[188] After a $250,000 park bond issue was passed in 1914, one of the most outstanding landscape architects in the country began work in 1915 to improve the Houston city park system.

George E. Kessler was born in Germany but grew up in Dallas. He returned to Germany, however, to study engineering and landscape gardening. Coming back to the United States, he worked briefly for Frederick Law Olmsted, then began his own practice. In 1891 he designed the plan for the suburb of Roland Park on eight hundred acres of land north of Baltimore.[189] He was invited to Kansas City, Missouri, to design a municipal park system; his outstanding achievement in this endeavor made his reputation in landscape design. Kessler moved to St. Louis in 1903 when he was invited to be the consulting landscape architect for the Louisiana Purchase Exposition in 1904. In 1910 he designed a plan for the Dallas park system, the first such plan for a Texas city. In 1915, at the instigation of J. S. Cullinan, the Houston park board engaged his services to design a landscape plan for a system of parks for Houston. He set about improving existing parks, designed a "parked thoroughfare" plan for Main Street, and began to implement the first stages of his plan for Hermann Park (fig. 147). Lack of funding meant that only a few moves were made toward developing the Buffalo Bayou Park, which was to reach from Shepherd's Dam to Market Square. After Kessler's death in 1923, Hare & Hare of Kansas City became the consulting landscape architects for the Houston park system. Ben Campbell had succeeded H. Baldwin Rice as mayor in April 1913, and fortunately for Houston, he continued the policy of strong municipal support for the development of the park system.[190]

In 1916 J. S. Cullinan persuaded George Kessler to design the private place neighborhood of Shadyside, on property he had purchased from the Hermann estate on Main Street between the Rice Institute and Bissonnet, which would be in harmony with the projected plans for the esplanaded Main Street and Hermann Park across the way. Kessler integrated the whole complex by extending Montrose Boulevard to intersect Main Street, both esplanaded boulevards, and placing a traffic circle at the conjunction with a drive across the way leading eastward into Hermann Park (fig. 148). His design imposed an order and a unity to the area which gives credence to the claim that landscape architecture is the most comprehensive of all the arts. His "architected space" in this area of Houston still retains a functional grace within a bustling city.

Houston was in the vanguard of urban planning in the United States during this period. A city planning commission, appointed by the mayor in 1921, was charged with formulating plans for a major street network, a civic center, beautification of the city's bayous, and a zoning ordinance. The commission was purely advisory, however, and recommendations would have to be authorized by the state, a situation that allowed room for political maneuvering. There was strong leadership on the commission and a great desire on the part of citizens to participate in the city planning process, as evidenced in Commissioner Will Hogg's coalition of volunteer groups in the Forum of Civics.[191] Hogg's untimely death in 1929 ended any further strong efforts in the direction of comprehensive city planning. Other cities across the nation instituted funding for parks and zoning laws, but Houston remained essentially static in these areas. Depression and war diverted both funding and citizen attention in the ensuing years, but there was also a political unwillingness to contend with private real estate interests. All of these circumstances brought about a reversal of policy in Houston with regard to city planning.

Nevertheless, much of the city's heritage of gardens, landscapes, and urban planning can still be seen today. Houston's rich alluvial soil and plentiful rainfall provided a hospitable climate for luxuriant gardens. The varied agriculture of the mid-nineteenth century, the horticultural sophistication of the Victorian era, and the civic design and planned neighborhoods of the early twentieth century all depended on this natural luxuriance. It was the bounty of the land itself, seen perhaps most clearly by the early settlers and travelers in Harris County, that provided the possibility of a beautiful city. Attractive individual gardens continue to be created in Houston. The future beauty of the city itself, however, will depend less on the natural beauty of an earthly Paradise than on the responsible decision of its citizens to revive the forgotten legacy of comprehensive planning.

2 The Development of Domestic Architecture

Barrie M. Scardino

Those who came to Texas in the 1820s seeking a fresh start brought with them knowledge of specific house forms and building techniques. Typically, Anglo-American settlements began with the construction of simple, rectangular log structures familiar from American Colonial traditions. The side-gable configuration of these narrow houses has been considered a British folk form brought to this country in the seventeenth century.[1] However, recent scholarship suggests that the single- and double-pen cabins common to the lowland South are as African in plan as they are European. The cabins of both slaves and white farmers found first along the southeastern Atlantic coast and later in such frontier settlements as Texas were so similar that it is difficult to distinguish them, except perhaps in size.[2] Many of Harris County's early Anglo-American settlers were from two distinct regions of the South: the Upper South (Kentucky, Tennessee, Missouri, and Arkansas, with antecedents from Virginia and North Carolina) and the Lower South (Mississippi, Alabama, Georgia, and Louisiana).[3] However, others who were influential in the early years, such as the Harris family, the Allen brothers, Ashbel Smith, and Erastus Perkins, came from New York and New England. Although many of these settlers left large, comfortable houses, they began their lives in Texas humbly.

The first families who came to what would become Harris County brought tents for temporary shelter and simple tools to build log cabins. These settlers relied on their knowledge of construction techniques and on available timber for their first houses. Much of Harris County is open coastal prairie interrupted by forested strips along the streams and bayous (fig. 2). Various types of wood were available for building, including loblolly pine, hickory, sycamore, pecan, willow, cypress, and post oak.[4] With axes, saws, and adzes settlers were able to cut trees and trim logs. They stacked hewn logs horizontally on foundation blocks two or more feet high and notched them in a variety of ways to fit together at the corners. When craftworkers and carpenters were not available for hire, building was a family affair; women and children often daubed clay mixed with moss or grass between the chinks. Four walls were thus constructed into a one-room "pen," the size of which depended on the length of logs.

In these simple folk houses the walls, roof, chimney, and front door were the chief elements. Neither time nor energy nor money for decoration was available. Early residents shared the goals of settlement, land clearing, and the establishment of farms. Available resources went into farms and businesses rather than better living quarters. John E. Milsap, writing of the early history of Harris County, describes his uncles' first houses: "Uncle Tom Marshall and his brother Haslem having secured land on Greens Bayou, built themselves log cabins and gave their attention to farming."[5]

In 1846 Ferdinand Roemer observed that James Morgan's house "is an unornamented, one-storey wooden structure of the architectural type common in this part of the south. . . . "[6] Indeed, these small wooden structures with a front porch were common and gave, in the first decade of settlement along Buffalo Bayou, little evidence of class or economic distinction. Typically, the roof was constructed on a ridge parallel to the front of the house and covered at first with interwoven branches, twigs, and grass, later to be replaced with sawed timber or shingles. Women wet and swept dirt floors to keep them "clean" until puncheon floors, like more durable roofs, could be installed once materials and tools to make them were available.[7]

The simplest type of wattle and daub chimney, called "mud-cat," was built at one of the gable ends[8] (fig. 3). Four posts, taller than the house, were sunk into the ground and inclined toward each other to make the chimney narrower at the top for better drafts. The builder tied cross-pieces of wood to the posts, one above the other, making a frame that he covered with several coats of a crude "plaster" made of clay and grass or moss. After the basic shelter and chimney had been constructed, a door was cut in the center of one side. Many cabins had no windows at first, or had only holes cut into the walls covered by solid battened shutters made like the door and hinged with leather straps (fig. 4). The single fireplace provided cooking and heating initially, but because of the danger of fire and the heat of Texas summers, most families soon constructed a separate kitchen outbuilding, which was also used for eating. Inclement weather made a covered breezeway or porch connected to the outside kitchen desirable.

Dilue Rose Harris described a house at Clopper's Point (later known as Morgan's Point) where her family spent the night of April 28, 1833, on their way from Galveston Island to Harrisburg: "There was a small log house near. It was vacant and had a fireplace, but no floor." When they reached Harrisburg they found that "most of the houses in Harrisburg were built of logs." After settling on the Cartwright farm about fifteen miles from Harrisburg, the Rose family attended a dance at the nearby Clement C. Dyer residence in April 1834, which Harris described as a "double log cabin with a passage between the rooms."[9]

The double-pen, or dog-trot, house, formed by connecting two pens with a covered passage between them, made a larger, two-room house. The passageway served a number of useful functions: a breezy place for summer living, a children's play area, shelter on rainy days, and winter storage for foodstuffs. One of the two rooms generally served for family living, while the other might be used for storage, housing farm animals in winter, and such domestic chores as spinning, weaving, and candle- or soap-making. In town the second pen could be used as a more public "office." Ornithologist John James Audubon recorded his impressions of the dog-trot house in Houston where Sam Houston briefly lived in May of 1837:

> This abode of President Houston is a small log house consisting of two rooms and a passage through, after the Southern fashion. The moment we stepped over the threshold on the right hand side of the passage we found ourselves ushered into what in other countries would be called an antechamber. The ground floor, however, was muddy and filthy; a large fire was burning, and a small table covered with paper and writing material was in the center; campbeds, trunks, and different materials were strewed around the room. . . . The President was engaged in an opposite room on some national business and we could not see him for some time. [After a brief tour of the environs] . . . he [Sam Houston] at once removed us from the anteroom to his private chamber, which by the way was not much cleaner than the former.[10]

In 1828 J. C. Clopper described life in Harrisburg, where there were six or eight houses scattered among tall pine and oak trees. "We pass the winter in a small log pen our fire in one corner. . . . Shoulder our axes and build a fine large warehouse with a shed dining room."[11] Dilue Harris remembered the rented Cartwright farm where her family lived from 1833 to 1835:

> The house was two stories high and was built of hewed logs. It had a brick chimney and two doors and three windows all fastened inside with heavy wooden shutters. The doors were made of heavy timber put together with wooden pins and with wooden bars across. No iron was used except in the fireplace and in nailing down the floor. . . . There were no stairs and we had to use a ladder . . . drew up the ladder and placed it over the opening. [12]

The second floor mentioned would have been attic space under a pitched roof, perhaps with windows in the gable ends. Children and servants slept in such a loft.

Lewis Birdsall Harris, son of the Austin colonist John R. Harris, left a remarkably complete description of early log construction in 1836. The Mexican army had burned the original Harris home in Harrisburg, and the following account was of the rebuilding of that house:

> After resting a while my brother and myself concluded to build a house on the site of the one burned by the Mexicans. The great difficulty was lumber. The sawmill built by my father in Harrisburg was burned by the Mexicans, but hearing that the Sawmill at Lynchburg about 20 miles below, at the mouth of Buffalo Bayou and the San Jacinto River, would soon be started up, we concluded to build of logs and by the time the mill would be ready we could get our cribs up and roof on and be ready for the flooring, etc. We procured four additional Mexicans [prisoners of war from the battle of San Jacinto] and axes and started them to cutting down pine trees of suitable size, and cutting them of the right lengths. It was amusing to see them use an axe, something they had never seen before. . . . We were rather aspiring in our ideas of a house and concluded to build it the same size and shape of our Grandfathers

house in Seneca Co., N.Y. only not as high, (that was 3 stories) which is 56 feet long by 36 feet wide, divided into four rooms 22 by 18, and a Hall thro' the center 12 feet wide. There was not a carpenter to be had in the country, the nearest to it was an old dutchman Henry Tierwester called "Dutch Henry" who was in the battle of San Jacinto. . . . We procured Henry to hew the logs which he did fairly well after they had been scored by the Mexicans. We finally cleared away the debris of the old house and set the Mexicans to preparing the foundations. . . .

I found one of the Mexicans quite handy with cattle and we broke in with the help of a yoke of gentle oxen enough others to haul our hewn logs to the place. We found it a more difficult matter to get our saw logs in to the water, but finally managed it, and got enough to make a raft, which by the help of two of the Mexicans who became expert oarsmen, we towed to the sawmill at Lynchburg, and had them sawed up into the flooring and boards and rafted the lumber back. We built our house on large oak blocks several feet from the ground, making "pens and a passage," until we got it to the proper height for the first story, when we cut our logs the full length 56 and 36 feet determined to have one room the full size of the house. [The second floor was one room.] The roof consisted of peeled pine poles hewed on one side, with split laths on which we laid split boards three feet long. . . . We also built a kitchen of logs about 18 x 20 with a loft, in which we lived for some time before our big house was ready to occupy. This had a large fire place in one end and a chimney of sticks plastered with clay.[13]

Surviving documents attest to the fact that log construction was usual in Harris County during the early settlement period, but little physical evidence remains because of the rapid urbanization that took place around Houston. Few log cabins were built in Houston after statehood in 1845, although this type of construction probably continued in rural areas of Harris County until after the Civil War, particularly for outbuildings or servants' quarters. Because early builders used extremely hard heartwood from old trees, their log structures did not rot or become infested easily. For this reason log cabins survived into the twentieth century in other parts of Texas when they were not torn down. On some farms and ranches they continued to be used as outbuildings for storage or animal shelter.

Timber-frame houses were also constructed during the settlement period. As Drury B. Alexander explained in *Texas Homes of the Nineteenth Century,* these early frames were constructed as a "heavy cage" of square-hewn logs. Although this type of frame posed more difficulties in construction because of its mortise and tenon joints, it required far less timber than the solid wood log houses and cabins. The first frame houses had exterior sheathing of uneven weatherboard, and inside the frame was exposed or covered with smooth board walls.[14]

The oldest known extant example of such a frame house in Harris County was built by John R. Williams possibly as early as 1825. It was located on upper Clear Creek about fifteen miles southeast of what is now downtown Houston, before being moved to Sam Houston Park and restored by the Harris County Heritage Society in 1971. The original rough-hewn cedar frame of the Williams house is covered with clapboard, perhaps dating from around 1850. The first covering of the frame is believed to have been moss, bark, and possibly pit-sawed lumber. It is now a single-room cabin with a mud-cat chimney and central doorway, which opens onto a porch extending across the front.[15]

Because of hot summers and mild winters even the first modest cabins in this part of Texas had such a front porch. There was no English or northern European antecedent for this type of porch, which was commonly found in the South. Architectural historian John Michael Vlach believes that such porches were inspired originally by the tropical heat and humidity of Africa and brought to this part of the world by slaves. Crediting a cross-cultural encounter, Vlach observes that "for almost 250 years the southern front porch has owed its existence mainly to the adaptive genius of local carpenters acting on African notions of good architectural form."[16] In 1846 Ferdinand Roemer commented on the necessity of front porches:

> The house of the planter who had invited us to dinner was situated on the high bay, surrounded by stately trees. It was built of wood in the same simple, unattractive style as the home of Mr. Morgan. Surrounding the house was a porch resting on wooden pillars about two feet above ground. A porch of this kind, at least on one side of the house, is a necessity in every Texas home. On it the occupants of the house spend the greater part of their time in summer, as it affords protection against the direct rays of the sun and at the same time permits the air to circulate freely. On a section of the porch, which was enclosed with boards on one side only, we were served a dinner of roast wild turkey. This would have been a rather cool place to serve dinner in Germany on January 14 but here we experienced no discomforts, due to the mild climate.[17]

Evergreen, built by Moseley Baker on Tabbs Bay, was typical of early houses built in this area (fig. 6). Surviving photographs of Evergreen, purchased by Ashbel Smith in 1848, show that it had a front porch incorporated under the main roof, an arrangement seen in the majority of drawings and photographs of early frame houses in Harris County. The roof was shingle-covered and gently pitched over walls of milled lumber, with a loft under the roof, evidenced by the shuttered window in the gable end. The house probably faced west, toward Tabbs Bay, and needed protection from the hot afternoon sun. This was haphazardly accomplished at Evergreen by nailing boards at the top of the porch for an awning effect, but no attempts at decoration were made.

Even though imported building materials were available in the 1820s, their expense precluded common use. Cut lumber was the norm. Sawmills were operating in Harris County in the mid-1820s, but the Harrisburg mill was the first steam-driven sawmill to be well documented.[18] In Adele B. Looscan's account "the sawmill, which was also a gristmill, stood nearly opposite [the Harris house] on the south side of Bray's Bayou, and was being run by David Harris and Robert Wilson, administrators [of the John R. Harris estate]. . . . The mill was doing good service, making lumber from the big primeval pine trees, rafted directly to the mill."[19] Other sawmills were in operation in nearby counties, and possibly a few more may have been located in Harris County, but the Harrisburg mill seems to have been the most important. It was burned by the Mexicans in 1836 with the rest of Harrisburg.

New Orleans was a three-day to one-week trip by boat, depending on the wind, and all building materials used there were available to people who wanted and could afford to import them. By 1830 window glass, shingles, milled lumber, and paint were being imported. Both William Fairfax Gray and C. Anson Jones left descriptions of the Singleton-Zavala house, which stood across Buffalo Bayou from the San Jacinto battlefield. Gray visited Lorenzo de Zavala in 1836 and observed, "the house is small, one large room, three small bed closets and a porch, kitchen, etc. . . . "[20] In 1876 Jones described the house more completely:

> In 1828 or 29 Philip Singleton settled on the north bank of Buffalo Bayou between the mouth of Old River and Carpenter's Bayou, on a hill nearly opposite where the Texian army camped the night before the battle of San Jacinto, and built a small log house afterward covered with plank, which is mentioned here because it is the first house in the county of which we have any account which was covered with shingles and had glass window sashes. . . . Singleton afterward sold it to, and it became the home of Lorenzo de Zavala, the distinguished Mexican refugee and Texian patriot.[21]

It was common for log structures to be overlaid with weatherboard, or narrower clapboard, for better insulation and to update their appearances. The roof of the Singleton-Zavala house was shingled because "plank" would have referred to the siding.

In 1830 Samuel May Williams was constructing a house in San Felipe, approximately sixty miles west of what was to become the town site of Houston, for which he bought one box of window glass in Brazoria, imported from New Orleans. In September 1830 William P. Harris wrote to Williams from Harrisburg that he needed two thousand feet of weatherboard and five hundred bricks.[22] There was a brickyard at San Felipe before one existed in Harris County. Brick was used for the kitchen floor, well, and fireplaces, but full brick buildings were not constructed in Harris County until several years later. Cypress shingles covered the roof, and milled lumber was used for siding. When completed, the Williams house was a white frame, story-and-one-half dwelling with imported window sashes, glass, and paint.

After the burning of Harrisburg and the battle of San Jacinto in April of 1836, Harris County's best hope for development seemed to lie with the town of Houston. Selection of Augustus C. Allen and John K. Allen's new town as provisional capital of the republic brought instant recognition and gave it a considerable edge over other Texas towns struggling to attract new settlers. Francis R. Lubbock, one of the first to arrive at the Houston townsite, in January of 1837, commented: "Houston, having been made the seat of government, at once became the attraction point of all Texas. Water communication was good down Buffalo Bayou to

Galveston, and vessels at once engaged in making regular trips to that city from New Orleans and other points. . . . "[23] This communication gave Houston the immediate access to building materials from the states that Harrisburg had previously enjoyed.

As early as 1837, precut house frames, lumber, and other architectural elements were available in Houston. An 1837–38 ledger from the mercantile firm of Doswell & Adams listed, among foodstuffs and furniture, lumber sales at seven cents per foot, kegs of nails, kegs of white lead for paint, brick, and a "house frame" sold to John O'Brian on February 21, 1837, for $550.[24] Another house frame was shipped by Samuel A. Roberts on the schooner *Annie* from Mobile on January 23, 1837.[25] Even the Capitol, built with lumber imported from Maine, was quite likely framed with precut timber. A building could be rapidly raised with such a framing system, which consisted of pieces of lumber precut to the right lengths for a specific plan or building size.

Firsthand accounts of Houston's beginnings differ very little. In January of 1837, when lots in the new town were first offered for sale, Lubbock says: "A few tents were located not far away [from the landing]; one large one was used as a saloon. Several small houses were in the course of erection. Logs were being hauled in from the forest for a hotel to be erected . . . by Col. Benjamin Fort Smith, who was the inspector-general at the battle of San Jacinto. A small number of workmen were preparing to build cabins, business houses, and this hotel."[26]

An anonymous account related that "in the latter part of March, the improvements consisted of a one-story frame, two hundred feet or more in length, which had just been raised, intended by the enterprising proprietors for stores and public offices [this was the Long Row, the exterior of which has been replicated in Sam Houston Park], several rough log cabins, two of which were occupied by taverns, a few linen tents which were used for groceries together with three or four shanties made of poles set in the ground and covered and weatherboarded with rough split shingles."[27] Zachariah N. Morrell, an itinerant Baptist preacher who held the first religious service in Houston, also described his impressions in March of 1837: "a city of tents; only one or two log-cabins appeared. John K. Allen's frame building [Long Row] was raised, covered and partly weatherboarded."[28] John J. Audubon arrived on May 4, 1837, and wrote, "as soon as we rose above the bank we saw before us a level of far-extending prairie destitute of timber, and rather poor soil. Houses half-finished and most of them without roofs, tents and Liberty pole with the capitol, were all exhibited to our view at once."[29]

When Mary Austin Holley visited Houston for the first time in December of 1837 the town had grown from the few scattered tents and log buildings that Lubbock witnessed in January. She wrote that two hundred houses had been erected "chiefly in the margin of the timber line, on the Bayou. . . . The houses generally are of 1 story a few have 2. 2 large hotels with galleries above and below."[30] Holley also sketched rather primitive, but informative, drawings of the buildings she saw. One, belonging to the secretary of war, Colonel Bee, was a one-story frame structure that looked much like Evergreen.

Before Sam Houston moved into the house constructed for the president by the government, he probably lived in a succession of small houses, including the dog-trot on Travis described by Audubon in May of 1837. Another, on Caroline Street between Preston and Congress, has been pictured and often mistakenly identified as the "Texas White House." Charlotte Baldwin Allen said that Houston lived in this house in the fall of 1837 and described it as a "crude little house with two rooms and a lean-to."[31] Houston wrote to a friend on February 1, 1838: "It is late at night, and I am freezing in a miserable open house, four windows in it and not one pane of glass nor shutter. . . . Is this not a "White House" with a plague to it? The Palace is not yet finished, but it is said to be in progress and will soon be completed. I have sent to New York for magnificent furniture, and when it arrives what a beautiful contrast shall I enjoy."[32]

Robert Boyce built the "Palace" on property that Francis R. Lubbock sold to the republic in November of 1837. Boyce described the president's house, located at the southeast corner of Main and Preston:

Among the early houses I built was a clapboard house as follows: Gallery 8 x 10 ft., main room 16 x 16, bed room 8 x 16, the first President's house in the Republic. . . . Market Square was then heavily [sic] covered with forest trees, Pine especially. There being no lumber in Houston at that time, I asked Mr. John K. Allen, the founder of the town, if I could have pine timber enough off the square to build the President's house. He replied that I could, but how was I going to use it, I replied, whip saw it, that I would send to New Orleans for a whip saw (which I did) and cut into lumber. Of course it was slow work through the fall and winter of 1837. I had the house finished except plastering, and my men slept in the building for solid comfort as there was two brick chimneys. . . . I finally finished the house [1838], Gen. Houston being in Nacadoches [sic] at the time. I said finished, not quite, there lacked twelve pains [sic] of glass, in a twelve light sash. . . . In due time the President returned and moved in his new house. . . . I called on him at his request, found him in one of the two front reception rooms, that was divided by two large doors, five feet wide each. . . . [33]

Robert P. Boyce (ca. 1816–90) was among the first builders who settled in Houston. Born near Cincinnati, he began as a carpenter's apprentice there at about age fourteen. When his mentor moved north, Boyce went south to Natchez and then New Orleans, where in 1835 he joined the Texas cause.[34] When the fighting was over, Bob Boyce moved to Houston, where carpenters were in great demand. With his eagerness and experience he was busy from the start. Boyce also intermittently held public office. He was city marshal in 1850, but in the 1860 U. S. census his profession was listed as "master builder."[35]

Another of Houston's early master builders had known Boyce in New Orleans. Thomas William Ward, an Irish immigrant, also left New Orleans in 1835 to join the fight for Texas's independence. He was called "Pegleg" Ward after losing his leg at the storming of Bexar in 1835. At the end of the war Ward went back to New Orleans, where he was hired by the Allens to return to Texas to build the Capitol for the new republic in Houston.[36] Ward apparently used extra lumber from the Maine shipment intended for the Capitol to build what is generally believed to be the first two-story residence in the new town. Judge Andrew Briscoe purchased this house from Ward in October of 1837, shortly after his marriage.[37] The Briscoe house, located on Main Street at Prairie Avenue, had a double gallery across the front supported by three tall columns (fig. 10).

The columned façade of the Briscoe house was characteristic of the Greek Revival style, which had been popular in the United States since the 1820s. The Greek Revival was introduced into both Houston and Galveston soon after the battle of San Jacinto in what architectural historian Gus Hamblett described as a "substantial and even urbane manner."[38] An academic rendering of the Greek orders, with measured proportion and ornament corresponding to Greek temples, was generally reserved for public buildings. Houses used only a modified application of these details, often in a very schematic way. Greek Revival attributes can be found on both one- and two-story houses in early Harris County, although the application of Greek details was vernacular.

In Harrisburg John Birdsall Harris is thought to have been the builder of a one-story house around 1850 that differed from the pre-republic structures only in its use of more formal columns across the porch front (fig. 8). This house was bought by John Grant Tod from Harris's widow about 1866. In 1888 it was incorporated as a kitchen wing in the rear of the Charles Milby house on Broadway[39] (fig. 68). By 1841 Jane Birdsall Harris, John's mother and the widow of John R. Harris, had made alterations to the log house built for her by Mexican labor following the battle of San Jacinto (fig. 9). The logs were covered with weatherboard, and two-story, Greek-type columns were used to support the galleries, which wrapped around the house on three sides. In the late 1840s DeWitt Clinton Harris, another son, purchased doors, windows, and brass hardware from a three-story brick house in New York City that was being razed. This house, built around 1808 at 349 Bowery Lane, was noted for its fine interior woodwork and had belonged to Daniel D. Tompkins, governor of New York from 1807 to 1817. These items were shipped to Harrisburg and installed on the first floor of the Harris house.[40] The Harris house was divided downstairs into four rooms separated by a central hall. The fact that this type of center-hall plan had found its antecedent in Mrs. Harris's Seneca Falls, New York, childhood home emphasizes the fact that Harris County's early domestic architecture was not necessarily southern in origin.

Gus Hamblett asserts that it is a mistake to think that the Greek Revival was brought to Texas by southerners, because many of the early builders were European immigrants who had previous experience in their native countries.[41] In Harris County this was true. Ward was from Ireland, Charles Grainger from England, the Bering brothers from Germany, and Michael DeChaumes from France. But these and American-born builders, such as Eugene Pillot from New York, were influenced by current fashions and the expectations of their clients as well as by their own training. The Greek Revival was most often given form locally with square-cut, box columns with Doric capitals, as opposed to cylindrical columns with Ionic or Corinthian capitals, because these were the simplest and least expensive to reproduce. Such columns became ubiquitous in Houston before the Civil War. Front porches on two-story houses had either a two-tiered gallery with superimposed columns on the first and second stories or tall, colossal columns that reached the full height of the house. Both types of porch, as well as the columned porch on smaller one-story houses, commonly stretched across the entire façade of the house. Other elements derived from the Greek Revival that can be recognized in local dwellings were symmetrical massing, molded cornices, double- or triple- hung sash windows, and, less often, a front-facing gabled roof.

In addition to these stylistic characteristics, houses constructed in Harris County before the

Civil War had relatively consistent typological forms. The center-hall floor plans of Greek Revival houses, prevalent in Harris County, were standard residential plans that had been in use since Colonial times. They were essentially an elaboration of the double-log houses (or dog-trots). Front porches were often inset beneath a side-gabled roof, particularly on one-story houses. Front-facing dormer windows, when not part of the initial structure, were often added. Two-story houses were generally three bays wide with a portico across the front; many had a low-pitched, hipped roof rising to a flat, balustraded deck or widow's walk.

A variation of the formal symmetry of the center-hall plan was evident in such early local houses as the Charlotte Baldwin Allen house, which was located at the corner of Main Street and Rusk Avenue (fig. 11). The entrance was placed to one side, opening onto a wide hall with the rooms lined up on the other side, toward the prevailing breezes. Basically a townhouse plan adapted from the English row house, this arrangement was suitable to the local climate. The Allen house is an uncharacteristic example of the Houston interpretation of the Greek Revival. With double galleries supported by Doric box columns, it had a front-facing "pediment," which was more stylistically correct than the hipped roof of the Capitol or the side gable of the Briscoe house. The house was large, with a two-story ell on the south at the rear. The double gallery extended across the front and along the north side of the house.

The Nichols-Rice-Cherry house, now located in Sam Houston Park, is an extant example of this type of plan. Built on Courthouse Square about 1850, it has several relatively sophisticated architectural features. Hinged panels below the first-floor windows that could be opened for additional circulation of air during hot summer months indicate concern with ameliorating climatic extremes. Hand-carved woodwork on both the exterior and the interior was more elaborate than that of most contemporary Houston houses. Of particular interest are the fluted Ionic columns and the front door and its lighted surround. During restoration in 1957, architect Harvin C. Moore discovered that the columns had been shortened, suggesting that they originally were intended for some other building or had been altered when the house was moved.[42] Both the 1873 *Bird's Eye View of Houston* and Thomas Flintoff's 1852 watercolor of Courthouse Square (fig. 149) illustrate the original three-sided porch. About 1886 John Finnegan, the third owner, moved the house to the back of the same lot to face San Jacinto Street. The porches were probably altered and reduced in size at that time.

Moving houses was a frequent and relatively uncomplicated endeavor. Houses were transported not only from one part of town to another but also to the corner of a lot after having been constructed in the center of the block; many were simply rotated on their sites. Houston houses were built on brick or wooden piers and could be wheeled away easily on wooden platforms wedged beneath them. After the structure was lifted and the necessary bracing was made, teams of oxen or horses were used to roll the house slowly to its new site, where it would be transferred onto previously constructed new piers. One account related that it took forty yoked oxen to move a two-story, eight-room house.[43] In those days there was little to get in the way—no overhead wires, or even large trees. The greatest difficulty was first getting the motion started and then stopping in exactly the right place.

Houses not only were moved frequently but also were enlarged and updated. The James T. D. Wilson house was a square one-story house with porches on two sides (figs. 42, 43). Dormers had been added by 1873 to convert attic space to living area.[44] W. D. Cleveland bought a raised cottage at 806 San Jacinto Street built ca. 1854 (fig. 40). When his first son was born in 1873, he added a new room and was said to have added another for each of his subsequent five children.[45] Attic dormers and both side and rear additions were used to enlarge outgrown houses in the nineteenth century, just as they are today.

The John D. Andrews house, probably not completed until mid-1838, was another early two-story, Greek Revival structure built of imported materials. The Andrews house was occupied for some time by two families simultaneously. It was built on land owned by Andrews' partner, Thomas M. League, who lived upstairs with his family until 1840, when the partnership was dissolved and Colonel Andrews received the house as part of the settlement.[46] Such shared accommodations were not uncommon. In fact many early dwellings housed not only extended families of several generations but also servants and boarders. Before apartment houses were built after the turn of the century, newcomers and bachelors, as well as visitors, often lived in hotel rooms or boarding houses. Some who owned businesses lived with their families over the store, but the single-family house, though often crowded, was the predominant type.

Houses during the first few years of Houston's development were scattered, and street numbers were not assigned until 1870. Residential neighborhoods were clustered along Buffalo Bayou, up Main Street, and around Courthouse Square. Quality Hill, located along Franklin and Congress avenues between Caroline and Chenevert streets, was the first elite residential area removed from the daily workings of the city. Large houses overlooking Buffalo Bayou were built there beginning in the 1850s, including the Cornelius Ennis house (fig. 20). The finest house constructed on Quality Hill was the William J. Hutchins house, built around 1850 at Franklin Avenue and LaBranch Street[47] (fig. 15). With fluted Ionic columns supporting a full entablature and a low-pitched pediment, the Hutchins house was the most high-style Greek Revival house built in Harris County. Its deep moldings, brick fabric, and monumental proportions suggest not only expensive construction but the hand of an accomplished architect-builder as well.

Photographs of houses built in the 1840s and 1850s show consistent similarity. Examples of larger houses built during this period were those of Benjamin A. Shepherd and Thomas W. House (fig. 14), built in town, and the suburban house of Robert Lockart[48] (fig. 19). In Harris County, rural dwellings and urban houses tended to conform to common models, indicating that land was plentiful and inexpensive enough to avoid the crowding that produced row houses with common walls in other cities. Houston did not have the extensive public services available in older eastern cities, and, therefore, space for numerous outbuildings in this self-sufficient period was important. Even neighborhoods with more crowded conditions contained free-standing, single-family houses. When commercial expansion and railroad construction eventually began to squeeze out residential areas, particularly in the densely populated area between Courthouse Square and Quality Hill, residents simply migrated farther toward the edge of town rather than build new houses closer together. Yet, even after extensive grounds were less of a practical necessity, Houston continued to have a suburban, garden-district atmosphere. Readily available land produced a sense of spaciousness that residents came to enjoy and expect.

One example of the early pattern of dispersed settlement was a German neighborhood called Frost Town, located on Buffalo Bayou downstream from the Allen brothers' town site.[49] There Matilda Erhard and Frederich William Heitmann built their house in the 1840s. Blanche Heitmann Strange recalled her father's description of this white frame cottage built of cypress as a square dog-trot with three rooms on each side of the central hall. A front porch the length of the house faced the road and was used as an outdoor living room for the family. A rear porch, facing Buffalo Bayou, was a workplace where butter was churned, vegetables were hulled, and servants could relax. The roof, sloping over the front porch, had a central dormer window on the front and back, which lit a loft accessible by a narrow, steep stairway. The kitchen was a separate building. There was a well house, smokehouse, wash house, chicken house, and barn.[50] These, in addition to a privy, were the typical outbuildings most houses had throughout the nineteenth century.

In *Early Days on the Bayou*, Ellen Robbins Red also described various outbuildings at the house of Emily and H. D. Taylor, which was constructed on Buffalo Bayou at Preston Avenue and Smith Street in 1851. Built on three and one-half wooded acres, the house was enlarged six different times, eventually containing ten rooms. A long porch stretched across the front and down the Smith Street side. In the rear, the kitchen and servants' rooms were separated by an open gallery on each side and connected to the main house ten to fifteen feet away by a covered walk. Just north of the kitchen was a separate smokehouse about twelve feet by twelve feet, and northwest of that was the barn, which had stalls for stock, a carriage room, and a feed and hay room. West of the barn was a fenced cow and horse pen; north of the barn was a vegetable garden. The whole place was surrounded by picket fences that extended down to the bayou.[51]

Early Houston houses, like many elsewhere, were built without contract drawings. While architects, designing in "drafts," produced scaled drawings, master builders used a practical planning approach. The owner's specifications were customarily detailed in the builder's contract. A rough sketch with the number of rooms and their relative sizes and placements might be all that a builder needed to begin construction. Builders' handbooks, such as those by Asher Benjamin and Minard Lafever, were standard texts for the design and construction of Greek Revival details.[52] Instructions for framing, reproducing moldings, capitals, and interior refinements were included, accompanied by drawings of plans and elevations. Details taken from such books were sometimes simplified in construction but not drastically altered. Use of patternbooks may partially account for the fact that many houses in early Houston looked quite similar. Although these books served as guides for planning houses, individual architectural elements, such as prefabricated window sashes, mantels, doors, and even whole staircases, continued to be imported. Although sawmills had long been in operation, Houston's first window sash and blind factory was not opened until 1850.[53]

One of the more unusual houses constructed in Houston before the Civil War was the Erastus Perkins house, locally referred to as the "Round House" (fig. 12). Its octagon-shaped plan came from designs published by Orson Squire Fowler in 1854.[54] Although Fowler stressed the superiority of what he called "gravel walls" (concrete or stucco), the Perkins house was wood. A one-room lantern or cupola stood atop the two-story structure, which had a wide veranda on the first floor stretching around four sides of the house, with simple, round columns supporting the porch roof. Attached to the main block of the house was a smaller, two-story octagonal wing in an offset position. Fowler visited Galveston in the spring of 1859 on a lecture tour, and the *Galveston Daily News* reported a large attendance.[55] The Perkins house, one of the few octagon houses built in Texas, was probably constructed soon after that visit.

By chance the names of such builders as Boyce, Ward, and Dalton are known; many others no doubt settled in Houston or traveled through as itinerant carpenters and builders. Other local builders were Maurice Birdsall, who designed and built the first county jail in 1837; L. J. Pilie, who advertised in 1839 as an engineer and architect; C. C. Woodward, builder of the W. F. Gray house in 1838; and F. Jacob Rothaas, architect of the George Allen house about 1845[56] (fig. 13). In the 1850 U.S. census, fifty-eight men listed their profession as "carpenter," but none was listed as "architect." One man, Charles J. Grainger, was designated "house carpenter." Grainger was the builder and possibly the designer for the E. A. Palmer house in 1858 (fig. 16). Others at that time involved in the building industry were five painters, four cabinet makers, six bricklayers, and one plasterer. [57]

The Palmer house was an ambitious adaptation of a Greek Revival country house built in 1858 on a full-block site facing Rusk Avenue between LaBranch and Austin streets. Similar to Abner Cook's Neill-Cochran house in Austin (1855), the Palmer house, called Spring Grove, was a large wood structure with high fluted columns across the front. Letters between Palmer and his father, Dr. Reuben D. Palmer, in Virginia discuss some aspects of the construction. In January 1858 the father wrote: "I was very glad to get a plan of your house. It will be very roomy and convenient. If the balconies are to be without a roof, somewhat like open balustrades, I would advise that the floor be double and of the very best hart [sic] timber, to prevent the ingress of water and consequent early decay."[58] The balconies were covered by the extended, high hipped roof when the house was finally completed at the end of the summer.

The first experienced architect to work in Houston was Michael DeChaumes. A native of Paris, DeChaumes brought his family to Houston in 1837 after having practiced in Norfolk, Philadelphia, and Washington, D.C. He remained in Houston until his death in 1871 except for a brief stay in Austin.[59] DeChaumes was the architect of the Houston Academy (1857), the second Harris County Courthouse (1861), and the Treasury Building in Austin (1851); he was superintendent of construction for the Capitol in Austin (1852).[60] However, there is no record of houses he may have designed in Houston. His son, Henry DeChaumes, lived in a large house built in the 1860s and located on a full-block site bounded by Caroline, San Jacinto, Hadley, and Webster (fig. 17).

It is possible that Michael DeChaumes designed this house for his son after returning from Austin.[61] The DeChaumes house differed from its local contemporaries in that the front porches did not extend all the way across the façade. The centered one-bay entrance portico was articulated with colossal square-cut columns below a brief pediment. Such houses were popular in other parts of Texas, but not in Houston.

By 1850 a wide variety of materials was available to these builders. Smith & Bauer announced the opening of a brass foundry in 1841, a year after A. McGowen began to advertise tin, sheet iron, and copper for sale.[62] Twentieth-century demolitionists have discovered wooden pegs in pre-Civil War houses, but iron and steel nails were plentiful.[63] In 1847 J. D. Groesbeeck advertised fifty kegs of assorted nails as well as fifty boxes of window glass in various sizes.[64] Kemeys & Sampson in 1848 advertised iron and steel nails and imported "English wrought nails."[65] Numerous blacksmiths and foundries that were established in the 1840s probably manufactured nails locally. Iron and brass cabinet hardware was also readily available.[66]

The Houston iron foundries in operation in the 1840s and 1850s made tools and machinery but did not produce ornamental work for fences and balconies until after the Civil War. Few houses in Houston were built with New Orleans-type wrought-iron balconies. A notable exception was the C. S. Longcope house, built in 1859, which stood at 109 Chenevert on Quality Hill (fig. 246). Longcope bought the house from its original owner, Peter Floeck, and remodeled it in the early 1870s, adding stucco to its brick façade and decorative iron balconies across the front.[67]

Until 1840 most roofs were shingled with cypress and pine, but as soon as tin was available it became preferable. Tin roofs were first used on commercial buildings, but were quickly adopted by those who could afford them for their residences.[68] In 1845 a new method of "cement roofing for houses" was recommended in a newspaper article explaining its application: "Osnaburg (strong cotton cloth) is tacked down. Rosin and Tallow are melted and mixed with North Carolina Tar, water and lime." Guaranteed for five years, this mixture was brushed over the cloth and allowed to dry for four days, and then two more coats were repeated at one-week intervals.[69] Slate roofs were not reported until the 1880s.

Paint and sealers were used from the beginning in Harris County, not only for decoration but also because another special requirement of Houston's warm, moist climate was the need to protect exposed wood from mildew, insects, and rot. The Doswell & Adams ledger indicates that F. R. Lubbock bought "6 kegs of white lead" on February 23, 1837, for $48. In 1838 they advertised thirty kegs of white paint for sale.[70] Houston attracted professional painters eager for work. L. S. Marguiret advertised in July 1837 that he was available for "house, sign and ornamental painting."[71]

The problem of dampness in walls was also addressed in the early years with the suggestion that paint should be made of 1/10 litharage, applied hot to make a wall impervious to moisture.[72] The most creative formula for durable paint was published in 1845: "Dissolve an old Indian rubber shoe of common size in three or four gallons of oil, by heating it, and put on the paint after being prepared, while it is warm. White lead and oil make an imperfect body and soon wash off. India rubber added to paint makes it glossy and durable."[73] Another suggestion was advertised in 1856: "Fire Proof Paint—chocolate and slate colors." [74] Fire was a major problem, with frequent reports of houses, and even whole blocks, being damaged or destroyed. In an attempt to reduce fire hazards an 1841 city ordinance was passed that specified "no shingle or board roof or shed roof as awnings shall be lawful. . . . " [75] In 1858 the city passed another ordinance forbidding the erection of any wooden buildings in the commercial district along lower Main Street.[76] Larger houses were less susceptible to destruction by fire for three reasons: better construction, often surfaced with tin roofs; larger sites, therefore not as vulnerable to fires next door; and more careful isolation of chimneys and cooking areas.

Clearly the best defense against fire was the construction of solid masonry buildings. Although brick buildings quickly became preferable for businesses, brick houses were never that popular, probably because of the high cost of bricks relative to easily available lumber.

A brick kiln was established in the summer of 1837 by a man named Hathaway on the banks of Buffalo Bayou at the foot of McKinney Avenue.[77] It is known from their ledger that Doswell & Adams were selling imported brick as early as February of 1837. In December of that same year they advertised: "100,000 superior bricks for sale, apply at the brick yard or to Doswell & Adams." [78] These bricks were no doubt used at first for foundation piers, chimneys, and well casings, but by 1838 sufficient quantities for whole buildings were being manufactured locally. The first brick buildings recorded were a firehouse constructed in May of 1839 and two months later, in July, a brick office, which doubled as the first town hall, built by A. C. Allen on Franklin between Main and Fannin.[79]

Although Andrew Briscoe built a brick house in Harrisburg in 1840,[80] the first recorded brick residence constructed in Houston was built by A.C. Allen in 1841. Only a description of its construction exists, with no location and no indication of what happened to the house:

> It is known that Valentine Dalton erected a brick residence for the A. C. Allens in 1841—and dug a well 43 1/2 feet deep at that site [not identified]—using 20,000 bricks; he furnished these bricks and laid them for $200.00, at the rate of $20s per thousand. He charged $55.00 for digging the well. It might be interesting to know that the Allens apparently paid for this work by furnishing Valentine Dalton with 574 pounds of pork at 6 cents per pound—$34; 2 beeves [beef] at $15.00 ; one roan horse at $30.00; one yoke of oxen at $60.00; one mirror at $15.00; together with several other items.[81]

By 1842 Nathaniel Kelly Kellum had a large brickyard near the site of Hathaway's brickworks.[82] This yard was adjacent to the property on which Kellum built a two-story brick house in 1847. Still standing on its original site, the Kellum-Noble house, as it is now called, was surrounded by broad porches and a wide overhanging hipped roof that resembled a Louisiana interpretation of West Indian houses unusual in Houston (fig. 261). The vestigial Greek details on the second-floor columns and front-door framing as well as the center-hall plan, however, were similar to other local houses of its period.

The house of William Fairfax and Millie Gray, one of the first constructed on Courthouse

Square (about 1838), was remembered in the twentieth century as having been covered with "concrete made of shells and lime obtained by burning some of the shells. . . . "[83] This mixture, known as "tabby," was curiously not common in early Houston, where oyster shells were plentiful. The first contemporary report of tabby was published in 1859: "We notice an experiment in the way of building being tried by Mr. L. B. Bearce. . . . He is putting up a concrete house of shells, sand and cement. We are inclined to believe it will prove cheaper than brick and fully as lasting."[84]

Although Houston was not attacked during the Civil War, all available resources were channeled to the Confederate effort between 1861 and 1865. New construction was impossible during this hiatus, but changes in thought and construction methods became evident when building resumed after the war. A report in the 1870–71 *Houston City Directory,* noting two large foundries, eight or ten brickyards, and eleven lumberyards in town, stated: "During the war the location of Headquarters [of the Trans Mississippi Department of the Confederate Army] here largely increased our population. A year or two after the close of the war, there was a temporary reaction when the city seemed to decline, still some pertinent improvements were made. Gas works were erected, and now the public buildings, and many business houses and private residences, and the leading streets have pipes, posts and fixtures for the use of gas light. A number of leading streets have been graded and the sidewalks shelled."[85] In 1873 the *City Directory* reported on the newly opened Houston Cement Company, which produced cement from the sand of the San Jacinto River. This was the first time cement drainpipes, flues, and "ornamental tops" were available, which quickly added to the efficiency of the sewer system, to fire safety, and to the appearance of local buildings.[86]

A wider range of construction materials available in the 1870s did not influence the look of all new houses. Although Greek-style houses generally were identified as antebellum, they continued to be built alongside the new styles that became popular after the Civil War. Examples of large houses built after the Civil War in prewar styles were the John Shearn and Emmanuel Raphael houses. Shearn built his house in the country at what is now the corner of Main Street and Polk Avenue in the late 1860s.[87] This wide structure had double porches with six first- and second-floor columns across the front. In 1871 Emmanuel Raphael built a large front addition to his 1868 L-shaped cottage, located on a three-lot site at the corner of Rusk Avenue and Hamilton Street[88] (fig. 21). Six colossal Greek-style columns supported the high front portico, but a side porch on the southeast interrupted the frontal symmetry of the house, hinting at its postwar construction date.

Judge James A. Baker built a house about 1877 on a full block at the northeast corner of San Jacinto Street and Lamar Avenue in a modified T-shaped plan with a projecting entry bay[89] (fig. 22). While the columns on its double front porch were typical of the Doric box columns seen on antebellum houses, the Baker house had closely spaced brackets under the eaves, another sign of a postwar construction date. The gently sloping, hipped roof that terminated in a flat, railed gallery is another feature of the Baker house that was used on many of the large, two-story houses from the 1850s through the 1870s.

A photograph, probably taken in the late 1860s, illustrates this same type of roof on the large, two-story Henry Sampson house, which faced the southwest corner of Courthouse Square (fig. 23). The image gives a clear picture of the intersection at Fannin Street and Preston Avenue, which was surrounded by various types of buildings. This mix of businesses and residences was common in the center of town until the late 1880s, when increasing numbers of house sites began to be sold for new commercial buildings.

The exact date of construction of the Sampson house is unknown, but it was probably built before the Civil War.[90] Nevertheless, its appearance was updated by the addition of double brackets under the eaves (fig. 24). A similar house was constructed by John Thomas Brady in the 1870s (fig. 94). The earliest photographs of the Brady house show simpler brackets, bay windows, and a two-story octagonal porch on the east. These types of decorations and forms broke the strict symmetry of Greek Revival houses and would become increasingly popular after the Civil War. However, both the Sampson and Brady houses were remarkably similar in plan to the earlier Allen house, the Nichols-Rice-Cherry house, and the Hutchins house. All five also had round, fluted columns, as opposed to the more prevalent box-shaped columns.

The 1867 Will Powars house was another postwar house with classical attributes (figs. 25, 26). With rectilinear massing and a lack of decorative ornament, its porches were of the Greek Revival type.[91] Like such earlier houses as the T. W. House house, the Ennis house, and the Perkins house, the Powars House had a separately roofed, offset wing. The appearance of such wings on Houston houses in the 1860s and 1870s was another local typological form recurring in many photographs of otherwise symmetrical, rectangular houses of this period. The reason for such a plan, which might appear to be an addition but often was not, was twofold. First, such an arrangement allowed the house to take greater advantage of prevailing breezes. Large houses built in a single block would have had rooms without multiple exposures, making them claustrophobic and hot during the long summer. Second, the offset wing, slightly separated but still connected to the main block, could house the kitchens and servants' quarters, a more convenient arrangement than having a completely separate outbuilding. On the Powars and Ennis houses, small corner porches linked the two blocks, which in these cases were equal in size to the main block.

The Samuel Ezekiel Allen Ranch house was the largest and most complex of the offset wing-type houses with Greek Revival characteristics (fig. 27). Called Oaklawn Place, it was constructed at the confluence of Sims and Buffalo bayous shortly after the wedding, in 1874, of Samuel Ezekiel Allen and Rosa Christie Lum. The house was built on Allen's father's cattle ranch, which the younger Allen eventually inherited and expanded to a 13,000-acre operation. Mrs. Allen was said to have designed the house after plantations in Natchez, Mississippi, which she had seen while visiting her paternal grandparents there.[92] At Oaklawn Place the setback wing contained the kitchen and servants' quarters. Grooved, two-story box-columns and closely spaced decorative brackets under the eaves added to the impressiveness of this structure, as did high third-story dormers in the main block.

Certainly not all houses, or even most of them, built in Houston during the Greek Revival period were imbued with classical columns. Many were still built with one-story, post-supported porches similar to early Harrisburg houses. Typical of modest houses that continued to be built with box-columned front porches into the 1880s was the Justine and William Ruppersburg house, now located in Sam Houston Park.[93] These German immigrants constructed their one-story cottage on San Felipe Road in 1868, hence its current appellation, the San Felipe Cottage. The German population in Houston was second in size only to the Anglo-American, but its influence in the architectural arena was less significant than in the German settlements in central Texas. Like other ethnic groups that settled in Houston, Germans did tend, at first, to cluster in their own neighborhoods. But as they became more affluent or developed business interests in various parts of town, they were assimilated into other Houston neighborhoods. Local German-occupied houses, from the outside, looked much the same as those of other residents. The Germans, however, often decorated their interiors with intricate stencil designs painted on ceilings and walls.

Houston entered the last quarter of the nineteenth century with new ideas, new technology, and new money that combined to produce a demand for new buildings which continued until World War I. By 1870 Romantic idealism had swept the country, providing a new set of principles on which American architecture was based. The Romantic Movement espoused two interdependent ideas that had an effect on architecture: a glorification of nature and a new emphasis on imagination and emotion. Victorian notions extolling a natural and "organic" way of life, as well as a desire to create something new and unconventional, were factors that motivated the appearance of the Victorian styles, with their muted colors and rambling, complex shapes. Individualism and a taste for the picturesque were equally powerful influences in the new forms that emerged after the Civil War.

The transition to more ornamented architecture began to occur just after the Civil War. Transitional houses were generally rectilinear in plan but kept current with fashionable applied ornament of the Victorian period. For example, Thomas W. House, Jr., built a rather straightforward L-shaped house in 1871; he added not only paired brackets under the eaves but also decorative scalloped brackets at the top of its first-floor porch columns[94] (fig. 41). Photographs of this house also hint at some decorative rooftop ornaments, which are in sharp contrast to the formalized and restrained classical styles of earlier decades. Older houses, such as the W. D. Cleveland house, were updated by the addition of bay windows or new porches with fancy millwork. Both large, two-story houses and one-story cottages continued to have this type of decoration, at least on the street front, through the 1890s.

While some Houstonians continued to build houses with Greek Revival characteristics as late as 1875, many, like citizens in the rest of the country, had changed their ideas about how houses should look. In July 1870 the *Houston Daily Telegraph* reported: "Somebody is building a tasty cottage, on the corner of Capitol and Fannin streets, and another is going up on Main in its western portion. By the way, it is time to abandon the miserable old fashioned box houses for the later and more elegant Italian villa style. . . . "[95] As early as 1868, such fancifully decorated houses as the Eugene Pillot house appeared—not quite an elegant Italian villa, but not an old-fashioned box house either[96] (fig. 28). Spindle posts replaced columns and scroll brackets replaced capitals. Bay windows became an important element in large and small houses alike, contributing to the voguish asymmetry. Victorian houses had more vertically accentuated proportions, floor-length windows with multiple panes, both rectangular and diamond-shaped, and more complex roof forms.

Andrew Jackson Downing (1815–52) emerged in the 1840s as the most widely read and influential American writer with respect to this type of Romantic suburban house design. In promoting his new landscape ideas Downing sketched and published dozens of dwellings that would be appropriate in these settings. His books remained influential long after his death. *Cottage Residences,* which continued to be reprinted throughout the nineteenth century, was not only a house patternbook but an ideological manifesto in which Downing sought to bring moral justification to his house designs. He equated truth and beauty in architecture with domestic contentment and moral righteousness.[97]

Downing's wooden houses used the Gothic pointed arch (hence the term "Carpenter Gothic") or, less frequently, Italian vernacular references. As popular as Downing became, few of the Carpenter Gothic or Italianate cottages that he promoted appeared in Harris County. This was partially because of the style lag that still existed in Texas. A notable exception was the house of A. J. Whitaker, the landscape gardener and horticulturalist[98] (fig. 31). Whitaker built a two-story cottage in the late 1860s that had pedimented window molds and a steeply pitched cross-gabled roof with a high third-story dormer over the entry bay suggesting a tower. Decorative brackets under the eaves and at the top of the porch added to the picturesque quality of the asymmetrical plan.

Another noted Houston horticulturalist, E. H. Cushing, built a large, asymmetrical raised house, called Bohemia, on a ten-acre site south of town between Austin and San Jacinto[99] (fig. 30). A native of Vermont, Cushing probably purchased this property soon after he arrived in Houston in 1856. If Bohemia was built before the Civil War, it was certainly one of the first local residences to depart radically from the Greek Revival. Even if it was not built until the late 1860s, its Italianate window ornament, similar to that of the Whitaker house, decorative porch spindles and brackets, and T-shaped plan mark Bohemia as one of the earliest Victorian houses in Houston.

James S. Lucas built a later Downing-like house around 1875[100] (fig. 32). Decorative bargeboards under the narrow eaves of a high-pitched roof, a one-story entry porch covered in vines, multiple gables, arched windows, and tall chimneys created the picturesque quality Downing advocated.

After the Civil War two divergent models for local residences began to emerge more clearly: houses of the affluent, designed to display wealth and standing in the community, and houses of people of more moderate means designed for economy, shelter, and comfort. Rows of similar or duplicated houses were built along the streets of middle- and working-class neighborhoods, while rather idiosyncratic houses, reflecting the freedom of expression in architectural taste allowed by a larger income, were built in affluent neighborhoods. Houses built for investment and those copied from books or ordered prefabricated from catalogs tended to be more uniform. The larger, expensive houses were more likely to express current architectural fashion; they were also more likely to have been photographed.

These large houses often took advantage of technical innovations that became available in Houston after the Civil War. In 1870 the Architectural Iron Works of New York advertised locally for the first time.[101] In Houston ornamental iron fences, in particular, were manufactured by the Phoenix Iron Works, which advertised in 1877 that they could "make castings of every description in brass and iron" and would supply anything "from iron house fronts to the garden gate and railing."[102] The Richardson Iron Works in the same year advertised balconies and railings "in a hundred handsome patterns."[103] In 1882 Henry House advertised a large stock of window sash, doors, blinds and trimmings, moldings, flooring, ceilings, lattice, and shingles.[104] Several local mills were by this time producing all of the necessary appurtenances for new houses, including fancy spindle posts, scrolls, and brackets.

Portland cement sidewalks were reported to have been installed first by L. J. Latham in front of his store on Main Street in 1873.[105] A. A. Van Alstyne advertised his Artificial Stone Works in 1880, the beginning of the cast-stone cement block industry that produced what became a popular material for foundations and fence and porch piers.[106] In 1884 Bayou City Marble Works was making Italian and American marble available locally.[107] Although this firm primarily made gravestones, it also provided marble for basins, tabletops, and fireplaces. In the same year Jerry Crowley, a plasterer, advertised his ability to produce "all kinds of plain and ornamental plaster work."[108] The first advertisements for roof slating seem to have appeared in 1884.[109] During the early 1880s asphalt and shell roofs were offered. Sanborn fire-insurance maps indicate that most houses were still being roofed with wood shingles; some dwellings, both large and small, had asphalt roofs, but larger houses had tin or slate roofs described as "fireproof." The Repsdorph Tent & Awning Company, founded in 1878, produced canvas awnings. Photographs of some Houston houses in the 1880s and 1890s show full awnings shading almost every window. Awnings, like window screens, were appreciated for functional reasons; they also added a decorative touch. In an eyecatching advertisement, Repsdorph asked: "Do you live in a House? If so, have Awnings put on your windows. If not, we can furnish you a tent at reasonable figures."[110]

During the Victorian era iron fences, cement sidewalks, the first paved streets, and awnings changed the look of some neighborhoods. However, less affluent areas continued to look much as they had before the Civil War, with poor drainage, unpaved streets, and small one-story clapboard houses built close together. But even small houses were affected by the arrival in the late 1870s of professional architects, who were instrumental in changing the architectural climate of Houston. Until this time houses were designed, with few exceptions, by artisans and builders of varying talent, usually with the help of builders' handbooks or patternbooks. After the Civil War wealthy clients wanted imaginative and individualistic houses. The demand for these, as well as the need for new commercial buildings and public structures, created a market for the services of professional architects. Although most houses were not designed by architects, the influence of professionally designed buildings was widespread because builders could copy forms and details firsthand. Architects not only designed specific local houses but also were responsible for plans and elevations that were widely circulated in patternbooks, catalogs, and periodicals. Design elements from innovative houses created by professionals quickly began to appear on smaller, simpler dwellings.

The earliest grand Victorian house reported in Houston was the Albert A. Van Alstyne house constructed in 1877 at 1216 Main Street (fig. 44). It was designed by Galveston architect N. J. Clayton, a native of Ireland who was educated in the customary apprenticeship system, rising from plasterer to marble carver to draftsman between the 1850s and 1871. Moving to Texas from Cincinnati, Ohio, in that year, he lived five months in Houston before settling permanently in Galveston. Clayton secured his first commission as a supervising architect in the fall of 1872.[111] His architectural reputation grew rapidly, securing for him posthumous fame as Texas's best-known late-nineteenth-century architect. Although Clayton's practice was based in Galveston, he received a number of Houston commissions for churches and schools. However, he is not known to have designed any other houses there. The Van Alstyne house was important in Houston's architectural history for several reasons: it was the first elaborate mansion constructed after the Civil War; it was the first to be designed by an acclaimed Texas architect; and it established Main Street as Houston's new elite residential thoroughfare.

The Van Alstyne house was the first in Houston to conform to a predominant type for large Victorian houses, the "towered villa." Stylistically, it would have been described at the time as "Modern French Renaissance."[112] The house, though, was oddly proportioned. Its tower was too attenuated and sat like an afterthought above the third story. In addition its awkward asymmetry produced a less than graceful example of the modern French style, identified by the mansard roof, classical moldings, and such details as roof cresting, quoins, cornices, and belt courses. Yet the Van Alstyne house, despite its shortcomings, was Houston's most sophisticated residential structure when it was built because of the attention to detailing lavished on both its exterior and interior.

Van Alstyne sold the house in 1882 to another prominent Houstonian, Judge James R. Masterson, whose family occupied it until 1900, when industrialist John F. Dickson bought it. Shortly afterward Dickson retained N. J. Clayton to remodel the interior[113] (figs. 175–77). The Humble Oil and Refining Company acquired the property in 1918 for the site of its office building and demolished the house.[114] This pattern of commercial development along Main Street was responsible for the demolition of all of the mansions built along this tree-lined thoroughfare during the last quarter of the nineteenth century. After selling their house sites for handsome profits, wealthy families who resided on Main tended to build new houses in the South End subdivisions.

At the time the Van Alstyne house was under construction, architect Eugene T. Heiner (1852–1901) arrived in Houston. He was born in New York and later moved to Chicago, where he received his architectural training through apprenticeship. Heiner moved to Terre Haute, Indiana, in 1873 and worked as a draftsman for J. A. Vrydaugh, one of Indiana's best-known nineteenth-century architects. After establishing a short-lived practice in Indiana, he came to Houston in late 1877 and began what was to become a prolific architectural career.[115]

The success of Heiner's first major Texas commissions, two Galveston commercial buildings in 1878 and 1879, gained him a solid reputation.[116] He designed at least twenty-two county courthouses and jails throughout Texas, as well as an equal number of large commercial buildings in Galveston and Houston. Heiner concentrated on commercial and institutional buildings rather than on domestic ones. However, he did design four notable houses in Houston, two of which conformed to the towered-villa type. The first of them, his finest, was for Charles S. House in 1882 at 1806 Main Street[117] (fig. 45). The House residence closely resembled the Van Alstyne house by Clayton, but it was better proportioned, particularly with respect to its tower, which was more carefully integrated into the overall design of the house. Although House spent $18,000, compared with the $20,000 invested by Van Alstyne, his residence was larger and had a more elaborate exterior with prominent roof cresting, a stylishly curved mansard roof, and ornate moldings. Heiner's penchant for polychromatic and textured surfaces overlaid with decorative ornament was evident in this house. It was this kind of exuberant architecture for which he was well known.

The House family lived there until about 1896. In 1899 the building was sold to Dr. William R. Eckhardt, who remained there until his death in 1913 or 1914, leaving Jesse H. Jones's Bankers Trust Company the agent for his estate. At this time the Houston Art League was looking for a permanent home for its fledgling art collection. When negotiations with both George Hermann and the city of Houston for land on which the League could build a museum failed, Mrs. Gentry Waldo negotiated a one year lease with Bankers Trust to rent the Eckhardt House for $75 per month.[118] The old C. S. House residence thus became the first home of the Houston Art League, the forerunner of The Museum of Fine Arts, Houston. The Art League's president, Albert L. Guérard, wrote in 1916: "When I returned from the Pacific Coast in October, I found a large house rented and under repairs. . . . In spite of the architectural monstrosity in which we were sheltered, we received last year several valuable gifts which might not have gone to a homeless organization."[119] By 1916 Guérard's assessment of a Victorian house—an "architectural monstrosity"—had become prevalent. Combined with the escalating value of urban real estate, this attitude gave such old houses no chance of survival in Houston. The Humble Oil and Refining Company, which had demolished the Van Alstyne house, was also responsible for the loss of the Charles S. House house. On its site one of Humble's first retail gasoline stations was constructed in 1919.[120]

Contract prices were reported in building announcements and sometimes in the *Houston City Directory*. The 1882 *Directory* reported the construction of two other houses by Heiner: his own residence for $3,600 and a house for George L. Porter for $13,500.[121] The amount that Heiner was able to spend on his own house would have built a small, one-story frame cottage with few embellishments. During the 1880s anything over $10,000 built a large, decorated dwelling. Another of Heiner's Houston houses, designed in 1884 for Dr. James H. Blake and constructed at 1517 Texas Avenue at Crawford, cost $9,000.[122] Compared with the C. S. House house, which cost nearly $5,000 more, the Blake house was plain. The more restricted budget did not give Heiner a chance to display his talent for façade ornamentation.

Dr. Blake, a physician, surgeon, and homeopath, had his office in a rear wing of the house, a customary arrangement in the nineteenth century. Two years earlier, in 1882, Dr. David F. Stuart had built a similar house for $8,000 diagonally across the street at 1116 Texas Avenue[123] (fig. 233). He saw patients in a red brick building constructed in his side yard. Although the Stuart house was not designed by Heiner, the roof cresting and finials, overlaid gable and porch work, and deep decorative cornices were like elements of Heiner's work seen elsewhere. Such mimicry was rampant during the Victorian period and explains how the arrival of professional architects in Houston influenced local architecture.

The year after Heiner arrived in Houston, architect George E. Dickey (1840-?) came from New Hampshire via Boston and Toronto. Dickey rivaled Heiner in both numbers of Houston commissions and proficiency. However, Dickey's practice included a much larger share of domestic buildings than did Heiner's. No architectural drawings for houses by these architects survive, but their work can be documented through photographs, descriptions, and published accounts. It is difficult to compare Heiner's and Dickey's domestic work because Heiner designed so few houses. However, Heiner's work was generally more rectilinear, while Dickey's houses were varied and picturesque. Heiner's emphasis on decorative brickwork might have been a result of his Chicago training, whereas Dickey's use of shingles, vertical and horizontal siding of different widths, and contrasting exterior paint colors indicated his Boston affiliations. Heiner's plans and forms were tight, while Dickey's were more fluid and expansive. Heiner seems to have formularized his elevations in a way that Dickey did not; Heiner's later buildings were much like his earlier ones, but Dickey's designs evolved gracefully with the times. Dickey was the more imaginative and accomplished architect of the two.

George Edwin Dickey was born in Wilmot, New Hampshire, and educated in public schools there before attending a technical institute in New London, New Hampshire. He then studied architecture in Boston before opening his first office in Waltham, Massachusetts, in 1868.[124] Two years later he established a practice in Manchester, New Hampshire, where the local newspaper reported: "Mr. Dickey, a new architect in this city has opened an office in Riddle's block. He comes well recommended, and will probably find work enough to do."[125] In Manchester Dickey received several commissions, including two churches that are strikingly similar to churches he designed in Texas.[126] Dickey appears in the *Boston City Directory* only for the year 1872.[127] Boston at that time was the center of architectural innovation in the United States. The first architecture school in America was established at the Massachusetts Institute of Technology in 1865. Although Dickey did not receive his training at M.I.T., he was exposed to the exciting Boston architectural community.

By 1873 Dickey had moved to Toronto, where he remained until coming to Texas in 1878. George Dickey intermittently took on partners during his twenty-five-year Texas tenure, but his houses were usually attributed to "George E. Dickey, architect," indicating that these other affiliations were for limited time periods or individual projects.[128] His busy practice and the fact that in 1892 he was elected president of the Texas State Association of Architects attest to the professional respect he was accorded.[129] Dickey left Houston in 1896 to practice with his son, Dura Anderson Dickey, in New Orleans, but returned to Houston in 1899 with several important commissions.[130] Dickey and his entire family abruptly disappeared from Houston in 1906. His last important Houston commission was a significant one—the 1904 Houston City Hall and Market.

Like Eugene Heiner, George Dickey received his first known Texas residential commission in 1882, and, also like Heiner, he began with a large, expensive towered villa. Dickey's house for Jehu W. Johnson stood on a two-block site at 710 Hadley Avenue at the edge of town (fig. 54). The Johnson house, later owned by J. O. Ross, had extensive gardens and a huge stable-servants quarters building, which added to its overall impressiveness. With walls four bricks thick, the usual construction for masony supporting walls, the residence had twenty-four rooms, six baths, and a large billiard room on the third floor.[131] Compared with the later Scanlan house by Eugene Heiner (fig. 55), the Johnson house was more elegant and less chunky.

In 1884 Dickey designed for Jedidah Porter Waldo his last square-towered villa [132] (fig. 51). Like the Johnson house, this residence had a tall tower over its entrance, an L-shaped double porch, and double-height protruding bays. The Waldo house was built at 1213 Rusk Avenue at the corner of San Jacinto. It was dismantled in 1903 when Mrs. Waldo sold the property for construction of a new United States Post Office. The house now stands at 201 Westmoreland Avenue, where it was rebuilt by the owner's son, Wilmer Waldo, a civil engineer educated at Princeton. According to recollections of Wilmer Waldo's sister, Virginia Waldo, every piece of the house was marked as it was dismantled. It took until 1905 for the reconstructed house to be completed. A full basement was dug, and reinforced concrete foundations were allowed to cure for almost a year to prevent later shifting.[133] The brick exterior was redesigned by Waldo in a modified Italianate manner with an arched loggia on the first floor. The mansard roof was reconfigured into a hipped roof, and the tower and third floor dormers were removed. These changes reflected the more subdued architectural atmosphere prevalent in 1905. Remarkably, the interior woodwork survived intact, leaving arched doorways, wainscoating, built-in bookcases and china cabinets, and a large hand-carved staircase off of the expansive entry hall. Marble basins from the original bathrooms were also transferred to the new location.

Because original architectural plans do not seem to survive for these buildings, it is difficult to be specific about the interior living spaces contained within the shells one knows from photographs. Published plans of similar houses, of course, relate general trends, but, as the only remaining large house of this period, the Waldo house is important because one can examine its plan and interior detailing fully. The centered entrance doors open into a wide living hall with dark wainscoating, stair rails, columns, and a massive brick fireplace. Elaborate woodwork throughout the house was fashioned from several types of wood: oak in the halls and dining room, maple in the parlor, and cherry in the library. The formal parlor, to the north, is a heavy, high room with a bay window on the west side. Directly behind the parlor, up two wide steps, is the dining room, separated from the front room with sliding pocket doors. The dining room has another large, leaded-glass west bay window. Massive built-in sideboards and cabinets are characteristic of the dark, heavy atmosphere of the whole house. The cherry-paneled library is to the right of the entry. A warren of kitchen, pantries, back halls, and a back stair completes the first-floor plan.

Henry-Russell Hitchcock has pointed out that asymmetrical massing forced asymmetrical planning, which encouraged a greater degree of functional differentiation that had rarely been seen in American domestic architecture before the Civil War.[134] The Waldo house, although not a rambling structure, is a good illustration of this observation. Rather than three or four large rectangular or square rooms on each floor, plans with bays and projections provided for more spatially varied room configurations, with nooks, storage places, and smaller subsidiary rooms, in addition to the large formal ones. The idea of a "living hall" was an innovation based on medieval architectural precedents, which served as a model for Boston architect H. H. Richardson and other Anglophile American architects who devised these new architectural types. What characterized many Houston houses was not necessarily a hall used as the main living space, but the presence of a fireplace and wide dimensions in the entry, alluding to these medieval origins in a symbolic way.

Another such symbolic allusion was expressed in the towers and turrets that became widespread in the 1880s and 1890s. The Queen Anne style transformed towered villas into more rambling houses with rounded turrets. This Victorian type was popular during the last two decades of the nineteenth century in Harris County, as it was in the rest of the country. Identifying features were steeply pitched roofs, patterned shingles and brickwork, bay windows, and asymmetrical massing combined with a partial or full-width porch, usually one story high. Flat, planar façades were avoided by the use of numerous shapes and sizes of windows and doors and overlaid decorative siding. Because the American Queen Anne was so varied, elements of it could be used for both large and small houses.

In 1888–89 George Dickey designed the grandest Queen Anne house built in Houston at 1416 Main Street for Samuel K. Dick, president of the Inman Compress Company (fig. 56). Its construction was fascinating enough that its progress was reported in the local newspaper.[135] The Dick house was sold ten years later to Captain James A. Baker, Jr., whose family occupied it until 1923, when he demolished it to erect a commercial building on the site. A variety of shapes, textures, and materials were combined with a panoply of chimneys, dormers, bays, gables, wrapped porches, stairs, arches, and a handsome round turret to achieve a remarkable complexity. Closely spaced rails, extensive spindlework, and shifting planes were used on the porches of this house to emphasize its asymmetry and to produce shimmering, light-and-shadow effects. What might have been a confused composition was unified by a high, dominant slate roof toward which the subsidiary roofs of porches, offset gabled bays, and dormers rose. The tall chimneys, turret finial, and roof cresting served to outline this complex compilation of architectural forms.

During the 1880s and 1890s Houston saw a wide variety of Queen Anne houses constructed with varying degrees of elaboration. The town's expanding middle class not only lived in relatively unpretentious houses, which mimicked aspects of popular stylistic conventions, but also discovered catalog houses that in many cases were as individualistic as those being designed for the wealthiest citizens by local architects. Although A. J. Downing had been one of the first advocates of patternbook picturesque dwellings, his particular stylistic modes were not adopted in Harris County. After the Civil War patternbooks began to proliferate, most notably those by A. J. Bicknell, who began publishing catalogs of his plans for Victorian houses in 1870, and William T. Comstock, who began as Bicknell's partner.[136] Downing, Bicknell, Comstock, and many others were widely acclaimed nationally for their publications, but no particular houses in Houston can be attributed directly to their plans. In fact, the designs of these architects were strikingly different from anything that was built locally. They are heavy, mostly stone or brick structures, with less emphasis on porches, fewer windows, and seemingly more prominent and more numerous chimneys. They were obviously designed for colder climates, and Houstonians did not take to them. They did, however, embrace the plans of another designer who became one of this country's most successful late-nineteenth-century domestic architects through his mail-order method of architectural practice—George Franklin Barber.

Barber was a midwesterner who understood the importance of mail-order catalogs to small-town residents and rural settlers. He also realized that previously published designs were not necessarily suited to midwestern and southern communities: "One great trouble with Northern books and periodicals on architecture is the lack of plans suited to Southern requirements."[137] Barber was successful in translating the color and texture of masonry buildings into wood, the most convenient material outside of New England. Not limited to architectural versatility, his genius devised the idea of a mail-order practice. He published inexpensive, illustrated catalogs with price lists and order forms for his plans, constantly stressing that his draftsmen would make any changes that his client wished. One would simply choose a plan and order the working drawings, which were produced as originals, drawn by hand for each order.[138]

Margaret Culbertson, architectural librarian at the University of Houston, has discovered several Barber houses that were built in Houston.[139] Some were constructed exactly according to the published plans, and others were so close to Barber houses that it is highly probable they represented individualized plans by Barber. The first documented local examples of Barber houses were built during the 1890s in the new suburban town of Houston Heights. Because five Barber designs, among the first houses constructed in the Heights, were engraved on the promotional map published around 1900, it seems likely that Barber was hired by the Omaha and South Texas Land Company, developers of Houston Heights, to supply designs specifically for the new development. Among them were the D. D. Cooley house at 1802 Heights Boulevard (fig. 76), the Newton L. Mills house, 1530 Heights Boulevard (fig. 77), the John A. Milroy house, 1102 Heights Boulevard (extant), and the similar Mansfield house at 1802 Harvard (extant). These houses were slightly modified from published Barber designs, but two other houses, at the corner of 16th and Rutland and on Heights Boulevard between 8th and 9th streets, were published on the Heights map directly from a Barber catalog.[140]

Barber wrote in 1898: "All over America, the idea is spreading that a new building must be original, not thereby meaning a freakish departure from well known principles of design, but one planned originally for the owner. This is right, and will do more toward the growth of an artistic taste and the establishment of content in the homes of the people than any other factor. . . . "[141] George Barber probably had as much influence on the designs of larger houses in Houston as any one local architect. He published more than eight hundred designs and is known to have produced many unpublished variations. Elements and plans of Barber houses seem to appear in many of Houston's Queen Anne houses. Although he is certainly not to be credited with all of these designs, many local architects and builders probably had copies of his catalogs, as well as those of others, and used them freely for inspiration.

More surprising even than the Heights-Barber connection was Culbertson's discovery that George Dickey seems to have sometimes relied on designs published by other architects. His J. M. Cotton house (fig. 79), constructed in 1882–83 and well documented as Dickey's work, looks on the exterior exactly like F. Egge's Cottage, published in George and Charles Palliser's *Model Homes* in 1878[142] (fig. 78). This design was reprinted three times, giving architects and potential clients throughout the country ample opportunity to copy it. Design no. 485, published in Shoppell's *Modern Houses* in 1887, seems to be an exact replication of the Charles Dillingham house (fig. 81) built in 1889 at 1214 Rusk.[143] Again Dickey clearly took credit for the plans. There are several possible explanations for such flagrant plagiarism: Dickey might have been a rather dishonest practitioner redrawing in his offices work of others and presenting it to clients as his own; or the clients could have seen the designs, liked them, and asked their architect to copy them; or Dickey could have been the original architect in the first place, having previously sold his own designs to catalog publishers. The strangest element in this puzzle is not that one architect would copy the published work of another, for that type of "inspiration" has occurred since Palladio's first publications in the sixteenth century, but that an architect who was so well regarded and apparently creative would have so closely copied another's work. Perhaps Dickey copied others' work more often than has been discovered, and he was particularly gifted in choosing and executing good designs. But this seems unlikely. His Houston houses have been scrutinized with reference to many publications of the time, and only the Cotton and Dillingham houses seem to have been copied. So perhaps the most satisfactory explanation is that these particular clients requested these specific houses.

Many large Houston houses that have not been attributed to a particular architect could have been based on sophisticated catalog designs. The houses built by Alexander Bergamini about 1885, Gustave A. Mistrot in 1895, and Michael DeGeorge in 1900, among others, were interesting

Queen Anne houses with various tower configurations in the manner of George Barber or other catalog architects. The Bergamini house had a squared tower that was not over the angled, off-center entry bay but placed to one side without reference to other parts of the house[144] (fig. 57). The Mistrot house had not only a tower-like dormer centered over the entrance but also a rounded turret to the right of and below it[145] (fig. 58). With gracefully curved millwork, spindles, shingles, latticework, and a cast-stone base, this was one of the most ebullient Queen Anne houses built in Houston. The DeGeorge house had a more typical tower placement, at the corner, with its effect enhanced by a curved porch[146] (fig. 59). All of these houses were two-story structures with elaborate ornamental millwork on double-tiered porches. Although their designs spanned a ten-year period, they were similar in decorative aspect, form, and size.

Illustrating the more exaggerated end of the Queen Anne spectrum was the Captain Thomas D. Cobb house, built around 1887[147] (fig. 60). This anomalous house was top-heavy, with a large bargeboard-draped tower that looked more like a Victorian hat than a house. Its multilayered porches, gables, and bays seem to be jumbled together and decorated with every type of lattice, millwork, and bracket that the local dealer had in stock. This house reveals the extreme limit of architectural imagination in Houston during the Victorian era.

Imagination was not necessarily limited by budget or house size. The H. W. Wood house was a simpler, one-and-one-half story frame cottage on which a hexagonal porch fanned out to enframe a small but prominent octagonal tower[148] (fig. 61). Another small cottage with a porch tower is still standing at 2009 Live Oak Street in the Third Ward (fig. 62). This house, located in a historically African American neighborhood, was probably built just after the turn of the century by an experienced black contractor.[149]

Many houses constructed during the Victorian era did not have towers and complex plans. Milton G. Howe's house constructed about 1880 at 918 Austin was a towered-villa type without the tower[150] (fig. 48). In 1885 Charles H. Milby built a large brick house in Harrisburg at 614 Broadway[151] (fig. 68). This house had no rounded forms, but was L-shaped, like the Howe house, to allow wide side porches on the first and second floors. Tall windows, decorative porch ornament, and high, shingle-covered dormer windows were all aspects of fashionable houses built during this period.

Farmhouses and houses built in the small communities that dotted Harris County in the late nineteenth century were never as sophisticated as those of their city neighbors in Houston. The reasons are several. Economic considerations usually precluded much decoration or innovation on rural dwellings. In addition people who lived in the country, like the first settlers, were more concerned with their farms and farm equipment than the architectural style of their houses. Large, fashionable houses were built for show, a pretension that country folk did not usually share with "city slickers." People who lived in Harris County outside of Houston, while certainly aware of the new styles, did not indulge themselves in this way. They built houses for comfort, and they lived in them longer. An example of such a country house was the Reed Singleton farmhouse, built in 1885 in Humble, which was photographed with the entire family lined up out front[152] (fig. 69). It clearly displayed its typological kinship with pre-Civil War houses, such as the early Ashbel Smith house in rural Harris County and the later Ruppersburg house (San Felipe Cottage, Sam Houston Park) in Houston, and it bespeaks the architectural conservatism of the countryside.

The B. C. Simpson house was typical of small, nineteenth-century houses, using brackets and spindle posts to support its front porch[153] (fig. 35). But the Simpson house also represented an important planning innovation in smaller, post-Civil War houses. Its T-shaped plan was popular for several reasons. Following widely published plans, such houses were easy to construct; mass-production of building materials made these small, wooden houses inexpensive; and the arrangement of rooms with multiple exposures and one or more porches was especially suitable in hot climates. Architectural historian Paula Johnson explained that, in its simplest form, the T house is a three-room, one-story dwelling with a front porch. The T configuration was formed by a projecting wing, usually two rooms deep, and a side wing, never more than one room deep. This type of house was oriented so that the gable end of the projecting wing and length of the side wing faced the street.[154]

A modification of the T-shaped plan was an L configuration in which the side wing became the main block of the house. L-shaped houses often had a center hall with one front room projecting beyond the entrance. This arrangement allowed for a more private front porch and more rooms inside. The I. C. Lord house was L-shaped, as is evident from its high, unifying, pyramidal roof.[155] In addition to decorative porch ornament, the Lord house had fishscale shingles in the gable end of the projecting wing, another favorite decorative device used during the Victorian era on both large and small houses.

These types of plans were used repeatedly in Houston, and examples can be seen today in several older neighborhoods, particularly in the Sixth Ward (now the Sabine Historic District), just northwest of downtown Houston, where working families lived in small, sparingly decorated Victorian cottages.[156] Such cottages were built by the hundreds and far outnumbered large, two-story Victorian houses. Spindle posts and brackets appeared even on tiny front porches of two- or three-room houses (fig. 71). Because they could not afford to buy the elaborate, ready-cut millwork used on larger houses, builders of small cottages in working-class neighborhoods often made their own from patterns. One of the most unusual types of brackets, seen in the Sixth Ward, was a bird pattern, believed to be German in origin and developed from a Germanic folk symbol[157] (fig. 70).

Even neighborhood stores, which often conformed to domestic building types, had Victorian ornament. The Nick D'Amico Grocery, located on Hamilton Street and Polk Avenue, was constructed to house not only the store but a large Italian American family (fig. 232). This kind of living-working arrangement was typical for many store owners. The grocery store was on the first floor, as was a small apartment for the owners, which had two bedrooms, a kitchen, and a dining room. Upstairs the porch extended around three sides of the house, with three doors coming off of the east side (back). Four large bedrooms, two smaller ones, and a kitchen-dining room housed seven boys and their sister, along with her husband and two children. There was one bathroom on each floor that was accessible only from the outside porch. The absence of any "living room" is interesting. The large kitchens and dining rooms were the living spaces for this family, almost all of whom worked in the store.[158] Built in 1904, the building was stylistically behind the times, with Victorian brackets and spindle posts that were not frequently used in Houston after the turn of the century.

In the last decade of the nineteenth century houses built by African American professionals and businessmen and women, like those of new immigrant groups such as Italians, were generally analogous to those of the white working and middle classes. There were, of course, exceptions. Shotgun houses were identified with nineteenth-century black neighborhoods even though whites occupied them, too. They were one room wide, one story tall, and several rooms deep, lined up in such a way that a shotgun could be fired straight through from the front to the back—hence the name (fig. 71). The entrance was in the gable end, with a perpendicular alignment of rooms that was a departure from Euro-American patterns seen in other small house types. This form was brought to New Orleans in the early nineteenth century via Haiti by slaves and is thought to represent a combination of native African architecture, indigenous Haitian forms, and European framing techniques.[159] Shotgun houses did not appear in Houston until the late 1880s or early 1890s, when scores of African American families migrated to the city to find work in new industries. White landlords built them by the hundreds because they were the cheapest and most land-efficient structures that could be thrown up to house their workers. Although rows of shotgun houses were built in Houston near railroad yards and factories in the Fifth, Sixth, and Third wards and in the Fourth Ward Freedmen's Town, relatively few remain today.

Before the Civil War most black men, both slave and free, were agricultural workers. The only trades in which they had a chance to become proficient were those of carpenters, masons, and blacksmiths. This influenced their ability after the war not only to build their own houses with some expertise but also to establish contracting businesses. One such enterprising man was Richard Allen, who had been born a slave in Virginia in 1846. During his tenure as a slave of J. J. Cain in Harris County, he acquired carpentry skills, which he used after the war. In 1870 the *Houston Union* reported that the "finest and most elegant mansion that once graced our city—[that of] Mayor J. R. Morris—was the handiwork of Honorable Richard Allen while he was a slave; not the mere mechanics only, but the design, the draft and all."[160] Between 1875 and 1879 Allen designed and built Antioch Missionary Baptist Church, which stands today at Robin Street and Clay Avenue as it was remodeled in 1895 by another black architect, Robert Jones.[161] It was not until 1910 that an African American was listed as a professional architect in the *Houston City Directory*. John T. Meredith, an architect and engineer, advertised that he could provide plans and specifications on short notice.[162] The first black member of the Texas State Association of Architects was Booker T. Washington's son-in-law, W. Sidney Pittman. Pittman lived in Dallas but designed several Houston buildings, including the Colored Carnegie Library in 1913.[163] However, no local houses have been attributed to him. The *Red Book of Houston*, published around 1915, listed six prominent contractors and pictured several houses occupied by African American families at that time.[164] One purpose of this social directory was to emphasize that some black

Houstonians had risen from the status of freed slaves, who lived in rent houses owned by absentee white landlords, to successful landowners, who built and occupied their own houses.

African American women had been relegated to domestic and agricultural work. After the Civil War some enterprising women became real estate investors and landladies; they did not have the option of entering the building trades like many of their male counterparts did. One house published in the *Red Book,* built about 1908 at 611 Hobson, was the home of Annie L. Hagen, a trained nurse and well-known midwife.[165] The Hagen house, raised on brick piers with lattice foundation skirts between the piers, had a front-facing chamfered bay to one side of its entrance (fig. 72). In plan this house was similar to the L-shaped B. C. Simpson house. Its elevation was like many raised cottages built in both black and white neighborhoods. Raised cottages were never as numerous in Houston as they were in Galveston, where flooding was a problem and where breezes blew more predictably. The H. M. Curtin house (fig. 73), built on Fannin Street about 1880, was a larger version of the L-shaped house.[166] Instead of a chamfered bay on the projecting wing, the Curtin house had a bay window, but both of these arrangements achieved the same effect on the interior.

Another variation of this architectural theme was the graceful James Lanier Britton house at 1010 Rosalie Avenue, built in 1903.[167] Its L-shaped porch was supported by bracketed spindle posts and arches enclosing delicate beadwork. Fishscale shingles were used to vary the texture in the gable ends that appeared on the front and side of the house. A wide, centered dormer and bracketed pediment marking the entrance were other devices used to vary the roofline. Leaded-glass, double front doors under a similar deep overlight, like those of the Britton house, were also popular in Victorian houses. The William A. Smith house, built at 3614 Travis Street, was a more complex raised house with side rooms added to the conventional L-shaped plan.[168] The Smith house, like the Britton house, had a wide, centered dormer at the front, but it also had a rounded turret over a curved porch, which extended into a screened section at the side. Screens, used in Houston since the 1890s, were at first confined to doors and windows, but by the turn of the century larger houses began to include screened porches that provided, on the first floor, outdoor living spaces without flies and mosquitos, and, on the second floor, equally more comfortable sleeping porches.

The Queen Anne style lent itself to wide interpretation, as can be seen in a series of wood houses overlaid with decorative framing members intended to imitate structural half-timbering of English Tudor houses and Swiss chalets. Wall surfaces were the main field of design on which boards were applied in horizontal, vertical, and diagonal patterns, and paint was used in contrasting colors. George Dickey designed such houses for James Cotton at 1018 Travis Street in 1882 and J. C. Hutcheson in 1887 at 1417 McKinney[169] (figs. 50, 169–74). The Cesar Lombardi house, which was built around 1890 at the corner of Austin Street and Rusk Avenue, combined fanciful porches with a profusion of decorative woodwork in the gable ends, between the first and second stories, and at the corners[170] (fig. 80). In the Charles Dillingham house wood-framed panels of narrow clapboard were combined with horizontal bands of shingles [171] (fig. 81). The heavier, more compact form of the Dillingham house indicated Dickey's architectural evolution toward a more orderly rendition of the picturesque. Another house that used contrasting clapboards and framing strips in its entrance gable was the W.H. Palmer house at 1116 Travis Street, built about 1884 [172] (figs. 82, 256). This house had a flatter facade than the most fanciful Queen Anne structures, and its large circular bay, which did not extend into a tower, was like one that Dickey designed for the Alexander P. Root house of 1894 [173] (fig. 49). The Root house provides another illustration of the evolution of Dickey's residential architecture. Although it had a vertical emphasis, its disciplined massing, low rounded columns, use of shingles, and wide, arched entrance were elements of the Shingle style.

The Shingle style was a combination of several architectural conventions: Queen Anne free-flowing plans and wide porches; Colonial Revival classical columns; Palladian windows; Dutch gambrel roofs; Richardsonian Romanesque arches; and stone or masonry substructures. Although H. H. Richardson became famous for his use of the arch, Vincent Scully emphasized Richardson's ability to express an asymmetrical freedom while retaining a unifying order in his domestic architecture.[174] This "unifying order" was created by lowered, expansive roofs that gave the archetypal Shingle-style New England country houses their exaggerated horizontality. In Houston, images of only two houses that could be loosely categorized as Shingle style are known. The Levi Kaiser house, built in 1902 at 1404 Rusk Avenue (fig. 83), and the similar Charles L. Desel house, built two years later at Main Street and Berry Avenue, displayed not only a more horizontal feeling but also monochromatic shingle cladding, Richardsonian arches, paired or tripled windows, Colonial-type columns, and masonry bases.[175]

George Dickey's first use of shingles and the gaping arch was in 1892, two years before the Root house was designed, for an extensive remodeling of the Thomas W. House, Jr., residence [176] (figs. 65, 66). By 1892 the residence that House built in 1872 (fig. 41) was clearly out of style. Increasing success in business and banking allowed House to do what his two brothers had done—build a larger, more up-to-date residence. But instead he chose to modernize his old house and hired George Dickey to design additions and a new façade. The remodeled version of the T. W. House, Jr., house, like the Waldo house, was a remarkable transformation. Clad with shingles and weatherboard, the graceful rounded forms of the turret, wrapped porch, and arches were echoed in a circular front drive. The projecting wing, porches, and new roofline were all part of Dickey's scheme, which enlarged the house by two rooms and a bath upstairs.

Another shingle-clad house was designed by architect J. Arthur Tempest, who was briefly in partnership with George Dickey. Tempest moved to Houston in 1891 from Toronto, where he previously may have known of Dickey's work.[177] The W. B. Chew house at 1206 Fannin Street, designed by Tempest in 1893, had some features that were analogous to New England Shingle-style houses [178] (fig. 84). In addition to the use of shingles, the brick first floor above a high cast-stone base is like the masonry or stone bases used in the Northeast, where such materials were readily available. The tower and columns of the Chew house showed movement away from Victorian spindles and high, pointed towers. An octagonal bay was kept below the high-pitched roof and topped with a helmet rather than a churchlike spire. Although the Chew house can be tentatively compared to Shingle-style houses of the Northeast for its tower bay, wide round arches, and tight massing, its overlaid stickwork, varied shingle shapes, and asymmetrical form with jutting gables, porches, and bays are elements of an earlier, more frenetic architecture.

As the nineteenth century waned, the most obvious changes in domestic architecture were tighter massing and the disappearance of towers, spindles, and brackets. The J. W. Jones house of 1893 at 1117 Main Street, like the Chew house, combined some elements of the Shingle style.[179] However, the tower was pulled in to become a round-roof pavillion centered on the entrance porch, and projecting bays were not evident, indicating that the rooms inside were mostly rectangular. The Lee B. Menefee house, located at 2106 Crawford Street and built in 1900, was a particularly unusual expression of some of these same elements: shingles, a short turret-type porch roof, and a masonry base[180] (fig. 85). Its upturned roof corners, wide eaves, and bulbous column porch supports with diminutive Ionic capitals stand out as adventuresome elements forecasting the bungalow forms from California that began to emerge in Houston after the turn of the century.

The final evolution from the Victorian era to the Colonial Revival period can be seen in a number of houses built in the 1890s and the first few years of the twentieth century, including the Frank Andrews, Howard Smith, J. H. Kirby, and Hugh Waddell houses. All four combined classical motifs with Queen Anne elements. The Waddell house, built in 1901 at 2404 Caroline Street, had a smaller gambrel gable with a round-arched window in its third story, but its tall round tower and wider eaves were more in keeping with earlier forms[181] (fig. 87). Likewise, the Smith house of 1893, located at 2204 Main Street, combined new and old with a pulled-in corner tower bay, classical columns, and wide arches set in a decorated asymmetric form[182] (fig. 46). The Kirby house, built by J. S. Price in 1893–94 at 2006 Smith and sold to Kirby in 1896, looks as if it had been designed by Dickey (fig. 118). It is interesting to compare this house with the remodeling, a year earlier, of the T. W. House, Jr., house (fig. 65). Similar materials and motifs were used, but the Kirby house was more "advanced." The Frank Andrews house, built in 1901 at 1508 Main Street, with even tighter massing, was the most successful of these transitional houses in presenting a cohesive façade.[183]

Another young architect, Olle J. Lorehn, arrived in Houston in the 1890s. He designed a house in 1903 for Jemison E. Lester at 3112 Main Street that was similar in scale and design to its contemporaries[184] (fig. 88). Its use of cast-stone blocks and quoins, in combination with narrow wood siding at the third level, as well as unconventional window configurations, resulted in a heavy, somewhat incongruous appearance. The Swedish-born Lorehn was educated at the University of Linkoping, Sweden, where he graduated as an architect and engineer in 1886. He came to the United States shortly after his graduation, and, after a year in a Swedish colony in Kansas, he went to work for the Anheuser-Busch Brewing Company in St. Louis. Lorehn came to Houston in 1891 to supervise construction of the American Brewery. He settled permanently there and established a successful architectural practice engaging in the design of commercial buildings as well as houses.[185]

Between 1899 and 1906 several Houston families built rather grand houses that were a departure from the Queen Anne and Shingle styles, but might still be considered Victorian. The Samuel Fain Carter house of 1899 at 1804 Crawford Street was designed by Dickey with more restrained Italianate features[186] (fig. 89). A second-floor loggia consisting of a series of arches linked two dissimilar towers, the tallest of which was square and topped with another open loggia on the third floor. The broad proportions of the lower round tower allowed the use of wide, curved single-pane windows. This stylish house also had wider bracketed eaves reminiscent of Italian villas.

Dickey designed another house in the same year for James I. Campbell at 2908 Main Street that was quite similar in organization to the Carter house but was detailed with a decidedly French accent[187] (figs. 90, 178–79). The tall stepped gable centered between two towers was a mark of the châteaus of the Loire Valley that had been a model for the extravagant and influential houses designed by New York architect Richard Morris Hunt in New York, Newport, and elsewhere for the Vanderbilts and other clients in the 1880s and 1890s. Almost symmetrical, the Carter and Campbell houses were a definite departure from the early, more fragile, and rambling Victorian structures.

Dickey was not the only Houston architect who was aware of the widely published Hunt designs. J. Arthur Tempest built his finest house for Henry S. Fox in 1893, next door to the Van Alstyne house on a prominent Main Street site[188] (fig. 91). The Fox house was symmetrical, with a centered third-story French gable. The grandest, and last, of the Houston châteaus was designed by Olle Lorehn for Abraham M. Levy in 1906 at 2016 Main Street[189] (figs. 92, 180–81). This symmetrical structure was built at a time when larger houses were beginning to be designed in the Colonial Revival style. The Levy house presented an imposing street front, with large corner towers and twin French-gabled dormers in between. It reportedly cost the huge sum of $150,000 and had twenty rooms, which were kept in order by as many as ten servants.

The only known Victorian residence built in Houston to exhibit Gothic detail was the second Christ Church rectory, designed by George Dickey[190] (fig. 270). Built on Texas Avenue in 1902 to fit with the Victorian Gothic church next door, the rectory was a massive brown brick building related to Houston interpretations of the French châteaus in its massing and symmetry. Tall pointed dormers and gables emphasized the verticality of the house. Round segmental and ogee-pointed arches were combined to produce a well-defined and imposing urban house. The rectory was one of the earliest brick veneer houses built locally. Its wood frame construction with brick facing gave the solid appearance of a brick building, but was far less costly. Alice Gray Sears, who grew up in this fifteen-room house, where her family lived from 1905 to 1926, described its interior: "There was a tremendous stove at the back of the house in the big center hall. The parlor was on the left of the hall with Papa's study behind it, and his study opened into a yard which led to the cloister and parish house." The living room–library was on the right with the dining room behind it. In back of that were the butler's pantry and kitchen, which opened onto a back porch that in turn led to the back yard, where a cistern and quarters for the rectory maid were located. Five bedrooms and two baths were upstairs. Sears also recalled that a lamplighter came every evening to light the gas lamps on the street corners.[191]

The World's Columbian Exposition of 1893 in Chicago was an architectural benchmark for the United States. This fair was laid out as a great "White City" where elaborately columned façades of white plaster were reflected in Frederick Law Olmsted's formal lagoons. Americans wondered at and fell in love with the grand scale and the columns. Henry-Russell Hitchcock believed that inspiration for this new American architecture was more academic than specifically Italianate. This he attributed to the influence of New York architects McKim, Mead and White, acknowledged leaders of the newly acquired American infatuation with the classical traditions of the École des Beaux-Arts in Paris, the premier architecture school of the western world.[192] Hitchcock noted the architectural paradox of the 1890s, when the academic triumph of the fair occurred at the same moment in history as the culmination of nineteenth-century high Victorian styles.[193] As has been demonstrated, some Houston houses tried to combine elements of both. These amalgamations were typical of transitional periods, when architects and their clients were reluctant to give up all vestiges of the old styles while trying at the same time to be current.

Classical forms filtered from Chicago, New York, and other American style centers had by 1900 produced major architectural changes across the country in both domestic and commercial buildings. Another important influence was the rise of the Progressive era. Reform in the political arena produced a new emphasis on rationalism and centralized control in government that allowed for planned urban development. These collateral developments, architectural and political, altered the look of American cities, including Houston. The houses that resulted were distantly related to antebellum Greek Revival houses, but they clearly adhered to a different set of architectural conventions. More complex architectural detail on both interiors and exteriors complemented the more elaborate orders. Rounded, sometimes fluted, and often paired columns with florid Ionic and Corinthian capitals looked quite different from the restrained square Doric columns of the Greek Revival period. Likewise, the floor plans of these neoclassical twentieth-century houses were more complicated than the center- and side-hall plans of Greek Revival houses.

Architects of the time described these new houses as Colonial Revival. Certainly classical features had been employed during the Colonial period in America, but never with such gusto and pretention as Colonial Revival houses exhibited. Ironically, the model for the new Colonial Revival craze was not a southern product but the Connecticut State Building designed for the Chicago fair in 1893.[194] Painted yellow with white trim and green shutters, the Connecticut house was accurately described by one contemporary commentator as "such a mansion as anyone could wish his grandfather had lived in before the Revolution, and could be certain that he did not."[195]

The term "Colonial Revival" is indeed a misnomer, and it appropriately describes the more modest shingle and clapboard houses with pedimented doorways and windows that became popular after World War I. However, because of its wide usage throughout this century, the label, like the term "Victorian," has come to represent a particular form in the minds of most architectural historians.

The first Colonial Revival house in Houston was built in 1902 for Jonas Shearn Rice at 2304 Crawford Street (fig. 107). The house was designed by S. A. Oliver and Company, who took over Eugene T. Heiner's practice after his death in 1901. Although the Rice house was well designed, Oliver received no important commissions after it; he apparently left Houston in 1913.[196] Detailed documents concerning the construction of the Rice house survive, including the building contract with D. A. Crawford for over $23,000, which did not include plumbing, heating, and site improvements.[197] Although the Rice house lacked a pedimented entrance—it was topped instead with a rather Baroque gabled dormer—its colossal Corinthian columns and its resolute symmetry gave it a markedly different appearance from the picturesque Victorian houses constructed before it.

For a decade following construction of the Rice house most of the large residences constructed in and around Houston were of monumental proportions with classical features described as Colonial Revival. The Edward R. Richardson house, built in 1903 in one of the new South End subdivisions represented an unusual attempt to be authentically "Colonial"[198] (fig. 108). Another noteworthy Colonial Revival house built during the first decade of the twentieth century closely resembled the Connecticut State Building prototype, with a combination of porches supported by both large and small columns—the William R. Nash house. Designed by H. C. Cooke and Company in 1905 at 217 Westmoreland Avenue, it is still standing[199] (fig. 109). Henry C. Cooke (1852–1920) received his architectural training in his native England and traveled in Italy. He came to the United States in 1885, established an architectural practice in Galveston in 1890, and moved to Houston in 1900. From 1905, the year the Nash house was built, Cooke's son, W. A. Cooke, managed the firm.

In 1903 Olle Lorehn was the architect for the Thomas L. Hackney house at 2210 Main Street, another of the earliest Colonial Revival houses in Houston[200] (fig. 110). The Hackney house had some decorative features that resembled those of the J. S. Rice house, notably the scrolled gable dormer, modillion brackets under the eaves, and railed porches. But it was far more ornate and included neo-Adamesque swags, extensive denticulation, urn finials on the second-floor balcony posts, decorative window moldings, and well-detailed Ionic capitals on both large and small columns. Curiously, the Hackney house closely approximates a design published by George F. Barber in 1898.[201] Barber's floor plans show what the interior arrangement of the Hackney house might have been (fig. 111). Whereas Victorian plans had large stair halls just inside the front door, often containing a fireplace, the Barber plan shows a more typical arrangement for Colonial Revival houses. A small vestibule led to a reception hall between the sitting room and the parlor, with a stair hall behind that was oriented not to the front door but to a side entrance that led from a porte cochere, or family entrance. Corner fireplaces, nooks, bay windows, and strange room configurations of Victorian houses had all but disappeared in the more symmetrical Colonial Revival plans.

Houston had dozens of these large Colonial Revival houses by 1915, including the Robert C. Duff house at McGowan and Milam streets (figs. 125–27, 199, 201) and the J. P. Carter house, 2602 Main Street (figs. 196–97). Given the symmetrical forms and formularized classicism of these Colonial Revival houses, less variety was to be expected than was found in Victorian houses, particularly those in the Queen Anne style. Therefore, many of Houston's Colonial Revival examples began to look alike. Two that were almost identical were built for Judge Sam Streetman at 2616 Louisiana Street in 1908 and for J. C. Bering on Holman Avenue the following year.[202] With only minor modifications of the side porches and dormers, the Bering house was a duplicate of the Streetman house.

All of these, like most of Houston's Colonial Revival houses, were wood. Brick was readily available and was often used on such houses in other parts of the country. A noteworthy exception in Houston was the Harris Masterson house in Westmoreland (figs. 128–29). The primacy of the lumber industry in Harris County might account for the popularity of wood there. The Sanborn fire insurance maps of 1907 show that remarkably few brick houses were standing in Houston at that time.[203] Only a small fraction of the housing stock in Houston was of brick construction, and probably not more than 5 percent of the large, expensive houses were brick.

By this time residential development in Houston had moved away from immediate proximity to the downtown area. No residences, according to the Sanborn maps, remained on Main Street below Rusk. But south of Texas Avenue a residential atmosphere prevailed, and new construction continued until the late 1910s. More densely populated neighborhoods, with as many as ten small houses facing the street on one block, existed on the north side of Buffalo Bayou, in the Freedmen's Town area of Fourth Ward, and to the extreme east, including residential areas around new industrial developments along Buffalo Bayou. The maps do not in many cases show property lines on these blocks, indicating that entire blocks were owned by one landlord who rented the shotgun houses to workers. The relative size of the small rent houses is dramatic when their sites, often twenty per block, are compared with even larger blocks on which only two to four large houses were built (figs. 112–13).

Sanborn maps and Houston city directories after 1908 also show that the west sides of the north-south streets were preferred for building sites. These lots were developed first, and the most expensive houses tended to be built on the northwest corners of intersections (southeast corner of the block). This allowed front rooms to face east, toward the morning sun rather than the hot afternoon sun, and toward the prevailing southeast wind. Photographs consistently show upstairs porches, including sleeping porches that became popular on large houses around the turn of the century, on the south sides of houses, whether they faced east or west. These porches were usually attached to master bedrooms that, therefore, also would have been placed on the south side of the house, where cooler breezes blew at night. On the streets that ran east-west, preferable lots were on the north side of the street facing south. Considerations of climate continued to exert influence on both the site of a house and the arrangement of rooms within.

By 1907 outbuildings had changed. Sanborn maps show many small houses still had one tiny outbuilding in back, which indicates that outhouses were in use even though indoor plumbing was by then widely available. Although some yards still had hen houses and barns, the largest newer houses generally had only one two-story outbuilding. This structure incorporated sleeping quarters for servants above a carriage house or automobile garage, wash house, coal bins, and storage rooms. Several of these properties show a "summer house," which was an open gazebo placed in the garden. At least five "greenhouses" were placed in backyard corners. One notation, on the Capt. James A. Baker property at 1416 Main Street (S.K. Dick house), read: "greenhouse with glass roof that slides." [204]

After 1905 several new materials and services began to be advertised. With the exception of new window types, most innovations for the house changed the interiors and made living arrangements within the houses more comfortable and efficient. F. B. Walcot was a manufacturer's agent for "prismatic glass, terra cotta face brick, roof tile, slate and granite roofing, interlocking rubber tile, ceramic tile and Venetian blinds."[205] The Texas Art Glass Company manufactured "art stained glass" locally.[206] These types of windows, which were used on both large and moderately sized houses, consisted of "prismatic glass," or beveled cut panes, and stained glass, or "art glass," that was popular for dining rooms, stair halls, and landings. Large plate-glass windows with both straight and curved panes were used as early as 1899 (figs. 89, 90). The most popular new window sash consisted of lozenge- and diamond-shaped panes set in a wood frame, which was also used from the 1890s (fig. 72).

Small window panes were also configured in orthogonal patterns like the entrance and parlor windows of the Benjamin J. Covington house at 2219 Dowling Street[207] (fig. 105). Built around 1908 with two colossal Corinthian columns set before a double porch, the Covington house was a simplified Colonial Revival house. Dr. Covington was one of the leaders of Houston's African American community and built one of the largest, most stylish houses in his Third Ward neighborhood.

The B. C. Simpson, Jr., house, built in 1908 at 3804 Fannin Street, can be compared with the Covington house.[208] However, the two colossal columns of the Simpson house were square without classically derived capitals and were set in front of an off-center entrance in an even more simplified example of the Colonial Revival. The A. Thomas Lucas house, built in 1905 at 2017 Milam, was another of the two-columned Colonial Revival houses[209] (fig. 114). But the Lucas house was clad in cast stone because the owner produced it at his brick and cement works. This house was not symmetrical and had a rounded porch and corner bay, producing an effect that was more Victorian than classical.

Cast stone was popular in Houston and was most often used for foundations and fence posts. The 1903 Louis C. Luckel house at 3016 Main had massive cast-stone piers in front of a squarish clapboard house[210] (fig. 115). The long, extruded porch gave the Luckel house a definite horizontal aspect. This house illustrates the fact that the Colonial Revival style was not only simplified but also susceptible to transformation into something less conventional and less historically dependent.

One of the most unusual houses to display an abstract classical derivation was built in 1911 by John Wiley Link, developer of the Montrose Addition[211] (figs. 100, 242). This large but tightly organized structure is faced with yellow vitrilized brick, limestone, and a variety of colored tile and glazed terra cotta decoration, which combine when sunlit to produce a sparkling effect. The colossal limestone-clad piers (as opposed to traditional columns) are topped with decorative pendants rather than capitals, and the deep cornices above the second floor have multiple bands consisting of herringbone brickwork, dentils, terra cotta cartouches, stone panels, barrel tiles, and several more rows of stepped-out brickwork. Behind the terraces the Link house rises to a third story with additional but different banding under the tiled roof.

Link built this showcase house on Montrose Boulevard as much to advertise his real estate development as to provide a home for his family. It was designed by Sanguinet and Staats and Alfred E. Barnes, a Fort Worth architectural firm established in 1902 that became well known throughout Texas. Their Houston office, opened in 1903 when they were commissioned to design the First National Bank Building, was managed by Barnes from 1903 to 1905 and again from 1907 to 1913.[212] Architectural historian Stephen Fox wrote that the flamboyant Link house belonged to a genre of Texas millionaires' establishments that were constructed in several Texas cities before World War I. "These were massively scaled showplaces meant to advertise their owners' worth and standing while also serving as family residences. This mixture of domesticity and public grandeur imparted a measure of architectural improbability to most of these houses, as though the owners' desire for opulent display had exceeded their architects' abilities."[213]

In contrast to the Link house, Houston in the same decade saw a decidedly unpretentious type also abstracted from the classicism of the Colonial Revival. The American foursquare, as it has become known, was a simple, unadorned, two-story, box-shaped structure with a low-pitched hipped roof. Front porches on the foursquare were usually one story high, supported by simple rounded columns or tapered piers. A good example of this ubiquitous architectural type was the J. F. Usner house located at 1415 Wichita Avenue in the Southmore Addition.[214] An early photograph of this house shows a detached garage next to the house at the front of the site, forecasting what was to become an integral part of the suburban landscape after 1920. Both foursquares and bungalows populated many of the new middle-class neighborhoods, like Montrose, that were being developed along streetcar lines around Houston's nineteenth-century core.

The name "bungalow" was derived from *bangala,* a Bengali word for a one-story, rural house with wide verandas adapted by British colonists living in India. From colonial India this house type spread to Europe and, around 1890, to the United States. It took hold most forcefully and gained its typological form in Pasadena, California.[215] The bungalow was characterized by broad, sloping rooflines, wide eaves overhanging generous porches, and expressed structure, such as projecting rafters. In plan these efficient, one-story houses were built around a large living room, which served as the center of the house. Halls were deleted in the interest of compactness; the dining room and kitchen were set, one behind the other, on one side with bedrooms, usually two and a bath in between, on the other.

The bungalow was the popular architectural expression of America's Craftsman Movement. Gustav Stickley's magazine, *The Craftsman,* from which this movement took its name, was widely circulated throughout the United States. Like Andrew Jackson Downing had done before him, Stickley based his architectural preferences on an ideology. He felt that the low, broad proportions of the bungalow fit more appropriately within the landscape, and its simple, straightforward rendering of structure, without decorative overlays, was morally superior to fanciful and false "Victorian" ornaments. The Arts and Crafts Movement in England had, through such designers as William Morris, advocated a return to medievalism and hand-crafted decorative arts. In the United States, Stickley led the movement as it developed beyond furniture and fixtures to architecture. Pasadena architects Henry and Charles Greene refined and elaborated the bungalow, bringing to this form their appreciation of Japanese and Swiss wooden architecture. Houses designed in Pasadena by the Greenes from 1893 to 1914 developed from simple one-story bungalows to large and elaborate two-story houses. The popularity of the bungalow spread rapidly from California eastward for several reasons. Ease of construction coupled with readily available plans from widely circulated patternbooks and magazines, low-cost, efficient use of space, and adaptability to a more casual way of life made bungalows universally attractive to Americans who could not afford large, architect-designed houses.

George F. Barber, who began his mail-order architectural practice with Queen Anne style houses in the 1890s, was producing not only Colonial Revival plans but also bungalows by the turn of the century. The George Westfall house, still standing at 303 Hawthorne Avenue in Westmoreland, was published in Barber's *Art in Architecture* in 1902.[216] The enclosed dormer in the original Barber design was changed to an open balcony more appropriate to the Houston climate; otherwise the unusual Westfall house was built exactly according to Barber's published plan. Barber would make such changes for an additional fee, but they were often made by the builder during construction.

Not only were hundreds of published plans available, but catalog houses could be bought complete with all necessary construction materials and instructions for assembly. In 1908, Sears, Roebuck and Company began to manufacture and advertise not only bungalows but other types of houses as well that could be ordered by mail. By 1925 thirty thousand houses had been sent from Sears by rail all over the country.[217] In Houston, E.L. Crain produced similar catalogs for his ready-to-assemble bungalows that were manufactured locally. Crain Ready-Cut houses were erected throughout Houston from the 1920s to the 1940s.[218]

A new breed of speculative builder latched onto the innovative bungalow form, which remained in vogue for small- and medium-sized residences through the 1930s. In Houston such new subdivisions as Westmoreland (1902), Woodland Heights (1907), and Montrose (1911), as well as the older Houston Heights (1892), generally had large houses on the boulevards. But lots along parallel and cross streets were smaller, intended for more modest houses, and hundreds of these sites were populated with bungalows. In his essay on Houston bungalows, William F. Stern said:

"Link never intended Montrose to develop as a garden suburb for the rich alone. The majority of his property was laid out in blocks of tree-lined streets between the boulevards. . . . And it was along these streets that the bungalow appeared, a new, modern house type within the economic reach of Houston's working and middle-class populations."[219]

Developer William A. Wilson built dozens of bungalows in Houston Heights, Woodland Heights, and Eastwood. Wilson published a local version of *The Craftsman* called *Homes,* in which he featured both his own company's speculatively built houses and others that were constructed in his developments.[220] The George W. Roff house at 3305 Morrison (ca. 1911) in Woodland Heights was typical (figs. 210–11). The clapboard siding of the low apron, which disguised the foundations, was painted brown, the main block was cream-colored, and shingles covering the wide gable ends were moss green. Wood trim under the wide eaves, projecting rafters, deep barge boards, and stickwork over the entrance were painted white.[221] Muted paint colors were the same as those advocated for early Victorian houses; rafters and brackets had a Japanese derivation; diamond-paned windows evoked an English medieval feeling; and dormers, roof shape, and gable stickwork were Swiss in origin. The interiors of this bungalow and others like it contained heavy, dark-stained false beams that matched the rest of the interior woodwork, as well as built-in furniture.

Houston bungalows were not limited to English-Swiss-Japanese conventions. In 1912 architect William A. Cooke built a California mission-type bungalow at 1724 Alta Vista in the Forest Hill Addition[222] (fig. 116). This house can be characterized as a bungalow because it conforms to the main precepts: low-pitched roof and dormers, exposed rafters, and compact plan. But its importance goes beyond its unusual stylistic features; it was one of the early indications that a new academic eclecticism was beginning to take hold in Houston.

Most prominently illustrating this eclecticism were the domestic buildings that Sanguinet and Staats produced in Houston between 1909 and 1913. They were based on a variety of historically derived ornament, but as Stephen Fox has pointed out, "these historical references were grafted consistently onto broadly proportioned, firmly planted, symmetrically massed houses, usually capped by hipped roofs with deeply projecting eaves."[223] In the same year that the Link house was built, 1911, Sanguinet and Staats designed a Mission-style house for William S. Wall at 3717 Main Street, which conformed to this basic formula[224] (fig. 117). The identifying parapets of the Cooke house, although much smaller, were quite similar to those of the Wall house. Although other examples of stuccoed, Mission-style houses were built in Houston, this Spanish-derived interpretation was never particularly popular there.

The Cottage, designed for Edwin B. Parker by Sanguinet and Staats as a temporary residence while his "big house" was under construction, was a large bungalow with the Progressive features described by Fox.[225] Built in 1909 and still standing at 2204 Baldwin Street, The Cottage has a tiled, hipped roof with wide, low dormers, and stucco walls framed by decorative timberwork above a high brick foundation, which is banded by continuous stone coping in the manner of Frank Lloyd Wright.

The Oaks, as Parker's large house was called, was completed in 1910 and has incorrectly been attributed to Frank Lloyd Wright[226] (figs. 139–141). When construction of The Oaks was announced, the architectural design was attributed to Sanguinet and Staats, but the announcement also said that "the style of architecture will be the plainest imaginable, of the Frank Lloyd Wright type, absolutely plain lines governing everything."[227] The Oaks was one of a very few houses constructed in Houston that might be considered an example of Wright's Prairie School. Stephen Fox observed that "the horizontal articulation achieved with the unbroken eaves line; the terrace coping stone; continuous molded bands at the sill levels of the first and second floor openings; the treatment of the porch supports as solid piers terminating in small, molded caps; and the dense files of vertical glazing bars in casement windows enclosing various porches" were Wrightian features.[228] However, Fox also pointed out that the interior was decidedly unlike those of Wright, and the exterior did not project into the landscape the way Wright's Prairie houses did. A low, horizontal form was an essential feature of the Prairie School houses designed to fit in with the midwestern prairie landscape.

Wrightian forms did not catch on in Houston during the 1910s, nor did the related Progressive forms with strict frontality, dominant front verandas, and absence of historical detail. Most new houses in Houston were classical or bungalow types. However, a showcase for new architectural ideas that would predominate between the wars also developed during this decade. Courtlandt Place(1906) was an elite enclave subdivision based on St. Louis's Private Places[229] (fig. 99). Between 1910 and 1914 nine large houses were constructed there for several of Houston's wealthiest families. The term "creative eclecticism" has been used to describe these types of houses, which combined historical elements with Progressive tendencies and contemporary typologies.[230] Renewed interest in scholarship, propriety, and correctness prompted architects to look more carefully to historic authenticity than they had done during the Victorian era.

Sanguinet and Staats with A. E. Barnes designed five houses in Courtlandt Place with decidedly different stylistic motifs. The Sterling Myer house (4 Courtlandt Place) was Jacobean; the James L. Autry house (5 Courtlandt Place) was grandiosely classical; the C. L. Neuhaus house (6 Courtlandt Place) had a Colonial New England aspect; the J. M. Dorrance house (9 Courtlandt Place) was Italianate; and the A. S. Cleveland house (8 Courtlandt Place) was more abstract, with both Colonial and Italian attributes.[231] This display foretold the wide variety of eclectic styles that would characterize Houston's domestic architecture after World War I. However, both large and small houses built after the war were more asymmetrical and picturesque in their front elevations than these prewar models, all of which had a distinct frontal symmetry despite their varying stylistic modes. This "cyclical oscillation between the picturesque and formal principles of design," as it has been so aptly described,[232] has occurred in Houston since the Civil War about every twenty years, or every other generation.

Although Harris County had come a long way in its first ninety years, it was not until after World War I that Houston began to emerge as a presence in the mainstream of American architecture. In terms of domestic architecture, it is important to note that Houstonians continued to prefer local architects and designers. Although some commercial and institutional buildings were designed by nationally known architects, these architects were not commissioned to build houses in Houston until T. J. Donoghue asked the New York firm of Warren and Wetmore to design his house at 17 Courtlandt Place in 1915.[233] Two years later Hugo V. Neuhaus brought Harrie T. Lindeberg from New York to design his house in Shadyside.[234] In contrast, George Sealy had commissioned McKim, Mead and White to design his Galveston house, which was completed in 1891.[235] It should be noted that this was an exceptional circumstance that failed to start a trend even in Galveston. On the other hand, Lindeberg went on to design other houses in Houston and in 1921 sent a young associate, John F. Staub (1892–1980), to supervise them. Staub settled there and by 1924 began his own firm, which was to have a significant impact on the architecture of Houston's upper-income neighborhoods after World War I.[236]

Several other architects who influenced the look of Houston after 1920 also began their careers before 1914. Alfred C. Finn (1883–1964) was the most notable Houston architect trained in the Sanguinet and Staats office. He joined the firm in Fort Worth as a draftsman in 1904 but was sent to the Houston office in 1911. Finn resigned the following year to establish his own firm, which became identified with the many commercial projects he designed for Jesse H. Jones's interests; he also designed several notable houses in the South End after World War I.[237] William Ward Watkin (1886–1952) came to Houston in 1909 as the supervising architect of the Rice Institute for Cram, Goodhue and Ferguson of Boston. He stayed to become the first professor of architecture at Rice and designed local buildings, including houses, after the war.[238]

The other influential and talented architect whose houses also dominated the enclave neighborhoods, and River Oaks after 1920, was Birdsall Parmenas Briscoe (1876–1971). Briscoe was related to one of Houston's first builders, Maurice Birdsall, and descended from John R. Harris and Andrew Briscoe. He was born in the old Harris house in Harrisburg and grew up on the ranch of his maternal grandparents near Goliad. Educated at Texas A & M College and the University of Texas, he received his architectural training in the office of the Houston architect C. Lewis Wilson. From 1904 until 1908 Briscoe was employed by Lewis Sterling Green, a commercial architect with whom he formed a partnership in 1909. Briscoe left Green in 1912 to begin a long and productive independent practice.[239] He was especially well known for his elegant detail and assured handling of materials.

In Courtlandt Place, Briscoe succeeded Sanguinet and Staats as the favored architect. By the time he designed the E. L. Neville house at 11 Courtlandt Place in 1914, his architectural talent was evident[240] (fig. 130). Stephen Fox said: "This large, graceful house, with its terraces, loggias, and balconies, demonstrates Briscoe's adeptness at reconciling English imagery with Houston's climate."[241] Despite its sophistication, Houston architecture still had to grapple with the elements—a last continuous link with the first Anglo-American pioneers. Briscoe received national recognition when the John W. Garrow house at 19 Courtlandt Place, also designed in 1914, was published in *Architectural Record*[242] (fig. 133).

In both the Neville and Garrow houses the disappearance of the prominent front porch is one of the most striking architectural changes that had begun to occur. On the Neville house two side loggias provided greater privacy and were incorporated into the architectural theme of the house, rather than standing out as prominent porches on earlier houses had done. In the Garrow house an architecturally elaborate but restrained portico took the place of the front porch. Floor plans of these houses reveal other functional innovations. The kitchen, pantries, and back stairs were set to one side, and in the Neville house (fig. 131) the dining room was at the center of the rear, with a view of the private, south-facing back garden, which had taken the place of the old, utilitarian, service-oriented back yard. Likewise, a screened "sunroom" was set on the back below a second-floor sleeping porch. These plans show more bathrooms and closets than did earlier houses (fig. 132). But they also reveal the continued use of fireplaces in all the main rooms, which, like screened porches, did not disappear until later in the twentieth century when more efficient heating systems and air-conditioning became available.

By 1914 houses in Houston displayed a range of styles, tastes, and means comparable to those in other American cities. A family's economic status was most palpably expressed in the quality and size of a house, but large and small residences alike reflected their time. In a general sense, the development of increasingly sophisticated architectural expression in Houston depended first on steady economic growth and second on changing stylistic preferences and innovations in construction techniques and building materials. The same progress that was responsible for replacement of early log cabins in Harris County caused the disappearance of Houston's elegant nineteenth-century mansions and Victorian neighborhoods. Harris County was settled by men and women who were willing to leave familiar places behind in seach of prosperity. This lack of loyalty to place and a fascination with the new have led Houstonians to build more contemporary houses at every opportunity; and the search for prosperity has been rewarded with profits realized from escalating urban real estate values. Economic gain and a spirit of newness and promise have held a far higher place in the value system of the community than have tradition and history. Middle-class aspirations for continually better living conditions have been a dominant force, which has existed in tandem with the drive to build Houston into a modern metropolis. In demolishing so much of the historic architectural fabric of their city, Houstonians have unsentimentally sacrificed artifacts embodying the collective memory and historical continuity of both individual families and the community as a whole.

1

Cedar Timber, Sarah Deel and Robert Wilson house

Clear Lake at Middle (now Armand) Bayou

This map of the Wilson property, drawn by P. Snell ca. 1837, included a primitive drawing of the home of Sarah Deel, second wife of Robert "Honest Bob" Wilson. The house appears to have been built atop one of the many Indian shell middens constructed along the bayous in this region long before European settlement. This raised site would have provided protection from rising storm waters. The hipped roof of the house appears to have a dove cote (roost for domesticated birds) or possibly a centered chimney. The name Cedar Timber indicates that native cedar trees probably grew nearby. Honest Bob was the father of James T. D. Wilson (figs. 42, 43).

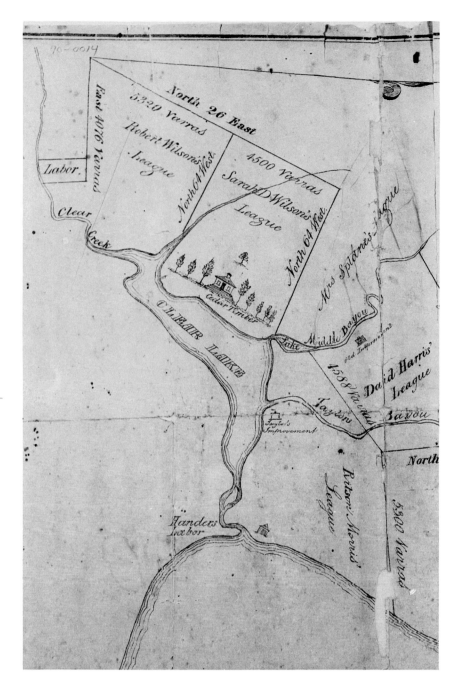

2
Buffalo Bayou at Magnolia Park

This late nineteenth-century photograph is an excellent far view of the curving Buffalo Bayou as it existed when Harris County was settled. The bayou was lined with dense native vegetation typical of the waterways running through the Texas coastal plain.

3
Unidentified log cabin with mudcat chimney
Harris County

This one-room log cabin shows typical early construction techniques: logs laid with decreasing diameters from the bottom; plank doors; a mudcat chimney with tall structural poles, inclined inward to narrow the chimney at the top for better drafts; and the cage, exposed here at the bottom, on which the cats were laid. The hunter in the foreground suggests that the cabin was used as a country hunting retreat when the picture was taken, probably around 1920.

4

Unidentified log house with board and batten addition

Harris County

The small and crudely built log house probably served as a slave cabin originally. The only opening was the doorway; it has a hand-split shingle roof and a log-cage chimney that was heavily chinked with mudcats. An attached board and batten house with sash windows was probably added in the latter part of the nineteenth century and shows a frequent solution to the need for slightly better accommodations.

5

Orange Grove, James Morgan plantation

New Washington, Clopper's Point
(now Morgan's Point)
built 1820s; burned by Santa Anna
1836

Orange Grove was named for the orange trees planted by Nicholas Clopper in the late 1820s. The plantation was bought by a New York real estate company, the New Washington Association, in 1831 and became the home of its agent, James Morgan. After the plantation was burned by the Mexican forces during the Texas revolution in 1836, Morgan "returned to the ruins of his home and soon he was able to send to his friends a number of oranges from his trees which had escaped the depredation of the Mexicans," according to Andrew Forest Muir. This house was unusually large and commodious for the time; it appears to have glass windowpanes, a center-hall plan, and an attached kitchen reached via the side porch.

This sketch has been attributed to J. J. Audubon, but it is much more like the work of Mary Austin Holley, drawn on her earliest visit to Texas in 1833. Morgan built a new, one-story house on this site in 1837, but he told Ferdinand Roemer in 1848 that "a much larger house and two store buildings [seen here] . . . once stood where today his dwelling stands."

6

Evergreen, Moseley Baker– Ashbel Smith house

Tabbs Bay, near Cedar Bayou
built 1830s; burned ca. 1890

Evergreen, purchased by Smith in 1848, might have been a log house later overlaid with weatherboard. It consisted of two rooms at the front and a narrow back room running the width of the house incorporated under the rear roof extension. Two mud and daub chimneys provided the only heat. What is probably the kitchen building can be seen on the right at the rear of the house. Another outbuilding, to the far left, could be slave quarters. The picket fence, outbuildings, and front porch supported by utilitarian posts were common features of early Harris County homesteads. A graduate of Yale Medical School, Dr. Smith was the first principal of the Houston Academy, and in 1881 he became the first president of the Board of Regents of the University of Texas in Austin. Smith was principally responsible for the establishment of the University of Texas Medical School in Galveston, and its first building was named for him.

7

Francis Richard Lubbock
Ranch house and garden

Sims Bayou (near Hobby Airport site)
built ca. 1847; demolished

8

John Birdsall Harris–
John Grant Tod house

Broadway at Elm Street, Harrisburg
built ca. 1850; incorporated into the
Milby house 1888; demolished 1959

Harris's widow and her second husband, A. W. Scoble, sold this house to John Grant Tod in 1866 when the Tods moved to Harrisburg from Richmond, Texas. Tod's daughter Maggie and her husband, Charles H. Milby, moved into the house not long after Tod's death in 1877. The thin, curved braces appear to have been added to the porch after the Civil War in order to make the old-fashioned Greek columns look more stylish. (Compare it to the porch of the Pillot house, fig. 28.) In 1885 the Milbys began construction of a new brick two-story house (fig. 68) on the same property. Maggie Tod Milby recalled the center-hall plan of the original house, which was resituated so that its front porch served as the back porch for the new house.

The Lubbock Ranch house was considerably more sophisticated and larger than Evergreen (fig. 6), but it nevertheless followed the same architectural pattern. Native oak trees and native grasses, scythed for a lawn enclosed by the fence, provided the usual residential landscape during the settlement period. The picket fence surrounding the house was unusual in the country, where rail fences were the rule. It is known that the garden around the house included bois d'arc trees and altheas; in a nearby field a vegetable garden supplied the household. A Texas Historical Marker, located at the intersection of Broadway and Sims Bayou near Hobby Airport, commemorates the site of the Lubbock Ranch.

9

Jane Birdsall Harris house

near the confluence of Brays and
Buffalo bayous, Harrisburg
built 1836; destroyed by fire 1888
oil by Mrs. Peter W. Gray, 1879

The Jane B. Harris house was constructed for the widow of John R. Harris on the site of the original Harris house, which had been built in 1829 and was burned by Mexican troops a few days before the battle of San Jacinto in April of 1836. The Harris house is historically important as the home of the family for whom Harris County was named and as the birthplace of the influential twentieth-century Houston architect, Birdsall P. Briscoe. Generalizations about contemporary construction practices can be made from several well-documented architectural features of the Harris house: detailed accounts of its plan and construction; the fact that its center-hall plan was copied after a New York family home as opposed to a southern antecedent; and the fact that interior architectural elements, including brass hardware, were imported. The garden may have contained native trees, but some trees and shrubs were obviously planted. For instance, large crape myrtles lined the entrance walk. The garden was enclosed by a Gothic fence like those widely used in New York state. In this house on August 18, 1837, the Harrises' only daughter, Mary Jane, was married to Andrew Briscoe.

10

Judge Andrew Briscoe house and garden

408 Main Street at Prairie Avenue
built 1837; demolished 1884
Thomas William Ward, builder
oil by M. Westcott

Architecturally, the Briscoe house was typical of many of Houston's first houses: a combination of straightforward box construction and Greek-type ornament (columns), added to show a measure of sophistication. A kitchen outbuilding can be seen at the rear. The simple landscaped yard inside the picket fence was also typical of early nineteenth-century gardens. The size of the large trees, including flowering magnolia, oak, and possibly hackberry, indicates that they were native. The smaller trees, probably planted by the Briscoes, appear to include flowering fruit trees,

crape myrtles beside the front walk, and a few rose bushes along the side of the house. In 1839 Briscoe sold the house to his wife's cousin, Judge John Birdsall, who was attorney general of the Republic of Texas and Sam Houston's law partner. W. W. Swain

bought the house in 1846, then sold it to Dr. Ingham S. Roberts in 1856. Roberts lived there for twenty-eight years before the house was demolished for the Prince Building.

11

Charlotte Baldwin Allen house

718 Main Street at Rusk Avenue
built ca. 1850s; demolished ca. 1915

Charlotte Allen's house was like many large houses built in Houston before the Civil War: wood frame and clapboard construction with brick chimneys; a two-tiered front porch; attenuated Greek-type, square-cut columns providing vernacular Greek Revival details; and rectangular, symmetrical massing (although this house, like others, did have a rear ell wing). Mrs. Allen, wife of Houston founder A. C. Allen, occupied this house from the 1850s

until her death at age ninety in 1895. After that it was a boarding house until it was demolished for the Pearce-Woolworth Building, with the Liberty Theater Moving Pictures on the

ground floor. The Gulf Building, constructed in 1937 and restored by the Texas Commerce National Bank in 1987, now stands on the site.

12

Erastus S. Perkins
house and garden

1508 Texas Avenue between
LaBranch and Crawford streets
built ca. 1860s; demolished ca. 1926
after plans by Orson Squire Fowler
(published 1854)

Erastus Perkins, a New Yorker who
arrived in Houston in 1838, built this
unusual octagon house, called the

Round House by Houstonians, on the
full-block site, which he had amply
landscaped. Possibly he had lived on
this site in a different house. Documents indicate that the grapevines
were planted by 1845. The house is
complemented by well-spaced trees
that appear to be principally fruit
trees in this 1869 engraving. Trees
outside the simple but handsome paling fence were probably native oaks.
X-shaped supports for Perkins's extensive grape vines can be seen in

the distance on the right. By 1908 the
house had been sold; the smaller
wing was demolished and the house
moved to the corner of the block. It
was a boarding house for the next
eighteen years until its demolition.
The World Trade Center now occupies this block across the street from
Annunciation Church.

13

George Allen plantation

east Harris County
built ca. 1844–45, demolished
watercolor by F. J. Rothaas, architect

It is evident here that native trees
and grass formed the main features
of the fenced area around the house.
Magnolia, cypress, and a chinaberry
tree can be identified, and other
plantings were added to beautify the
entrance: three blooming white
crape myrtles, three white altheas
with rose pink centers (Rose of
Sharon), and pomegranate bushes.
On the house itself, both vertical and
horizontal siding were used for decorative effect. The outbuildings were
kept well away from the main house
to avoid the danger of fire and the inconvenience of excessive heat from
stoves. The barn was fenced separately to keep livestock away from
the decorative gardens, and slave
quarters were screened by a substantial trellis. George Allen was
the younger brother of Houston's
founders.

14

Thomas William House, Sr., house and garden

706 Smith Street at Capitol Avenue
built ca. 1845; demolished 1933

T. W. House (1813–80) was born in England and found his way to Houston in 1836 in time to fight in the last battle of the Texas revolution. House began to build a substantial fortune by shipping cotton to English markets. In the 1840s he established one of Texas's first and most successful banks. He married Mary Elizabeth Shearn, the only daughter of his partner, Charles Shearn; they had four sons: T. W., Jr., John H. B., Charles S., and Edward Mandell, all of whom, like their father, were community and financial leaders. T. W. House, Sr., eventually accumulated vast Texas real estate holdings, including a large sugar plantation at Arcola, Texas. The English love of horticulture was evident in the early planting of bulbs in the House garden. The "white narcissi," described as having been planted in a wide bed across the whole width of the property, were probably paperwhites, which naturalize and multiply in the Houston area. After Mrs. House died in 1914, her home became a boarding house. It was severely damaged by fire in November 1932 and was finally demolished in April 1933. Today the Bob Casey Federal Building and United States Courthouse stands on the property. A Texas State Historical marker commemorates the site as the birthplace of Edward Mandell House, adviser to President Woodrow Wilson.

15

William J. Hutchins house

1416 Franklin Avenue at Caroline Street
built ca. 1850; demolished ca. 1930

Hutchins was born in 1813 in New York, grew up in New Berne, North Carolina, and moved to Houston as a young man from Tallahassee, Florida, in 1843. He became one of Houston's pioneer merchants and built a fortune from his railroad investments and shipping interests. His house was perhaps Houston's most elaborate Greek Revival building. His daughter, Ella, and her second husband, Seabrook Sydnor, inherited the house from her father and lived there until about 1914. It stood vacant until 1930, one of the last survivors on Quality Hill.

16

Spring Grove, Edward Albert Palmer house

1410 Rusk Avenue between Austin and LaBranch streets
built 1858; moved to corner ca. 1900; demolished 1927
Charles Grainger, builder

E. A. Palmer's letters to his father in Virginia during 1858 document the construction of this Greek Revival house, which is said to have been called Spring Grove after his father's plantation in Virginia. Deed records show that Palmer traded the house to W.R. Baker for $8,000 plus a house on Main between McKinney and Walker in 1860. Palmer, a lawyer who had come to Houston in 1847, died in 1862. W. R. Baker was a railroad investor who platted the early additions to Houston in the early 1850s near his railroad yards on the north side of Buffalo Bayou and in the Fourth Ward area. Baker, who was mayor from 1880 to 1885, lived in the house until his death about 1892. It was then moved from the middle of the block to the corner and became a boarding house until it fell into terrible disrepair and was finally demolished for an auto repair shop. During the Civil War the house was used by General John Bankhead Magruder as Confederate army headquarters in Houston.

17

Henry Michael DeChaumes house

2203 San Jacinto Street at Webster Avenue
built ca. 1867; demolished ca. 1955

Henry DeChaumes was the son of the first experienced architect to settle in Houston, Michael DeChaumes. According to the *Houston City Directory*, Henry lived with his father at the corner of Main and Dallas until 1867, when he moved to this house. The Wood map (1869) shows this house in the middle of the block, and early accounts relate that a barn was built at the back, and the DeChaumes had a pasture across Hadley Street. The crape myrtles on either side of the entrance walk provide vertical structure framing the entrance, texture in the deeply furrowed smooth bark, and flowers for color in summer months. Sanborn maps drawn in 1907 show the house moved to the corner of San Jacinto and Hadley; and other houses were built on the block for family and rental income. It was lived in by the DeChaumes's unmarried daughters until about 1945, when it became a boarding house until its demolition.

18

Houston street scene, ca. 1856

400 block of Main Street, looking
south from Preston Avenue

This photograph by R. L. Morris is
one of the earliest extant photographs of Houston. The pitched roof
of the Capitol can be seen in the far
distance on the left. The columned
house in the foreground stood at
the corner of Main and Preston and
was probably the house of Thomas
William Ward, the builder responsible for the Capitol and the Briscoe
house. The Odd Fellows Lodge was
founded in Ward's house in the 400
block of Main in 1838. The house was
bought in 1846 by Dr. Ingham S.
Roberts, who sold it in 1856 to Alex
ander Sessums. The trees planted
along the street outside the sidewalk
were probably water oaks transplanted from the native forest and
carefully boxed with plank structures
until they were well established.

19

Robert Lockart house

2915 Commerce Avenue at
Ennis Street
built ca. 1847; turned to face Ennis
1903; demolished 1927
oil by Walter Sies Finnil, 1872

Walter Sies Finnil was one of the
itinerant painters who roamed the
countryside painting houses and
landscape scenes in hopes of selling
them later (see also fig. 149). Robert
Lockart (1814–86) built this house in
the country and grew cotton on its
surrounding thirty-eight acres. The
rail fence was usual for property in
the country (as opposed to picket
fences in town). The house, however,
was similar to those built in town
(see figs. 11, 14, 20, 22). Surrounding
the house were magnolias, oaks, and
smaller pecan trees planted during
the Civil War. Spanish moss can be
seen hanging from the limbs of the
oak trees. The grazing horse demonstrates one early method used to
keep the lawn cropped; the only alternative was the hot, tedious work
of scything. The Lockart house was
built before city streets extended
from town that far, but in 1903, when
Ennis Street was graded nearby, the
house was turned on its site to face
the street and was renumbered 19
North Ennis Street. The house was
demolished when the property was
sold to J. C. Means for development
as the Lockart Addition.

20

Cornelius Ennis house

1618 Congress Avenue at
Jackson Street
built ca. 1871; demolished ca. 1935

Ennis moved to Houston in 1839
from New Jersey and formed a partnership with George Kimball in the
drug and mercantile business. In
1841 Ennis and Kimball exported the
first bale of cotton to Boston. After
the Civil War the Ennises bought this
house on Quality Hill. Architecturally, the house has both features of
prewar Greek Revival houses (rectilinear massing and columns) and
decorative elements that became
popular during the Victorian period
(paired brackets under the eaves). In
the garden evergreens provided a
green accent in the winter landscape.
Massed shrubbery near the entrance
walk across the front porch and a
hedge along the side fence were unusual features in Houston gardens
just after the war. The family lived
here until the death of Mr. Ennis
in 1899; the house was then sold to
Solomon Brown, a local businessman with seven children. When the
Browns moved in 1918, it was subdivided for rental rooms. In 1926 a furniture company occupied the building, followed by a succession of small
businesses, including the Tampico
Cafe, before it was finally left vacant
and demolished.

21

Emmanuel Raphael house

1820 Rusk Avenue at Hamilton Street
built 1868; additions 1871;
demolished 1925

Raphael's original four-room raised
cottage was expanded into this two-
story house surrounded by extensive
plantings of oaks and elms by the ar-
boriculturist Charles Albrecht. The
Raphael garden was the site of many
publicized musicales in the late nineteenth century. Its tree-shaded lawns
even served as the "Forest of Arden"
in a production of *As You Like It* by
the Old Shakespeare Club. Emmanuel Raphael was an attorney, banker,
and school board member who became one of the original trustees of
the Rice Institute. He organized the
Houston Electric Light Company in
1882 and, as its initial president, exhibited in 1883 the first incandescent
lights ever seen in Houston.

22

Judge James Addison Baker house

1104 San Jacinto Street at
Lamar Avenue
built ca. 1876; demolished 1930

James A. Baker, Sr., moved to Houston from Huntsville, Texas, about 1876 to join the law firm founded by Peter W. Gray in 1840 (later known as Gray, Botts and Baker). In 1887 when his son, Capt. James A. Baker, joined the firm, it became known as Baker, Botts and Baker. It is interesting to note not only usual architectural features such as the columned porches, shutters, hipped roof, railed widow's walk, and fenced yard, but the one-story porch to the right, unusual in itself, has an atypical side entrance. The elder Baker is pictured here on the far left looking at a nurse holding his grandson, the son of Capt. James A. Baker. Baker died in 1897, and the house was probably sold. Richard H. Gray, an architect, lived there from 1907 until his death in 1915. The house was demolished shortly after Gray's widow sold the property and moved in 1930.

23

Houston street scene, 1860s

Preston Avenue at Fannin Street,
south end of Courthouse Square

This photograph documents the
original appearance of the Henry
Sampson house (fig. 24), the large
Greek Revival house on the right,
and gives a good impression of the
Courthouse Square area as it appeared in the late 1860s with a mix
of commercial and residential structures, muddy streets, shell sidewalks,
and fenced yards. The utility poles
were for telegraph lines installed between Houston and Galveston shortly
before the Civil War. Electricity was
not available in Houston until 1883.

24

Henry Sampson house

1104 Preston Avenue at Fannin
Street
built ca. 1860; demolished 1906

Henry Sampson, a general commission merchant, probably built this
house facing the southwest corner of
Courthouse Square just before the
Civil War. It was updated with the
addition of brackets under the eaves
(not evident in fig. 23) in the 1880s or
1890s by the time this photograph
was taken. By 1899 Dr. Max Urwitz
had acquired the house and built a
large two-story addition onto the rear
for his offices. When Urwitz died, the
house was sold and demolished for
the Stewart Building, erected in
1906. The site is now a parking lot.

25

Will Powars house, south and west (front) elevations

1206 Brazos Street at Dallas Avenue
built 1867; demolished 1907

Will Powars, a civil engineer, is shown here with his family and his surveying instruments on the second floor at the back of the house. The double porches on the right were at the front of the house, facing Brazos, and had centered doorways on both floors. Two features of this garden were typical of gardens in the countryside: the rail fence, of which this is a particularly elaborate one; and the leafy "China tree," the most popular ornamental tree planted during the settlement period. On a triangular block of land near the Kellum-Noble house (fig. 261), the Powars house was constructed in a sparsely populated area at the intersection of the Houston grid and the true north-south Freedmen's Town grid platted as an addition to Houston in the 1850s by W. R. Baker. The Powars house site is now part of Allen Center.

26

Powars house, east elevation (rear and side)

The fences at the back of the Powars house were more utilitarian than those on the more public street façade (fig. 25). The barn was located outside the fence. The one-story at-tached block seen in this photograph was the kitchen. Even on two-story houses, attached kitchens were only one story well into the twentieth century to avoid fire and unnecessarily hot rooms above them. The Powars house was demolished by Will Powars, Jr., when he built a new house on the same site.

27

Oaklawn Place, Samuel Ezekiel Allen Ranch house and garden

Confluence of Sims and Buffalo bayous
built ca. 1875; moved to LaPorte 1917; demolished ca. 1935

Allen was the grandson of Ezekiel Thomas, a member of the Old Three Hundred, who came to Texas in 1822 from South Carolina. A straight, live-oak–lined lane led to the house site, which was bounded by a white picket fence. Numerous outbuildings included a large barn and stables; an orchard and a carriage house (not visible here) stood behind a boxwood hedge at the rear. In 1917 Mrs. Allen sold seven hundred acres surrounding the house to the Sinclair Oil Company (now Atlantic Richfield). The house was moved to her bayfront property at LaPorte, next to Sylvan Beach. In 1921, encouraged by her grandson, Robert C. Stuart, Mrs. Allen offered her summer home to Bishop Quin for his Episcopal church camp. The name Camp Allen still identifies the large diocesan-owned camp at another site. The Allen Ranch house was torn down after having served from 1921 to 1927 as the original Camp Allen.

28

Eugene Pillot house

1803 McKinney Avenue at Chenevert Street
built 1868; moved to Sam Houston Park 1965; extant

Eugene Pillot was from New York, where he learned carpentry from his father, Claude N. Pillot. The thinned porch supports and curved bracketing illustrate emerging Victorian-type porches, which by the late 1860s had begun to supplant chunkier Greek Revival details. The Pillot house has been moved to Sam Houston Park, restored, refurnished, and opened as a museum house. This photograph is of the house on its original site.

AFFLECK'S

SOUTHERN RURAL ALMANAC,

AND

PLANTATION AND GARDEN

CALENDAR,

FOR

1860;

BEING LEAP YEAR;

AND UNTIL THE FOURTH OF JULY, THE EIGHTY-FOURTH YEAR
OF THE INDEPENDENCE OF THE UNITED STATES.

BY THOMAS AFFLECK,

NEAR BRENHAM,

WASHINGTON CO., TEXAS.

PUBLISHED BY

DAVID FELT, New York, and H. G. STETSON & CO.,
54 Camp Street, New Orleans.

29

Title page of Thomas Affleck's *Southern Rural Almanac and Plantation and Garden Calendar* for 1860

Copy No. 264 of a limited edition. A Texas Sesquicentennial project by the New Year's Creek Settlers Association, Washington County, Texas, 1986 (Houston: The Beasley Company, 1986)

Thomas Affleck was born in Scotland and lived in New York and Indiana before moving to Cincinnati, where he was agricultural editor of the *Western Farmer and Gardner.* He established the Southern Nurseries near Natchez, Mississippi, and later Affleck's Central Nurseries at his plantation, Glenblyth, near Brenham, Texas. His plants were for sale in Houston at the home of J. H. S. Stanley, 406 Capitol Avenue. *Affleck's Southern Rural Almanac* became the standard text of the reconstitution of southern agriculture after the Civil War.

30

Bohemia, Edward Hopkins Cushing house

6-block site between Holman and Elgin avenues, Austin and San Jacinto streets
built ca. 1858; demolished before 1900

E. H. Cushing moved to Houston in 1856 and shortly thereafter built this house. Bohemia stood on a ten-acre site south of Houston now bordered by Elgin, Holman, Austin, and San Jacinto streets. Cushing's flower garden was a horticultural collection of more than two hundred varieties, and his vegetable garden included vegetables that were new to Houston. A formally landscaped area near the house included a circular rose garden edged with violets. The house itself was one of Houston's first with Victorian aspects, including Italianate window moldings, decorative porch trim, and an L- or T-shaped plan.

31

Alfred Whitaker house and garden

South end of Houston near Main Street and Holman Avenue
built ca. 1865; demolished before 1900

Alfred Whitaker, an Englishman and another of Houston's early landscape gardeners and horticulturists, built this house south of town near Cushing's property. The newly planted evergreens drawn on this 1869 engraving demonstrate Whitaker's special and atypical interest in them as landscaping elements. The house is closely related architecturally to the suburban villas advocated by A. J. Downing, with decorative trim, fanciful bargeboards, and romantic entry trellises. This house type was not popular in Houston.

32

James S. Lucas house

818 Chartres Street at
Walker Avenue
built ca. 1875; demolished 1917

Emily and James S. Lucas moved to
Galveston from England in 1870 and
to Houston in 1873. In 1884 Lucas
was the contractor for the first Cotton Exchange building. He may have
both designed and built this house,
which was one of the few brick residences in Houston in the 1870s. Its
decorative bargeboards under the
eaves, ocular attic windows, entrance, and arched apertures were
all unusual for Houston at the time.
The Lucas house is related to the
earlier Whitaker house (fig. 31) in
architectural style and in garden
planting. Lucas died in 1888, but his
widow continued to occupy the house
until 1917, when family members re-
call that the house was torn down
after she died.

33

William Joseph Settegast house and garden

Gentry Street (later 2218 Sherman,
now Valentine) between Hadley and
McGowen avenues
built ca. 1879; demolished 1950s

The Settegast brothers, William and
Julius, acquired a large tract of land
south of the city across from the Fairgrounds probably shortly after the
Civil War. Both were living there by
at least 1877. It is thought that this
was the house occupied by W. J. at
the time of his death in 1895. According to family sources, this house

was moved a couple of blocks away
to 102 McGowen Street and remodeled by J. J. Settegast about 1910. At
that time the site was purchased by
E. B. Parker for his new house, The
Oaks (figs. 139–41). The landscape
illustrates pollarding, a European
pruning technique. Architecturally,
the house was of the type most popular in Houston before the Civil War;
however, its unusual porch railing
was indicative of a later period.

34
Christ Church rectory

1119 Texas Avenue at San Jacinto
Street
built 1857; dismantled 1902

The first Christ Church rectory was built behind the church (which at that time faced Fannin) for the Reverend Mr. and Mrs. W. T. D. Dalzel. The $3,240 contract with Bering Brothers stated that the main part of the house was to be a two-story rectangle with a sixteen-foot square room on each side of the central hall and staircase. A one-story back wing, finished with thinner plaster and simpler boards, housed the kitchen and rector's study. It was connected to the main house, but access was only via a gallery that ran along the inside of the wing. An outdoor, two-room privy was also specified in the contract, with one room to be "neatly ceiled and finished." Typical of many two-story houses built in Houston before the Civil War, it was accommodating but modest, not as elaborate as the high-style Greek Revival houses erected by wealthy Houstonians. The rectory porches were opened to the south and east to take advantage of prevailing gulf breezes, and shutters provided both climate control and privacy. In 1874 an Englishman, John Julyan Clemens, arrived as the new rector. During his tenure (until 1885), he set church finances in order and made major building and landscaping improvements. A second floor was built above the kitchen of the rectory, and a bathroom at the top of the stairs, said to have been one of the first in Houston, was added. The original picket fence that enclosed the church property may also have been replaced about this time by the wrought-iron fence seen in this photograph. Clemens landscaped a large mud puddle between the church and the rectory with shell paths and a large English rose garden. English ivy, some say grown from Westminster Abbey cuttings, softened the façade of the church and shaded the front of the rectory. This rectory was divided, sold in two separate parts, and moved to nearby sites in 1902 to make way for the new large brick Victorian Gothic rectory constructed that year (figs. 269, 270).

35

Benjamin Charles Simpson house and garden

Youngs Avenue (now Riesner Street),
Sixth Ward
built ca. 1873; demolished

B. C. Simpson came to Houston before the Civil War from New York and married Rebecca Wheeler in 1873. This house, probably built shortly after the wedding, was located north of Buffalo Bayou in the vicinity of the current Houston Police Department. The Simpson family, seen here on the front porch, lived there until 1882, when they moved to a fashionable new house on Main Street (fig. 36). Hundreds of such one-story, L- or T- shaped clapboard cottages were built in Houston neighborhoods in the last decades of the nineteenth century. The primitive state of outlying residential areas, even as late as the 1880s, is evident. Street trees had been planted, but planks had to be placed across the open gutter for access to the house from the unpaved street. The wood trellis between the corner of the house and the front fence, roses planted inside the yard at the fence base, a planter box placed on the porch railing, and the small arched arbor on the opposite side of the front walk all indicate the Simpsons' interest in their garden.

36

Simpson house and garden

804 Main Street at Rusk Avenue
built 1882; demolished 1906

The Simpsons built their new, larger, and more stylish house across the street from Charlotte Allen (fig. 11) on a corner site of the full block owned by Daniel Greenleaf Wheeler. Wheeler gave lots to each of his daughters as they married, creating a family compound surrounding the site of the original Wheeler house, which had stood in the center of the block but had burned. In the flower bed between the house and encir-cling sidewalk rose bushes and violets grew luxuriantly. Climbing roses covered an arbor framing a rear side door. This elaborate, well-kept garden was made possible by a dependable supply of water from the city waterworks, established in 1878. The water faucet, visible in the smoothly mown lawn, is evidence that water was finally being supplied to residential neighborhoods as Reconstruction ended in Houston. According to family accounts, the wrought-iron fence was made in Houston by the Phoenix Iron Works, of which Mr. Simpson was an owner.

37

Unidentified house with swept yard

Houston, Texas

This house of an African American family demonstrates the "swept yard" of smoothly packed dirt, some say a feature of African life transported to America with the slave population. The practice was a matter of cleanliness, not an indifference to the beauty of plants; the carefully boxed climbing rose in this front yard is evidence of an appreciation of decorative planting.

38

John Miles Frost house, swept back yard

406 Gray Avenue
built ca.1900; demolished ca. 1936

Next door to the Frost house at 404 Gray, this house was probably built as a rental. Utilitarian back yards of affluent homes were kept clean and orderly by the house servants, many of whom had been slaves. The swept yard, common around the houses of African Americans (fig. 37), was therefore a natural practice. The cistern for rainwater with a pipe into the house assured pure drinking water for the family; underground brick cisterns were also widely used. Water for gardens was at first hauled from the bayous or used sparingly from cisterns, but after artesian water wells were drilled in 1888, water was available from individual water wells, and the city water pressure became more reliable. Cisterns were used even after piped city water was available, however, because of possible contamination and intermittent problems with water pressure.

39
Samuel Maurice McAshan
house and garden

1315 Main Street at Clay Avenue
built ca. 1876; demolished 1907

S. M. McAshan (1829–1905) came to Texas from Virginia in 1844 with his parents. In 1863 he moved to Houston and began a career with the T. W. House bank. This house that McAshan built for his family after he was well established had elements of both prewar Greek Revival houses (columns and massing) and postwar Victorian houses (eave brackets, tall windows, and window moldings). The most interesting and unusual features of this house were the two front windows configured as semicircular bows. The cape jasmines in the McAshan garden were famous for their size and necessitated a stepladder for cutting the highest blossoms. The typical division of front yard from back yard utility area was accomplished by both fencing and planting. The house was demolished by the McAshan family, and on the site they erected the McAshan Apartments with 21 "flats" in 1908–1909.

40

William Davis Cleveland house

806 San Jacinto Street at Rusk Avenue
built ca. 1854; remodeled several times after 1873; demolished 1917

Born in 1839 in Alabama, W. D. Cleveland moved to Austin County, Texas, with his parents in 1840. He made his first trip to Houston at age fourteen and stayed in this house, which must have just been completed. In 1859 Cleveland moved to Houston as a clerk for a drygoods merchant and eventually became one of the city's wealthiest wholesale grocers. By 1870 he had started his own cotton business and bought this house. Cleveland married Tina Latham and raised six children , the first of whom, W. D. Cleveland, Jr., was born in this house in 1873. The house was enlarged several times to accommodate the large Cleveland family; the decorative brackets and porch railings were additions made after 1870.

41

Thomas William House, Jr., house and garden

1010 Louisiana Street between McKinney and Lamar avenues
built 1872; remodeled 1890; demolished 1936
George E. Dickey, architect for remodeling

Four years after his marriage, T. W. House, Jr., built this house, an excellent example of transitional Victorian architecture seen in Houston just after the Civil War. It has a rectilinear plan and pedimented roofline like the older Greek Revival houses (figs. 10, 11, 13, 19), but it also has a bracketed double front gallery and paired brackets under the eaves typical of more highly decorated Victorian styles (figs. 36, 39, 46). The garden boasted a star-shaped flower bed in the middle of the front lawn planted with pansies and centered with a palmetto in an urn. Another early Victorian garden feature was the vine-covered arbor next to the front porch. On the opposite side of the lawn stood a large magnolia tree and an evergreen framing the front view of the house. This house was substantially altered in 1892, when it was "modernized" by George Dickey (figs. 65, 66).

42

James Theodore Dudley Wilson house and gazebo

608 Rusk Avenue between Louisiana
and Smith streets
built 1857; demolished ca. 1916

J. T. D. Wilson (1820–1902), the son
of Robert Wilson (fig. 1) and his first
wife, Margaret Pendegrast, who died
in 1823, was born in St. Louis. He
came to Texas in 1835, served as a
private in the Texas army in 1836,
and moved to Houston the following
year. He married Mary Adeline Cornelia Cone in 1855, built this house
two years later, and reared six children there. Although he built his fortune from real estate investments,
Wilson procured supplies for the
Confederate army from Mexico during the Civil War, and afterward
became Houston's first mayor following Reconstruction. Architecturally
this house has several features that
were typical of many larger Houston
houses built before 1860: railed widow's walk, hipped roof, and simple,
boxed columns. The lattice foundation covering may have been a later
addition, as the gardens and the gazebo certainly were. The elaborate
Wilson gardens (including the gazebo), trellis screens, and star-shaped
bed seen in this photograph were
probably added by Wilson's sons who
inherited the house (fig. 43).

43

Wilson house and entrance gardens

Harvey T. D. Wilson, the Wilsons'
oldest son, lived in this house all his
life. Owner of the Forestdale Nurseries, Harvey clearly was the family
member responsible for the great
horticultural diversity of the Wilson
gardens that occupied a full-block
site. The wide front path was bordered on either side by long beds
with luxurious clumps of flowers,
outside of which were beds containing widely spaced rose bushes. Tall
oak trees shaded the expansive front
lawn except in one area that held a
round bed of enormous elephant
ears. After Harvey's death, his youngest brother, Hubert Wilson, continued to live in the house until about
1914. After lying vacant for a couple
of years, the house was demolished.
The Houston Lighting and Power Company headquarters now occupies this
block across from Tranquility Park.

44

Albert A. Van Alstyne– John F. Dickson house

1216 Main Street at Polk Avenue
built 1877; demolished 1918
Clayton and Lynch, architects

This 1918 photograph depicts the Van Alstyne–Dickson house shortly before it was demolished, demonstrating the state to which many of Houston's nineteenth-century mansions declined (for comparison with its original condition see fig. 53). This important house was the first known in Houston to be designed by an experienced professional architect, Nicholas J. Clayton of Galveston. Its ornamented architecture, large scale, and heavy masonry construction were new to Houston when this house was constructed. Sanborn maps show not only that the kitchen was in a separate building attached by a porch to the rear of the house as late as 1907, but also that the property had numerous outbuildings including a hen house. Judge James Masterson bought the house in the 1890s and held there a highly publicized reception for Winnie Davis, daughter of Jefferson Davis, during the Confederate reunion in 1895. John F. Dickson bought the house in 1900 and hired Clayton to make interior alterations (figs. 175–77). Henry Dickson, son of John F. Dickson, salvaged many interior furnishings when the house was demolished and commissioned architect Alfred C. Finn to incorporate them into his new house on Montrose Boulevard, which also has been demolished.

45

Charles Shearn House house

1806 Main Street at Jefferson Avenue
built 1882; demolished ca. 1920
Eugene T. Heiner, architect

Charles S. House was one of four sons of T. W. House, Sr., all of whom built impressive residences. Charles House was president of the Houston Street and Railway Company when this house was constructed. Although the Van Alstyne house (fig. 44) was the first of the towered villas, this house was probably Houston's best example of the American Victorian interpretation of the French Second Empire style. After Dr. W. R. Eckhardt, the second owner from ca. 1904 to 1913, died, this house became the first home of the Houston Art League, forerunner of the Museum of Fine Arts, Houston. The garden is a good example of the Victorian principle of "scatter" planting in which each specimen was widely separated so that it could grow to horticultural maturity and be viewed from all sides like a piece of sculpture.

46

Howard F. Smith
house and garden

2204 Main Street at Webster Avenue
built ca. 1893; demolished ca. 1924

Howard Smith owned a company
that sold heavy hardware, iron, steel,
railroad and mill supplies, and eleva-
tors. He built this house out on South
Main before many houses were constructed there. The typical pattern of
nineteenth-century cement walkways
is seen clearly in this photograph: the
wide entrance sidewalk coming from
the street and a narrow walk encircling the house inside the fence. The
lattice fence separating and screening the utility back yard added a
decorative touch. By 1920 the house
had new owners, and it was demolished several years later for the
Piggly Wiggly Grocery Store # 4.

47

Edward Andrew Peden house

1017 Bell Avenue at Fannin Street
built ca. 1890; demolished ca. 1927

E. A. Peden came to Houston from
Griffin, Georgia, in 1883 and with his
father and two brothers established

Peden Iron and Steel. It became one
of Houston's foremost industries and
prospered during the boomtown
days. The handsome iron gates and
fence railings might have been manufactured at Peden Iron and Steel. Cement was used as a decorative element in this garden with a distinctive

molded fence and fence posts. The
corner entrance gate, another popular fashion in Victorian garden design, was reflected in the corner
porch entrance. Such interworking of
asymmetry and diagonals in the house
and garden was carefully planned for
a stylish effect.

48

Milton Grosvenor Howe house and garden

918 Austin Street at
McKinney Avenue
built ca. 1880; demolished 1922

A Massachusetts native, Howe graduated from Andover and Dartmouth and came to Houston in 1859 as a civil engineer with the Houston and Texas Central Railroad, from which he retired in 1900. As a captain in the Engineering Corps of the Confederate army, he improvised two of the six cannon used to repel Federal troops in the battle of Sabine Pass, in 1863. He was married in 1873 to Jessie Wade Briscoe, daughter of Judge Andrew Briscoe and Mary Jane Har-

49

Alexander Porter Root house and garden

1410 Clay Avenue at Austin Street
built 1893–94; demolished 1925
George E. Dickey, architect

Root was a Yale-educated banker whose daughter, Cora, married E. A. Peden (fig. 47). Although Root bought this full-block site in 1882 and lived here from at least 1884, this house was not constructed until 1893. The earlier house must have been demolished or partially incorporated into this one. This house was typical of Houston's later Victorian houses, with some vertical emphasis but more disciplined massing, low rounded columns, and a wide-arched entrance

ris (fig. 10). The Howe house was a more heavily ornamented version of the house type built by E. H. Cushing (fig. 30), indicating its later construction date. A lattice fence extending from one side of the house to the side picket fence probably screens the

back yard. Widely spaced planting filled the narrow foundation beds surrounding the house. A decorative wire fence enclosed the front and side yards—a light touch similar in feeling to the decorative roof cresting.

reminiscent of the Shingle-style houses of the Northeast. In contrast to utilitarian back yards, this hedged back garden, entered through a tall arched arbor, provided a private area for family recreation. The children and grandchildren of A. P. Root

gave this property to the city of Houston for Christmas in 1922, and the house was demolished three years later. The live oak trees seen here still stand in Root Memorial Square—one hundred years older and still defining the area with shaded dignity.

50

Joseph Chappell Hutcheson house and garden

1417 McKinney Avenue at
LaBranch Street
built 1887; demolished 1927
George E. Dickey, architect

Hutcheson was a Virginia native who graduated from the University of Virginia Law School before moving to Houston in 1874. The Hutcheson house presented a combination of light decorative elements and heavier, oversized architectural statements, which exaggerated the three-dimensional quality of the building. A variety of surface materials and shapes were used to create a picturesque composition. Victorian latticework enclosed the gazebo (behind the house to the right), a favorite place to sit in the shade and visit with friends while enjoying a long dahlia bed planted every spring.

51

Jedidiah Porter Waldo house and garden

1213 Rusk Avenue at Caroline Street
built 1884–85; moved to 210
Westmoreland and remodeled
1904–1905; extant
George E. Dickey, architect

The Waldo house, one of Dickey's early Houston commissions, was one of the square-towered villas built in Houston in the 1870s and 1880s (see also figs. 44, 45). The open lawn and geometric planting of the street trees emphasized the vertical lines of the house. Sparse foundation planting and the iron fence were typical of the Victorian garden, but the unbroken lawn surrounding the house was a new development in garden design that appeared in Houston in the 1880s. The Waldo house was moved when the Rusk Avenue property was condemned for a new U. S. Post Office that still stands on the site.

52

Houston street scene, 1890s

1200 block of Main Street

The Van Alstyne house (figs. 44, 53) and the Henry Fox house (fig. 91), seen in the foreground, occupied this entire block on the west side of Main Street. This street scene with spacious front gardens, grass-lined sidewalks with oak trees shading the street, and carriages proceeding leisurely along the thoroughfare evokes a vision of the gracious pace of that earlier time when Main Street was Houston's elite address. This Fox–Van Alstyne block is now occupied by the Humble Building, Humble Tower, and a Modern pavilion, built on the Fox House site, that was constructed for an Air France ticket office in 1963.

53

Van Alstyne–Dickson house and garden

The Van Alstyne house was famous for its architecture (fig. 44), but the garden was also greatly admired. Tall oak trees shaded the sidewalk along Main Street, and the low wrought-iron fence allowed passersby an excellent view of the garden. Banana trees flanked a front oriel window, and low shrubs of several varieties framed the corners of the house. A tiered bird bath at the side of the house in the front garden partially obscured a gazebo behind it. Both bird baths and gazebos were popular garden ornaments of the Victorian age.

54
Jehu W. Johnson–James Oliver Wesley Ross house

710 Hadley Avenue between Milam
and Louisiana streets
built 1882; demolished 1938
George E. Dickey, architect

J. W. Johnson, who established the
original *Houston Post* in 1880, built
this grand brick house for $50,000.
Johnson and his wife, Penelope Bor-
den, moved into the house before it
was painted, and, according to one
story, Mrs. Johnson died of painter's
colic shortly thereafter. In 1904 the
house was bought by J. H. Burnett for
his daughter Ellen and her husband,
J. O. Ross, a realtor. This house, like

the Scanlan house (fig. 55), was a
version of the square-towered villa
less French than other houses of this
type built in Houston (figs. 44, 45,
51) primarily because of its pitched
rather than mansard rooflines. Of all
these houses the twenty-four-room
Johnson-Ross house was the largest
and most highly decorated. It was
particularly well appointed inside,
with inlaid floors, mahogany panel-

ing, mantels, and stair rails, etched bronze and copper hardware, hand-painted murals, and art glass windows. The stables-servants quarters was itself a fine two story, L-shaped brick building with corner turrets, arched second-story windows, and a stonework base. In addition to stables and tack rooms, it had twelve servant rooms and baths. The landscape plan encompassed the whole property and included a gated entrance walk laid out on the diagonal from the corner, extensive flower beds, walkways, wrought-iron fencing, and fountains. The beds lining the diagonal walk were always of one variety, one of the fashionable practices in Victorian gardening. In the spring the beds were always filled with poppies. Ross heirs converted the house into a rooming house, and finally sold it to W. W. Fondren, who demolished it to subdivide the property. St. Paul's Methodist Church was organized in this house in 1905, and the Rosses donated the property on which the first St. Paul's Church was built.

55

T. H. Scanlan house

1917 Main Street at Pierce Avenue
built 1891; demolished 1937
Eugene T. Heiner, architect

Scanlan, Houston's famous Reconstruction mayor, had seven daughters, all of whom lived with him in his Main Street mansion and none of whom married. The elaborate residence and its garden reflected Scanlan's business success. The delicate wrought-iron fence revealed low cape jasmine bushes on either side of the entrance walk, and low shrubs were widely spaced at the foundation of the house. The tall tiered bird bath in the center of the lawn space in front of the veranda was a popular garden ornament in Victorian Houston (fig. 53). Paths branched from the entrance walk on both sides of this front lawn and joined a serpentine walk running beside two huge magnolia trees at the side of the house toward the back yard. The other side lawn was open but bordered with large shrubbery. It is interesting to compare the Scanlan house, Eugene Heiner's most elaborate residential design, to the Dick house (fig. 56) and the Johnson-Ross house (fig. 54), two of Dickey's largest and most elaborate commissions.

56

Samuel K. Dick– Capt. James A. Baker house

1416 Main Street at Bell Avenue
built 1888–89; demolished 1923
Dickey and Allen, architects

George E. Dickey was commissioned by S. K. Dick, president of Inman Compress Company and member of the Houston Cotton Exchange, to design this house, which became a local landmark and was widely photographed. A later photograph reveals a new, heavier wrought-iron fence set on a cement base punctuated with white cement posts. Dick sold the house ten years later in 1899 to Capt. James A. Baker, who was a partner in his father's law firm. The junior Baker won renown as the personal attorney and friend of William Marsh Rice who represented Rice's estate in the litigation concerning the disposition of Rice's fortune and the establishment of the Rice Institute. Baker was the first chairman of the board of trustees of the Institute and remained in that post until his death in 1941. The house was demolished in 1923 when the Bakers moved to The Oaks (figs. 139–41).

57

Alexander Bergamini–Simon Peter Coughlin house and garden

1203 Milam Street at Dallas Avenue
built 1894; demolished ca. 1930

Bergamini owned a popular saloon in the Rice Hotel. When his daughter Carrie married Simon Peter Coughlin in 1899, the Coughlins took over the house and remained there until 1919, when it was leased as a funeral home to Lawrence Morse Undertakers until the Coughlin family had it demolished about 1930. Note the fashionable Victorian corner entrance leading to the front steps and the decorative cement footings for the main posts of the wrought-iron fence. The large bed in the front garden was probably a domed bed favored by Victorian gardeners. Such beds were usually planted with bright flowers or bulbs, while shrubs were widely spaced along the foundation of the house.

58

Gustave Antoine Mistrot house and garden

1504 Clay Avenue at LaBranch Street
built 1895; demolished ca. 1960

G. A. Mistrot moved to Houston from Louisiana in 1879. He was a partner in Mistrot Brothers (later Mistrot-Munn), a chain of early department stores founded by his father, a French immigrant, in 1850 in New Iberia, Louisiana. Several features of this garden design were typical of the period: the cement entrance walk and secondary walk curving around one corner of the house, and the decorative lattice fence dividing front and back yards, painted the same color as the house trim. In its later years the Mistrot house was subdivided into rental units before it was demolished for an auto parts dealership.

59

Michael DeGeorge
house and garden

918 Bagby Street at
McKinney Avenue
built 1895; demolished late 1950s

The DeGeorge family had wide-ranging real estate interests in Houston and erected several hotels, including the now restored Lancaster Hotel (originally Auditorium Hotel). Michael DeGeorge came to the United States from Italy in 1870 and, after a decade in New Orleans, moved to Houston. He eventually built a grocery store next to this house site at the corner of Walker and Bagby. By 1895 he could afford to build this ten-room house, which stood across Bagby Street from City Hall. The garden was Victorian with evidence of spaced foundation plantings of evergreen and deciduous shrubs. With unusually handsome gate posts at the entrance, the DeGeorge house was surrounded by a wrought-iron fence. The DeGeorges moved out in 1939, the year City Hall was completed,

and the house stood vacant until it was demolished. The City Hall Annex, built in 1967, now stands on the site.

60

Thomas D. Cobb
house and garden

1904 Main Street at Calhoun Avenue
built 1887; demolished ca. 1922

Captain Cobb, the first owner of this house, was an attorney with Baker, Botts and Baker. He sold the house in 1893 to E. J. Wilson, who remained in it only a few years before selling it again about 1900 to the attorney B. F. Bonner. The encircling driveway and elaborately roofed porte cochere were new design elements in Houston houses and gardens in the late 1880s. The house was demolished for the Batterson and Crawford Auto Tire Company built on the site by 1923.

61

Hosmer W. Wood house

409 McKinney Avenue
built ca. 1894; demolished ca. 1927

H. W. Wood, proprietor of the Excelsior Steam Laundry, built this house for his family, who lived in it until the 1920s, when it was purchased by E. A. Epley. This house stood across Bagby Street from the DeGeorge house (fig. 59), on the site of Houston City Hall (1937) across McKinney Street from the Houston Public Library.

62

Cottage

2009 Live Oak Street
built 1890s; extant

This small house, still standing, is probably nearly a hundred years old. It is not possible to trace reliably the history of this house, because many houses in the neighborhood have been moved for nearby freeway construction. Also, houses in this neighborhood changed hands frequently and were not often owner-occupied.

In 1908, the earliest date to which the house can be traced, Jesse Wilson, a black railroad worker, lived there. Because of its tower, the house looks as though it was constructed in the 1890s when some houses were standing in this area, though they are not recorded on Sanborn maps.

63

Kutschbach Florist,
farm and greenhouse

Old Katy Road

In 1880 Mary Proetzel and August Kutschbach opened one of Houston's early florist shops in their home at 2526 Washington Avenue, which was conveniently located across the street from the entrance to Glenwood Cemetery and near a hospital. The Kutschbachs owned sixty acres in Houston Heights and eventually had twenty-two greenhouses: seven next to their house on Washington Avenue, a few nearby on Center Street, and the rest on their large farm on Katy Road, where they grew most of the flowers and plants they needed for their floral decorating business. Hardy annuals, like the daisies seen here, were planted in open fields to provide enough flowers and varieties for the increasing number of social occasions in Houston for which Kutschbach Florist supplied the decorations.

64

**John Joseph Atkinson
house and garden**

817 San Jacinto Street at
Walker Avenue
built mid-1880s; remodeled 1890;
demolished ca. 1927

J. J. Atkinson was a ship captain with
the Charles Morgan Line. The Atkin-
sons bought a one-story cottage on
this property in 1890 and incorporated it into their new two-story
house. The garden at the Atkinson
house was planted to provide a constant supply of blooming flowers (see
also fig. 257). There were few trees
in the garden because the flowers
needed sun. Fortunately, the warm
climate in Houston allowed a succession of blooms most of the year.

65

House, Jr., house and garden

The new gardens, designed after 1890, were quite a change from the earlier, more rigid plantings of this house before it was remodeled (fig. 41). The expanse of lawn seen here was planted with a row of California fan palms in the side yard. Roses were set in a rectangular bed between the fence and the line of palm trees; there were two hundred rose varieties in the House collection. A greenhouse behind the house in front of the two-story servants' house provided shelter for many of the plants used in "bedding out" as well as many of the new exotic plants so exciting to Victorian gardeners. The T. W. House, Jr., house was sold to the state of Texas for use by the Transient Bureau, and it housed around a hundred men before it was demolished. The curving, green-glassed Allied Bank Tower (First Interstate Bank) now stands on the full-block site once occupied by the House estate.

66

House, Jr., garden on tour

This image of the House driveway planting appeared in a Houston newspaper along with photographs of other gardens that were on a tour during the Fruit, Flower and Vegetable Festival of 1898. The graceful rounded forms of the turret, wrapped porch, and arches of this house were echoed in the curving drive and lush, free-flowing landscape.

67

Josiah F. Crosby–
James Bute house

1016 Milam Street at Lamar Avenue
built ca. 1875, demolished ca. 1925

68

Charles H. Milby house

614 Broadway at Elm Street,
Harrisburg
built 1885–88; demolished 1959

Charles Milby, a financier, and his
wife, Maggie Tod Milby, lived in her
family home (fig. 8) until 1888, when
this new two-story brick house was
completed on the same property.
Because the porous brick allowed
dampness to seep through and damage the plaster interior walls, the
exterior was sheathed in cast stone
about 1908. The center-hall plan allowed for a parlor and library on one
side and a dining room and guest
bedroom on the other, downstairs.
Four bedrooms were located upstairs, with built-in closets, unusual
for this time. From the wide front
porch, which later extended across
the south side of the house, the Milby

Judge Crosby constructed this house
across the street from the T. W.
House, Jr., property (figs. 41, 65, 66).
In 1895 James Bute, founder of the
Bute Paint Company, bought it and
probably laid out a new and classic
Victorian garden. The domed bed,
around which the driveway circled,
was planted in the popular ribbon
bedding manner and crowned with
a round water basin mirroring the
sky. Lush plantings of mixed flowers
edged the outer rim of the drive. A
running figure of Mercury on a pedestal was silhouetted by a luxuriant
growth of vines on a trellis in front of
the porch. Low shrubs filled a bed at

the foundation around the front and
side of the house. The leafy young
pear tree would have been covered
with showy white blossoms in the
spring. Although the house lacked a
square tower, architecturally it exemplified the earlier, more massive
Italianate-style houses with brick
load-bearing walls overlaid with
scored stucco, wide eaves under a
low-pitched roof, formal balance,
brackets, quoins, and hooded, arched
windows. Mrs. Bute lived in this
house until 1921, after which it lay
vacant until it was demolished. Today the Tenneco Building stands on
the site.

family could see Buffalo Bayou, and
through the decades they witnessed
the progress of the ship channel as
paddle-wheelers were replaced by

oceangoing cargo ships. The family
occupied the house until Mrs. Milby's
death in 1942, after which it stood
vacant until it was demolished.

69

Reed Singleton farmhouse

Humble, Texas
built 1880s; burned ca. 1916

This house has drawn interest from folklorists because the infamous outlaw John Wesley Hardin is said to have stayed here with his wife and ill baby. The baby died and was buried on the Singleton property. It is unclear if Hardin was a friend of the family, a paying guest, or an intruder. Family members pictured here are (from left to right) Reed Singleton, Sr., his wife, Margaret (or Marguerite) Huffman Singleton, and their children, Henry, Jim, Maggie, Ada, Joe, Reed, Jr., Martha, Cinda, Allen, and Jeff. When the house burned, Mrs. Singleton, then a widow, moved to Houston Heights to live with her daughter, Cinda Singleton Williams.

70

Bird porch brackets

2212 Decatur Street, Sixth Ward
built ca. 1890; extant

Said to have been adapted from a German folk symbol, these brackets were cleverly designed in bird patterns and were probably carved locally, not mass-produced in large factories elsewhere. Most of the wood trim elements used on Victorian houses were stock items that could be ordered from catalogs or bought at a local hardware store. These bird brackets appeared on several small houses in Houston neighborhoods where working German families lived.

71
Shotgun houses

Freedmen's Town
built ca. 1880s

Few of the long rows of nineteenth-
century shotgun houses still stand in
Freedmen's Town.

72

Annie L. Hagen house

609 Hobson Street
built ca. 1908; demolished

Considered one of the best nurses and midwives in her community, Annie Hagen was representative of black women who achieved respect and relative affluence before World War I. Trained by the Houston doctors for whom she worked, Hagen qualified for an Experienced Trained Nurse Certificate and organized the Trained Nurses Club. She owned this raised cottage, three nearby rent houses, several city lots, and some farm property. Plants in the photograph indicate an interest in gardening: elephant ears, climbing roses, pot palms on the porch railing, and hanging buckets of ivy between porch posts.

73

Henry M. Curtin house

2111 Fannin Street at
Webster Avenue
built 1880; turned on site early
1900s; demolished 1940

This raised cottage was built by George and Mary Botts Fitzgerald facing Webster. When Henry Curtin married Georgia McKinney in 1891, he purchased the house for $5,000, turning it to face Fannin sometime after 1900. Curtin was the Harris County tax assessor. This was one of the first houses built in the South End, and Mrs. Curtin recalled that early in the twentieth century there were no houses between it and Emancipation Park two miles away, and that nearby on the future site of St. Agnes Academy stood only "powder houses," where gun dealers stored ammunition away from the city. The house had five large rooms and boasted a copper bathroom tub housed in a wooden casing; at the time of construction it had only gas lights and a wood-burning kitchen stove. The Curtin family occupied the house until its demolition for a used car lot.

74

Houston Heights plat map

ca. 1890

This plat was prepared in Boston perhaps at the behest of Bostonian F. L. Ames, one of the investors in the Omaha and South Texas Land Company. Ames family members were major stockholders in the Union Pacific Railroad, which had its headquarters in Omaha. A Massachusetts law at this time imposed a heavy tax on excess profits that were not reinvested; therefore, much of the capital for new real estate developments throughout the U.S. came from Boston. The park indicated on this plat was never built; the area was included in the grounds of the waterworks, which was attractively landscaped, however. A later map was published without the park and with completely different (and more numerous) engravings. It is on this map, which was reprinted in Sister Agatha's *History of Houston Heights*, that the houses match published Barber catalog plans.

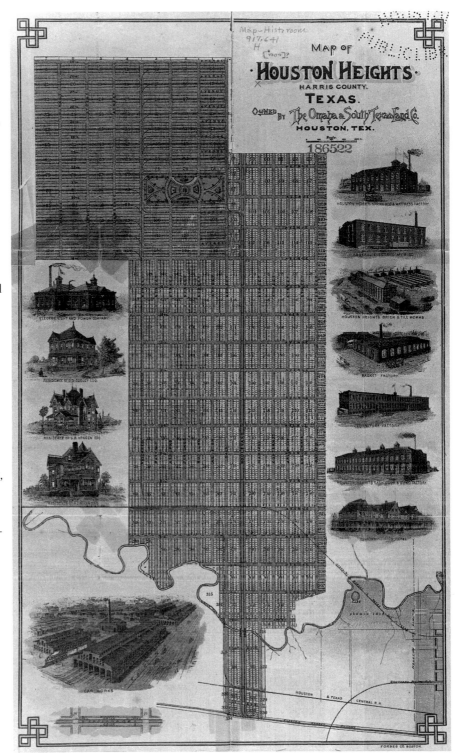

75

Heights Boulevard

1904

L. D. Folse, a florist and nurseryman, provided and installed the plants for the Heights Boulevard esplanade. An attractive low hedge followed the outer contours of the esplanade, and oak trees were placed at equidistant intervals along the street edge. Pyramidal evergreens were spaced just behind and at midpoint between the trees. Crescent-shaped beds of shrubbery accented by a single palm in the curve moved down the whole length of the boulevard in even cadence. Such public neighborhood planting set high standards for private gardens.

76

Daniel Denton Cooley house and garden

1802 Heights Boulevard, Houston Heights
built 1892–93; demolished 1965
attributed to George F. Barber, architect

D. D. Cooley was a New Yorker who founded the Omaha and South Texas Land Company in 1887 with O. M. Carter. He moved to Houston in 1892 as general manager to develop the company's newly acquired property. A pioneer in oil production in the Goose Creek area, Cooley served on many boards and financed worthy causes, including the first school in Houston Heights. The Cooleys had three children: Denton, Arthur, and Dr. Ralph Cooley (father of heart surgeon Denton A. Cooley). Cooley's house was the first completed on Heights Boulevard, and when the electric trolley was installed on the boulevard, Cooley hooked up to it to provide his house with the first electric lights in the area. Built over a full basement, the six-bedroom house was constructed almost entirely of cypress. When Arthur Cooley, the last occupant, died in 1962, the house lay vacant until the family had it demolished. Original landscaping included large native trees, part of the natural woods that covered the area. Wider entrance walks and luxuriant vines framing the porch entrance added to the sense of spaciousness and ease in this shaded garden. The site remains empty except for pecan and magnolia trees planted there by the Cooleys.

77

Newton L. Mills house

1530 Heights Boulevard, Houston Heights
built 1893; demolished ca. 1938
attributed to George F. Barber, architect

This was one of several large houses built for advertisement and investment on Heights Boulevard by members of the Omaha and South Texas Land Company, developers of Houston Heights. Mills was superintendent of the real estate department and sold this house the year after it was completed to Nelson Baker. Wil-

liam A. McNeil, another realtor with Omaha, bought the house in 1909, and his family lived there until the house was demolished around 1938. Along with the Cooley house (fig. 76) and a dozen others, the Mills house appears to have been built from plans designed and published by George F. Barber.

78

View of Egge's cottage
1878

This drawing was published by George and Charles Palliser in one of their 1878 catalogs. When comparing it with the J. M. Cotton house (fig. 79), one sees that George Dickey freely used the Palliser design in planning the Cotton house.

79

James Madison Cotton house
1018 Travis Street at Lamar Avenue
built 1882; demolished ca. 1927
George E. Dickey, architect

This photograph of the side elevation of the Cotton house was taken in May 1885, three years after construction. Cotton was a fire insurance agent with S. O. Cotton and Brothers. The architecture of this rather delicate house shows the influence of the Swiss chalet, often imitated in American Victorian houses. Although George Dickey frequently took full credit for this house design, an almost exact rendition was published by George and Charles Palliser in 1878 (fig. 78). The logical explanation is that Dickey kept catalogs in his office from which his clients could choose a design; Dickey then probably drew up a set of plans based on the exterior appearance and modified the original according to his client's wishes and budget. It is also possible that Dickey ordered and copied catalog plans. The Dillingham house (fig. 81) was another Dickey house for which a published set of plans has been discovered.

80

Cesar Maurice Lombardi house

806 Austin Street at Rusk Avenue
built 1890; demolished ca. 1920

Cesar Lombardi, a Swiss native, came to New Orleans in 1860 and after the Civil War to Houston, where he gained prominence in local business affairs. William Marsh Rice credited Lombardi with the idea for the Rice Institute, and asked him to be a member of the first board of trustees. As president of the Houston school board, Lombardi had asked Rice to fund construction of a new high school, but Rice decided instead to endow an institute of higher learning. Lombardi was married to Carrie Ennis, daughter of Cornelius Ennis (fig. 20). The Lombardi house was demolished around 1920 for the Kanawa Apartments. The Houston Center garage now occupies the site.

81

Charles Dillingham house

1214 Rusk Avenue at Caroline Street
built 1889; demolished 1916
George E. Dickey, architect

Born in Vermont in 1837, Dillingham was the son of Paul Dillingham, a two-term governor there. He moved to Houston in 1885 with his family and became a successful attorney, railroad investor, and banker. The building permit for this house was issued in November 1889 for $7,000, and published sources listed George Dickey as the architect. However, a close copy of the Dillingham house had been published two years earlier in *Sheppell's Modern Houses*. The Dillinghams moved to 3214 Austin Street in 1914, leaving their three-story, once stylish house on Rusk Avenue as a boarding house. It was demolished about two years later. The Medical Arts Building was built on the site of the Dillingham house in 1925–26, but it in turn was demolished in 1987 for a parking lot.

82

William Henry Palmer house

1116 Travis Street at Dallas Avenue
built 1884; demolished ca. 1930

83

Levi M. Kaiser house

1404 Rusk Avenue at Austin Street
built ca. 1901; demolished ca. 1928

Levi Kaiser was in the cotton business with his brother Ike. The Kaiser house was, for Houston, unusual in its kinship to the Shingle-style houses of the Northeast with a low, horizontal aspect, neoclassical decorative devices, shingle cladding, and a stone base. The garden was a simple classic example of a Houston garden in the Victorian tradition: cement sidewalks circling the house, low foundation plantings, hanging baskets, and a lattice side fence screening the back yard where a lattice gazebo provided a private outdoor seating area. The house was demolished for a Shell gasoline station.

W. H. Palmer (1847–1907), the only son of Edward Albert Palmer (fig. 16), was a wholesale grocer and cotton factor at the time of construction of this house, but a few years later he became associated with the First National Bank. Palmer Memorial Church was built in memory of his son, Edward Albert Palmer II (1883–1908), who accidentally drowned while saving the life of his sister, Daphne, who married Edwin L. Neville (figs. 130–32, 256). Palmer's widow, Manilla Shepherd Palmer (1856–1920), continued to occupy the house until her death; it was demolished ten years later. Foley's garage now occupies the site.

84
William B. Chew house

1206 Fannin Street at Dallas Avenue
built ca. 1894; demolished ca. 1920
J. Arthur Tempest, architect

W. B. Chew was president of the Commercial National Bank and the Houston Land and Trust Company, treasurer of the Houston Oil Refining and Manufacturing Company, and a member of the Houston Cotton Exchange. The Chew house became a well-known landmark, and at the beginning of the twentieth century photographs of it were published often. It was demolished for a tire and battery company, but the site now stands empty, used for parking across from the old Sakowitz store downtown.

85
Lee B. Menefee house

2106 Crawford Street at Gray Avenue
built ca. 1900; demolished 1940s

The Menefee house was located next to the Rockwell house (fig. 86) and was strikingly similar to it in massing, in detail, and particularly in the upturned roofline. Both houses were surrounded by the same geometric-patterned wrought-iron fence with square cement posts. The Menefee garden was well tended, and numerous potted plants on the porch railings indicate an interest in growing things. Menefee sold the house to lumberman J. M. West, Sr., the father of oilmen "Silver Dollar" Jim and Wesley W. West. The West family occupied the house for at least a decade. It was demolished in the 1940s during World War II.

86

James M. Rockwell house

2116 Crawford Street at Webster
Avenue
built ca. 1900, demolished ca. 1980

J. M. Rockwell (1863–1931) was
born in Indiana and came to Houston
with his father in 1877. He joined the
lumber business with M. T. Jones
(fig. 90). At the height of his career
Rockwell owned twenty-four lumber
yards over a three-state area and had
significant banking interests as well.
Rockwell and his wife, Sara Wade
Richardson, were married in 1889.
They moved into this house just after the turn of the century. Like the
Menefee house (fig. 85), the Rockwell
house was more overtly picturesque
than other post-1900 houses and was
more closely related to the emerging
bungalow styles than the classically
derived Colonial houses that were
also popular at this time.

87

Hugh Waddell house
and garden

2404 Caroline Street at
McIlhenny Avenue
built ca. 1901; demolished late 1940s

Hugh Waddell was the owner of
Waddell's Furniture Company, formally founded in 1881 but actually
successor to L. J. Latham's furniture
business begun in the early 1840s.
The Waddell house represents the
transitional houses sometimes called
late Queen Anne–style that had
some Victorian-type ornament, more
rambling Victorian plans, and verticality combined with neoclassical
decoration and rounded porch columns. The simple garden around the
house on its large lot included vines
on a trellis and the popular lattice
dividing front and back yards. This
house was rented out after the family
vacated it in the 1920s. It became the
George Lewis Funeral Home and was
demolished in the late 1940s.

88
Jemison E. Lester house

3112 Main Street at Elgin Avenue
built ca. 1903; demolished ca. 1924
Olle J. Lorehn, architect

J. E. Lester was a cotton factor with the firm of Gohlman, Lester and Company. Built across Elgin Avenue from the current site of Walgreen's on South Main, the Lester house was considered far from town when it was constructed. Like the Waddell house (fig. 87), the architecture of the Lester house had transitional qualities, but it was more compact and heavier than the rambling Victorian styles. The oversized posts and wrought-iron gates provided an impressive entrance to the unusual vine-filled Victorian garden. Standing a mere twenty years, this house was always occupied by the Lester family.

89

Samuel Fain Carter house

1804 Crawford Street at Jefferson
Avenue
built 1899; demolished 1965
George E. Dickey, architect

S. F. Carter, a banker and lumberman, moved to Houston in 1892 from
Beaumont. The Carter house was
George Dickey's interpretation of the
Italianate. Its frame structure stood
on five-foot brick foundation piers
and was covered with wood block cut
to look like stone. The interior had
sixteen rooms and six fireplaces with
marble mantelpieces imported from
Europe. Its most unusual and interesting interior architectural feature
was an eight-paneled, leaded and
stained-glass dome that stood thirty-
five feet above the first floor in a ro-
tunda opened through the second
floor. A clear glass skylight on the
third floor protected the dome and
the gas (later electric) lights installed
above it, which lit the dome at night.
Although the garden was basically in
the Victorian tradition, the absence
of a fence and fuller shrubbery foundation planting were more typical of
twentieth-century landscaping. Carter's wife, Carrie Banks Carter, died
at eighty-three in 1944 and left the
house to the Bluebird Circle, who
sold it the next year to the Palm
Funeral Home, named for the palm
trees out front. The Carter house was
demolished after serving for twenty
years as a funeral home.

90

James I. Campbell–Martin
Tilford Jones house

2908 Main Street at Anita Avenue
built 1899; demolished 1937
George E. Dickey, architect

Like the Carter house (fig. 89), the
Campbell house was faced with cypress blocks cut to look like stone. It
also shared a similar plan with the
Carter house, but in this case was
rendered with French rather than
Italian stylistic details (see also figs.
178, 179). The house was purchased
just a few years after its construction
by M. T. Jones, founder of the Jones

Lumber Company. His nephew Jesse
Jones, who moved to Houston to
work with his uncle, lived in the
house from about 1902 to 1907 while
he was settling his uncle's estate. One
story relates that the stables were
converted to a garage when Jesse
Jones purchased a new Pierce-Arrow,
said to have been the first automobile
in Houston. In 1907 Mrs. Jones sold
the house to Settegast-Kopf for a funeral home, and it was sold again in
1915 to the Arabia Temple (Shri-
ners), who occupied the twenty-room
house as its headquarters for about
fifteen years. In the 1930s the house
became a rooming house until it was
demolished.

91

Henry S. Fox house

1206 Main Street at Dallas Avenue
built 1892–93; moved 1913;
demolished ca. 1927
J. Arthur Tempest, architect

This shingle- and wood-block-clad
chateau was built next door to the
Van Alstyne house (figs. 44, 53) for
Henry Fox, president of the Houston
National Bank. The most notable feature of the typically Victorian garden
was the pair of weeping mulberry
trees on either side of the entrance
walk. When Fox died his son moved
the house back and turned it to face
north at 906 Dallas. The Lanoma
Apartments were put up in the back
yard, and the Fox Apartments were
constructed on the original Main
Street house site with shops on the
ground floor. The Fox house, owned
by the Fox family until its demolition,
was a rooming house for its remaining years.

92

Abe M. Levy house

2016 Main Street at Gray Avenue
built 1906; demolished 1938
Olle J. Lorehn, architect

Abe and Haskell Levy established
Levy Brothers Drygoods in 1881 with
Abe Levy president. After Abe's
death in 1924, a biographer called
him the "Merchant Prince of Houston." He, Haskell, and their sister
Harriet built this grand house—
the most impressive of the Houston
châteaus, a French-derived type
popularized by Beaux Arts–trained
American architects such as Richard
Morris Hunt. The three siblings, none
of whom ever married, shared this
house for the rest of their lives. The
front entrance walk circling around a
center flower bed and the two urns
flanking the walk were the height of
fashion in garden design during the
first decade of the twentieth century.
A niece, Adelina, and her husband,
Leopold Meyer, lived in the house
with "Miss Harriet," and following
her wishes, they demolished the
house a year after her death. The
Meyers built a high-rise apartment
known as 2016 Main, which is still
standing, on the site. Their pent-
house apartment there contained
many furnishings from the old Levy
house.

93

Magnolia Park map

ca. 1889

Magnolia Park, owned by J. T. Brady (fig. 94), was opened to the public in 1890. Improvements included a pavilion-type clubhouse and docking facilities for pleasure boats. This map reveals the location of Magnolia Park in relation to the city of Houston, the port of Houston, and Harrisburg. The park design, with curving drives cut through the tall native magnolia trees, reflected the curvilinear planning that began in parks and cemetery parks (like Glenwood in Hous-ton) and later became fashionable for suburbs (like River Oaks). This type of more graceful, naturalistic planning was first advocated in the U.S. by Frederick Law Olmsted in parks and suburbs such as Central Park in New York and Riverside near Chicago. Magnolia Park became a popular recreation area outside Houston—just the distance for a Sunday drive and picnic by the bayou under the trees.

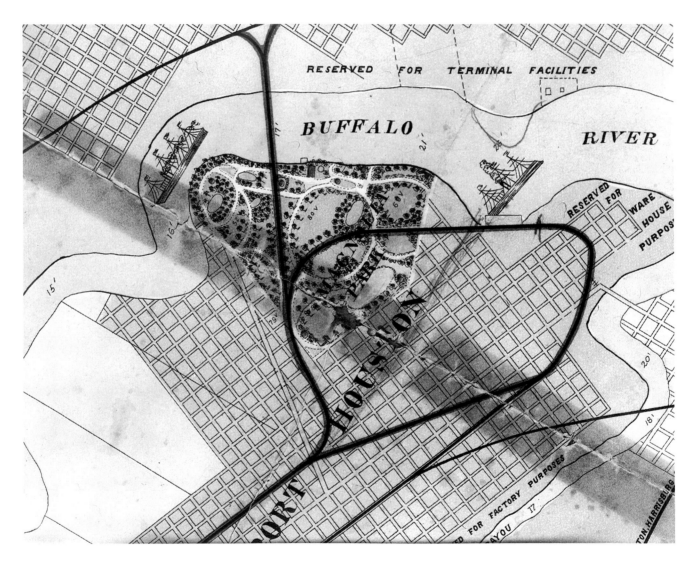

94

John Thomas Brady
plantation house

Milby Street at Harrisburg Boulevard
built ca 1870; moved; burned 1990

J. T. Brady was one of the most active
entrepreneurs on the Houston scene
in the latter part of the nineteenth
century. He owned one of the two
trolley lines in Houston as well as a
vast expanse of property along Buffalo Bayou toward Harrisburg, including Magnolia Park (figs. 2, 93)
near which he built this Greek Revival house where native oak trees
and evergreens graced the lawn.
Shrubs were spaced attractively
around the house and entrance walk.
Brick-lined rose beds flanked the
grass-covered drive leading to the
house. Although the Brady house was
moved about a block from its original
site and significantly altered, it survived with its tall, dignified columns
and remained in use as a residence
(multifamily rental property) longer
than any other Greek Revival house
in Houston.

95

City Park
(now Sam Houston Park)

Buffalo Bayou at Allen Parkway
near Bagby Street
ca. 1900

The natural beauty of the area along
Buffalo Bayou, even this close to
Houston development, with many native loblolly pines and water oaks is
obvious in this photograph. Two pa-
vilions, one on the winding drive for
carriages and one down the slope of
the land toward the bayou, give an
intimation of the pleasant prospects
available to Houstonians in the
downtown area at the turn of the
century. This land, donated along
with the Kellum-Noble house (fig.
261), was the first public park in
Houston. Still owned by the city, the
park is now the site of several museum houses maintained by the Harris County Heritage Society.

96

Gazebo at Bay Ridge

Morgan's Point
built ca. 1895; demolished

This large gazebo was constructed
by the Bay Ridge Park Association,
founded ca. 1890, as a recreational
pavilion for the families who built
summer homes on Morgan's Point
along this shoreline of Galveston Bay.
Like the popular garden gazebos in
town, this open structure provided
an ideal protected spot from which to
gaze at the bay.

97

John Thaddeus Scott bay house, entrance garden

711 Bay Ridge Road, Morgan's Point
built ca. 1900; extant

J. T. Scott, Sr., came to Houston in
1886 and married Martha Rebecca
Campbell in 1893. The Scotts were
famous for their hospitality; at the
bay friends enjoyed Sunday lunch or
sailing picnics on an island or singing
together on the pier in the moonlight.
Behind the houses at Morgan's Point,
where the driveways entered from

the road, more tender plant varieties
could be placed where they were
better protected from the sun and
sea. The J. T. Scott entrance garden
was unusual in its formality, more
like town gardens. It had a round
raised bed in the center of a circular
driveway planted with flowers and
ground cover.

98
Harry S. Filson bay house

835 Bay Ridge Road, Morgan's Point
built 1911, remodeled 1923; extant
Sanguinet, Staats and Barnes,
architects
Alfred C. Finn, architect for
remodeling

The Filson garden, planned in conjunction with the house during remodeling, was in the naturalistic tradition with clumped bulbs planted in the lawn and tropical plants and ferns near the house. This type of landscape, with low-maintenance plants, was well suited to a house at the bay not constantly occupied.

99

Courtlandt Place east gateway

built 1912; extant
William Ward Watkin, architect
Arthur Seiders, landscape consultant
ca. 1907

The east entrance to Courtlandt Place differed from the west entrance only in that it was designed with an inviting crescent-shaped curve, and handsome lanterns instead of large orbs topped the gateposts. Today the west entrance is permanently closed, and a locked iron gate across the east entrance gives access only to residents. Such architectural gateways were popular all over the country; they graced both private, enclave subdivisions and the main entrance streets to much larger and more public developments.

100

John Wiley Link–Thomas Peter Lee house

3812 Montrose Boulevard
built 1912; extant
Sanguinet and Staats, architects

Built as a showcase house by the developer of Montrose, J. W. Link, this house now serves as the administration building for the University of St. Thomas. The landscaping around the house was sparse and had a classical balance. (See also fig. 242.) The esplanade (now gone) in the foreground was an important element of new suburban developments encouraged by the City Beautiful movement. Along with public landscaping and green, parklike areas, these esplanades showed that the area was dedicated to developing the landscape as part of an integrated environment.

101

Magnolia Park Addition

1909 promotional advertisement

Although it was used by the public, Magnolia Park (fig. 93) was on privately owned land. The Magnolia Park Land Co. began offering lots for sale in June 1909. It is interesting to observe the successive uses of this area where magnificent magnolia trees had greeted the first settlers (fig. 2). The proximity of the turning basin for the deep-water port helped assure the successful development of Magnolia Park as a residential subdivision. Most of the magnolia trees were cut down when roads were built and lots were readied for construction. The houses built here were modest. Magnolia Park and Houston Heights vied to attract new residents. Today this area is almost completely devoid of vegetation; industrial facilities along and near the Ship Channel have replaced most of the early twentieth-century houses built in the Magnolia Park Addition.

102

Park Place Addition
1912 promotional advertisement

Park Place was located southeast of Houston on Sims Bayou. The advertisements extolled the virtues of living in the "natural beauty of the landscape" combined with up-to-date utilities and transportation to town. Despite its idyllic setting, by 1914 Park Place had only fifty houses, probably because it was nine miles from Houston. In new subdivisions where public transportation did not materialize, sales were slow, and in some cases new developments did not survive. In contrast, building boomed in places like Houston Heights, Woodland Heights, and the South End additions, where streetcar lines provided transportation into the city.

An October Picnic at Park Place

Simms Bayou in the Vicinity of Park Place

103

Houston street scene, ca. 1910

1100 block of Milam Street

Good landscape design was admired
and imitated in many areas of the
city. Neighborhoods that were not
necessarily part of a planned development also reflected the parklike
atmosphere created by a succession
of green lawns and sidewalks shaded
by rows of trees. Five blocks along
Milam and Louisiana between Lamar
and Leeland were known informally
as the "Bering Settlement" because
so many Bering relatives lived there.
The large house to the left with
double-height Doric columns and
denticulated eaves (1118 Milam) belonged to Henry William Cortes, who
was married to Mary Bering. Mary's
brother, Julius Cornelius Bering,
lived at 1112 Milam, the second
house from the left. J. C. Bering was
married to Mellie Cortes, Henry's sister, making these neighbors double
in-laws. Together H. W. Cortes and
J. C. Bering founded the Bering-
Cortes hardware business in 1885.
The E. W. Gruendler house is in the
foreground.

104

W. E. Miller house and garden

310 Robin Street, Fourth Ward
built ca. 1910 ; demolished

Professor W. E. Miller graduated
from Prairie View College in 1890
and moved to Houston's Fourth Ward
in 1892, where he built this house
around 1910. The Miller house was
more substantial than most of its
neighbors, and the fenced garden
was carefully landscaped. The vines
on the decorative picket fence and
porch railings, along with the well-
spaced hanging baskets of Boston
fern, created a warm, well-tended
atmosphere in the Miller garden.
The upstairs screened porch was no
doubt used as a sleeping porch during the hot summer months.

105

Benjamin Jesse Covington house

2219 Dowling Street at Hadley Avenue, Third Ward
built 1911; demolished 1980

Benjamin Covington, M.D., moved to Houston in 1903 after graduating from Meharry Medical College in Nashville, Tennessee. He was an influential leader in Houston's African American community. The Covingtons hosted Booker T. Washington in this house in 1911 soon after it was completed. Architecturally, the house was similar to many large neoclassical houses built in Houston between 1910 and 1915. The Covington garden was simple, with climbing roses on the porch railings and the side entrance doorway; a statue of the classic figure of Flora on a pedestal in the side front garden provided a fashionable touch. Dr. Covington died in 1961 at the age of eighty-nine. Although it was listed in the National Register of Historic Places, the Covington house was demolished in 1980.

106

The Rossonian

913–919 McKinney Avenue at Fannin Street
built 1910; demolished ca. 1952
Sanguinet and Staats, architects

J. O. Ross built this eight-floor luxury apartment hotel with 246 rooms and fourteen apartments and named it for himself. The inclusion of a roof garden with pergolas where one might sit in the shade and enjoy the outdoors indicated the popularity of private gardens in Houston. This sophisticated building was a grand addition to the city, and its Beaux Arts classicism was compatible with the new architecture of Houston banks and office buildings that began in 1904 in a movement parallel to the construction of neoclassical Colonial Revival houses. In the 1940s The Rossonian became the Ambassador Hotel and Apartments, which had eighty-five units.

107

Jonas Shearn Rice house

2304 Crawford Street at
Hadley Avenue
built 1902–1903;
demolished ca. 1933
S. A. Oliver, architect

J. S. Rice was a member of the complicated Baldwin-Allen-Rice family so visible in early Houston's public life. The oldest of ten children, he was named for his great-grandfather, Jonas Baldwin of Baldwinsville, New York (the father of Charlotte Baldwin Allen, considered the mother of Houston). Rice's obituary on March 12, 1931, called him Houston's pioneer financier. His varied business interests centered on banking and lumber, and his house was the first large Colonial Revival one to be constructed in Houston. Rice lived there until his death, and it stood vacant for about two years before it was demolished by the trustees of his estate.

108

Edward R. Richardson house

1311 Holman Avenue
built 1903; moved to 3307 Austin
Street 1926; extant

E. R. Richardson was a partner in Cargill and Richardson, a cotton and grain brokerage firm. He died soon after the house was completed, and it was sold. The Richardson house is a more restrained and more academic interpretation of the Colonial Revival style than two other prominent Houston examples: the Rice house (fig. 107) and the Nash house (fig. 109).

109
William R. Nash house

217 Westmoreland Avenue
built 1905; extant
H. C. Cooke and Company, architects

The Nash house was built by an enterprising rancher who wanted a showplace for a home. The exuberance with which the neoclassical has been expressed here borders on the baroque; ornament exists everywhere from the denticulated frieze, to the modilion brackets under the eaves, to the garland swags above the windows. The Nashes owned the house until 1944 even though they did not live there consistently and they intermittently rented it out. After 1928, however, the house was occupied by the family until Mr. Nash died in 1931 and his widow moved back to their ranch permanently. Since 1944 the Nash house has had several owners.

110

Thomas L. Hackney–
James J. Sweeney house

2210 Main Street at Hadley Avenue
built 1903; demolished 1968
Olle J. Lorehn, architect

This house was occupied by a succession of prominent Houstonians. In April of 1903 Hackney bought $2,622 worth of furniture from Waddell's to furnish his new house. But the next year he sold it to Mrs. J. I. Campbell, who was recently widowed. She kept the house only eight months, selling it to lumberman James M. West. Three years later, in 1907, West sold it to jeweler J. J. Sweeney. The Sweeneys, who owned the house for nearly fifty years, constructed a rear addition with a fifth bedroom but never changed the character of the house. In 1936 it was leased to the Working Girl's Club, and in 1959 it was leased to Mrs. C. V. Robinson for her new Bertha's Mexican Restaurant, which became a Houston institution. Bertha's moved out of the old house, and it was demolished in 1968.

MODERN DWELLINGS

FLOOR PLANS (A) FOR DESIGN No. 1

111

Floor plan, design no. 200

Modern Dwellings (1898)
Barber and Klutts, architects

The façade (not pictured) of this Barber plan is remarkably similar to that of the Hackney-Sweeney house (fig. 110). This coincidence indicates that, like George Dickey, Olle Lorehn based some of his designs on published catalog plans. Although these floor plans may not be exactly like those of the Hackney house, they were surely similar enough to use for illustration. Another point of coincidence between the Barber plan and the Hackney house is that the $25,000 figure that Barber said would build his version was precisely the amount for which Hackney sold the house three years after construction.

112

Sanborn fire insurance map

1907
Freedmen's Town, shotgun houses
1500 block George (now Victor)
Street and O'Neil Street
built ca. 1880s; partially demolished

Six of these houses on the south side
of Victor Street, 1502–1512, are still
standing. Note the narrow streets
and small lots.

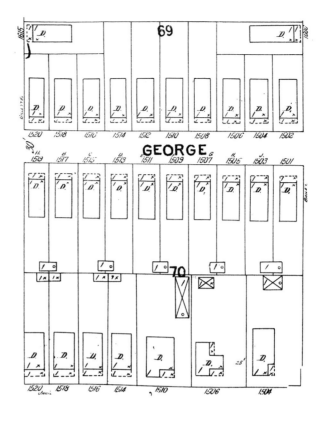

113

Sanborn fire insurance map

1907
2303 Main Street—
William L. Rogers house
2317 Main Street—
Frederick A. Gieseke house
2316 Fannin Street—
Dr. James H. Bute house
1010 Hadley Street—
Lynch Davidson house

Comparing this Main Street block
with a Freedmen's Town block (fig.
112), which was considerably smaller,
one sees the relative density of the
two neighborhoods. Not only are the
houses themselves much larger, but
the outbuildings are more numerous,
larger, and expected to serve more
complex functions.

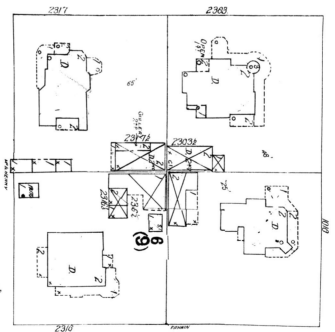

114

Alfred Thomas Lucas house

2017 Milam Street at Gray Avenue
built 1905; demolished 1961

Alfred Thomas Lucas was the son
and partner of James S. Lucas (fig.
32) in the general contracting firm,
James S. Lucas and Son. The family
owned brickyards and cement works
as well as a large construction business. This house was unusual in
Houston for its overall cast-stone veneer (see also fig. 214). After Lucas's
death his widow, Maria Langham,
married the Hollywood film star
Clark Gable (1931–39).

115

Louis C. Luckel house

3019 Main Street at Rosalie Avenue
built ca. 1903; demolished ca. 1922

The Luckel house was one of the few
large Main Street houses built on the
east side of the street. The house appears much larger than it actually

was because of the heavy cast-stone–
clad piers and long porches. The
Luckel family occupied this house
until it was demolished.

116

William A. Cooke house

1724 Alta Vista, Forest Hill
built 1912; extant
W. A. Cooke, architect

William A. Cooke became manager of his father's busy firm, H. C.
Cooke and Company. He designed
this bungalow for his family in an
unconventional style for Houston,
demonstrating his own architectural
sophistication.

117
William S. Wall house

3717 Main Street at Alabama Avenue
built 1911; demolished 1960
Sanguinet and Staats, architects

The Spanish Colonial Revival architecture of the Cooke house (fig. 116) and the Wall house was not popular in Houston, but these images represent just one of the wide range of house styles considered acceptable. The Wall house became a doctor's office in 1929.

118

Inglenook,

John Henry Kirby house

2006 Smith Street at Pierce Avenue
built 1893–94; remodeled 1897–
1900; incorporated into new house
1925

James Sterling Price erected this
typically Victorian, three-story, shingle-clad house on a full-block site
and sold it to the Kirbys in 1896. This
photograph, probably taken around
1898, shows the Kirby house shortly
after it was purchased and painted.
The garden, planted by the Prices,
was a fashionable Victorian one that

used the principle of "scatter" planting. The circular greenhouse was also

a fashionable and practical structure
for those interested in horticulture.

119

Inglenook,

side view looking north

The addition of a conservatory on the
west side of the remodeled Kirby
house was a sign of elegant living at
the turn of the century.

120
Inglenook,
fountain and lily pond

The elaborate baroque water parterres filled with water lilies added a touch of prestige because of the elegance of garden design and the rarity of water lilies. These plants had been brought to England from the Amazon by Sir Richard Schomburgh in 1837; they were first grown successfully there in the conservatories of Sir Joseph Paxton at Chatsworth. Requiring large pools and a high temperature, they were well suited to a Houston garden.

121
Inglenook, pergola

At the turn of the century, the fashion for arbors and gazebos gave way to pergolas, a development probably brought to the attention of Americans by Charles Platt's 1894 publications on Italian villa gardens. The pergola was one of the many features of this garden that earned it the designation "Italianate."

122

Inglenook, greenhouse

Not only did the Kirbys' gardener
tend the greenhouse and the gardens, including the propagation of
new plants (note the stakes), but he
also was responsible for the vegetable
garden and care of the milk cows.

123

John Henry Kirby natatorium

2006 Smith Street at the rear of the
Kirby house
built ca. 1901; demolished

The natatorium, built behind the
house, was an immense building constructed about 1901 in the current
neoclassical genre. It had a huge
domed ballroom on the second floor
(fig. 223) above an enclosed swimming pool on the first (fig. 224). The
Boston landscape gardener Joseph
Henry Curtis made the plans and
suggested native plants for the Kirby
garden after consulting a professor at
the University of Texas. He used palmettos (native) and altheas (a hardy
introduction) as the screening plant
material around a parterre rose
garden.

124

Inglenook, Mirror Lake

The practice of having a "rustic" garden feature evolved during the nineteenth-century Romantic movement when a desire to return to Nature pervaded not only gardening, but art, architecture, and belles lettres. Curtis used the idea of a small lake crossed by a rustic, curving bridge and surrounded by weeping willows to create a particularly romantic setting.

125

Robert Crews Duff
house and garden

803 McGowen Avenue
at Milam Street
built 1910; moved to face 2421 Milam
1937; extant
George Freuhling, architect and
builder

The Duff house was another of Houston's grand Colonial Revival houses. The center planting in the entrance sidewalk was a popular design feature in the gardens of this period, and the equidistant spacing of plants on either side of the front walk emphasizes the architectural symmetry of the house. A succession of shallow terraces gives an impression of height to the house, and a feeling of greater distance is accomplished by the rows of plants that follow the architectural lines of the house and balustrade. The Duff house and gar-

dens were the site of the numerous publicized soirees Mrs. Duff, a musician and patron of the performing arts, hosted. Subsequently the house served as the headquarters for the City Federation of Women's Clubs. Although the exterior of the house has not been maintained, the interior is sound and still contains many of its original appointments. The library is unchanged and has its original wall-coverings, but the sparkling beveled and leaded-glass front doors look out onto a much-changed city.

126
Duff house, side gardens

Trees and shrubbery follow the straight lines of the house and sidewalks. The expanse of the Duff gardens can be appreciated from this view, which shows the first St. Paul's Methodist Church building (now demolished) in the background.

127
Duff house, Psyche garden

The connotations of the classical figures placed in the Duff garden were romantic: Psyche, the human soul, is attended by Venus, the goddess of love, and Faunus, the god of untouched Nature. These statues as well as the balustrades and urns that defined the terraces and a pair of lions that guarded the front entrance were carved by Oswald Lassig in 1916. Lassig, an Austrian stone carver, was brought to Houston to work on the sculptural relief at the Rice Institute.

128

Harris Masterson house, maze garden

3702 Burlington, Westmoreland
built 1906–1907; demolished ca.
1959
R. D. Steele, architect

The hedged maze was used in the seventeenth- and early eighteenth-century court and manor gardens as a decorative and entertaining puzzle planting. Here it performed the same service for the Masterson grandchildren. The Colonial Revival Masterson house was a bit unusual for Houston in that it was brick and its entrance pavilion was an elegant semicircular porch rather than a straight gabled one.

Low hedging provided a decorative
frame for specific play areas in the
Masterson gardens and gave an artistic unity to the design of the whole
outdoor space.

130

Edwin L. Neville house

11 Courtlandt Place
built 1914; extant
Birdsall P. Briscoe, architect

Briscoe probably designed the garden of the Neville house. A grass terrace extended the built terrace and was a connecting link between the house and garden, which are well integrated but with primary emphasis on architecture.

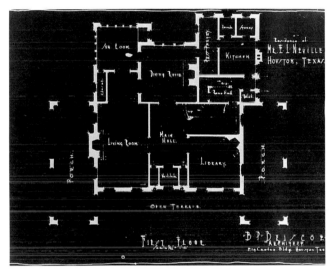

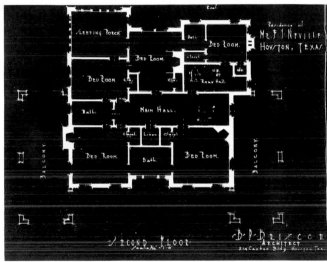

131

Neville house, first-floor plan

132

Neville House, second-floor plan

133

John Wanroy Garrow house

19 Courtlandt Place
built 1914; extant
Birdsall P. Briscoe, architect

New houses in Courtlandt Place, such as the Garrow and Neville houses, were designed with a variety of stylistic references, the eclectic architectural fashion that recurred around 1914 signaling an end to the Colonial Revival preference. These new house styles were more historically accurate than their Victorian counterparts had been. Note the exclusion of the front porch, an architectural evolution. The garden at the Garrow house was planted in the typical Briscoe manner of straight lines following the architecture; variety was obtained only by contrasting the vertical and the horizontal or by plant texture.

134

Miramichi, Edward Andrew Peden lake house

north shore, Clear Lake
built ca. 1850s; remodeled ca. 1907;
demolished 1940s

Miramichi is a river in New Brunswick, Canada, that runs through a favorite vacation area with country lodges and salmon fishing. The Peden family must have had a connection to this resort to have named their summer home in Harris County after it (see also figs. 135, 160, 212). The typical and beautiful waterfront planting was planned by Edward Dewson and installed by Edward Teas in 1911.

135

Miramichi, entrance drive

Behind the Peden lake house, native oaks hung with Spanish moss bespeak a natural environment. The few shrubs and low planting along the drive enhance that impression.

136
Henry Thomas Staiti house and gardens

421 Westmoreland Avenue, Westmoreland
built ca. 1905; remodeled 1915; moved to Sam Houston Park 1988; extant
Alfred C. Finn, architect for remodeling; Edward Dewson, landscape architect

Henry T. Staiti, son of an Italian immigrant, moved to Houston and built this house in 1905. A successful pioneer in Texas oil, he extensively remodeled and relandscaped his house after it was badly damaged in the 1915 hurricane. The wide expanse of lawn gave a feeling of spaciousness to the Staiti gardens. The pergola provided privacy to the parterre rose garden and greenhouse behind it and architecturally framed the border flower garden. A decorative bench is centered on the screening wall that divides the front lawn from the utility yard. The Staiti heirs donated the house to the Harris County Heritage Society, and it was divided into two parts, moved to Sam Houston Park, and reassembled and restored for use as a museum house.

137

Staiti house, landscape plan

The Staiti gardens were installed almost exactly as drawn by the landscape architect in 1917. Only the fan-shaped parterres in front of the garden bench were omitted. Dewson was the only professional landscape architect living in Houston before the 1920s. These gardens went untended for many years and were destroyed when the house was moved to Sam Houston Park.

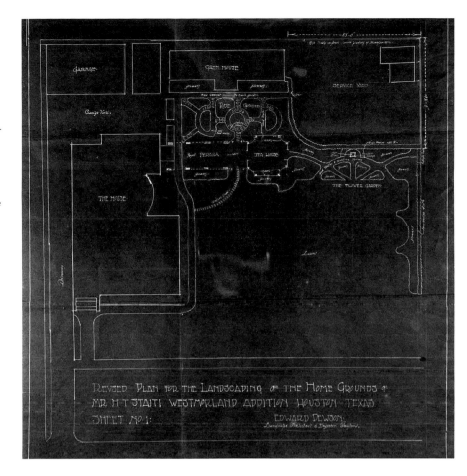

138

Staiti house, parterre garden

Both the tea house and the greenhouse on the opposite side of the geometric open parterre for roses can be seen in this photograph. The paths and beds were made decorative with narrow cement edging. The garden is flanked by plantings of cape jasmine edged with violets.

139

The Oaks, Edwin Brewington
Parker–Capt. James Addison
Baker house

2310 Baldwin
built 1909–1910;
demolished ca. 1955
Sanguinet and Staats, architects

This seven-acre site had eighty native live oak trees for which Parker
named his estate. With its "Modern"
Wrightian architecture, the house
was very avant-garde for Houston.
The house was purchased by Capt.
Baker in 1923 after his law partner,
Parker, died. In 1941, when Baker
died, he left the property to the Rice
Institute, which transferred it to M.
D. Anderson Hospital. For six years
The Oaks provided an eighty-bed
hospital and research facility for this
fledgling institution. It was demolished shortly after the hospital moved
to the Medical Center in 1950.

140

The Oaks, entrance

The twentieth century reintroduced
the basic garden design principles of
the natural landscape garden popular
in the eighteenth century. At The
Oaks a simple landscape of grass and
trees was considered the best complement to good architecture.

141

The Oaks, back garden

Flowers need not be neglected in such a "Modern" landscape. In the Parkers' back garden, flowers in neat raised beds provided lavish color. The compartmental divisions of the garden expressed the Wrightian philosophy of functionalism in garden design. The unity of the house and garden exemplified the integration of architecture and outdoor surroundings into a single unit for domestic living.

142

The Country Place, Walter Benona Sharp house, entrance

4301 Main Street between Eagle and Wheeler avenues
built ca. 1895; demolished 1938

W. B. Sharp (1870–1912) came to Texas from Tennessee with his widowed father in 1878. By the age of eighteen Sharp was contracting to drill water wells in the Dallas area, and from this experience he became a successful driller in Corsicana, considered to be the first commercial oil field in Texas. He married Estelle

Boughton the following year, and they moved to Houston in 1905, when Sharp organized the Producers Oil Company, which later became a subsidiary of the Texas Company (Texaco). Sharp was also a founding partner of the Sharp-Hughes Tool Company, but he sold his interest to Howard Hughes before it became a multimillion-dollar operation. In late 1906 the Sharps bought the house, a 35-acre estate south of town near the Aransas Pass Railroad, from Gustav F. Sauter. The Sharps improved the property, installed extensive gardens, and built tennis courts. From 1917 to 1922 R. L. Blaffer, a founder of Humble Oil Company (Exxon), leased this house from Mrs. Sharp before he built his mansion in Shadyside. The house was vacant before it was converted to offices that were rented by some of Houston's best design professionals: architects John Staub, Kenneth Franzheim, Claude Hooton, Harry D. Payne, Maurice Sullivan, and Birdsall Briscoe; the Houston Studio Garden, landscape architects; and Clare Deman, a sculptor. The Sharp house was demolished for Sears and Roebuck, which opened in 1940 and still stands on the site.

143
The Country Place, lawn opening

The open glade near the house was reminiscent of Jens Jensen's "sun openings." The principles Jensen advocated—use of native plants, hardy introductions arranged in natural plantings, and attention to plant textures and patterns of sun and shade—are the cardinal qualities of the Sharp garden.

144
The Country Place, specimen pittisporum

This specimen pittisporum was impressive and a tribute to the horticultural expertise of the gardener. Although pittisporum was (and is) widely used in Houston gardens, such large specimens were rare and are no longer observable. Other such specimen plants were nurtured in the Sharp garden, including a large date palm (fig. 143), which thrives in the semitropical climate and also resists the devastating effects of hurricanes. The Sharp house was nearly hidden by the lush vegetation. It was a rather large but typical rambling, two-story frame house with Victorian details.

145
The Country Place, screened porch

The Sharps' screened porch projected into the gardens with open views of the landscape on three sides. This type of room, usually with two exposed sides, served as a summer living room where cross-breezes could mitigate the stultifying Houston heat.

146

The Rice Institute, Academic
Court hedge planting

South Main Street
planned 1909; installed 1912–15
Cram, Goodhue and Ferguson,
architects

The long lines of clipped hedges in
the courtyard simulated the water
canals of eastern Mediterranean gardens. The strong horizontal lines of
the hedges in this photograph were
not yet matched by the verticals of
the cypresses, but the intended balance was evident.

147
Hermann Park site plan

South Main Street
1916
George Ks-4essler, landscape architect

A beautiful mixture of formal land-scape design at the entrance of Hermann Park, donated to the city of Houston by George Hermann, created a line of sight into the park down an esplanaded boulevard and across a long reflecting pool to a "grand basin." A circling drive enclosed a wooded area around the reflecting pool and a circular parterre with straight paths radiating through the woods. The shape of the grand basin was irregular, probably following the topography, and the proposed avenues through the park, though esplanaded, were winding. In this plan, based on the ideas of Frederick Law Olmsted, formal areas for public gatherings and naturalistic settings are well integrated.

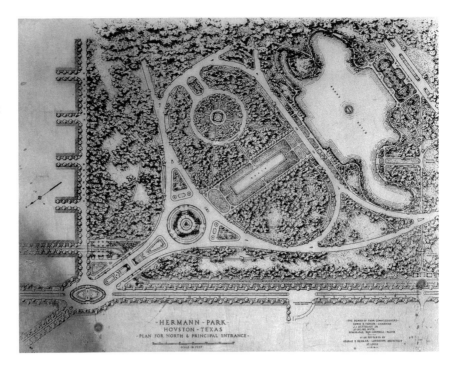

148
Aerial view of Shadyside and traffic circle

South Main Street between Montrose and Sunset boulevards

The advantages of civic planning are abundantly clear in this area south of downtown. Not only is the area one of the most beautiful in Houston, but traffic still moves efficiently and gracefully after eighty years of growth and development. Joseph S. Cullinan, who was responsible for bringing George Kessler to the attention of the board of park commissioners, purchased thirty-seven acres

from the Hermann estate in 1916 on which he commissioned Kessler to design the new subdivision of Shadyside. The Cullinan house (demolished), designed by the architect James P. Jamieson from St. Louis, was the first constructed there in 1917–19. The Cullinan house is visible in the lower right corner. The first section of the Museum of Fine Arts appears in the triangle between Main and Montrose.

149

E. B. Nichols–William Marsh Rice–D.B. Cherry house

Courthouse Square, facing north
built ca. 1850; altered and moved
several times; moved to Sam Houston
Park 1957; extant
watercolor by Thomas Flintoff, 1852

Thomas Flintoff was an itinerant painter known for his oil portraits. Flintoff painted five scenic watercolors on his visit to Houston, leaving the earliest known images of public buildings and churches. The impressive Nichols-Rice-Cherry house was included by Flintoff in the background of this watercolor of the recently completed Harris County Courthouse and Courthouse Square. Unusual for Houston at the time were the Ionic columns, which are clearly visible in this picture. The painting confirms that the porches of the Nichols-Rice-Cherry house originally wrapped around three sides of the structure. The house survives in Sam Houston Park with porches only on its façade.

150

Houston Art Glass Company

1718 Congress Avenue
Business Album of Houston
The McKay Company, comp.
(Houston, ca. 1911)

151

John McClellan & Co., Inc.

ca. 1911
1012 Texas Avenue

153

Japanese Art Store

ca. 1911

715 Main Street

154

Lottman's improved mosquito net bar frame, no. 3

C. F. Lottman Mattress Catalogue,
January 1, 1912

By 1900 most beds sold in Harris County were manufactured in other parts of the country and were not equipped for mosquito netting. C. F. Lottman found a way to satisfy the local market by adapting a mosquito net bar to contemporary bed frames.

SLEEP ON A SOUTHERN QUEEN 30 NIGHTS FREE.

Lottman's Improved Mosquito Net Bar Frame

No. 3 Bar Frame

We enamel any color desired.   Made any size —single or double.
We also finish in Vernice Martin.

Price with ordinary size clamps . . . . $25.00 per dozen
Price with 2-inch clamps . . . . 27.00 per dozen
Vernice Martin finish 50 cents each each extra list.

TRY OUR COTS NEXT TIME—SEE DIFFERENCE.

155

Mother (Cora Root Peden)
with baby Stella Alexandra
Peden

August 21, 1906

Although baby Stella's mother is putting her into a fairly plain, painted
iron crib, its half-tester is gracefully
covered with lacy mosquito netting.
The netting served a genuine purpose, as it had in Houston since the
1830s.

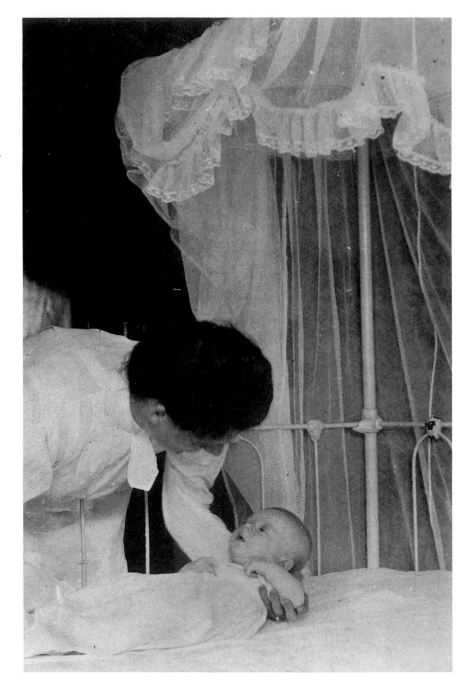

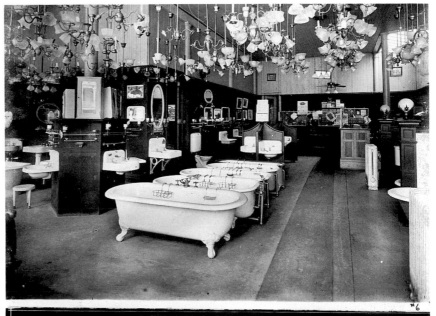

156

Rocking chair

ca. 1907

E. A. Hudson

*The Standard Blue Book of Texas
Who's Who Edition De Luxe of
Houston*
(Houston: Who's Who Publishing,
ca. 1907), 51

Wicker, rattan, and cane furniture
appears in numerous Houston interiors and on porches. It was cool to
sit upon, lightweight, stylish, and reasonably inexpensive. It lent a light,
airy quality to rooms that might otherwise have been overwhelmed by
monumental furnishings and elaborate upholstery. This rocker seems to
be a later version of the one used by
Mrs. T. W. House, Jr., in her bedroom (fig. 166).

157

Keithly Company, Inc.

ca. 1911

811–813 Main Street

158

*S. Karpen & Bros.,
Chicago, Ill.*

Upholstered Furniture
(Chicago: privately printed, 1900?),
cover

The Colonial Revival was so important to turn-of-the-century decorative
arts that S. Karpen & Bros. Furniture
Company put these two "colonial"
figures on the cover of their 1900
catalog. The characters obviously approved of Karpen's wares, although
the chair that they are inspecting
more closely resembles a classical
model from the 1820s than one made
fifty years earlier. The John Kirby
family owned Karpen furniture (figs.
184, 185).

159
Ed. C. Smith Furniture
Company
ca. 1911
1009 Texas Avenue

The Arts-and-Crafts–style desk in
the foreground is similar to the type
made by the Lifetime Furniture Company of Grand Rapids, Michigan.

ED. C. SMITH FURNITURE COMPANY
PHONE PRESTON 1260   1009 TEXAS AVE.

160

Fireplace: Stella Peden reading, Miramichi

ca. 1912

Although this is a twentieth-century photograph, it documents the interior of a simple cottage (figs. 134, 135) built on Clear Lake before the Civil War. The large wood-burning hearth framed by a midcentury board mantel contains a cooking pot suspended from a chain. The scene's simplicity is appealing: bare floors made of wide, loose-fitting planks covered with a rag hearth rug, a favorite photograph or two, perhaps a betty (fat burning) lamp hanging under the mantel next to a mammoth paper wasp's nest, and on the shelf miscellaneous undistinguished ceramics and metalwares, including a Chinese export, blue-and-white, willow-pattern plate.

161

Parlor, Simpson house

ca. 1900

The Simpson house (fig. 36) parlor is
a comfortable blend of old and new.
Its furniture, according to family tradition, was purchased in Cincinnati
by Rebecca Wheeler Simpson at the
time she and her husband moved
into the home. It is typical of the Renaissance Revival furniture associated with Charles Locke Eastlake
and made by midwestern factories.
The sunflower repeat wallpaper
frieze done in the manner of the English designer Walter Crane, the sunflower motif inlaid in the mantel pi-
lasters, the coal-burning hearth, gas
chandeliers, pier and over-mantel
mirrors, the hall stand visible through
the right door, and the comparatively
narrow doors all indicate a home of
the early 1880s. However, the art
pottery on the mantel and on the pier
table appears to have been made
about 1900 at Sophie Newcomb College in New Orleans. The rolltop
desk, the wicker and deep rockers,
and an elaborate portiere superimposed on a small door all point to a
turn-of-the-century photograph of a
well-maintained older interior.

162

George W. Collings–
Almeron F. Amerman house

35 Collings Place, north side
Buffalo Bayou
built late 1870s; demolished 1928

163

Dining room, Collings–Amerman house

ca. 1900

Almeron F. Amerman and his wife, Cornelia, lived north of downtown Houston on the banks of White Oak Bayou in a nice but not grand home. According to Houston city directories, the property was occupied by George W. Collings, a brickmaker, as early as 1877, although the exact date for this house is unknown. Mrs. Amerman's immaculate dining table is an extension model that rolls on efficient, unpretentious casters. Her dining chairs are economical, too. With their pressed crest rails, they were probably made of oak and were perhaps bought from a local purveyor of moderately priced furniture. Although both gas and electricity were available in Houston at this time, the Amermans continued to depend on their hanging kerosene lamp. The Amerman dining room is photographed from the adjacent parlor, which contains a fireplace (probably coal) with a ready-made surround. These elaborate mantels were made in factories elsewhere and shipped to local suppliers like C. L. and Theo. Bering (fig. 152).

164

A. Earl Amerman, Collings–Amerman house

ca. 1900

Not all Houston houses had handsome, gilt-framed paintings suspended from picture moldings decorating their walls; many probably more closely resembled this interior. Amerman is standing in an unidentified room in his parents' home (fig. 162) before what appears to be a simple two-color wallpaper. A print is tacked directly onto the wall, as are two series of photographs carefully laced together. Laced photos both make an attractive pattern in themselves and eliminate a number of tack holes in the wall. At the time of this photograph, Amerman was probably just finishing law school. Mayor of Houston from 1918 to 1921, either he or someone else must have decided that three of the wall decorations were inappropriate, for the glass negative from which this photograph was made was reworked, thereby obscuring the images.

165

Drawing room, House, Jr., house

ca. 1890

So impressive was the T. W. House, Jr., house (fig. 41) that the *Galveston News* carried a detailed description of its interior: "The drawing room is entered by a door on the right of the hall, and here you are struck at once by the dainty effect of the white and gold which prevails, in strong contrast to the grave tones of the hall. The furnishing of the room is artistically planned, for the carpet of soft brown and wood shades forms the basis from which the tones gradually lighten until the pale tints of the ceiling are reached. The furniture is upholstered in tapestry of a paler shade of brown, tinged with a woody green, and finished with silk plush of the green. A handsome étagère of French gilt lined with mirrors, and a double stand of white onyx and gilt brighten the room. To the left of the stand is an easel in white and gold, holding a panel picture framed in the same colors. On the stand and étagère are handsome pieces of royal Worcesterware, and on the mantel, which is of white and gold, with brass firedogs and fender, are more vases and bowls of the same ware in white and gold. The chandelier is of oxidized silver, and fine lace curtains cover the broad windows."

The Worcester is probably the soft paste porcelain variety made by the Royal Worcester Porcelain Company in England in the 1890s. Hanging above the étagère is a pleasant painting that may be a regional landscape. The still-life print displayed on the easel is noteworthy not so much for the print but for its molded gold and white Aesthetic-style frame.

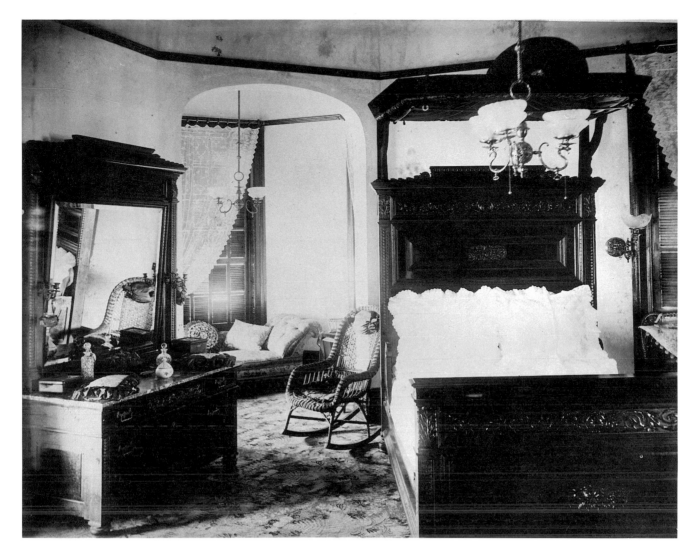

166

Master bedroom, House, Jr., house

ca. 1890

Mr. and Mrs. House kept their older mahogany furniture when they refurbished their bedroom. A late 1870s half-tester, devoid of mosquito netting but retaining its mosquito bars, looms above their bed. Mrs. House's toiletries rest on the marble-topped bureau that is outfitted with two candle brackets, two small pillows (pin cushions?), two boxes, a ceramic jar, and two fancy bottles. In the alcove is an ottoman or daybed. The alcove and bedroom have hanging gas lamps; a third gas lamp is mounted on the wall. However, during the course of remodeling George Dickey and the owners may have elected to wire the house with electricity, for two of the chandeliers' arms have pull chains. The owners, like so many others of their age, participated in the Industrial Revolution by going from candles and kerosene to electricity in one generation. New multicolored, fern-patterned carpeting and a demure rocker complete the scene.

167

Daughter's bedroom, House, Jr., house

ca. 1890

A journalist described this daughter's bedroom after remodeling as being "in bamboo, white and maple, with blue ornaments." The Houses had probably owned the bed and cheval glass for several years, for its "faux bamboo" style was fairly common in better homes in the 1880s. To this set the owner has added two lightweight wicker rockers, a Louis XV revival fall-front desk, and a richly upholstered ottoman, which, in conjunction with floral carpeting, probably introduced the aforementioned blue. In the cheval glass, itself a nineteenth-century form, one sees Miss House's mantel.

168

Daughter's bedroom, House, Jr., house

ca. 1890

The second House daughter had an equally attractive room. The *Galveston News* described this room as "antique oak with yellow decorations," having "been made very beautiful by the skill of the young occupant, who has frescoed the ceiling with graceful trailing vines, the design being her own" (for source see fig. 165). Although it is doubtful that this room contains "antique oak" furniture—the style of the bedroom suite has more in common with the 1880s, and the little fall-front desk seems to be a dark wood version of

her sister's (fig. 167)—Miss House's ivy garlands add a definite sense of style to her room, as does the garland that is twisted around her gasolier. According to the article, Miss House also decorated porcelain. She is a Houston example of the lady painter/decorators who appeared throughout the United States during these years.

169

Entrance hall, Hutcheson house

ca. 1897

The Hutcheson house (fig. 50) entrance hall was imposing but welcoming. Broad enough to accommodate a desk and a Windsor-style rocker in the middle of the room, but made intimate by abundant wood trim, a herringbone-pattern wood floor, and cozy furnishings, the entrance hall welcomed visitors without overwhelming them with conspicuous display. The two *stuhls* (seventeenth-century Swiss or German chair forms) in the foreground were ideal for the hall since they were not harmed by wet rain gear. To the left of the hall were the two parlors; the back parlor's wallpaper is just visible. To the right, beyond the pair of sliding doors and double-hung portiere, are the library and the dining room. The staircase at the rear has two newel posts, each with a lamp. The large carpet is probably Persian, while the furs may be carefully pieced hides from the fox family. This photograph is one of several (figs. 170, 171 among them) probably taken at the same time. The photographer moved furniture from one room to another to enhance his composition.

170

Parlor, Hutcheson house

ca. 1897

The Hutcheson parlor is one of Houston's best examples of a room designed to entertain the women in a family: lightly colored plank floors and walls delicately laced with floral garlands encase fragile furniture, including an upholstered settee. The furniture was probably painted white or gold. A classically inspired fireplace surround embellishes the hearth. Lacy curtains and a flowered portiere, which is in marked contrast to the bolder Turkish brocade portiere in the men's library across the hall, complete the scene. The furniture in the parlor was probably arranged for this photograph, for it is unlikely that a wicker seat would be so close to the doorway or that the footstool on the right would be away from the chair. The richly upholstered velvet or mohair side chair on the left was probably part of the suite of seating furniture in the other parlor or music room seen through the doorway.

171

Parlor or music room,
Hutcheson house

ca. 1897

Although the Hutchesons may have
referred to this room as the parlor or
the music room, it could just as easily
have been called the aesthetic room,
for a number of the objects in it communicate—perhaps consciously on
the part of the owners—a family at
ease with the arts. Beneath the gas
chandelier is a baby grand piano,
probably the most universally accepted symbol of musical luxury
found in a home. To the left of the
piano, past the *stuhl*, stands a metal
easel carefully draped with a lacy
stole and holding a framed object of
art. Beneath the patterned ceiling
and complex wallpaper frieze, each
in a different embossed pattern, hang
two white biscuit plaques. *Night*,
modeled after Danish sculptor Bertel
Thorvaldsen's 1815 marble version,
hangs on the left; *Day* probably
hangs on the right. Near them, neatly
tucked behind a tufted leather armchair, is a firescreen, conspicuously
Japanesque and sympathetic with the
Aesthetic Movement of the 1880s.
A table to the right of the screen,
laden with cups and plates and a
substantial silver pot, is ready for
entertaining.

172

Parlor or music room,
Hutcheson house

ca. 1920

Although decorated for a wedding
reception, the Hutcheson parlor
graphically shows the radical change
in taste that this house, like many
Houston houses, underwent in the
1920s. With one window sealed, it
has been stripped of its embossed
wallpapers, heavy dark moldings,
elaborate draperies, and wall-to-wall
carpet, and most important, of its

eclecticism. Its new version is subdued: muted wallpaper, white trim,
bare plank floors with oriental scatter rugs, more lightly framed chairs
in Chippendale styles, and a neoclassical mirror hanging over a demilune,
neoclassical-style table. The room
represents a standard that conservative Houstonians continue to admire.
Through it all, however, certain older
artifacts remain: the piano, the Thorvaldsen plaques, and the chandelier,
now wired for electricity, stand side
by side with a Victrola and a pole
lamp with a jaunty fringed shade.

173

Second-floor hall, Hutcheson house

ca. 1897

Although the Hutchesons may have entertained on the first floor, they congregated in this comfortable second-floor sitting area. Four rocking chairs and a bed strewn with pillows provided ample seating; the worn carpet no longer commanded the careful respect it required when new. The room contains numerous mementos as well as a packed bookcase. Other books casually lie on the table as though they were in use and not intended for display. A hose carries fuel from the gasolier to the table lamp, and the telephone hangs on the wall to the left of the bookcase.

174

Bedroom, Hutcheson house

ca. 1897

This lacy bedroom probably belonged to Rosalie, the Hutchesons' only daughter. Like one of the House family daughters (fig. 167), she furnished her room in "faux bamboo." Her lace-trimmed sheer curtains relate to her elaborate bed hangings. The delicate (probably pastel) wallpaper with its slightly darker border continues the floral theme introduced in the draperies. The ceiling is papered in a moire pattern. Miss Hutcheson's room is decorated with a large glass-and-silver dressing table set and many mementos: family photographs, an initialed cowhide on the mantel, and a Princeton pennant.

175

Entrance hall, Van Alstyne–
Dickson house

ca. 1900

176

Dining room, Van Alstyne–
Dickson house

late 19th century

The massive scale and attention to detail lavished by N. J. Clayton on the exterior of this Second Empire–style house (fig. 44) was also lavished on its dining room. This seemingly octagonal room is resolutely symmetrical. Its oversize, heavily molded doors with transoms echo its tall, arched windows. A massive mantel flanked by Egyptian caryatids and a huge over-mantel mirror complement and reflect the large double doors, which are hinged to open into the room. With the help of two large candelabra on the mantel, a sophisticated two-tiered gas chandelier suspended from an elaborate plaster rosette illuminates the room. A patterned carpet assembled from strips and framed by a border covers the floor; a large sideboard dominates the end of the room. Although this room has a deeply sculpted ceiling molding, it has no wallpaper. Instead, the walls are decorated with paintings, including one in the roundel of the cellarette on the right.

The Dickson house (fig. 44) hall must have been one of Houston's most memorable rooms. It is typical of the eclecticism that pervaded many late-nineteenth-century homes. Here one sees an interior that retains its original door frames, black enamel paint and gilt mirror, and newel post (also with gilt highlights); however, the room has been dashingly updated with a creative mixture of goods. The painting, a neo-Gothic gasolier, the coats of arms, and the armor all convey a medieval theme. These objects are counterpointed by a Moorish jardiniere supporting a Chinese censor adapted to serve as a planter and an intricately carved Chinese chair, settee, and screen that obscure the area beyond from public view. Not obscured are the handsome oriental area rugs, the grand staircase, and the parquet floor, which is made from several colors of wood. The painting hanging at the landing had previously hung in the dining room (fig. 176).

177

Drawing room, Van Alstyne–Dickson house

after 1900

Sometime after purchasing this home, the Dicksons decided to remodel its double parlors by knocking out the common wall between them to make one large drawing room. In the process they created one of Houston's grander formal spaces. The room is perfectly symmetrical: two pairs of double doors, two fireplaces, and pairs of windows at either end. A bay window flanked by pairs of Ionic columns, a handsome electric chandelier, and a cabinet define the room's center. The columns, the delicate neoclassical plaster frieze, and the bracketed ceiling moldings are all historical references to the eigh-

teenth century, as is the handsome Aubusson-style carpet, which was no doubt ordered for this room to mirror the ceiling's plaster work. Among the unusual furniture in the room is the Savonarola-style chair on the left, an early sixteenth-century Lombardy design, the fragile (gilt?) side chair on the right, and the bergère with its companion footstool at the end. To their credit the Dicksons updated but did not abandon many of the original architectural features of the room. The doors, pier glass, over-mantel mirror, and mantel all seem to date from the 1870s, although they have been painted a light color (possibly white) in an attempt to make them appear more modern. The sofa and matching armchairs in the Renaissance Revival style also date from the 1870s, although their brocade upholsteries are reminiscent of the eigh-

teenth century and were probably applied during the remodeling.

The Dicksons were world travelers and among Houston's earliest art collectors. John F. Dickson, Jr., was an early supporter of the Museum of Fine Arts, Houston, and a lay member of New York's Grand Central Art Galleries. Like many of their contemporaries, the Dicksons displayed both copies of masterpieces and original works of art side by side. In this room a copy of *Venus Italica* by Antonio Canova stands in the bay, while another Canova copy, *Cupid and Psyche* (1787–93), sits on the mantel. A large mid-nineteenth-century Hudson River School–style landscape hangs adjacent to the Italianate sideboard, while a copy of Italian Baroque artist Guido Reni's fresco of *Aurora* (1613–14) hangs above it.

178
Parlor, Campbell–Jones house
ca. 1904

What began as a simple parlor in this house (fig. 90) has been enlivened considerably by the addition of a gilt-highlighted fireplace surround and the ambitious use of wallpapers and textiles. Silks and satins appear to predominate, and Mrs. Jones's fringes and tassels are the most elaborate seen thus far in any Houston interior. Her new Persian carpet and ladies' fans in the vitrine add even more texture to the room. The portrait on the left appears to be after Sir Joshua Reynolds's portrait of Mrs. Robinson (1782).

179
Dining room, Campbell–Jones house
ca. 1904

Like the parlor (fig. 178), the Jones house dining room unites a variety of materials and textures. From the embossed wallpaper above the plate rail to the opulently carved sideboard and dining table to the Persian-style carpet on the floor, the room is abundantly decorated. This room also illustrates the importance of decorative ceramics and glass during the period. The sideboard is laden with an elaborate cut-glass punch bowl, while decorative plates surround the room. The three ceramic figures on the right forming the base of a fruit stand are probably the Three Graces.

180

Parlor, Levy house

after 1906

It comes as little surprise that the owners of Levy Brothers Dry Goods, known for its quality and good taste, would live in a home with the same high standards (see fig. 92). The parlor was an intimate room furnished in Louis XVI Revival furniture. More than any other Houston interior, it seems to personify the styles espoused by Edith Wharton and Ogden Codman, Jr. The upholstery in the room, as well as the frieze and ceiling decorations, incorporate floral bouquet and swag motifs, both inspired by Louis XVI decoration. The handsomely figured carpet appears to have come from Persia.

181

Dining room, Levy house

after 1906

This room distinguishes itself from other known Houston dining rooms by the narrative tapestry frieze above the plate rail. Like the Joneses and Kirbys (figs. 179, 187), the Levys elected to use grape-cluster shades on some of their lights. Here the grapes dangle randomly as they might in an arbor.

182

Entrance hall, Inglenook

after 1906

Inglenook's staircase was as impressive as the house's exterior (fig. 118). It stood at the back of the entrance hall. By day sunlight streamed through its elaborate stained-glass windows; by night figural lamps, one on the newel post and one on the landing, lit its steps. There was a square grate on the floor to the right of the newel post, no doubt for a hot-air heating system. The chair to the right of the grate and the swags hanging from the banister are part of the Moorish nook installed beneath the stairs.

183

Moorish nook, Inglenook

With a flair for the exotic that was a bit unusual for Houston, the Kirbys had a Moorish nook nestled under the staircase in their entrance hall. The Kirbys' interest in the Near East was part of a national and international fascination with North Africa and the eastern Mediterranean in the late nineteenth century. Within the confines of a nomad's tent are elaborate pillows casually strewn on a Turkish (Kilim) throw. The heads hanging within the tent are possibly inspired by powerful bronze and onyx portrait busts like *Negro in Al-*

gerian Costume (1854) by Charles-Henri-Joseph Cordier. The figure in the tent on the right is a Guanyin or Kwannon, a Buddhist deity of compassion sitting on an elephant's head

bracket. A Near Eastern chair and a hexagonal low table similar to a taboret, each carved and inlaid, and a bronze vase sit in the foreground upon a Caucasian carpet.

184

Drawing room (first view), Inglenook

The Kirby house drawing room was probably situated in the house's projecting bay under the tower on the right side of the entry (fig. 118). It was an elaborate room decorated in a robust Louis XV Revival style. The room contained an ornate white marble caryatid-decorated fireplace surround and sculpture, including a figure known in the family as the Goddess of Chance. Elaborate rococo-style moldings filled the walls and ceiling. The walls were covered in at least three intricately decorated patterns, while the windows were protected by shutters, lacy curtains, and elaborately tasseled brocade draperies. The pair of figures standing before the window are probably ceramic variations on the popular Pierre Auguste Cot painting *The Storm*. At least part of the drawing room furniture was supplied by S. Karpen & Brothers, a well-regarded Chicago firm that distributed furniture throughout the Southwest, including to Joske's in San Antonio. The suite, a rose vine pattern that the firm called "L'art nouveau" was available in either mahogany or "Genuine Gold Leaf." The Kirbys chose the gold version. It cost $660 when purchased with the best grade of upholstery (fig. 186).

185

Drawing room (second view), Inglenook

A Karpen L'art nouveau side chair stands to the left of the drawing room mantel. The furniture barely visible to the right of the mantel is probably the sofa from the same suite.

186

L'Art Nouveau Suite, No. E1502

Karpen Furniture Company
(Chicago: privately printed, 1906)

187

Dining room, Inglenook

fall 1906

Beneath the painted and stuccoed ceiling and the grape-cluster lights, seated at a mahogany table surrounded by an expensive silver service, crystal, and eleven of her friends, and enjoying a seven-course luncheon, Bessie May Kirby announced her engagement to James Schuyler Stewart by giving a rose from this centerpiece, bearing the couple's names, to each friend. Certainly the elaborate social ritual surrounding the Kirby wedding found a sympathetic setting in this formal, opulently draped interior.

188

Library, Inglenook

ca. 1906

No one knows who helped the Kirbys decorate Inglenook, but the person was obviously aware of the work of the New York decorator/designer Louis Comfort Tiffany. The mosaic fireplace surround is in the Tiffany style as is the hanging metal and leaded-glass lamp, but more to the point is the twelve-light pond lily desk lamp that Tiffany advertised in 1906 for sale for $100. (The lamp is no. 382 in Louis Comfort Tiffany's "Bronze Lamps," published in 1904, and in his "Price List," published on October 1, 1906. See Robert Koch, *Louis Tiffany's Glass-Bronzes-Lamps* [New York: Crown, 1971], 124, 170.) The room also contains

a partners desk in an eighteenth-century revival style, a portrait bust of George Washington after one by Jean Antonio Houdon, and a new carpet from northwest Persia. Kirby has also added a number of personal items: a letter rack on the small fall-front desk against the wall, a die on the larger desk, and a cuspidor on the floor beneath it.

189

Bessie May Kirby's bedroom
(first view), Inglenook

ca. 1906

Bessie May Kirby's bedroom was outfitted in painted (probably white with
gold) furniture in a pseudo-French
style. Her bed, barely visible in the
chest-of-drawers' mirror, is a substantial brass model with half-tester.
Miss Kirby has hung a number of
photographs from her picture moldings rather than tacking them to the
wall. Although the Kirby entrance
hall may have had forced-air heating,
this bedroom depended on a radiator
to warm it.

190

Bessie May Kirby's bedroom
(second view), Inglenook

ca. 1906

191
Bathroom (first view),
Inglenook
ca. 1906

This Kirby house bathroom was every bit as luxurious as the rest of the house. It was spacious, attractively tiled and decorated, illuminated, and gleaming with chrome. Its auxiliary copper bathwater heater was an added luxury. (The Willis-Moody mansion in Galveston had similar copper heaters. They were used to raise the water temperature when the house's hot-water heater was far from the bath.) This room also had a shower, a relatively rare and desirable fixture in 1906. The water closet on the left probably had an elevated tank and a long, dangling pull chain.

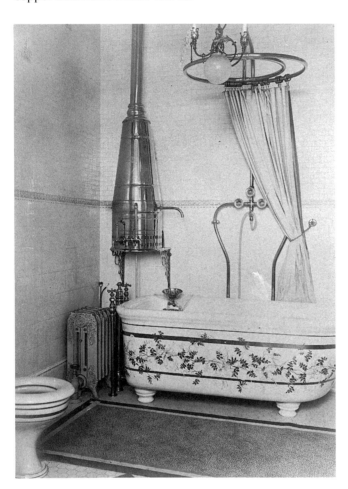 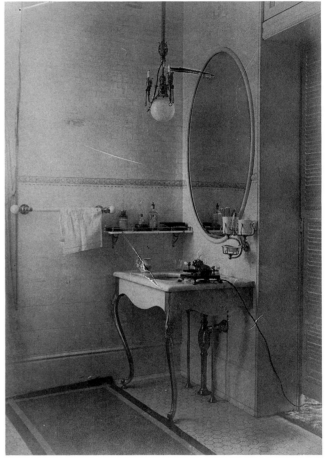

192
Bathroom (second view),
Inglenook
ca. 1906

The bathroom lavatory is as stylish and as well done as the rest of the room. The tall glass bottle on the marble shelf contains violet toilet water. The bulldog appliance on the sink holds a hair-curling iron.

193
Dining room, The Country
Place
ca. 1907

In contrast to many of the smaller Arts and Crafts bungalows built in Houston, The Country Place (fig. 142) was a large dwelling surrounded by several acres of land and situated far out (at least in its day) on Main Street. Nonetheless, the dining room is progressive and distinctly in the Craftsman idiom. The sideboard, hanging cabinet, vitrine, slat-back chairs, and electroliers could have come directly from Gustav Stickley Craftsman Workshops or from one of his competitors. The copper pitcher, tall and full-chested, standing on the plate rail is also a common Arts and Crafts shape. The room's subdued colors, beamed ceiling, wall decoration, and meticulous attention to detail make it one of the best Houston Craftsman interiors known to date.

194
Butler's pantry,
The Country Place

ca. 1907

The Sharps' butler's pantry was probably situated between their dining room and kitchen. Butler's pantries were utilitarian spaces where tablewares were washed and stored.

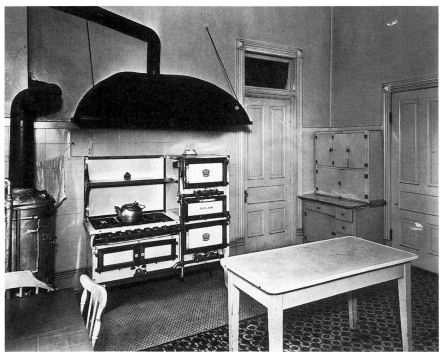

195
Kitchen, The Country Place

ca. 1907

In its day this kitchen was probably one of the best equipped in Houston. It had a large water heater and a prominent stove hood, which vented into the water heater's chimney, and an impressive gas-burning combination stove and oven. Its tile walls and floor and its enamel-topped work table were easy to maintain. A sitting area and built-in storage further aided the cook. The sink and icebox are probably just out of the camera's range.

196

Joseph P. Carter house

2602 Main Street at McGowen
built 1910; demolished
C. D. Hill & Co., architects; D. A.
Crawford, builder

Hardware by C. L. & Theo. Bering, Jr., Inc.
Millwork by Texas & Louisiana Lumber Co.
Mantels and electric fixtures by Brown-
Woods Electric Co.
Decorative glass by Texas Art Glass Co.
Furnishings and decorations by Waddell's
Lone Star Concrete and Acme Plaster by
W. L. Macatee & Sons Co.

It is most unusual to know so many
of the suppliers for a house. The Carter residence, however, was featured
in an article in *Southern Architectural Review* that listed the names.

197

Entrance hall, Carter house

ca. 1910

As in the Duff house entrance hall
(fig. 199), the gentle arch framing the
staircase alludes to eighteenth-century
Georgian interiors (fig. 200). In this
interior, however, Waddell's outfitted
the room with Chinese rather than
Colonial Revival furniture.

198

Dining room, Carter house

ca. 1910

The dining room is fundamentally an
Arts and Crafts interior, with the
ceiling and moldings comparable to
many fine Prairie School interiors of
the day. The andirons, perhaps from
Bering's, are sympathetic to the
space. Waddell's furniture and
Brown-Woods's mantel, however,
have very different roots: The mantel
appears to have been made of boldly
veneered wood decorated with contrasting Gothic arches. Beneath it the

fireplace hood closely resembles half
of an art nouveau Tiffany lampshade.
Waddell has placed Queen Anne Revival side chairs in the room, while

the flowered wall-covering and portiere of undetermined origin add
other textures to the scene. (See fig.
196 for a list of suppliers.)

199

Entrance hall, Duff house

1911

This photograph of the spacious entrance hall in the Duffs' Colonial Revival house (fig. 125), perhaps more than any other, summarizes the revolution in Houston interior design in the years immediately preceding World War I. The change is even more apparent when this entrance hall is compared with the Kirbys' Moorish nook (fig. 183) and the Dicksons' hall (fig. 175), each done during the preceding decade. The Arts and Crafts appreciation for stained-wood interiors and uncluttered simplicity lends itself to a reinterpretation of the elegant Georgian hall, like the Palladian-inspired one at Carter's Grove in Virginia (fig. 200). The Duffs extended the conceit by using caned high-backed chairs in their hall, which at this time were probably thought to be American products dating from about 1700. (In reality the majority of these chairs were made in England, not in the United States.) The two shield-back chairs in the parlor beyond are later variations on New York chairs made between 1795 and 1800 after designs associated with England's George Hepplewhite. The parlor's fireplace reverts to the twentieth century, however, in its tiled surround and stained-oak mantel with flowered frieze above. The carpets in both rooms appear to be commercially produced patterns inspired by oriental ones.

200

Entrance hall, Carter's Grove

James City County, Virginia
built 1750–53; extant

201

Library, Duff house

Like the entrance hall (fig. 199), the
Duff house library combines historical allusions with Arts and Crafts
stylishness. The over-mantel woodwork is directly inspired by ornamental strapwork of the type used in
Holland and England in the second
half of the sixteenth century. The
glass encased bookshelves, the wall
paper frieze of abstracted trees, and
the simplified valance and tailored
draperies also contribute to this
seemingly muted interior.

202
Fred E. Ward house

3301 Morrison Avenue, Woodland
Heights
built 1912; extant

203
Living room, Ward house
1912

Fred Ward's bungalow was one of
many built before World War I in the
Woodland Heights subdivision
slightly northwest of downtown. For
$4,000 (a considerable sum in 1912)
Ward was able to buy a three-bed-
room, one-bath house with living and
dining rooms, den, and kitchen. Like
other Arts and Crafts interiors, this
one offered a simple floor plan, extensive built-ins, large open areas,
and polished wood, in this instance
characterized as "stained Flemish
oak." In the dining room over the
sideboard is a large leaded-glass
window.

204
Den, Ward house
1912

The Wards combined a typical Arts
and Crafts interior with a vivid wallpaper covering the ceiling, walls, and
frieze. The furniture is decorated
with pierced cutouts in the style of
the Charles P. Limbert Company
of Grand Rapids, Michigan.

205

Gustav G. Heyne house

4008 Austin Street
built 1912; extant

206

Kitchen, Heyne house

ca. 1912

The author of an article describing this house referred to it as "a high-class bungalow." No doubt its kitchen, while state-of-the-art, is more typical of most Houston kitchens of the period than the Sharps' (fig. 195). It is smaller, spare, devoid of built-ins and a stove hood, and, as befits a smaller house, has a smaller gas range and water heater. In lieu of tile, this kitchen has "white Sanitas wall covering" and probably a linoleum floor.

207

Dining room, Staiti house

January 10, 1912

Here the Staiti dining room is festively decorated for Jeanette Reisner's marriage to Ewell H. Jackson. When the house (fig. 136) was newly finished, this room was published in *The Houstonian* (Aug. 5, 1905) as "one of the prettiest dining rooms . . .

ever seen" with "two-toned green carpeting . . . wall tapestry of appropriate fruit design," and draperies supported by a continuous pole spanning seven windows.

Although the ceramics, glass, and oak furniture in this room are traditional for the day, the wallpaper, frieze, and draperies are very progressive. Both the ceiling and the wall are decorated with a paper in a

moiré (watered) design. A strongly patterned fruit border frames it. Most noteworthy, however, are the draperies, devoid of valances, tassels, and fringe, and printed in a pattern that seems to have come from the reform designs of Charles Rennie MacIntosh and the Glasgow School of Art.

208

Joel Stuart Boyles house

1217 Fannin Street at Polk Avenue
built ca. 1904 ; demolished ca. 1925

209

Christmas, Boyles house

1912

Left to right (top row): Joel Stuart
Boyles, Fannie Bob Matthews Boyles,
Frances Stuart Boyles (baby), Media
Davis Matthews, Letitia Matthews;
(bottom row): Sam Davis Matthews,
Louis Thomas Matthews, Toodles
(dog).

Family photographs takens at holi-
day gatherings are rituals in the
United States. Here the squirming
child, the apprehensive mother, the
blinking grandmother, the family pet,
and the stoic men are surrounded by

objects indicating a prosperous but
not wealthy home: striped wallpaper,
pretty (but not ornate) curtains, a
fringed electric lamp with tinted but
not leaded glass, family photographs,
and an austere two-drawer library
table with a man's jacket piled upon
it. Five family members sit on a
tufted leather couch. To the right of
the couch is a relatively new household appliance, a Victrola.

210

George W. Roff house

3305 Morrison, Woodland Heights
built 1912; extant

211

Bathroom, Roff house

1912

This bathroom, which was quite
modern for its day, is probably much
more typical than the Kirbys' elaborate one (figs. 191, 192). With a linoleum floor, "dainty white enamel,"
rag rug, straightforward window
shade, and utilitarian appliances, the
room is functional and efficient.

212

Front porch, Miramichi

April 27, 1913

Left to right: unidentified servant, Stella Root Williams, Chaille Jones Brady, Lucy Brady Hunt, Edward A. Peden, and three unidentified guests.

Houston's turn-of-the-century summer social season was centered in recreational houses around Galveston Bay, where formality in dress and social customs carried over from the city. The wicker chairs and Arts and Crafts settee rocker were very stylish.

213

John Henry Kirby stables and servants' quarters

Pierce Avenue at Brazos Street, northeast corner
built ca. 1901; demolished

This, with the Johnson-Ross stables (fig. 54), was one of the largest private stables and quarters buildings known in Houston. It was probably built at the same time as the natatorium (fig. 123), given the similar neoclassical detailing, although the cornered turret is pure Victorian.

214

A. T. Lucas house

Mrs. Lucas and her daughter, George Anna, pose on the upstairs porch (ca. 1914), which served as an extension of the living area, especially in warm weather (see fig. 114).

215

Parlor, Richard A. Giraud house

ca. 1895
1718 Main Street at Jefferson Avenue
built ca. 1880; moved ca. 1908; demolished

Left to right: Edythe Giraud, John Dickson, Will Kendall, unidentified man, Stella Giraud.

High five, hearts, five hundred, euchre, forty-five, and bridge were popular card games at the turn of the century both for casual evenings at home and for elaborate women's card parties. The mischievous participants in this game staged the photograph to depict as many vices as possible (note the dice and wine). The velvet table covering at left, the material draped on the mantel at right, and the stereoptic viewer in the basket were fashionable parlor accoutrements. The window is raised but the shutters are closed to let in the air while keeping out the insects.

216

Billiard room, Inglenook

The Kirbys' billiard room was on the third floor of Inglenook. The heavy table, probably made of golden oak, was similar to furniture made by the Tobey Furniture Co. of Chicago. Square legs and carved decoration were often found on reform furniture of the Progressive era made in the Middle West. Note also the swivel armchair, upright piano, and carpet borders devoid of a center surrounding the table. Such recreational rooms in large turn-of-the-century houses were popular retreats for men following dinner parties as well as for family entertainment.

217

William Fulton house

early 1900s
1507 Rusk Avenue between
LaBranch and Crawford streets
built ca. 1859; demolished ca. 1920

Left to right: Mary Frances Wickes Pettit (Mrs. William A.), Imogene Pettit, Daisy Pettit Elgin (Mrs. Robert Wilson), Mary Alice Elgin (baby), Alice Mae Pettit, Willie Ada Pettit.

A retired steamboat captain and native of Pittsburg, Pennsylvania, William Fulton became a Houston cotton merchant in the 1840s. He built this house in the middle of the block bounded by Rusk, Capitol, Crawford, and LaBranch before the Civil War. To the right of the large entry hall were double parlors, each 20′ by 20′, said to have been furnished identically. Large pocket slid-

ing doors between them opened to combine the rooms, which with the entry hall provided excellent circulation for large parties. According to the custom of the day, the Fultons gave the corner lots to their children, who built houses for themselves and rental houses for investment income. About 1901 Thornwell Fay bought the original house and moved it forward almost to the sidewalk.

218

Benjamin Francis Weems house

1616 Rusk Avenue at Jackson Street
built 1875; moved to face 816
Jackson ca. 1908; demolished 1970s

B. F. Weems (1839–1923) was a
businessman from Virginia who
bought this property in 1874, built
the house in 1875, and married Maria Nash Carrington in 1876. The
house resembles many that were
built just before or after the Civil
War. This photograph gives an excellent view of a typical downtown
street-corner in the late nineteenth
century. By 1963 the house and its
outside kitchen had been turned into
twelve apartments. Today the portion
of Jackson Street next to the property has been closed and the site has
been incorporated into a parking lot
near the George R. Brown Convention Center. Note the city street signs
attached to the fence here and in
figure 219.

219

Judge Presley Kittredge Ewing house

1103 Clay Avenue at Fannin Street
built ca. 1893; demolished 1947

Reared on a Louisiana plantation,
Judge Ewing came to Houston in
1882 after graduating from the University of Mississippi Law School. In
1883 he bought this property and
built a small, two-story house, which
he moved to adjacent property on
Clay about 1893, when this house
was constructed. A connoisseur of
fine food and wine and for many
years president of the ZZ Club, Judge
Ewing, together with his wife, entertained lavishly and frequently, counting William Jennings Bryan as a
close friend and houseguest. Mrs.
Ewing, first president of the Houston
Parent Teacher Association and an
advocate of women's suffrage, made
her home a center of civic as well as
social activity. In 1905 Judge Ewing
was named chief justice of the Su-
preme Court of Texas. The Ewing
house was a wonderful example of
the large Queen Anne/Eastlake–style
houses that were built in Houston.

220
Birthday party, Ewing house, front porch
April 27, 1910

J. Kittredge Vinson celebrated his first birthday at the home of his grandparents. Left to right: Mrs. Cochran and Jane, Mrs. Renn and Philip, Mamie Wren and Clark, Vesta Vinson and Kittredge, Mamie Shearn Forbes and Lila, Maggie Mildred Buschardt and Bolling Eldridge, Mrs. Charles Shearn and Maggie, Mrs. J. R. Christian (?), Mrs. Harry Pennington and Harry, Jr., Bessie Kirby Stewart and Betty.

221

Birthday party, Ewing house, back yard

April 27, 1910

Left to right: Jane Cochran and Ruby, Clark Wren and nurse, Philip Renn and nurse, Kittredge Vinson and Willie, unidentified baby and nurse (seated), Bolling E. Buschardt and nurse (seated).

In families with servants, nurses accompanied small children wherever they went, even to parties with their mothers. Kittredge Vinson's first birthday party was as much for the elaborately dressed mothers as for the babies, who in this photo have been handed over to the nurses.

222

Spencer Hutchins and Mary Root

ca. 1895

Spencer Hutchins, youngest son of William J. Hutchins and the acknowl- edged arbiter of Houston society from the mid-1880s until his death in 1906, was most noted as leader of the ZZ Club. A master of the most complicated nineteenth-century dance figures, he could direct hun- dreds of ballroom dancers with a small whistle. Also a superb eques- trian and a collector of fine carriages, "he was the personification of the ro- mantic nineties, and when he went to his grave in 1906, people cried in the streets as though not only a man's life but an epoch had come to an end" (*Houston Press*, May 27, 1934).

223

Ballroom, Kirby natatorium, second floor

November 12, 1906
2006 Smith Street at the rear of the Kirby house
built ca. 1901; demolished

The wedding of John Henry Kirby's only child, Bessie May, to James Schuyler Stewart on November 14, 1906, was one of the most elaborate in the history of Houston. The Kutschbach Florists decorated Christ Church with several thousand chrysanthemums and other flowers, using ladders borrowed from the fire department. Mrs. Kirby served midnight meals to the crew, including one of quail on toast. At Inglenook they strung incandescent lights in the gardens, along the bridge spanning Mirror Lake (fig. 124), and in the shapes of giant butterflies in the ballroom and over the swimming pool. On November 12 the Kirbys entertained out-of-town guests with a prenuptial cotillion in the ballroom.

224

Swimming pool, Kirby natatorium, first floor

November 12, 1906

225

Butchering hogs in north
Harris County

ca. 1900

226

Making sausage in north
Harris County

ca. 1900

Before refrigeration was available in rural areas, pickled and smoked meats and sausages made from cattle and hogs butchered on the coldest winter days could be consumed most of the year. Fresh meat was available in summer to members of the Butcher Club in the Klein community. Once a week, on Saturday, a cow or steer was killed and the meat divided equally among the members, each receiving a different cut each week until he had received all parts of the animal.

227

Orena Jane Francis Berry
rolling dough, James Berry
house

ca. 1900
2617 Loraine Street, Fifth Ward

The work table appears to be covered with a piece of carpeting to keep the dough board from slipping. The window is raised to let in the air, but the shutter is closed to keep out the insects and the hot sun. Heavy pots and a kettle rest on a Bucks brand cookstove, with the stovepipe venting through the wall to the left. Saw-toothed or dentilled shelf paper decorates the pantry.

228

Orena Jane Francis Berry
feeding chickens, Berry house

ca. 1900

Note the wooden cistern on brick stilts to the left. The utilitarian portion of the back yard was kept bare and swept or raked clean. The chickens are enclosed by a picket fence.

229

**"Auntie" Jordan with milk
cow, Frank Lee Berry house**

ca. 1908
3002 Austin Street at Anita Avenue
built ca. 1905; demolished ca. 1973

Although the majority of household
servants were black, a number of
young German women from rural
Harris County worked as housekeepers in Houston. However, Auntie Jordan, the Berrys' housekeeper, was
Belgian. Many families continued to
keep cows, chickens, and horses in
fenced areas at the back of their
properties through the 1920s.

The side of the Ida V. Sternenberg
house appears in the background.
The stained-glass window was probably along the side of the front stairwell, a typical feature in houses of
this period.

230

**Horse in fenced lot behind
Lester house**

ca. 1910

Even after the introduction of the automobile, horses were kept for pleasure. Lubbock's Grove and Merkel's
Grove on the northeast edge of town,
the banks of the bayous, Glenwood
Cemetery, Magnolia Park, and the
surrounding prairies were reached
on horseback. For decades picnicking, picking dewberries, and gathering wildflowers in these areas were
popular recreation for Houstonians.
Hayrides by moonlight avoided the
heat.

231

Holsmith and Isensee Grocery

ca. 1900
LaPorte, Texas

Many people lived in apartments
over their business establishments,
which probably was the case here.
Horsedrawn delivery wagons were
among a household's greatest
conveniences.

232

Nick D'Amico Grocery

1219 Hamilton Street at Polk Avenue
built 1904; demolished 1960s

The large D'Amico family lived over
this corner grocery store. The architecture of this building, and of
most neighborhood establishments
like it, was domestic rather than
commercial.

233

David Finney Stuart house

February 14, 1895
1116 Texas Avenue at San Jacinto Street
built 1882; demolished ca. 1907

A native of Gay Hill, Texas, David Stuart graduated from Jefferson Medical College in Philadelphia in 1859. In 1872 he and Dr. Thomas Joel Boyles founded one of Houston's few nineteenth-century hospitals, the Houston Infirmary, which operated until 1913. Dr. Stuart's office in a separate brick building adjacent to his house is visible at right. The photograph probably was taken following the historic blizzard of February 12–15, 1895, when almost two feet of snow fell on Harris County, a phenomenon not recorded before or since.

234

Knox Briscoe Howe
on moving day

ca. 1909

Following the typical pattern of migration from downtown neighborhoods to the new subdivisions in the South End, the Joseph Milton Howe family moved from 918 Austin Street at McKinney Avenue to 1112 Elgin Avenue at San Jacinto Street about 1909.

235

Dining room, Root house

ca. 1895
1410 Clay Avenue at Austin Street
built 1893–94; demolished 1925
George E. Dickey, architect

Left to right: Mary Porter Root, Laura Shepherd Root, unidentified servant, Stella Root, Cora Valentine Root, and Alexander Porter Root.

Victorian Americans believed that furnishings and family rituals created an environment in the home that influenced the character and morals of family members. Since most rituals were centered around food, the furnishings of the dining room reflected a family's values. Fine damask table linens and sterling silver flatware were considered essential accoutrements of gracious living. Linen "diaper" was purchased by the yard, then cut to size, hemmed, and monogrammed by hand. The formality of daily life for affluent Houstonians is illustrated here also by the "classic" trumpet flower vase, two cut-glass water decanters on the table, the presence of the butler, and the formal daytime clothing of family members.

236

Sitting room, House, Jr., house

early 1890s

Left to right: Thomas William House, Jr., Mrs. House, Mary House, Ellen House, and Edith House.

In the nineteenth century the family gathered informally in the sitting room, or back parlor, for conversation, reading, and playing parlor games or cards. The neo-Gothic bookcase reflected in the mirror holds some of the family's fine private library. Reading aloud together was a favorite pastime. The center table is positioned under the gasolier, from which a gas line feeds the reading lamp around which all activity revolves. According to family sources, this house was the first in Houston to be equipped with a gas line.

The corner fireplace is at an angle to share the chimney with a fireplace behind it (also at an angle) in the next room. Wicker furniture is used in combination with an upholstered Renaissance Revival side chair at left. Art tiles and pseudomedieval tiles decorate the fireplace under the mantel. The carpeting is highly patterned and brightly colored.

237

Mrs. Michael Louis
Westheimer knitting in her
living room

1612 Hadley Avenue at
Jackson Street
built before 1907; demolished ca.
1963

Hand work, like reading, was done in
the middle of the room, for the lamp
cord had to reach the socket in the
chandelier. This was probably the
only electrical outlet in the room,
a carryover from the era of the
gasolier.

238

Lucy Collins and House
children, House, Jr., house
ca. 1900

The enormous cistern in the background furnished water for the large
House estate, which covered an entire city block.

239

Roberta Westcott with her
goat and cart, Robert Morris
Elgin house
ca. 1902
1404 Texas Avenue at Austin Street
built ca. 1870; demolished ca. 1928

Many children had pet goats which
they hitched to store-bought buggies
like this one or to wagons improvised
from wooden crates and wheels. In
1890 W. R. Sinclair, the "Goat Editor" of the *Houston Post*, challenged
two children to race their goats down
Congress Avenue to the courthouse.
This began a midsummer tradition
known as Children's Day, which included not only goat races, but foot
races, bicycle races, potato races, dog
races, a greased pig chase, and a
pretty baby show. Also traveling photographers took goats hitched to buggies from house to house to use as
props for taking children's pictures.

240

Maud Gray Hester in
playhouse, Louis Gray Hester
house
ca. 1914
1102 Elgin Avenue at Fannin Street
built ca. 1907; demolished ca. 1955

The architecture of the playhouse reflects that of the main house in the
background.

241
Christmas, Bergamini–Coughlin house
1911

Left to right: Iris Coughlin, Charles Coughlin, Marie Coughlin.

As late as 1839 the German traveler Gustav Dresel noted with dismay that Christmas and the New Year were not celebrated by Anglo-Americans in southeast Texas. Undoubtedly the large German population that emigrated to Harris County beginning in the 1840s promoted these holidays, for they were popular by the late 1850s. The candles on the tree were lighted once, usually when the family held its main celebration, on Christmas Eve for Germans, Christmas Day for Anglos. Christmas dinner could include oysters, gumbo, oranges, apples, celery sticks, wild turkey and other game, traditional eggnog, whiskey punch, plum pudding, fruitcake, and mincemeat pies. Christmas night and New Year's Eve were celebrated with firecrackers, Roman candles, and skyrockets.

A Tiffany glass hanging lamp appears in the upper left corner of the photo. Jewel glass like that on the Bishop's Palace in Galveston decorated the Bergaminis' front door, which cost $500 when the house was built.

242

Link–Lee house

ca. 1916

Left to right: Thelma Lee, Maud Lee, Marjorie Lee, Ethel Lee, Essie Lee, Thomas Peter Lee, Maxine Lee.

  John Wiley Link, lumberman, entrepreneur, developer of the Montrose Addition, and eventual president of Dr. Pepper, built this showcase house as an example of the grand architecture he hoped would characterize Montrose Boulevard. Located in the center of a full block, it was constructed of Missouri lime-stone, with a full basement and third-floor ballroom. On Sunday after-noons his teenage daughters and their friends received groups of boys who came to call, play the piano, and sing. At least a hundred friends and neighbors sought refuge here the night of the 1915 hurricane. About 1916 Link sold the house to oilman Thomas Peter Lee.

243

Back yard, Lester house

ca. 1914

Despite advancements in technology, utilitarian outbuildings, cisterns, and pumps continued to dominate back yards even in the most expensive neighborhoods well into the twenti-eth century.

244

Boys from Emma R. News
Boys Home, Bismark Park
Natatorium

ca. 1915
6512 Harrisburg Road

Shortly after the discovery of artesian water in the city the *Houston
Daily Post* reported on July 1, 1887,
"Houston is the only city in Texas
with a swimming bath." Natatoriums
fed by artesian wells opened in
amusement parks around the city, ca-
tering to a new interest in sports and
the outdoor life inspired by the Progressive movement. Bismark Park
was later called Eden Park.

245

Dancing at Beatty's truck farm, Sunday afternoon

ca. 1900
North Post Oak Road at Woodway,
north side of Buffalo Bayou

Left to right: Harry and James W. Kennedy, Archie and Mitty Beatty, Sam Kennedy.

Truck farms located on the outskirts of Houston produced fruits and vegetables that were sold from the farmers' wagons at the City Market on Market Square. Noted for its superior watermelons, the Beatty farm abutted Post Oak Road and Camp Logan (now Memorial Park) on the east. On Sunday afternoons Archie and Mitty Beatty entertained their friends with dancing under the pine trees. During hot weather the refreshments included watermelons iced down in large barrels.

246

Michael Floeck–Charles S. Longcope house

ca. 1897
109 Chenevert Street at
Congress Avenue
built ca. 1859; demolished ca. 1949

Michael Floeck, a German baker, built this brick house about 1859 near the boundary line between two of Houston's earliest neighborhoods, Frost Town and Quality Hill. Later he deeded it to his son, Paul Floeck. In 1865 Charles S. Longcope, a Mississispppi River steamboat captain, bought the house. At great expense he added the custom-made iron grill-work from New Orleans, covered the brick with stucco, and constructed a two-story frame addition in back to create a ballroom across the whole width of the structure. From the balcony Captain Longcope read the Emancipation Proclamation to his slaves and announced that he had set aside a lot for each of them in the Fourth Ward, later known as Freedmen's Town. By 1897 the house had become the headquarters for the Lord's Cycle Club, one of many groups of enthusiastic bicyclists to emerge during the Progressive era.

247

Henry Franklin Ring
bay house

ca. 1894
Bay Ridge, Morgan's Point
built ca. 1890; demolished

Left to right: (back row) Mrs. Cage, Mrs. Ring, Mrs. E. L. Dennis, Mrs. Crane, Mrs. Chew, Mrs. B. F. Weems; (front row) Bartlett Chew, Rufus Cage, Roland Ring, Wharton Weems.

In 1890 twelve Houston families formed the Bay Ridge Park Association to build summer homes along the bayshore line near Morgan's Point. Mrs. Henry Franklin Ring described the first summer: "We built a barn immediately and we moved down early in the summer with two tents, the horse and cow. Aunt Sallie and Uncle Jerry [probably servants] lived in the new barn and the horse and cow lived out of doors. Mr. Ring took charge of the preliminary work. Men and teams were employed to fill up gullies and terrace the bluff. Bermuda grass was planted on the slopes. The lodge for the caretaker, the pier, and the bath house were built that summer. Several homes were begun. A man and wife were employed to care for the grounds and to serve meals for the Park owners. An artesian well was bored and we had a fine supply of splendid water."

248

Risdon D. Gribble bay house

811 Bay Ridge, Morgan's Point
built 1894; extant

This house, more enclosed and more elaborately decorated than most other bay houses of its period, was characteristic of houses built in the city.

249

Daniel E. Kennedy bay house

427 Bay Ridge, Morgan's Point
built 1896; extant

Approximately half the living space in this house is outdoors on the large porches. The open tower in the center of the roof was probably octagonal and gave an excellent view of the bay. The festive painted shingles and the towerlike projections at the four corners of the roof were appropriate to a vacation house.

250

Children on stile in front, John Stadtler and William E. Humphreville bay houses

ca. 1910
Bay Ridge, Morgan's Point

Left to right: (front row) George Humphreville, McIver Streetman, Billy Holtkamp; (back row) Susie Humphreville, Flora Streetman, Estelle Streetman.

Houston general contractors John Stadtler and William E. Humphreville built their bay houses next door to each other. Stiles like this one between the Stadtlers' yard and that of Judge Sam Streetman were used in lieu of gates for access between properties. Fences were necessary to restrain livestock, which were herded down to the bay from Houston for the summer.

Long-sleeved dresses of checked gingham that opened down the back were called aprons and served as summertime playclothes for girls. Even boys wore long-sleeved shirts for protection from the sun. Children always went barefoot at the bay.

251

Horse-drawn lawnmower, Miramichi

ca. 1908

252

John Grant Tod bay house

2510 Todville Road, Seabrook
built before 1900; extant

Judge Tod was the son of Capt. John Grant Tod (fig. 8), who served both as secretary of the Navy and as commodore of the fleet during the Republic of Texas. The younger Tod entered Yale Law School, from which he graduated in 1885. In 1900 Judge Tod, his brother-in-law, Charles H. Milby, and Andrew Dow built a compound of summer homes along Todville Road on part of an original Mexican land grant issued to Ritson Morriss, an ancestor of Tod's wife. The properties are contiguous, but each had a private pier, a boathouse, a kitchen, and servants' quarters. Evidently designed at the same time by the same person, the three residences are similarly constructed. All three still stand. Two are owned by descendants of their builders. The compound expanded as friends and relatives of these families built bay houses along Todville Road.

253

Cora Root Peden crabbing
at Miramichi

Crabbing, bathing, fishing, sailing, boating, and "autoing" occupied the long summer days in the Galveston Bay area. Women and children covered themselves from head to toe for protection against the sun and insects. From the net scarf covering her entire head to her long gloves and thick white stockings, Mrs. Peden is fortified against the elements.

254

Entrance hall, William Gray Sears–Herman E. Detering house

June 11, 1913
1417 McGowen Avenue at
LaBranch Street
built ca. 1908; demolished ca. 1966

For the wedding of Alice Gray Sears to James Butler McGee, the deep moldings and Ionic columns of the Georgian-style interior trim were enhanced with palms, plumosa ferns, and shasta daisies banked in every available space. Tulle and white maline bows were entwined with ferns in the chandeliers. Southern smilax festooned the stairway and pink gladioli in tall crystal vases stood in the reception hall at either side of the entrance to the parlor, where the wedding ceremony was performed in an alcove banked with palms and ferns (fig. 255). These decorations were typical for weddings and formal parties held at home from the 1870s through the 1920s.

255

Front parlor, Sears–Detering house

June 11, 1913

For a typical home wedding, the music was provided by a pianist, a violinist, a harpist, or an orchestra. In a two-story house the bridal party assembled upstairs, then proceeded down the stairs and through an aisle improvised with ribbons and flowers to form a semicircle around the altar in the parlor.

256

Dining room, William H. Palmer house

February 19, 1912
1116 Travis Street at Dallas Avenue
built 1884; demolished 1928

This scene greeted guests at the wedding reception of Daphne Palmer and Edwin L. Neville (February 19, 1912) as they entered the dining room for cake and refreshments. The heavy built-in mirror over the mantel was typical of the early 1880s when this house was built. The vitrine on the left, containing Mrs. Palmer's collection of cut glass, and the sideboard at right, embellished with carved caryatids, are banked with vases of flowers. Silver and crystal candlesticks, the lace tablecloth, ribbon streamers attached to the chandelier and bridal bouquet, and a profusion of ferns and palms complete the decorations. Exotic imported flowers such as the lilies of the valley were available by the turn of the century because of improved refrigeration and faster transportation by rail.

257

Atkinson house

For many years Mrs. Atkinson, seen here on her front porch, provided Easter lilies from her garden to decorate Christ Church on Easter Sunday (see also fig. 64).

258

Wisteria, August Jantz house

5209 Telephone Road

This particularly graceful wisteria draped the entrance to the home of August and Augusta Jantz. Jantz, a German immigrant, was the proprietor of Interurban Park, located at the Brookline station of the Interurban Railroad. In 1935 this house, which had been renumbered 1009 Telephone Road, was moved around the corner to become 4916 Stimson.

259

August Charles Bering, Sr., house

3402 San Jacinto Street at
Francis Avenue
built ca. 1906; demolished ca. 1963

Josephine Pauska Bering (Mrs. A. C.) is seen here resting on a bench in her famous garden. Although she grew many types of flowers and plants, her daisies proliferated; not only did they fill a wide bed in front of the house, they filled an empty field next door. At the corners of the Bering property (not visible) Mrs. Bering had grafted crape myrtle trees together to create a trellis-type arbor. When her garden was in full bloom, as it was in this photograph, people passed by all day to see it.

260

The Gables, Samuel K. McIlhenny house

1314 McKinney Avenue at
Austin Street
built 1889; moved and remodeled
ca. 1901; demolished ca. 1935

Samuel K. McIlhenny, a wholesale dry goods and cotton merchant, built this house with lumber salvaged from a hospital built on the same site before the Civil War. Shortly after his wife and daughters, Rosalie and Anita (for whom streets were named), died in the 1900 hurricane, the house was sold to Col. and Mrs. James E. Newton, former owners of the Sour Lake Hotel and its surrounding 1,000 acres where oil had just been discovered. The Newtons moved the building to the middle of the block, enlarged it adding gables, and turned it into a fashionable boarding house known as The Gables. The young William Ward Watkin, supervisor of construction for the Rice Institute and the first professor of architecture there, lived in The Gables with his mother from 1909, when they arrived from Boston, until his marriage in 1914.

In later years the building was known as the Drummers Home and as the YWCA. Barbados-type shutters, unusual in Houston, were installed on the dormer windows, and the upstairs porch was screened.

261

Nathaniel Kelly Kellum– Zerviah Kelley Noble house

Sam Houston Park
built 1847; extant

This is the oldest known house in Houston still standing on its original site. Constructed with brick made in the Kellum brickyards on the property, it was sold in January 1851 to Mrs. Abraham W. Noble, a Connecticut widow who had married Noble in April 1849. They were divorced in 1865. In 1851 Mrs. Noble opened a private school in the house. In 1871 it became the first free public school to be operated by the Harris County School Board under the auspices of the state in the city of Houston, and, as the teacher, she became a county employee. In 1877 the city passed an ordinance assuming control of free county schools within the city limits. Mrs. Noble continued her career

with the city public school system, as both teacher and principal. The house has a center-hall plan, the most common type for Greek Revival houses, with a two-room ell in the rear. The second floor is reached only from the side porch, there being no interior staircase. Mrs. Noble died in 1894 and the city of Houston acquired the property in 1899. After serving as headquarters of the city zoo, then as a storage barn, the house was restored in 1958 and is now a museum house operated by the Harris County Heritage Society.

262

The Rev. Jack Yates's Houston Academy

ca. 1885
Bell Avenue at San Jacinto Street

About 1884 the American Baptist Women's Home Mission Society of Chicago sent the Misses Peck and Dysart to Houston to work with the Rev. Jack Yates. Together they established the Houston Academy for black children in the residence pictured here known as the Cooper Place, which they moved to the corner of Bell Avenue and San Jacinto

Street. In 1894 the school was reorganized and moved to what is now the 3200 block of West Dallas, where it existed until 1921.

263

Professor Christopher Welch's Houston Academy

ca. 1912
2215 Caroline Street at Hadley Avenue

One of several nineteenth-century private schools known as the Houston Academy, Professor Welch's school opened in 1896 on Polk Avenue at Jackson Street. In 1906 Professor Welch moved his school and residence to 2215 Caroline Street, where both remained until the school closed in 1921.

264

Houston Golf Club (later Houston Country Club)

ca. 1904
San Felipe Road (now West Dallas),
south side of Buffalo Bayou

Domestic architecture was adopted for private clubs, which served as extensions of the members' homes. Begun informally at the suggestion of Lionel Hohenthal, the Houston Golf Club was officially organized in 1904. Years later the Jefferson Davis Hospital was built on part of the 45-acre site of the first clubhouse and nine-hole golf course on the south bank of Buffalo Bayou, which the club leased from the Rice Institute.

In July 1908, the membership was reorganized into the Houston Country Club. A new clubhouse was built in the Shingle style of residential architecture at a site on Wayside Drive and Brays Bayou, where boating down to the Houston Launch Club became a popular sport. A few bedrooms were available for overnight stays.

265

Clear Creek Fishing Club

ca. 1900

Architecturally, small fishing and hunting club buildings were indistinguishable from neighboring private bay houses, as seen here in the Clear Creek Fishing Club. Among these sometimes whimsically named groups was the Houston Left-handed Carnival Fishing and Hunting Club,

organized in 1887, with a house at Morgan's Point.

The Houston Yacht Club was organized in 1898 with a clubhouse at Seabrook, and the Houston Launch Club was organized in 1906 at Harrisburg. Members' yachts were used to transport senators, congressmen, and engineers on inspection tours in connection with establishing the Houston Ship Channel. In 1927 the Houston Launch Club and the Houston Yacht Club combined their mem-

berships and built the present clubhouse of the Houston Yacht Club at Shore Acres on Galveston Bay. Bedrooms accommodate overnight guests.

266

Greenwood Sanitarium for Nervous and Mental Diseases

9218 Old Main Street Road (now Fannin) at Old Spanish Trail
built 1912; demolished 1951

One of the first private hospitals for mental illness in Texas, Dr. James Greenwood's sanitarium was located on six acres backing up to Brays Bayou. The main building, pictured here, had forty-two rooms for patients plus rooms for nurses on the third floor. The separate two-story men's building had twenty-two rooms. A furnace house with a boiler room, an artesian well, tennis courts, and a croquet field were also on the property, as well as woods where Dr. Greenwood's sons hunted quail, doves, and prairie chickens.

267

Emma R. News Boys Home

ca. 1916
1600 Washington Avenue

Miss E. Ferdinand Trichelle, copublisher of the Houston railroad employees' newspaper, the *Railroad Echo*, founded the Emma R. News Boys Home for orphaned and homeless boys in 1910. She named it for her mother, Emma R. Gilbreath. In 1912 she was joined by Alice Finrock (fig. 272), secretary, manager, and in-house doctor. The home operated at various locations from 1910 until about 1922. In 1913 Mayor Ben Campbell gave to it the old Dow School, pictured here at 1600 Washington Avenue, just west of Houston Avenue, which the home occupied until 1919.

In 1913 Miss Trichelle was appointed juvenile probation officer so that she could receive a salary from the city. That spring 452 boys occupied the home.

268

Baptism in Buffalo Bayou, Sunday morning

ca. 1900–1904
South bank of Buffalo Bayou, opposite Henderson Street and east line of Glenwood Cemetery

The minister (center with pole) is about to immerse the woman who has been escorted into the water by two deacons. Others wait their turn on the bank in the background. Following immersion, the service took on the character of a religious revival as members of the congregation chanted spirituals (from a letter by Lucy Powers Dei to George Fuerman, April 11, 1955).

269

Maypole dance, Christ Church
May Fete

ca. 1910
1117 Texas Avenue

One of the oldest traditions in Houston, the Christ Church May Fete,
dates to at least 1855. As early as
1849 the women of Houston organized citywide May celebrations on
the banks of Buffalo Bayou, where
rustic thrones were constructed beneath the live oaks and magnolia
trees. Youthful May queens with attendants decked in flowered garlands
and evergreen wreaths were crowned
with flowers. Nurses came along to
care for the small children and help
protect their finery.

270

Christ Church rectory

1119 Texas Avenue at San Jacinto
Street
built 1902; demolished 1949
George E. Dickey, architect

This Victorian Gothic house was built
on the site of the earlier rectory
(fig. 34). It ceased to serve as a rectory and was used for church offices
before it was demolished for the Latham Building that now stands on
the site.

271

King Nottoc and his court

November 1907

Left to right (front row): Judge Presley K. Ewing, Virginia Dorrance, H. M. Garwood (King Nottoc), Alice Graham Baker (Queen), Hortense Lorenzen, Marguerite White Dickson, Daphne Palmer; (second row): Alma Miller Womack, unidentified, Bettie Taliaferro, unidentified, unidentified.

During the Gilded Age wealthy Americans often held pageants and masquerade balls to which they wore elaborate costumes. These costumes were designed to imitate historical figures from the European aristocracy, allowing those who wore them to identify with elegant court manners. No-Tsu-Oh (Houston spelled backward) was the city's annual cotton carnival held from 1899 through 1915. A prominent businessman was crowned King Nottoc (cotton spelled backward), and a debutante was crowned queen. In a series of tableaux, members of their court enacted an elaborate allegorical myth that centered on water transportation, the point of which was to show how important the ship channel was going to be to the Houston economy.

272

No-Tsu-Oh flower parade

ca. 1915

Left to right: E. Ferdinand Trichelle, Alice Finrock, Jo Ross Trichelle (baby), and Emma R. Gilbreath.

Parades of flower-bedecked vehicles were popular in the United States during the last quarter of the nineteenth century and into the twentieth. Southern flower parades usually were public affairs associated with agricultural festivals or commemorative historical events. In Houston annual flower parades celebrated No-Tsu-Oh, the blacks' corollary known as De-Ro-Loc, and Juneteenth. They also were held in honor of visiting dignitaries.

273

Jane Cochran with doll carriage, William Shepherd Cochran house

ca. 1915
4004 Brandt Street

The Juvenile Flower Parade at Sam Houston Park was a feature of No-Tsu-Oh week. Children participated with decorated doll buggies, baby carriages, and donkey and pony carts. Similar events were popular fund-raisers for organizations such as Faith Home and the First Presbyterian Church.

274

Martha Yates Jones and Pinkie V. Yates, William E. Jones house

319 Robin Street, Fourth Ward
built ca. 1890s; demolished ca. 1964

This picture of the Rev. Jack Yates's daughters was taken in 1908 probably before the flower parade celebrating Juneteenth, the anniversary of June 19, 1865, when news of the Emancipation Proclamation reached Texas.

275

Glenn Morgan Harris house

ca. 1903
Red Bluff Point, Galveston Bay
between La Porte and Seabrook
built ca. 1832; moved ca. 1833;
remodeled 1872; extant

William Plunkett Harris, a brother of
John R. Harris (fig. 9), received a
Mexican land grant at Red Bluff in
1832. Within the year he built a two-
story frame house, which burned in
January 1855. Because of subsidence,
the site of the first house is now in
Galveston Bay.

In February 1855 Harris's widow,
Caroline Morgan Harris, her second
husband, William Beazley, and her
children, Glenn Morgan Harris and
Eugenia Harris, moved into the original portion of the second house, pictured here, which had been moved
onto the property about 1833. Family
sources and the correspondence of
William P. Harris indicate that the
original one and one-half room section of this house was constructed by
Harris early in 1832 under a contract
with the Mexican government dated
January 31, 1832, as part of the customs house complex on Galveston Island. Possibly moved to Red Bluff by
Harris in 1833, when the customs
complex was abandoned, it was built
of cypress with a hipped roof.

In 1872, before his 1873 marriage,
Glenn Morgan Harris added three
bedrooms, a living room with a fireplace, an attic, and porches, all made
of cypress and resting on a cypress
foundation and handmade brick
piers pointed with tabby. The original
building became the dining room.
Staples like flour and sugar brought
by boat from Galveston were stored
in barrels in the attic. The house and
property, once renowned for the
beauty of its orchards and gardens,
remain in the family today. After the
death of Glenn Harris's widow, Leah,
in 1912, its function became primarily recreational. In 1924 part of the
property became the El Jardin
subdivision.

3 *Interiors*

Katherine S. Howe

The settler who came to Harris County in its earliest years was, as one of them so eloquently described himself, a "newcomer to a land whose civilization dates from yesterday."[1] Whether from the United States, Europe, or Africa, immigrants came to a land on the edge of civilization, verdant, wet, flat, hot, and insect-infested, but with promise for the future. Dependent upon their own abilities—economic, physical, and mental—settlers created homes on the basis of their own standards, past experiences, and means, tempered by the natural resources of what became Harris County. Of course, tales of people who endured enormous privations accompany all such migrations, and this one is no different. For example, there is an account of three impoverished Germans who were found in Houston "in a compartment constructed in the corner of a smithy . . . the mother-in-law, wrapped in a cloak, grief in her face, a bundle of laundry under her head, lying on the floor. . . . No bed, no table, no chair, not even the least convenience for resting after so many hardships."[2] Settlers like these, however, seemed the exception rather than the rule.

Located on waterways, Harrisburg and, later, Houston gave settlers access to the markets of the world from the outset. John R. Harris's store on the banks of Buffalo Bayou at its confluence with Brays Bayou offered a wide variety of imported goods for sale. At the time of his death in 1829, an inventory of his store and personal property included a crate of earthenware with six dozen plates, nine dozen bowls, and two dozen pitchers; forty-two dozen painted cups and saucers; ten chamber pots; 4½ dozen cups and saucers, a teapot, five pitchers and ten bowls in blue printed ware; dozens of soup, dinner, and breakfast plates; eight stemmed glasses; one coffee boiler; two boxes of window glass; 8½ dozen printed tumblers; 9½ dozen plain tumblers; 6½ dozen "Indian looking glasses"; 1½ dozen glass knobs; five small tin lamps; six candle snuffers; eighteen quart decanters; twelve pieces of hanging paper (wallpaper); two iron candlesticks; one turning lathe; turning tools; one crosscut saw; twenty-five blankets; nine pillows; and countless other necessities for home, carpentry, and farming.[3] Harris's goods tended to be sturdy, immune to water damage, and utilitarian. He did not seem to have stocked furniture, possibly because of its bulk and fragility. Perhaps, too, at this point in Harris County's history most settlers brought their furniture with them, ordered it, or made do with chairs, tables, and other basic furnishings made from local materials.

Almost immediately after the founding of Houston in 1836, local newspapers began to advertise supplies delivered from New York, Philadelphia, Boston, New Orleans, and London. If they had the patience and the means, and it seems as though a number of people did, Harris County householders had access to the latest styles and goods from worldwide manufacturing centers. Houston, with one foot in the wilderness and the other in the industrialized world, became the funnel for commerce for southeastern Texas. Shipments arriving on Buffalo Bayou were both sold in Houston and shipped out to rural communities and to planters, whose business was cheerfully solicited by local merchants. This is not to say that domestic products were never made in Houston; indeed, bedding, chairs, furniture, ceramics, and candles were manufactured locally by the late 1840s. Unlike more isolated areas, such as the rural Texas German farming communities west of Harris County where transportation was impeded by overland routes dependent on dry weather for horses and ox carts, Houston seems to have relied from the very beginning on imports more than on locally made products.

While Houston certainly had some destitute immigrants like the aforementioned family, there were also a few families on the other end of the economic spectrum. In 1833 Mary Austin Holley, the adventurous Connecticut-born cousin of Stephen F. Austin, counseled those contemplating a move to Texas to "bring with them all indispensable articles for household use, together with as much common clothing (other clothing is not wanted) for themselves and their children, as they, conveniently, can. . . . If, on arrival, they find a surplus on hand, it can be readily disposed of to advantage; for trade, by barter, is much practiced, and you buy provisions, with coffee, calico, tea-kettles, and sauce pans, instead of cash." Holley also cautioned settlers to bring disassembled chairs and bureaus with them, knowing that tables could be made locally. And with admirable New England practicality she cautioned, "The maxim here, is, nothing for show but all for use."[4] In other words, prepared immigrants brought what they could for their homes, planned for a long stay, and knew from the beginning that they were dealing with the basic elements of civilization. The finer points would come later.

Those immigrants who arrived with fully equipped households tended to be from the United States. Allen C. Reynolds (ca. 1775–1837) was just such an early settler. On April 23, 1831, before the Allen brothers bought the grant on which they founded Houston, Stephen F. Austin granted this Connecticut-born New Yorker one league of land "on the right bank of the arroyo called Buffalo Bayou," west of what would become the Allen tract, in the area now known as River Oaks, Greenway Plaza, and the City of West University Place. To claim the land, Reynolds had to be married, which he was—to Harriet Baird of New York—and to live on the land, which he had been doing since at least February 1830.[5]

Reynolds chose to ship a fully equipped household from New York to Texas. In spite of the distance, in 1832 he also ordered supplies from Roger Shatzel of 171 South Street, New York. (South Street in lower Manhattan served New York's harbor and was a commercial center.) In addition to London mustard and 75 gallons of wine and liquor, Reynolds ordered eight boxes of spermaceti candles (the finest candles then made), pickled oysters, Java coffee, and "400 Havanna Segars." On March 14, 1837, after moving near the town of Washington-on-the-Brazos, approximately sixty miles from his Harris County tract, Allen C. Reynolds died. Washington County probate records show an impressive estate valued at $95,305.93. It included a bureau, three beds, bedding and bedsteads, brass andirons and shovel tongs, a hearth brush, two ink-stands, a card table, a large looking glass, four oil paintings, fourteen yards of carpeting, a kitchen table, nine chairs, four brass candlesticks, one lot of queensware (glazed white earthenware), one lot of china, glasses, one set of britannia ware (lathe-spun pewter), forty-four dinner plates, three large dinner dishes, two glass decanters, one lot of tinware, one lot of candle molds, and several books, including one set of Rollins's history, *The Federalist* (possibly *The Federalist Papers* [1788] by Alexander Hamilton, James Madison, and John Jay), and Ovid.[6]

The Reynolds tract was just one of several farms and ranches that radiated into the countryside from Houston and Harrisburg, although it seems to have been one of the best equipped. In the 1830s and 1840s newspaper advertisements sometimes referred to such tracts as plantations and to their owners as planters. The terms did not have the grandiose connotations then that they do now, and plantations in the Harris County area were considerably smaller than those of the Deep South or the Texas Brazos River area.

Ashbel Smith, who served as the Texas army's surgeon, also owned a plantation. As mentioned in earlier chapters, it was named Headquarters and was located on Goose Creek in Harris County in what is now the center of the city of Baytown. Smith bought it "to have a house in the country with all the profusion, the hearty comforts and appliances for field sports that such a life affords." He bought the land in 1840 and by the end of June in that year had completed his new home.[7] The nineteenth-century German geologist and chronicler Ferdinand Roemer described the "manor house" of Headquarters as

> a common two-roomed log cabin, built of partly-hewn logs. The simple furniture consisted of a bed, a table, and a few chairs, the seats of which were made by stretching a calf skin tight over them. On the wall near a huge fireplace, in which logs four to five feet in length could be placed, hung an American rifle with a long, heavy barrel, and a shot gun. In the corner of the room stood a tall cabinet, whose contents contrasted sharply with the surroundings. It contained chiefly books which formed a small but carefully selected library. Not only were the Greek and Roman classics represented, but also the best and choicest selections of English and French literature. . . . Near the manor house stood a small insignificant house which was inhabited by the negro family in charge of the farm.[8]

Although Roemer does not say in which rooms the furniture was placed, it is obvious from the list that Smith's two rooms served multiple functions, including sleeping, eating, and reading. Roemer has described a more modest planter's interior: spare, functional, unfinished, but graced with a library useful to an educated settler. Such versatility was as common in those simple interiors as it has been in small homes in North America since the seventeenth century. Indeed, most antebellum Texas homes must have had very flexible room arrangements. Some professionals like doctors and lawyers maintained offices in their homes, while most homes must have needed to accommodate house guests and many children within finite living, eating, and sleeping quarters.

In his observations Roemer referred to Smith's chairs with calf-hide seats. These chairs were variations on the typical slat-back side chair that has been common in the United States since the eighteenth century. Instead of having more usual rush or splint seats, these early Texas chairs have hides tightly stretched between the chairs' legs. Hide-seat chairs seem to have been staples in many Texas homes, both in Harris County and as far west as Fredricksburg.[9]

Roemer also mentioned a bed. It, too, may have been locally made and similar to the type described by Lewis Birdsall Harris in his journal. Nestled in a corner, cabin walls supported these early bedsteads on two sides. Two rails supported by a post framed the other two sides. Boards laid across the rails completed the beds, and bed ticks stuffed with materials like prairie grass, Spanish moss, and horsehair lay upon them.[10]

The furnishings of Smith's Headquarters do not seem to have been appreciably different from those in the house of Jonathan B. Frost, who died in Houston in 1837. Frost left one "burran" (probably a bureau), a table, one dozen chairs, "matrasses" and bedstead, two pots and an oven, one corn mill, and one churn, for a total appraised value of $120.75. His total estate, including $3000 in slaves, came to $6668.75.[11]

Although coastal Texas is not immune to cold weather and bitter winter days, from the very beginning hot humid summers and intense sunshine alternating with cloudbursts have played a far greater role in the development of Houston interiors. Some of the earliest interiors afforded the barest protection from the elements. Frequently made of rough-hewn logs and as rudimentary as "a small log pen" with a fire in the corner, they provided marginal first shelter for settlers establishing a toehold on this raw land and were probably well beneath the settler's previous standard of living.[12] In 1831 a German settler living near San Felipe in Austin County recalled "a miserable little hut covered with straw and having six sides which were made out of moss. The roof was by no means water-proof, and we often held an umbrella over our bed when it rained at night. . . . My father had tried to build a chimney and fireplace out of logs and clay, but we were afraid to light a fire because of the extreme combustibility of our dwelling."[13]

From the beginning multiple exposures and good cross-ventilation dictated room arrangements. Porches and galleries served as shady rooms without walls. Well into the twentieth century, they were warm-weather living spaces where families played, ate, entertained, and watched the world go by. They were flexible spaces used as parlors, reading rooms, dining rooms, bedrooms, workrooms, and for any other required function.

Because there were so few artists in early Texas and because indoor photography was slow and cumbersome at best, only a few tantalizing clues survive to document early Harris County interiors.[14] These clues are largely gleaned from newspaper advertisements, which usually provided the following information: the name of a retailer whose Houston office was often a branch of a New Orleans or Galveston concern; the name of the ship delivering the merchandise, its origin, and a list of contents to be sold; and the terms of payment, which might be Texas or U. S. dollars or credit against crops. On February 19, 1838, the merchants Doswell Adams ran a fairly typical advertisement:

> Just received per Schooner Isaac W. Norris from Philadelphia, a cargo of sundry merchandise, consisting of the following articles, viz: . . . assortment of queens ware; assortment of tin ware, consisting of buckets, dish and bake pans, coffeepots, tin cups, funnels, lamp feeders, wash bowls, coffee mills, cullenders [colanders?], bowls, scoups [sic], measures, pepper boxes, kettles, Japanned canisters, tea pots and lanthorns [lanterns?]; complete sets of brittania [sic] ware, consisting of coffee, tea, sugar and cream pots, and slop bowls (6 pieces); which they offer for sale at the lowest prices for the promissory notes of the government.[15]

Christopher H. Pix and Company, at Number 6 on the Strand in Galveston, ran similar advertisements in Houston, identifying themselves as "Importers of English Goods Direct from London" but adding that they paid the "highest price for any quantity of perfect cotton delivered here in exchange for . . . splendid goods, lately imported from London." In one particular advertisement Pix went on to state that he had "again been absent to, and remaining in Europe six months, for the sole purpose of superintending the manufacture of the articles which comprise this shipment . . . to the wants, . . . and fashion of the inhabitants of Texas."[16]

The Houston-London connection was so well established that by 1841 Archibald S. Ruthven of the English Importing House advertised "two first rate British manufacture Piano Fortes . . . in rose-wood and mahogany, just imported, and will be sold cheap for cash or trade." Ruthven continued to import European goods and by 1850 seems to have had a substantial inventory in European metalwares, including "from the Manufacturers in Sheffield, England, a large assortment of Hardware and Cutlery," such as knives and forks, spoons in both tin and silver plate, cupboard locks, japanned latches, fine steel scissors, and joiners' planes. He also advertised German steel handsaws and German silver table- and teaspoons.[17]

By 1858 Houston could support T. E. Thompson, a dealer in gold and silver, watches, and jewelry. In addition to "jewels and precious stones," he carried a variety of silver objects that he "warranted equal to coin" silver. His stock seemed quite extensive and included pitchers, castors, napkin rings, soup tureens, salvers, fruit and cake baskets, sugar tongs and shovels, and candlesticks.[18] The bulk of this hollowware undoubtedly was made in the eastern United States and was ordered by Thompson to be sold either in Houston or in his Galveston store.

Furniture also flooded into Houston. There seems to have been a specific Houston/New York furniture association during those years, for Jesse F. Randel on Main Street advertised a recent shipment from New York, this one via the brig *North*. The shipment included "Mahogany Sideboards and Sofas, Mahogany, Cherry, and Black Walnut Bureaus, Mahogany and Cherry Work and Dressing Tables, Mahogany, Cherry, Walnut and Maple Bedsteads, Writing Tables and Desks, Wash Stands, Foot Benches, Reed, Flag [flax?] and Wood Bottomed Chairs, Rocking Chairs, Settees, Looking Glasses & c, & c.[19] As early as 1838 Dr. Henry Evans, a druggist at Number 5 Mercantile Row with medicines "fresh and direct from New York," advertised for sale "A handsome SOFA, BOOK CASE, DRAWERS and SHELVES for a physician's office, eight Chairs, round Mahogany Table, 4 post bedstead and Mosquito Net, A Counter and Drawers, handsome family Medicine Chest, Writing Desk inlaid with Brass, [and] Ladies Dressing Stand."[20]

The same paper carried an advertisement from John Cornick, Jr., who had newly arrived "FURNITURE of superior workmanship," including "2 bureaus with Looking Glasses, a Sofa with loose [horse] hair cushions, Music Stools and others of an ornamental pattern, Work Table and a Work Box, 1 Portable Writing Desk, 1 Spanish Gaiter [sic], 1 Billiard Table complete, 3 Medicine Chests with directions, abd [and] a few Paintings."[21] It was fairly common in the United States at this time, and probably in Houston also, for furniture dealers to have items for sale in a showroom and to maintain an active special-order trade as well. In addition, Cornick may have actually imported oil on canvas paintings for sale in Houston. It is also plausible that his paintings were actually lithographs or engravings after originals similar to Henry Kesler's, who in 1837 sold "A SPLENDID variety of plain and colored Engravings and Lithographs . . . at low prices for cash" at the Houston Exchange.[22]

In their advertisements, Evans, Cornick, and Randel were probably describing furniture of the type made before the Civil War in great quantities in eastern cities, particularly New York, and sold throughout the United States in the 1830s and early 1840s. Often constructed of mahogany or rosewood, and dependent on thin, figured veneers and lathe-turned decoration, the furniture was in the style now called Restoration, or pillar and scroll. Manufacturers shipped pieces to Texas in a knocked-down state, and dealers assembled them locally. The styles were also sometimes executed in Texas by Texas-German furniture makers working from Houston to the Hill Country more than two hundred miles to the west.[23] Later imports of the 1840s and 1850s doubtless incorporated romantic revival influences such as Gothic, Italianate, and French (today sometimes called "Belter," after John Henry Belter, the New York cabinetmaker most often identified with the style).[24] Simpler spool-decorated versions of these styles, known as cottage furniture, were also sold in Houston. James H. Cooke, a New York furniture dealer, went so far as to advertise his wares in Houston, including high-post, cottage, and French beds. He promised "Particular attention paid to the boxing and shipment of goods, which is done by most experienced hands."[25]

In 1848 James A. Sauters, who had stores in both Galveston and Houston, also promoted up-to-date styles. In two separate advertisements in 1848 Sauters advertised "Mahogany French and half French Chairs . . . mahogany and marble top bureaus." He also advertised a full range of domestic accoutrements, including "Carpeting, Matting, Oil Cloth, Mats, Lamps, and Willow Ware," and "China, Glass, Crockery Ware . . . Painted Window Shades and Blinds," which he purchased in New York and Boston. Sauters's was perhaps Houston's first home-furnishings store.[26]

In part because Houston was a growing community and probably because of tariffs imposed by the Republic of Texas between 1836 and 1842 on many imported goods, in the 1840s a few products began to be made locally.[27] One example is earthenware made by the Shaben and Brother earthenware company, which advertised under the headline "Encourage Home Manufacture!" The Shabens offered "a large assortment of that splendid Earthenware manufactured by them in this city," with the tantalizing note that "Our Stone and Crockery Ware will be ready in a few Days."[28] One year later another firm, the Houston Pottery, advertised "Stone Ware at New York prices" as well as an immediate need for good potters.[29]

At this time a number of Houston merchants probably sold manufactured goods and marketed their own wares as well. During this period it was fairly common to see hardware, cooking stoves, tin, and copper all sold by the same merchant.[30] Alexander McGowen, a tinsmith elected Houston's mayor in 1858, was probably typical. In addition to selling cooking stoves, he carried "a large assortment of Tin, Sheet Iron, and Copper-ware, which owing to the reduction of duties, in consequence of annexation, he is enabled to offer for sale at *greatly reduced prices*. . . . The subscriber also manufactures at his shop . . . sheet iron and tin ware."[31]

Among the largest trade groups serving Houston homes at this time were the furniture makers, who came from a number of different places: Belgium, France, England, Ireland, Prussia, Baden, Holstein, Hesse, South Carolina, Louisiana, New York, and Texas.[32] Some, like P. William Lang[33] who was working in Houston in 1837, both made and repaired furniture; others, like the firm of Grainger and Ackerman, combined cabinetmaking and turning with building and carriage making.[34] Others practiced a combination of cabinetmaking and retailing, in much the same way as did McGowen, the tinsmith. In 1843 S. D. Staats, for example, advertised that he "has on hand and is constantly manufacturing all kinds of Cabinet Ware" and proceeded to list fourteen different furniture forms.[35] His advertisement suggests either that he owned a very large manufacturing and retail business (a doubtful situation) or that he combined imported goods with those of his own or local manufacture. Another example was Frederick Allyn Rice, who, while not a cabinetmaker, sold an extensive line of home furnishings in 1858, including "furniture now on hand, and being received by every boat."[36] How strange, then, that he would advertise bedsteads made of magnolia and sycamore, trees indigenous to Harris County that are unusual woods for furniture, unless the beds were made in Houston or in the near South.

Beds, of course, were necessary to any household. The four-poster, tester, and half-tester beds so loved in the twentieth century for their grace and romantic connotations were coveted in the nineteenth century not only for their beauty but also for their ability to support mosquito netting, a desirable protection from Harris County insects. Netting was used in Texas at least as early as 1831, when Mary Austin Holley cautioned that "every emigrant should use mosqueto [sic] bars. . . . They are indispensable in the summer season, and are made of this species of muslin, manufactured for the purpose."[37]

Mattresses, too, were adapted to the climate and the materials available. Because feathers were expensive ($50 per pound in 1848) and in spite of cotton being touted in some circles, Spanish moss, which hung in profusion from local deciduous trees, seems to have been a preferred material.[38] Nineteenth-century citizens were concerned with mattress maintenance, for they considered mattresses and bedding sources of yellow fever and other diseases:

> Few persons are aware that diseases of a dangerous or fatal character may be caused by sleeping on moss or hair mattrasses [sic], that have been long used. . . . It is important, therefore, that all old mattrasses, intended for summer use should be opened and the hair or moss washed, cleaned, and repacked after it is well dried in a clean tick.[39]

Spanish moss continued to be used in mattresses well into the twentieth century. As a result, their manufacture and improvement were of some interest locally. In 1889 the Houston Machine Mattress Factory (Lottman Brothers) even patented a new method for processing the moss. At that time one of the employees recorded the traditional method:

> The old Process of curing moss is very slow and not wholly satisfactory—The moss (green) is placed in pits or piled in large piles and kept wet until it is cured —that is until the bark is rotted from the fiber—It is a rotting process to clear the fiber from the bark—Of course must this [sic] have close attention otherwise the fibers will rot and become worthless—
>
> The bottom moss in pits or heaps will of course rot faster than that on top. This necessitates repeling [sic] every few weeks, which is enormous work as the moss is wet and has to remain in process for two (2) to three (3) months. . . .[40]

Moss mattresses continued to be advertised in Houston through 1895 and to be used by rural blacks, at least in nearby Louisiana, into the 1920s.[41]

While some merchants outfitted homes, others tailored the interiors: walls, ceilings, draperies, upholstery, and floors all required specialized workers. These men (painters, carpet layers, plasterers, woodworkers, and upholsterers) often did custom work dictated by room sizes and the owners' tastes and resources. Walls were, of course, a fundamental interior concern, as John R. Harris's 1829 probate reference to twelve hanging paper rolls attests; but paint, at least in the early years, seems to have been the preferred wall treatment. White paint, to which painters could add colored pigment, was sold by the keg as early as 1838 and continued to be offered in this way for years to come.[42] Houston has always had a dampness problem, and in at least one instance newspapers recommended a paint made of one part beeswax, three parts boiled linseed oil, and one-tenth part litharge (oxide of lead) applied hot to avoid mildew and peeling on stone or brick walls.[43] Some Houston families, however, preferred more elaborate treatment such as graining, that is, applying paint to resemble wood. Martin K. Snell, a "House, Sign, and Ornamental Painter," who did "Imitations Of Wood, And Marble, Gilding, Glazing & c. & c." in 1840, was probably representative of this craft.[44] The wood-graining in the Nichols-Rice-Cherry house, built around 1850, is typical of this type of mid-century painted decoration.

Wallpaper was also common. Joseph S. Taft informed the public in 1855 that he had 10,000 pieces of "paper hangings" in stock, costing from 12½ cents to $3.00 each, while a competitor,

James Burke and Company, announced that he carried wallpaper manufactured by Hart, Montgomery and Company of Philadelphia.[45]

Large functioning windows, of course, were mandatory in hot, humid Houston. Sash windows were not only efficient and attractive but, when large ones opened onto a porch, they could be used in lieu of doors. By 1850 James A. Thompson manufactured window sashes and blinds in Houston. Two horses powered the machinery Thompson used to make cypress sashes, blinds, and doors. Cypress, a local wood, remains highly desirable for its resistance to rot and termites.[46]

By the mid-1850s Houston windows received increasing attention. Taft, the paper hangings purveyor, also sold window shades and curtains. His references (and those of New Orleans dealer T. D. Dameron, who advertised in Houston) to shutters, cornices, and such drapery materials as brocatelle (a variation on damask), damasks, lace and muslin curtains, pins, cords, and tassels indicate that Houston's window treatments did not vary noticeably from those in comparable houses in other North American cities.[47] In a formula that did not seem to change appreciably until the end of the century, shutters hung immediately adjacent to the sash windows, with a window shade sometimes taking the place of indoor shutters. Shutters afforded privacy, air circulation even during a rain, and shade, as well as an extra measure of protection against severe storms and stray animals. Sheer curtains, in nineteenth-century parlance sometimes called glass curtains, which hung between shutters or shades and the heavier brocades, too, lent privacy and diffused sunlight, and made it more difficult for mosquitoes and flies to enter (fig. 165).

The interior draperies of brocade and silk trimmed with cords and tassels not only provided insulation, keeping heat in during winter and out in summer, but also made an undeniable statement about the taste and income of the householder; they were far more common in first-floor public rooms than upstairs in bedrooms.

Some drapers also did upholstery work. John B. Conrad advertised his diverse skills by offering to upholster lounges, sofas, tête-à-têtes, and easy chairs and to make window and bed curtains, as well as doing wallpapering.[48]

Floor coverings, too, contributed to the overall appearance of interiors. Practical Houstonians (and those on more limited budgets) bought floor or oil cloths, decorated area mats made of painted and sealed canvas.[49] Floor cloths offered modest insulating properties but, perhaps more important, were easy to keep clean. Others could purchase grass and rope matting which in more affluent homes was put down in the summer months in lieu of carpeting.[50] Woven carpets, however, were more elegant. By 1855 both Wilton (cut pile) and three-ply carpeting could be bought in Houston as could Brussels (a loop-pile weave), hearth rugs, and stair rods to secure carpeted stairs.[51] Since these carpets were seldom more than thirty-six inches wide, carpet strips were sewn together to make large area or wall-to-wall carpets (fig. 176).

By the 1840s Houston's acculturation pattern was established in a way that would continue until the Civil War: new arrivals lived in temporary quarters until they could find or build permanent houses. They furnished their houses as best they could with a mixture of locally made and imported products, and if they did not like what was marketed locally and could afford to do so, they ordered goods from elsewhere.[52] Some homeowners lived in substantial residences with formalized room arrangements, including parlors, dining rooms, and multiple sleeping rooms.[53] By 1855 even some rural houses, like the one located twenty miles from Houston belonging to a Judge Buckley, compared favorably with houses elsewhere in the nation. Buckley's house was a "fine two-story brick house with a handsome portico. On the first floor there were five rooms with folding doors between, as elegant as any Ohio house. The parlor was furnished with a sofa, a marble-topped table, mahogany chairs, gilded cornices at the windows, and 'all the usual ornaments of a city house.'"[54]

A growing sophistication resulted from improved economic conditions, rising cotton prices, and a more settled community, but it was also because Texans were beginning to experience the first wave of the Industrial Revolution, which had an impact on household amenities as well as on factory production.

Interior lighting also progressed. Spermaceti candles and oil (whale by-products that gave the cleanest, most desirable light) had long been available in Houston; merchants also stocked parlor, side, and suspended lamps, girondoles, and mantel ornaments, but by 1844 Houston had lard oil and stearine candle-manufacturing companies, too.[55] Not only did these firms provide good products, but they also provided a ready market for Harris County's cattle and swine, two heretofore undervalued local commodities.[56] In 1847 a Mr. Hall demonstrated a "portable gass [sic] light." He told his audience that "eight lights of the size and intensity of an ordinary spermaceti candle, can be furnished for only 1/4 cent per hour" and "that there is not the least danger that the materials may explode," a possibility with camphene, an extremely volatile liquid fuel also used in lamps at this time.[57] After 1859 kerosene, one of petroleum's first commercial products, became the preferred fuel for lamps in homes without access to natural gas or electricity, a status that it maintained into the twentieth century (fig. 163). In all probability some kerosene lamps were in use in Houston in the early 1860s, for post-bellum advertisements for kerosene stoves presuppose knowledge of them.[58]

In 1859 Houstonians saw their first demonstration of gas lighting from a private generating plant. The account does not say what fuel created the gas, but in 1868, thanks to oyster shell and coal by-products, the Houston Gas Light Company formally, if somewhat erratically, introduced gas service to the city.[59] Like kerosene, gas produced soot that discolored ceilings, walls, draperies, upholstery, and rugs. Ironically, improved lighting simultaneously created more dirt and made it easier to see.

Muddy streets, mosquitoes, and yellow fever epidemics notwithstanding, there was (by 1860) an undeniable feeling that Houston was, at least in some fortunate circles, a civilized place to live on the edge of the frontier. The Civil War, however, interrupted domestic progress. The Union blockade prevented importation of most manufactured goods. With rare exception, local newspaper advertisements for goods and services ceased, supplanted by news about the war and appeals to the populace for war supplies. When merchants advertised goods they were such staples as blankets, bleached cotton yardage, "Yankee notions," broadcloth, tools, thread, and needles.[60] Not until Reconstruction did extensive advertising resume and were merchants able to restock their shelves.[61]

After the war merchants resumed trade with manufacturing centers and offered new domestic wares like more efficient stoves and ample supplies of kerosene. Economic recovery was well on its way by 1870. One measure of returning prosperity was the number and diversity of exhibitors at the 1870 state fair held in Houston. Exhibitors came from throughout the United States to show the latest products, including those for the home. There were twenty-one entries in the cooking stoves, ranges, and heating apparatus category alone, which Texans gratefully embraced as alternatives to open hearths and wood-burning fireplaces (fig. 160). No doubt some of these cooking stoves, which were probably of the free-standing cast-iron coal- or wood-burning variety, were similar to the "Southern Home," "Cotton Bale," and "Belle of the South" models that were advertised as being "Suitable to the TEXAS MARKET."[62] One of the exhibitors, joiner August Bering, founded a hardware business that continues today.[63]

As it was elsewhere in the United States, the Civil War marked a turning point for interior design in Houston. Although Harris County never had tremendous houses comparable to those built in some northeastern and midwestern cities and resorts, a number of substantial and conservatively stylish houses were built locally. In discussing these post-Civil War interiors, however, one must remember that it is Harris County's most substantial houses, which often belonged to civic leaders, that are the best documented. They imply that all urban residents enjoyed a very high standard of living. Not everyone did. However, these stylish houses, clearly visible on Houston's major streets, served as arbiters of taste and models for subsequent domiciles. In addition, local newspapers and occasionally magazines recounted parties in private houses in great detail. They described not only the social event, menu, and decorations but houses' interior decoration as well.[64] Trends were aided by retailers who supplied their customers according to what was popular locally and what was recommended by suppliers, periodicals, and catalogs. Oriental carpets are fine examples of the dissemination of taste. Carpets imported from the Near East for an upper-class house (fig. 169) might be reinterpreted as an English or American woven copy of an oriental carpet in an upper-middle-class house, or an oil cloth with an oriental pattern in a middle-class one.[65] Of necessity a modest house probably made do with a bare floor.

After the Civil War local newspapers less frequently advertised the curvaceous furnishings so often featured in antebellum issues. Furniture became more rectilinear and less dependent on deeply sculpted carving. Floriforms such as daisies and chrysanthemums were reduced to stylized patterns used as repeats in woodwork, tiles, and wallpapers (fig. 161). In other words, Houstonians in the 1870s began to purchase furniture and interior accoutrements like those popularized by Charles Locke Eastlake in his best-selling book, *Hints on Household Taste*, the most important guide to interior design in the 1870s and 1880s.[66] Eastlake popularized aesthetic interiors of the style endorsed by English designer William Morris and his circle. The style was strongly influenced by medieval furniture forms, oriental decorative motifs, and Renaissance architectural moldings. In Houston, the Eastlake style was most readily apparent in parlor and bedroom suites (fig. 166). These suites, with all components made of the same wood (often walnut or maple turned and stained to resemble bamboo; figs. 167, 174), incorporated consistent design motifs throughout. A bedroom suite included a bedstead (often outfitted with a half-tester for mosquito netting), a bureau with mirror above and often with marble top, and, in homes that did not yet include built-in closets, a wardrobe. Bedrooms also could contain other amenities: a washstand with bowl and pitcher, a towel rack, a rocker, chairs, and for a child or the woman of the house, a desk.[67]

Later in the century Houstonians used wicker furniture in bedrooms, in parlors, and on porches (figs. 168, 170, 212). It was cool, lightweight, comparatively inexpensive, and comfortable (fig. 156).

By 1877 a new furniture specialty appeared in city directories: furniture dealers.[68] Furniture makers either made or assembled furniture locally; furniture dealers sold furniture made by others, usually in factories. There is little doubt that Houston customers, like those in other American cities, now shopped at furniture dealers who probably bought their wares in the Midwest—in Grand Rapids, Cincinnati, and Chicago (figs. 184, 185)—as well as in the eastern United States.[69] Stiff competition from factories elsewhere made it increasingly difficult for local furniture makers to compete. According to family history, Rebecca Wheeler Simpson actually traveled to Cincinnati in about 1882 to buy the furnishings for her home, including the parlor (fig. 161).[70] In addition, a major Cincinnati manufacturer, Mitchell and Rammelsberg (active 1847–81), operated a New Orleans outlet as early as 1866. Given the close trade relations between New Orleans and Houston and the presence of Robert Mitchell and Company's furniture in the McFaddin-Ward house in Beaumont and the Willis Moody mansion in Galveston, it is highly probable that Mitchell and Rammelsberg furniture was also sold in Houston.[71]

Although Houston does seem to have followed the mainstream of American interior design—in fact surviving photographs indicate that the city was not very adventurous—it did have access to two highly idiosyncratic forms of regional furniture: state penitentiary and horn furniture. The inmates of the state prison in Huntsville made furniture that was available in Houston in 1873. Ward, Dewey and Company advertised that "owing to our facilities we can sell cheaper than any other firm in the State."[72] Horn furniture, including a divan, piano stool, and chairs, was made by Joe White of Houston. It was probably a local version of the type of longhorn furniture made by Wenzel Friedrich in San Antonio, which Friedrich marketed nationally.[73] Horn and antler furniture was popular throughout the United States and Europe during this period. It was yet another way by which nineteenth-century industrial societies in Europe and North America romanticized the vanishing wilderness and attempted to incorporate it into their middle- and upper-middle-class worlds. It was this same kind of wistful remembrance that led a number of Houston homeowners, like others throughout the United States, to have bear, mountain goat, fox, and coyote or wolf pelts scattered on their floors as runners, hearth rugs, and area rugs (figs. 169, 201).[74]

More elaborate and more specialized furnishings were designed for the era's stylish and increasingly structured houses. Although larger new houses still relied on a prominent stair hall flanked by rooms, the rooms were often irregularly shaped: oriels, bays, and other projections relieved what otherwise might have been very ponderous interiors (figs. 166, 168, 178). At the same time these projections provided additional sources for daylight and air circulation, while spacious stairwells doubled as natural flues for vertical ventilation systems, drawing warm air upward from high-ceilinged first- and second-story rooms through the attic and out attic vents and dormers.

After the Civil War spacious entrance halls with massive stairs and imposing newel posts took on increased importance as a formal bridge between the world outside and the sanctity of the home (fig. 175). The public rooms of large, new houses were very specialized. Parlors, libraries, dining rooms, conservatories, drawing rooms, and music rooms, each with a specified function in keeping with more formal social customs developing during the late nineteenth century, were not uncommon.

In the most substantial houses these rooms also had gender-specific uses prescribed in a formula that continued in traditional households through the end of the century. In houses with central entrance halls, parlors and drawing rooms were "feminine" rooms in which women of the home received and entertained their guests. Where there were front and back parlors, the rooms were separated by large sliding pocket doors that could be opened to accommodate large parties (figs. 169, 170). Front parlors and drawing rooms were the houses' airiest ones, decorated in colors with lighter palettes and containing more lightly framed accoutrements. Often they were decorated in revivalist French styles that were much more faithful interpretations of genuine Louis XV and Louis XVI (fig. 180) furniture than the top-heavy Rococo Revival versions seen before the Civil War. Often the parlor contained a piano. Back parlors were more casual spaces informally furnished and reserved for family, not public, purposes, much as dens and family rooms are used today.

The entrance hall (figs. 169, 175), a neutral area in the house, became an imposing space neither masculine nor feminine, in which, in wealthier homes, visitors were greeted by a servant and waited in hospitable surroundings to be received by hostess or host. Here, too, visitors might make a formal call, leaving a card or conducting a brief bit of business. The entrance hall was used by social equals only; service people, household employees, and children at play used a rear door. By the end of the period the entrance hall in some houses evolved into a reception area, a broad living space, often with a fireplace and comfortable seating, which could be used both for entertaining and as an entrance to the house.[75]

Later in the century, when staircases within the entrance halls grew more important, builders relocated them from the side of the hall to the back. Broad and imposing, they often made one, and sometimes two, right-angle turns as they ascended to the second floor. A prominent newel post often anchored the stairway, giving it an air of importance while at the same time serving as a base for an impressive torchiere. The stairwell was often the location of a decorative device new to this era, stained glass (fig. 182). Tall, multicolored windows were installed in stairwell landings, where they cast warm light over otherwise dark passageways. Stained and leaded glass was used throughout turn-of-the-century homes in front doors, transoms, and sidelights, as well as in stairwells. The windows were either shipped in or fabricated locally by such firms as the Houston Art Glass Company (fig. 150) and the Texas Art Glass Company (fig. 196).

Opposite the parlor or drawing room lay the "masculine" room, the library (fig. 201). Often the dining room was behind it. In photographs of surviving Houston libraries, the rooms were hearty spaces with half-height bookcases made of dark woods and containing deep, comfortable upholstered seating and, of course, a desk. This was the man's retreat within the home, where men retired after dinner to enjoy their pipes and cigars and used their cuspidors (fig. 188). Women, of course, withdrew to the drawing room, hence the room's name.

The dining room (figs. 179, 181, 187, 193) shared many of the features of the library: it was dark and heavily trimmed. Often it had ponderous, richly carved serving boards with shelves above to display ceramics and other small objects, a plate rail encircling the room, and a circular dining table with a richly carved pedestal (fig. 179). The tables could be enlarged by the addition of numerous leaves. Three of Houston's elaborate dining rooms from the late 1890s, which are documented by photographs, also share another decorative accoutrement: glass grape-cluster electric light shades (figs. 179, 181, 193). The Houston Electric Light and Power Company was franchised in 1882 and by 1884 was providing at least occasional power to the city, although wary homeowners continued for some years to depend on gas as a backup.[76] Although incandescent light offered brightness never before enjoyed in homes, its brilliance and visible filaments posed difficulties. Grape-cluster and leaded-glass lampshades, of the type associated with Louis Comfort Tiffany (fig. 181), were two ways that Houstonians softened this new source of illumination.

Behind the dining room and the stairs lay the service area with the kitchen (fig. 195). Even in the best houses service areas and kitchens were rudimentary by today's standards. Only affluent turn-of-the-century householders could have hot and cold running water, electric lights, a wood- or, later, gas-burning stove, and an icebox. Older, more modest, and rural houses made do with less: cold water carried indoors in buckets to be heated on wood or kerosene stoves, kerosene lamps, and little or no refrigeration.[77]

In proximity to the kitchen lay the butler's pantry (fig. 194), the buffer zone between kitchen and dining room where fine dishes, silver, glass, and linens were kept. By 1900 Houstonians filled their butler's pantries with a wide variety of goods, most of which could be purchased locally. Retailers like John McClellan (fig. 151) stocked fine cut glass, porcelain dinner services, metal wares, art pottery, and flatware. C. L. and Theo. Bering, Jr. (fig. 152), in addition to providing mantels, hardware, and stoves, stocked fine china, including French porcelain made and decorated by Haviland and marked expressly for "C. L. & Theo. Bering Jr., Inc., Houston, Texas."[78] By 1911 the Japanese Art Store (fig. 153), located on Main Street, sold imported ceramics and metal wares to an interested public.

The back stairs, the utility porch containing laundry equipment (if there was no wash house) and cleaning paraphernalia, and any other amenities that owners could afford also lay near the kitchen. A back door leading from the utility porch to the back yard was used by servants in their daily routine. Deliveries were made to a side entrance, which sometimes was located under a porte cochere. The basement, or half-basement, which contained the furnace and central heating equipment, had a separate entrance as well. The Waldo house, Edwin B. Parker's The Oaks, and a number of houses on Courtlandt Place are examples of Houston houses that had basements. Householders could choose either hot-air (fig. 182) or radiant-heating systems (fig. 189), with radiators warmed by either hot water or steam. Hardware supply companies, such as the F. W. Heitmann Company (established 1865), carried a variety of heating equipment like furnaces and hot-air registers.[79] The proposal made by J. B. Collins in 1902 to heat the J. S. Rice house at 2304 Crawford may have been fairly typical: "We propose to do the Steam Heating in your Residence Bldg according to plans and specifications submitted for the net sum of $950.00 . . . or we will heat the building with a Hot water system for the net sum of $1350.00." In a separate proposal submitted the same day, Collins went on to price a drying room in the Rice house basement: "We propose to furnish all materials and labor necessary for the erection of a Steam Heated Dry Room to be located in Laundry Room in Basement to measure 5–0" Deep, 17–0" Long and 6–0" High with steam coils, drying racks, . . . and sliding doors, automatic steam trap, supply and return main from steam boiler that is to be used for house heating. This plant to cost complete, ready for use, $300."[80]

In two-story houses the bedrooms, of course, were upstairs. Before bathrooms, many functions associated with bathrooms were performed in the bedroom, for household plumbing was primitive at best, and wash basins, pitchers, and "slop sets" were necessary to personal hygiene. Bathtubs were portable and could be set up wherever convenient—kitchen, porch, bedroom, or anywhere with easy access to water. In more modest neighborhoods, such as Freedmen's Town, plumbing remained problematic well into the 1930s. One former resident recalled that her family and her grandparents, who lived next door, shared the "woodshed," a detached building containing a water closet. Their home had no running water but instead had a faucet next to the back porch from which they drew their household water.[81]

Mosquito netting was still necessary as wire screens were not introduced until 1894.[82] After the turn of the century, families who could afford it often had an additional upstairs amenity, a sleeping porch. Screened on the sides from floor to ceiling to allow maximum air circulation, this simple enclosure was a communal sleeping area where family members could be as cool as possible on muggy summer nights. If affordable, each family member had two beds, one in the bedroom and a simpler one on the porch. Sleeping porches continued to be important to many Houston homes until air-conditioning became prevalent after World War II.

Houston families with smaller houses engaged in another form of communal sleeping on hot Houston nights. In the Freedmen's Town section of the Fourth Ward, southwest of downtown, and probably in other parts of the city as well, some families slept on pallets laid in the path between the front and back doors. There they took advantage of drafts blowing through the house.[83]

Often, in larger Houston houses the third floor was also finished, though less elaborately detailed than the floors below. Here children played, family members put on amateur theatrical performances, and guests at large parties sometimes danced. Occasionally billiard tables were on the third floor (fig. 216), if not in the basement, as they were at The Oaks. Guests ascended the front stairs to a large second-floor–hallway-sitting room area, then continued up to the third floor. In such floor plans the upstairs front hall served as a semipublic area (fig. 173) and a buffer to the privacy of the bedrooms.

Because nineteenth-century domestic life could be so formal, children's activities tended to center around the less visible (and therefore less breakable) private areas of homes: the third floor, service areas, back stairs, children's rooms, playrooms, and, of course, porches and the outdoors.

One thing about Houston houses in the late nineteenth century is apparent: their interiors were more complex. For the first time, owners of large houses required the help of a decorator to coordinate the army of tradesmen, painters, paperers, upholsterers, and other artisans necessary to complete an elaborate interior. Unlike New York, where decorators like Gustave and Christian Herter and Leon Marcotte emerged from the ranks of furniture makers to do entire interiors, or unlike Galveston, where a few families engaged New York interior designers to work on their homes, known Houston decorators seem to have come from the frescoing, painting, papering, or drapery trades or from home-furnishing stores.[84]

The term "interior decorator," as we use it, first appeared in the 1905–1906 *Directory of the City of Houston* in an advertisement for J. P. January, "Interior decorator & frescoer," although Galveston architect Nicholas J. Clayton's father-in-law, D. W. Ducie, was known for his decorating services in Galveston long before then and George M. Kuhn, a painter and decorator, was in Houston as early as 1892.[85] By 1912 Karl W. Hille and William Kremeskoeter, directors of the Houston Decorating Company, described themselves as "artistic interior decorators" who had decorated "hundreds of homes, business buildings, churches, and halls," including the new Isis Theater.[86]

"Artistic" was a word often used in the late nineteenth and early twentieth centuries to describe decorative arts that aspired to elevated taste. Many nationally known examples were illustrated in *Artistic Houses,* an influential compendium of high-style interiors first published in 1883.[87] Although the houses featured in *Artistic Houses* are far more elaborate than even the most ostentatious Houston ones of the 1880s, they share a number of common traits: conspicuous historical references, elaborate woodwork, complex and richly textured competing patterns, abundant bric-a-brac, and, in addition to sliding main-floor interior doors, portieres, that is, heavy draperies suspended from doorway lintels with which one room could be separated from another (fig. 169). These interiors also were dependent on extravagant textiles used both in draperies framed by elaborate lambrequins and in richly upholstered furniture. In some of these interiors, such as Mrs. Martin Tilford Jones's parlor (fig. 178), the room itself was a container to which the decorator applied his or her talents independent of the architecture of the room itself.

Hugh Waddell owned another important decorating firm. Founded in 1881 as a furniture dealer and sewing machine representative, Waddell's was the successor to L. J. Latham. Waddell's grew to become a complete home furnishings store.[88] Among many projects, they are credited with outfitting the Joseph Presley Carter house at 2602 Main Street (figs. 197, 198) and, in 1912, the Rice Hotel, where they supplied the furnishings, draperies, and floor coverings for this 525-room edifice. For the hotel Waddell bought the fittings in the eastern furniture market and in Chicago as part of a contract that totaled almost $250,000.[89]

With decorators emerging from the ranks of Houston painters and paperers, one can be certain that walls and wallpaper received considerable attention in Houston homes. In elaborate houses elsewhere, up to five different patterns could be used in a single room, beginning with the dado and rising to the middle or fill area of the wall and then to the frieze and ceiling.[90] In surviving photographs of Houston interiors, however, a wallpaper dado was rarely, if ever, used. In its stead one sees deep floor moldings (fig. 161) and wood dadoes (fig. 184). Houstonians loved friezes (fig. 204) and were not averse to papering their ceilings as well (fig. 207). As in other parts of the United States, some Houston houses of the 1880s also had heavily embossed papers patterned in relief of the type known as either Japanese leather or Lincrusta Walton (figs. 171, 179). Japanese leather was actually a thick, embossed paper pulp. Lincrusta Walton was an embossed, solidified linseed oil. Both simulated much more expensive tooled leathers such as those featured in the aforementioned *Artistic Houses*.[91] Colored in warm earthen hues, these wall coverings were sometimes highlighted with gold paint.

In addition to local painters and paperers, some home owners employed artisans who hand-decorated their walls. J. A. Sweeney and Company offered this service from the store at 93 Main Street. Sweeney advertised in 1880 "PAINTERS, DECORATORS AND DEALERS IN Sign & Ornamental Painting. ALL KINDS House, SIGN, SCENIC AND FRESCO PAINTING."[92] The Marble Palace, a saloon that opened in 1895 at 414 Main Street, was decorated in faux marble by an artist named R. E. Lee.[93] On an amateur level, a daughter of T. W. House, Jr., painted garlands in her bedroom (fig. 168). Charles Martin Meister (1875–1935), the Texas German decorative painter, lived in Houston Heights beginning in 1906 and plied his trade until 1919, when he gave up his craft to become a painter for Gulf Oil Company.[94] In addition, the parlor ceiling of the F. A. Heitmann house at 1118 Dallas was hand-decorated.[95]

By 1900 new Houston houses reached a technical plateau where they would remain until after World War II, when air-conditioning would revolutionize Houston's floor plans and way of life yet again. With electricity, bathrooms and kitchens with hot and cold running water, stoves, iceboxes, ceiling fans, natural gas, and, in some cases, steam or forced-air central heating, Houston houses achieved a level of comfort that, compared with earlier domiciles, was truly modern (fig. 195).[96]

A revolution in interior ornament was also underway. On a national level this movement was led by Edith Wharton and Ogden Codman, Jr., whose 1897 book *The Decoration of Houses* quickly became a classic.[97] In it the authors lamented that interior design had been removed from architects and placed in the hands of decorators to the degree that design simply became "a labyrinth of dubious eclecticism." The authors argued against the very sensibilities that were so coveted fifteen years earlier: overdone upholstery, "artistic" furniture, heavily draped windows, and patterned carpeting; and they argued in favor of more systematic architectural detailing with fewer colors, less wallpaper, little or no draperies, no portieres, more oriental rugs, and less contrived furniture.[98] In short, Wharton and Codman wanted more harmonious interiors. To the authors, harmony largely meant French eighteenth-century styles. In Houston these two approaches (artistic versus architectural) came head to head when the Albert A. Van Alstyne–John F. Dickson house was remodeled soon after 1900. Nowhere are the differences in philosophy more apparent than in the contrast between the entrance hall (fig. 175), overwhelmed with a competitive array of objects and textures, and the drawing room (fig. 177): cool, pale, classical, and with abundant architectural detailing. Like the Dicksons, the Levys also decorated their parlor in a manner sympathetic to the Wharton and Codman philosophy (fig. 180). Certainly the number of surviving photographs of parlors outfitted in white or gilt Louis XV or Louis XVI furniture indicates the popularity of this style in Houston.

Among all the homes decorated in Houston during this era, one stands out: Inglenook, belonging to lumberman John Henry Kirby (fig. 118). When Kirby's daughter Bessie May was married on November 14, 1906, her wedding reception was held at home.[99] In conjunction with this event, Inglenook was professionally photographed. Photographs prove that the Kirbys were well traveled, experienced shoppers who lived in one of Houston's most elaborate houses. Their house contained furniture made in Chicago by the Karpen Furniture Company (fig. 186), a Louis Comfort Tiffany art nouveau lamp (fig. 188), a mosaic of the Colosseum in Rome (not shown), a copy of Jean Antoine Houdon's bust of George Washington (fig. 188), and a uniformly opulent interior. It even had a Moorish nook (fig. 183). However, like other Houston houses, the parlor was in a French Louis XV Revival style, the Kirbys' study was darkly paneled and masculine, and the dining room was equally dark and impressive. The house was imposing, formal, and conservatively adventuresome, a monument to conspicuous consumption and an example of entrepreneurial materialism of the sort identified by the controversial economist of the day Thorstein Veblen as a measure of one's standing in the community and personal success.[100] It was probably Houston's most complete domestic response to the Gilded Age.

Codman and Wharton's definition of architectural historicism and their interest in the eighteenth century were also compatible with another theme seen in Houston interiors at the turn of the century: the Colonial Revival. This theme, which was first identified nationally in association with the Philadelphia Centennial in 1876, by 1900 became clearly recognizable in Houston exteriors (fig. 125) and interiors. Just as architects of Colonial Revival houses reconfigured classical orders to make their exteriors sympathetic with turn-of-the-century expectations and floor plans, so too were colonial interiors redefined. Nowhere is it more apparent than in Robert Crews Duff's entrance hall (fig. 199), a beautifully detailed Georgian-inspired room in the manner of Carter's Grove, the 1750–53 plantation house in James City County, Virginia (fig. 200). The Duffs acquired Colonial Revival furniture for their interior: William-and-Mary–style armchairs in the hall, and shield-back Federal-style chairs in the parlor beyond. Although the hall shares Carter's Grove's symmetry, texture, and restraint, it combines these Georgian elements with a number of early twentieth-century characteristics: square newel posts, hanging multi-armed electric lights, and in the parlor an efficient tile fireplace surround in place of a more formal, carved Georgian mantel.

The Duff house combines Colonial Revival with a second reform movement, this one anti-historical and a bit more avant-garde, known as Arts and Crafts. Occasionally, as in the entry and library of the Duff house (fig. 201), the two styles converged. In architecture, Frank Lloyd Wright in Chicago and Charles and Henry Greene in Pasadena, California, are by far the most important names associated with this movement, but in interiors Gustave Stickley became its leading theoretician, publicist, and purveyor of furniture, lamps, and textiles. Houston embraced this style.

Stickley's own publications were surely available in Houston, but in addition Arts and Crafts values were publicized locally in monthlies like *Homes* magazine and in the *Houston Post*, which in 1914 ran an occasional column titled "The Home." In an article published in 1914, the *Post* advocated "more sane and simple living." The article went on:

> In spite of the recent vogue for modern art colorings, the room in one color scheme, especially the living room, is mostly in favor, because of its restful effects, not a monotony of one shade, but tones of one color with phasing touches of contrasts. Brown, say with tan, is unusually happy; brown woodwork and furniture; tan wallpaper; creamy tan window hangings that sift the light into tents of softened sunshine . . . .

In addition, the article praised cretonné, the boldly embroidered cloths (often linen) that were used for table scarves and as borders for bed tables and linens.[101] Surely F. E. Ward's Arts and Crafts cottage built in 1911 (figs. 202, 203) is the embodiment of this image.

Photographs of a number of Arts and Crafts bungalow interiors survive, as well as a 1911 photograph of the Ed C. Smith Furniture Company on Texas Avenue, which shows a large assortment of Arts and Crafts furniture readily available and reasonably priced (fig. 159). These Arts and Crafts interiors share dark (usually oak trim) shoulder-high chair rails or plate rails, wide frescoes, beamed ceilings, and simple hearths often decorated with art pottery tiles made by firms like the Rookwood Pottery of Cincinnati, Ohio.[102] They often have hanging brass electric lights with armatures that are square in cross-section, each light having its own shade (fig. 204).

From impressive brick and stucco houses in the Montrose area to smaller wood bungalows, Arts and Crafts interiors survive in virtually every turn-of-the-century quarter of the city. They were built by individuals and developers alike to be furnished by stylish purists in Arts and Crafts furniture or by others in older or more conservative styles.

By the 1920s Houston's interiors changed markedly (fig. 172). Decorators like MacMillen of New York worked in concert with local architects John F. Staub and Birdsall P. Briscoe to introduce more restrained upper-class housing and a broader architectural view to Houston. They left a legacy that permeates Shadyside, Broadacres, and River Oaks and continues to have a profound effect in Houston's monied, conservative circles. As early as 1920, Houston philanthropist Ima

Hogg bought her first American eighteenth-century chair, thereby beginning a love of Americana that remains one of her many legacies to the city of Houston. The years of rough, make-do shelters and the formalized, monumental, dazzling, unrestrained interiors of Houston's Victorian youth were past. The Colonial Revival style that began at the turn of the century as an affirmation of national heritage is the one continuing thread that survives from the city's boisterous adolescence into its middle age.

4 *Domestic Life*

Dorothy Knox Howe Houghton

During the nineteenth century, the Harris County area developed relatively sophisticated patterns of domestic life as a result of being the location of a southern port and trading center. The Gulf Coast region blended characteristics of frontier wildernesses and long-settled urban centers. The county's growth and its role in the development of Texas stemmed from its transportation system, water and later rail, which linked it to southern and eastern states and to other countries where local residents had business, social, and family ties. In consequence, the area reflected changes occurring across the United States, modified by its climate and other locational features. Before World War I the region's place in sparsely settled Texas promoted interconnected family relationships and a lifestyle largely centered around the home.

Stephen F. Austin's colonists settled on Mexican land grants, usually a league (4,428 acres) and a labor (177 acres) of land. Isolated from one another by thousands of acres, their log houses faced waterways feeding into Galveston Bay, such as the San Jacinto River or Buffalo Bayou. The quickest access between homesteads was by boat. Harrisburg, founded in 1826, was for the next decade the political, judicial, and trade center for the surrounding region, known under Mexican rule as the Municipality of Harrisburg. The early settlers had to be self-sufficient. Most of the things they used in their daily lives were homegrown or homemade: food, clothing, household provisions, and medicine. Men hunted and fished, tended and slaughtered animals, built fences and repaired buildings, and raised food crops. Boys hauled water, chopped wood, cleaned out-buildings, and helped the men. Women and girls tended gardens, milked cows, churned butter, gathered eggs, prepared food, made candles and soap, wove and dyed cloth, and made and washed the clothes. Most of the time the children worked like adults. They encountered the outside world on trips to Harrisburg or by visits from neighbors and travelers, who paced a day's journey by the distances between homesteads.

The early settlers constructed their own houses of logs from the primeval forest, sometimes with the help of neighbors. The houses typically had one room or two rooms separated by a dog trot, a sleeping loft, and front and back porches. The rooms provided shelter from the elements and wild animals, a place to sleep, and headquarters for the owners' businesses. By the late 1820s the steam sawmill at Harrisburg supplied boards to cover the logs, both inside and out, and John R. Harris's store provided such luxuries as wallpaper to those settlers who could afford them.[1]

Since log houses with few windows were hot and dark, during the warm months most activities took place outdoors where there were breezes: on the porches, in the dog trot, or in the back yard. The fire hazard posed by ill-constructed chimneys and overturned oil lamps was another reason to perform most domestic tasks outside or in outbuildings. Those who could afford it constructed kitchens as separate buildings. Barns, smokehouses, outhouses, and servants' quarters (for those who had them) were also separate log buildings. Settlers who came from areas where the climate and geography differed greatly from that of the Texas Gulf Coast had to adjust their housekeeping to local conditions. For example, the traditional method of digging a root cellar into the side of a hill was impossible on Harris County's flat terrain. Instead, homesteaders dug a four-foot-deep round pit and used cypress to build walls, a slanting door, and a shingled roof over it. The structure was completely covered with clay, and grass grew on the resulting mound. The structure maintained an internal temperature of 60 degrees or less, providing a cool place to store food. It also doubled as a storm cellar.[2]

The prairies, woods, and streams held an abundance of native fruits, vegetables, seafood, wild game, and waterfowl, which provided settlers with an adequate diet until they could raise their own crops and domestic livestock. Although their numbers and species are drastically fewer today, these food sources remained plentiful throughout the pre-World War I period, providing sport and recreation long after most residents had converted to domestic food supplies.[3] Ferdinand Roemer described the waterfront on Galveston Bay as seen from Col. Morgan's house (fig. 5) at New Washington (Morgan's Point) in 1846: "In many places the surface of the water was completely blackened by myriads of wild ducks. Whole rows of white swans resembling silver bands from the distance, clumsy pelican, geese and various diving birds without number completed the swarms of the feathered denizens. A confused noise, composed of a thousand-fold cackling and screeching rose up from the water as if coming from a huge poultry yard, and this continued unabated throughout the night."[4]

In 1845 the *Telegraph and Texas Register* recorded thirty-eight varieties of seafood harvested from Buffalo Bayou and Galveston Bay.[5] Oysters were a particular favorite. The salt necessary for preserving many foods, such as pork, was extracted from water found in salt springs, marshes, and salt "lagoons" all over Harris County or purchased from merchants in Harrisburg and Houston.[6] Hogs were butchered in cold weather to prevent the meat from spoiling (figs. 225, 226). The pickling or curing process for salt pork involved submerging the meat "in a barrel of water, salt, sugar, salt-peter, and potash."[7] Ham, bacon, and sausage were hung to cure slowly in the smokehouse. Ground meat not used for sausage-making was molded into patties, fried, and then layered in crocks with hot lard. When cool, the lard formed a seal that preserved the meat for weeks.[8] Native materials provided tools as well as food. For example, gourds, introduced to

European immigrants to America by the Indians, were cleaned and dried in the sun for use as storage containers, milk strainers, large ladles or dippers, and bird houses for martins, who helped control the mosquitoes.[9]

Guidelines for all types of domestic tasks had been passed down orally through the generations in most countries. The more complicated ones were written down by women in manuscript housekeeping notebooks to which they added recipes gleaned from published cookbooks and newspapers. By the 1830s instruction manuals for daily living, known as encyclopedias of domestic economy and intended for use by the growing middle classes, were published both in England and in America. Harris County's early settlers undoubtedly brought such housekeeping aids to Texas with them. As they did with the root cellar, they often had to modify or completely change certain household procedures either because some necessary ingredient was unavailable or because it didn't work locally.[10]

Insect control was an example. Anglo-Americans were accustomed to using citronella oil to repel mosquitoes. Europeans sprinkled the dried and crushed leaves of the daisy fleabane plant to discourage fleas. When these repellents were not available, early residents had to settle for local alternatives. The Indians repelled mosquitos by rubbing themselves with animal grease, alligator fat, and shark oil, which became rancid in the heat. They also used pine straw to skim crude oil from the surface of ponds into which it had seeped and stripped it off into containers for later use on their bodies. To the settlers these methods would have been a last resort, and they developed alternatives from materials on hand.

Sulphur dust sprinkled over the body fended off mosquitoes, chiggers, and ticks. Billowing smoky fires made of damp grass or leaves burned in heaps upon the ground or in smudge pots placed around the front porch repelled mosquitoes, while long-handled pots of smoking rags cleared them from the house. The floor-length skirts, long sleeves, high necklines, gloves, thick stockings, and net scarves across the face worn by women and the comparably complete clothing worn by men, gave mosquitoes fewer opportunities to bite (fig. 253). Stagnant water, including puddles formed in wagon ruts and animal hoofprints, was treated with oil (kerosene by the late 1850s) to prevent the breeding of mosquitoes. Castor beans planted around the house were also thought to be helpful. The indigenous southern wax myrtle or bayberry tree, with its pungent-smelling leaves, was an effective natural flea repellant.[11] Not only was mosquito netting draped on beds, but by 1855 "ladies had little mosquito net houses built in their parlors, in which they sat to sew."[12]

Social life often centered around domestic tasks. Neighbors arrived by boat, wagon, and horseback to help a family build a house or barn, roll logs, husk corn, or do almost any chore. When the work was done, a party began that lasted all night. In his "Reminiscences," Cornelius Cox described a quilting bee in early Harris County:

The quilt was stretched in the primitive way . . . between four slats and drawn out to the full size . . . the four corners each suspended by a rope to the ceiling—in the best room. Now all the ladies are expected to come early as the quilt has to be finished before the real fun begins. The quilters soon take their places—and the work begins on all sides. The gents on the ground are expected to roll up the sides as fast as needed, to pass the thread and scissors—and with anecdotes and small talk to entertain the workers. In the meantime things are getting hot in the kitchen, the biggest turkey on the place is basting its back before a huge log fire. A little porker had folded his feet under him and laid down in the bottom of a great oven, and with dressings of parsley and pepper and other accessions is enjoying the warmth of a covering of coals. Pies and cakes of all sizes and makes mingle their perfume with the odor that arises from every part of the preparation. Chicken, eggs, butter, milk, preserves, etc., etc. all gather in and take their place. While the busy hostess flits in and out, now with a word to the meddlers and a look of gratified pleasure and pride, and then back to the regime in which all hearts are centered. At last the wonderful quilt is finished. The frames are removed, the table spread, the company all in, and joy unconfined rules the hour—the third act is yet in store for us. The shades of night have settled upon the scene, where the fragments of the feast are all cleared away—but the sound of the violin expedites further preparations—and now change your partners and "we'll all dance a reel". . . .

At last the morning dawned, the fiddler fled, and after coffee and cake all round, with reluctant partings, the company scattered. . . . [13]

Such Texas hospitality bound scattered neighbors together into a close-knit, interdependent community. Friends or strangers, invited or not, guests were welcome for meals and to spend the night. The full moon lit up the prairies so that nighttime travel home from nearby social affairs in good weather was fairly easy and pleasurable, although moonless and overcast nights could be black as pitch. The sounds of cicadas, tree frogs, chuck-will's-widows, night hawks, owls, and even panthers and cougars pierced the air, while hundreds of fireflies flashed in the dark.[14]

Country weddings were major social events that could last for several days. Vows were exchanged in the front room or wherever the most guests could be assembled. The alcalde (chief political and judicial authority of the municipality) or, after 1836, the justice of the peace frequently officiated, since there were few ministers and no church buildings until the 1840s. The house and grounds were decorated with flowers and foliage from gardens, woods, and fields. As on most social occasions, feasting and dancing were the main entertainments. On the day after the wedding, the groom's family held a dinner called an "infare" at their house to which the bride wore her second-day dress (traditionally blue). Wedding and second-day dresses ranged from homemade lawn and homespun to custom gowns ordered from New Orleans or New York.[15] Later in the century, when more leisure time and improved transportation made honeymoons possible, the second-day dress became the going-away dress (also traditionally blue).

The early water transportation system connecting Buffalo Bayou with ports in Mexico, New Orleans, New York, and Europe allowed settlers to special-order household supplies and furnishings, clothing, agricultural necessities, and luxury products. New immigrants bought cattle, pigs, chickens, and seeds during a stopover in New Orleans on the way to Texas or ordered them from

Mexican agents once they arrived.[16] The inventory of imported goods for sale in John R. Harris's Harrisburg store at the time of his death in 1829 included ready-made clothing and bolts of cloth, shoes, candles, soap, spices, books, and even lace, gilt buttons, and silk vests. Like other nineteenth-century Texas merchants, Harris often accepted cotton, sugarcane, and hides as payment.[17] By the late 1830s newspapers in the new city of Houston included advertisements by merchants and tailors in New Orleans and New York for direct mail order. Specialty foods such as fancy dried and preserved fruits, spices, condiments, European wines and cordials, gourmet coffees, and teas were available in stores in Houston, Galveston, and Harrisburg.[18]

Home industries also produced goods for sale or barter such as eggs, butter, and clothing. Rosa von Roeder Kleburg, whose husband, Robert Justus Kleburg, later became manager of the King Ranch, turned to home industry while living in Harrisburg during the winter of 1835: "My sister and I took lessons in sewing from a Mrs. Swearingen, and made clothes for Moore's store. We were all unused to that kind of work, but we felt that we must save our money; and, when required by necessity, one learns to do what one has never done before."[19] She also made clothes for the Indians in exchange for moccasins.

Not everyone could afford the comfortable lifestyle these store-bought items offered. Some households had luxury goods and many servants, some used purchased supplies to supplement what they made for themselves, and others struggled to survive. Since Harrisburg, a town of one to two hundred inhabitants, had no public buildings or hotels, civic and political gatherings took place in the houses of prominent and influential citizens. Travelers routinely stayed as paid guests in settlers' houses.[20] The Harrisburg municipality's most famous resident, Lorenzo de Zavala, had been one of Mexico's most prominent statesmen. During his career he was representative of the State of Yucatán to the Spanish court in Madrid (prior to Mexican Independence), governor of the State of Mexico, and minister to France.[21] After joining the Texans in opposing the dictatorship of his former friend, General Santa Anna, he attempted to maintain some vestiges of his former lifestyle. He staffed his house with a young Irish woman who served both as chambermaid and as nurse for his three small children, a black cook, a French valet for his eldest son, and two or three men of French descent to care for the animals, garden, and grounds.[22] Following the battle of San Jacinto his house, located across the bayou from the battlefield, was used as a hospital for wounded soldiers.

Point Pleasant, on a peninsula just above the present docks at Exxon's Baytown refinery, was the house of entrepreneur William Scott. Although no picture or verbal description of the house survives, an anonymous visitor in 1837 referred to it as "among the many things which delight the eye as you ascend the river [Buffalo Bayou], . . . as remarkable for the beauty of its situation as it is for the hospitality of the proprietor and his amiable and interesting lady."[23] It was one of the most comfortable local houses, and in 1824 Stephen F. Austin chose it as the meeting place where he issued the first Mexican land grants to settlers in what would become the Harris County area. Austin again chose it for his meeting on February 5, 1832, with Mexican official Juan Davis Bradburn, whose closure of Texas ports was a contributing factor to the Texas Revolution. Scott's hospitality depended in part on his servants. In 1826 he hired the cook, Jimmie, from the schooner *Augusta*. When Scott died in 1837, the inventory of his estate listed thirteen Negro slaves, several of whom probably were employed in the house.[24]

On the other end of the socioeconomic scale were the servantless households of the Earles and the McCormicks, two Irish families. The Earles' many children must have shared domestic and farming responsibilities. William Fairfax Gray noted in March of 1836, just after Texas declared independence and legalized slavery, that Earle was trying to sell some land in order to buy slaves; productive laborers would improve the family's circumstances. Although Gray found Mrs. Earle's butter the best he had tasted in Texas and her hospitality cordial, he considered the family "civil, but coarse." The Earles' neighbor, Peggy McCormick, was a widow. Troubles with neighbors in business affairs were aggravated by the hardship of having to rear two sons alone. To make matters worse, the battle of San Jacinto on April 21, 1836, was fought on her land.[25]

For three weeks before the battle the provisional government of the new Republic of Texas was headquartered in the house of Jane Birdsall Harris at Harrisburg. The president and the cabinet escaped down Buffalo Bayou to Galveston Island, most on board William P. Harris's steamboat, *Cayuga*, just as the Mexican troops reached the town. Infuriated, Santa Anna ordered his men to burn the town's cluster of log buildings. His troops marched downstream burning most of the houses, barns, and outbuildings in their path until Sam Houston's troops stopped them at San Jacinto.[26] Residents fled their houses quickly, taking with them only their most valuable papers and a few belongings. Although the town and many of the homesteads were rebuilt soon after the battle, including the Harris house (fig. 9), few primary sources survive that describe the houses or life in the Municipality of Harrisburg in the era of Mexican rule.

Beginning in the fall of 1836, the Allen brothers' advertisements for the new city of Houston attracted curious travelers and would-be residents from Europe and America. Gustav Dresel, a German traveler, described the city's population in August 1838:

> At that time fifteen hundred to two thousand people, mostly men, were living together in Houston in the most dissimilar manner. The President, the whole personnel of the government, many lawyers who found ample means of support . . . a large number of gamblers, tradesmen, artisans, former soldiers, adventurers, curious travelers from the United States, about a hundred Mexican prisoners who made suitable servants, daily new troops of Indians—all associated like chums on an equal footing.[27]

The population surge spawned a building boom that lasted until the capital was moved to Austin in October 1839. After an economic slump of several years, the city rebounded to become a point of entry for immigrants and a center of trade and transportation for southeast Texas, roles previously held by Harrisburg. Construction resumed at a steady pace until halted by the Civil War.

The pattern of settlement in Houston established before the Civil War was dictated by economics and by ethnic concerns. From Buffalo Bayou south along lower Main Street and around

Market Square, people lived in apartments over or connected to their places of business. Around Courthouse Square (fig. 149) and immediately east in the area known as Quality Hill, larger houses were built by many of the city's influential families. North and east of Quality Hill a German neighborhood developed from a small area known as Frost Town. The eastern city limits were bordered by several large tracts, including Merkel's Grove and Lubbock's Grove, favorite spots for large picnics and festivals. North of Buffalo Bayou on the west side of town a densely populated and fairly self-sufficient neighborhood grew up in what would become the Sixth Ward, along Washington Avenue near the Houston and Texas Central Railroad yards. Railroad employees lived there to be near their work. Small cottages housed builders, carpenters, artisans, grocers, cobblers, and needleworkers. Many of these people were also German.[28]

Surrounding the more densely populated core of the city, houses were scattered in all directions on tracts ranging in size from a small lot to many acres. With their outbuildings, orchards, vegetable and flower gardens, and pastures for horses, cows, and goats, even the outlying estates of city dwellers resembled small farms. The eastern and western edges of the city were punctuated by the Robert Lockart house (fig. 19) and the Kellum-Noble house (fig. 261). West of Houston Germans and Italians established farms along the south side of Buffalo Bayou in the area that would become Freedmen's Town after the Civil War. On the southern edge of the city, along what is now Holman Avenue, were Bohemia (fig. 30), the ten-acre estate of Edward Hopkins Cushing, the estate of Gustav Forsgard, now the campus of Houston Community College, and the home of Alfred Whitaker (fig. 31). As streets were platted between the business district and Holman Avenue, some people such as William Fulton (fig. 217), Edward A. Palmer (fig. 16), Erastus Perkins (fig. 12), Henry DeChaumes (fig. 17), and Daniel Greenleaf Wheeler (fig. 36) bought entire blocks of land and built their houses in the center of their properties. Despite the beginnings of economic and ethnic concentration into neighborhoods, the imposing houses of the wealthy stood side by side with modest cottages or nondescript houses built for rental.

Professional builders and contractors, rather than the owners themselves, constructed many of Houston's first houses. These new houses, with glass windowpanes, wooden floors, and brick chimneys, were more tightly sealed and better insulated than the earlier log houses, better ventilated, easier to keep clean, and better lit by larger windows. One or two rooms no longer served all purposes; specific rooms were designated for sleeping, dining, business, and entertaining, which promoted a more formal lifestyle. Back parlors were used for family activities, while front parlors were reserved for entertaining and for family gatherings on Sundays. Libraries doubled as home offices for many men.[29] Sleeping lofts became attics or finished second floors. Kitchens continued to be detached buildings, and many domestic tasks were still performed in the back yard.

Housing types and household size varied widely in the city, in contrast to the fairly uniform accommodations of the county's earliest settlers. Tents provided temporary shelter during Houston's first years while permanent housing was being constructed: free-standing single-family residences, boarding houses, apartments over or attached to businesses, and hotels. It was common for single-family houses to hold three or four generations over a period of many years. Households could include unmarried aunts and uncles, impoverished cousins, the elderly, the ill, and even the insane, along with infants, teenagers, several live-in servants, and middle-aged couples in the prime of their business and social lives. Each member of the household helped with domestic tasks, especially in servantless homes. Individual privacy was a rare luxury, but the family provided security and a sense of belonging.

Some families, particularly those of widows, augmented their incomes by accommodating roomers and/or boarders. Roomers rented rooms in private homes; boarders took their meals in a private home or in a boarding house but might lodge elsewhere. Boarding houses, which provided both rooms and meals for long-term guests, were commercial establishments whose owners did not necessarily live on the premises. Such arrangements were well suited to single men and to newly arrived families who had not yet built a house (fig. 260). Gustav Dresel lived with the Gerlach family during his stay in Houston from August 1838 until January 1839.

> The front of our house was provided with a porch, that is, a gallery, which furnished shade and served the neighborhood as a happy gathering place in the evening. At that time [August 1838] as seen from here, the gay-colored, wild, and interesting city of Houston looked very picturesque. The few cabins, the numerous tents, the Capitol, the President's Mansion, and the many camps of recently arrived immigrants offered a novel and peculiar sight. The streets and squares that had been laid out were still covered with trees and stumps that obstructed the way, especially at nighttime.[30]

Although less expensive than hotels, rented rooms were not always cheap. Edward A. Palmer wrote to his father in 1848: "The man [J. E. Wade] with whom we are boarding has raised on us and we are going to move. Have to pay $40 per month at the house we are going to and buy our water to wash with. This is ruining me unless I can make money."[31] At her house on Courthouse Square, Mrs. William Fairfax Gray provided both lodging and meals for many of the officials of the Republic of Texas.[32]

Many people lived in the hotels clustered along Congress and Franklin streets near the steamboat landing. The Houston House (Main at Franklin), the Mansion House (northeast corner of Congress and Milam), and the Alabama House (corner of Congress and Fannin, later known as the Pierce House) were popular. When the government of the republic moved to Austin in 1839, the old Capitol building (corner of Main and Texas Avenue) was converted into the Capitol House Hotel. In 1881 the original building was replaced by a new Capitol Hotel; in 1913 this was replaced in turn by the Rice Hotel, which remained one of Houston's most prestigious addresses until the 1960s. For one hundred and thirty years, the successive buildings on this corner served as the social and political hub of Houston.[33] In 1840, while Gustav Dresel was living in the City Hotel, he often visited a friend, who lived at the Capitol Hotel with his family. They spent the evenings singing German songs, and "while Theodore Miller played on the flute, we waltzed around on the gallery of the Capitol of Texas to the tunes of Strauss and country waltzes."[34] The Fannin House was a favorite with Confederate officers during the Civil War. In 1859 the proprietor, T. B. J. Hadley, advertised: "I have added to the heretofore roomy house twelve new rooms 14 by 15 feet with fire places in each, they are all well furnished and ventilated with halls and promenades. The dining room will be extended and other improvements made. I promise the best fare and comfort, and if I don't comply, I make no charge."[35]

In 1867 the elegant Hutchins House Hotel was opened by William J. Hutchins at the corner of Franklin and Travis on the site of the old City Hotel. It featured a Turco-Russian bath, two regular plain bathrooms on every floor (one for men and one for women), and an artificial ice machine. An elegant parlor on the second floor was furnished with red velvet drapes, a red carpet, and a white marble fireplace over which hung a large oval mirror in a gilt frame.[36]

Residents of rural Harris County remained more or less self-sufficient before World War I. In the city, however, one could choose to be self-sufficient or could take advantage of domestic services offered by rooming or boarding houses or hotels. The average Houston family had vegetable gardens, fruit trees, poultry yards, and pastures for cows, horses, goats, and pigs either adjacent to the house or on neighboring city blocks (figs. 228–30, 239). Some people patronized dairies and farmers in the country for fresh eggs, milk, and vegetables. Others owned tracts of land outside the city where they planted crops. August, Conrad, and Charles Bering owned among them about two thousand acres in the area now known as Tanglewood and bordered by Westheimer, Chimney Rock, Buffalo Bayou, and Fountainview, which supplied their households.[37]

Food preparation both in the country and in the city continued to include picking fruits and vegetables, shelling peas, milking cows, churning butter, and killing and dressing poultry. It was a necessary daily process, regardless of economic level or access to city markets. By the 1840s both private enterprise and Houston's city government began regulating domestic services. An 1841 city ordinance defined butchers and victuallers as persons who sold meat in pieces smaller than a quarter of an animal, required them to be licensed by the mayor, and limited the practice of their trade to the City Market.[38] In the absence of refrigeration, daily visits to the Market were necessary. Baked goods, fish, vegetables, and fruit were sold from rented stalls in the Market House, while farmers from the country sold produce from their wagons parked in the square (fig. 245).

Delivery wagons were additional conveniences. Among the first in Houston were those that sold clear, pure drinking water by the gallon from Buffalo Bayou and from Beauchamps Springs on White Oak Bayou.[39] Horse-drawn wagons and carriages also delivered milk, vegetables, baked goods, fuel, and other commodities to the home (fig. 231). By 1866 J. O. Johnson and Company delivered groceries and supplies free of charge to any part of the city.[40] In addition to perishable foods from the market or delivery wagons, homemakers continued to purchase staples such as flour and sugar from general import merchants, who also sold luxury foods, ready-made clothing, and dry goods.

By the time Houston was founded, ice cut from New England rivers and lakes during the winter was a luxury regularly shipped to Gulf Coast ports. To minimize melting during shipping, the ice was insulated with salt hay, straw, sawdust, tanners bark, charcoal, or wood shavings. Upon arrival it was stored in commercial above-ground ice houses.[41] In July 1841 ice was selling in Houston for three cents a pound.[42] Ice houses did not deliver until insulated wagons and ice boxes became available, around 1870, so ice had to be bought frequently and in small portions.

To conserve his inventory, James House offered the hundred tons of ice he received from Boston in May 1851 for sale only between 9:00 and 10:00 A.M. and between 5:00 and 6:00 P.M.[43] Access to ice made possible the manufacture of ice cream, a favorite antidote to Houston's hot climate from the 1830s. Molded into fanciful shapes, ice cream was the climax of many festive parties.[44]

Houston's easy access to the gulf encouraged the import of many goods that were once made at home. By 1840 Houston merchants such as Charles Power were importing all manner of ready-made clothing, household and table linens, and luxury fabrics directly from England and France.[45] Clothing also could be custom-ordered from merchants and tailors in New York or New Orleans. In 1846 Gentry and Company Express advertised: "the ladies can be provided with the latest fashions direct from the great metropolis of the South. Gentlemen can have entire new suits of fashionable clothing, etc. by entering their orders in the Express Books at our office [presumably in Houston]. Try it and see."[46]

Of course, quantities of all imports were limited, and disruptions occurred in transportation schedules.[47] So, in addition to the imports offered by local merchants, businessmen who made trips to the East Coast or to Europe brought back such luxuries as custom-made clothing, jewelry, silverware, linen damask fabric for tablecloths and napkins, and ready-made dresses for their households.[48] In 1851 Christel L. Bethje wrote from Houston to Wilhelm Quensell, who was planning to come to Houston from Germany:

> Table linens and . . . bed linens . . . are not to be had here for money. . . . I request you earnestly to bring with you for me: modern heavy silk material for a dress for a grown person . . . 10 or 12 dozen pairs good woolen socks; several pounds of wool yarn the color of the socks, . . . an overcoat for me in the finest forest uniform green; and 100 or 120 ells of heavy, unbleached trouser ticking.[49]

Local tailors and dressmakers advertised their services by the 1840s.[50] Houston women could also make their clothes at home, keeping up with the latest styles through periodicals such as *Godey's Ladies Book*.[51] Fabrics and notions were available through local stores or from traveling salesmen known as drummers.[52] Making one's own clothing, an ordinary domestic task for the settlers of the 1820s, came to be considered a money-saving alternative in just a few decades. In 1850 Edward Albert Palmer wrote to his father, "Pat is making Willie's summer clothes. She makes all his clothes and her own dresses. We are as economical as possible, trying to save enough to travel home [to Virginia]."[53] By 1858 F. A. Rice and C. W. Hurley and Company were selling sewing machines in Houston.[54] This 1846 invention was the first of the home appliances that would revolutionize domestic life. For those who could afford the service, individual seamstresses moved from house to house with hand-operated sewing machines. In rooms set aside for their work, they outfitted entire families for the coming year.[55]

The concentration of people in Houston encouraged social, cultural, and educational opportunities that were seldom possible in the isolation of rural life. Because of the lack of public meeting places, however, such activities took place in private houses. Everyday social life included formal calls on friends and neighbors for afternoon tea. Informal dinners with friends often ended with singing and dancing. One of Houston's most popular mid-nineteenth-century hosts was Edward Hopkins Cushing, whose large telescope, facility with foreign languages, and diverse accomplishments made his house a gathering place for the intelligentsia.[56] In addition to such purely social gatherings, civic organizations began to form. One of the first was Lone Star Lodge Number One, the first Odd Fellows Lodge in Texas, organized on July 28, 1838, in the house of Thomas William Ward in the 400 block of Main Street[57] (fig. 18). On November 22, 1840, at the boarding house of Franke and Lemsky (Prairie Avenue at Travis Street), the German Society of Texas was established to promote the welfare of German immigrants.[58] The Houston Turnverein was founded in 1854 in the house of Peter Gabel on Preston Avenue. This group later organized the city's first fire department and the Turner Rifles, a citizens' militia, to keep the peace.[59]

Women opened their houses for all types of church-related and charitable activities. Between 1844 and 1847 the women of Christ Episcopal Church (now Christ Church Cathedral) organized numerous fairs at which they sold needlework, baked goods, and other homemade items to raise funds for the congregation's first church building on the corner of Fannin Street and Texas Avenue. At least one of these fairs was held in a house formerly occupied by the president of the Republic of Texas.[60] In 1862, during the Civil War, women from Houston and Galveston coordinated their war relief efforts in the Ladies' Aid Association, which met at the Houston residence of W. W. Stiles.[61] On Christmas Eve of that year, Mrs. Andrew Briscoe participated in a statewide effort to raise funds for Dr. Bryan's hospital for wounded Texas soldiers in Quitman, Mississippi, by holding a "Soiree Musicale and Tableaux Vivants" in the Harrisburg home of her mother, Jane Birdsall Harris (fig. 9). The effort yielded $251.[62]

Education for the early settlers' children was their parents' responsibility. Beginning in the era of the Texas republic, small private schools opened in towns throughout the county. Those children fortunate enough to attend rode horseback or drove a buggy to school, carrying lunches from home packed in tin buckets.[63] Well-to-do rural families could choose between several Houston schools that took students as boarders or arranged for boarding in private homes nearby. For example, in 1848 an advertisement for the Houston Academy (on the grounds of Christ Church) noted that "each young lady [boarder] must be furnished with mattress, bedding and towels." She was charged for fuel and washing.[64] Governesses and tutors in the home were other options for affluent rural parents. Adele Briscoe Looscan remembered being tutored in Latin by John Angier of Boston, treasurer of the Buffalo Bayou, Brazos and Colorado Railroad, while both her family and Mr. Angier were living in the house of her grandmother, Jane Birdsall Harris, in 1860.[65] In 1862 a family with seven children that lived twenty-five miles from Houston advertised for a governess who could care for the children as well as educate them in both academics and music.[66] These situations were the exception rather than the rule. An adequate education was difficult to acquire in the country, where as late as 1914 the curriculum for Harris County public schools emphasized training in agriculture rather than academics.[67]

City residents had more choices. In addition to a succession of schools named the Houston Academy, Houston had a number of teachers who ran schools in their houses.[68] The advertised curricula covered everything from a college preparatory education, including Latin, Greek, and other languages, to instruction in various types of instrumental music, and in fine needlework. Many children who attended private "classical" schools in teachers' houses completed their educations at eastern preparatory schools and/or colleges. Most returned to become leaders in the Houston community and to influence domestic life by their example. Two such children were Mary Frances Blake and Alexander Porter Root. Probably at the suggestion of Rev. Charles Gillett, her rector at Christ Church and a native of Hartford, Connecticut, Miss Blake (later Mrs. Robert Cummins Stuart) attended the Hartford Female Seminary from 1853 to 1857. This school was founded in 1823 by Catharine Beecher, whose impact on women's education, domestic economy, and household design was far-reaching.[69] Root attended the Williston Academy in Massachusetts and Yale University in his father's native Connecticut, graduating in 1861.[70]

Following the Civil War, the number of Houstonians attending eastern schools increased dramatically. The colleges later collectively known as the Ivy League and the Seven Sisters, as well as southern colleges such as Hollins, the University of Virginia, and the University of the South at Sewanee, Tennessee, were popular with Houstonians. A desire for the best available education, a family tradition of attending certain schools, and an interest in having children establish ties with their parents' native states were factors in these decisions. That so many parents were able to choose from the best schools in the country for their children probably explains why no college was established in Houston until the Rice Institute opened in 1912.

Business or family ties in Europe prompted some prominent businessmen, such as cotton merchants Cornelius Ennis and T. W. House, to send their children abroad to study. This custom was prevalent throughout Texas and the southern states, probably because of the strong economic ties between the South and Europe. Sons such as William H. Palmer and T. W. House, Jr., who studied abroad brought back a better knowledge of international business as well as a sophisticated cultural awareness, polished manners, and the disciplined habits that living in a foreign environment required. Laura Shepherd, Ella Hutchins, Tina Latham, Mary Van Alstyne, Emma McCraven, Libbie Randon, and Cornelia, Jeanette, and Caroline Ennis were among the Houston girls who studied in France before or during the Civil War.[71] Known at home as "The Parisians," they imparted the cultural advantages they had received abroad through their social circle and the cultural organizations they supported. For example, Laura Shepherd, who became Mrs. Alexander Porter Root, created a home in Houston where education and the arts were top priorities (figs. 49, 235). Reared in this environment, two of her daughters graduated from the New England Conservatory of Music. Although they never performed professionally, they regularly performed in their homes for family and friends. One daughter, Mary Porter, was president of the Women's Choral Club, which helped organize the Houston Symphony Society in 1913.[72] The legacy of this family's educational tradition, perpetuated in the home environment, lives on in the Shepherd School of Music at Rice University.

The concentration of population in Houston, which offered so many opportunities, had its drawbacks as well. Chief among them was the easy spread of disease. Before the Civil War a general ignorance of nutrition, hygiene, and the causes of disease resulted in frequent illnesses and epidemics, especially in the hot, damp Gulf Coast climate where mosquitoes were prolific. Yellow fever and cholera threatened the area every summer from Houston's first year until World War I. Many died from the diseases, and trade was disrupted as stricken areas were quarantined by neighboring towns. "Noxious miasmas," or atmospheric poisons arising from polluted water and decaying organic matter, were the suspected cause. Bleeding, purging, patent medicines, and home remedies were the most frequent cures prescribed by physicians.[73] The dearth of hospitals required patients to be nursed at home.

Houston bookstores stocked numerous medical books designed for sickroom attendants (usually members of the household). Among the offerings of J. S. Taft in 1848 were *Dungleson on New Remedies, Ewell's Medical Companion, Gunn's Domestic Medicine*, and *Charley's Midwifery*.[74] Medical advice was also found in the newspapers. That year an editorial touting Rockwell and Sauters Restaurant stated: "We would remind all invalids who are troubled with dispepsy, diseases of the lungs, etc. that a small dish of fresh oysters, taken regularly twice a day, affects those diseases more beneficially than all the quack medicines that were ever manufactured."[75]

Newspaper instructions on bathing, public sanitation, and avoiding tainted foods show that astute observers suspected a connection between hygiene, wholesome food, and disease control as early as the 1840s.[76] Nevertheless, remedies like C. E. Quensell's instructions to his son Wilhelm, who had just emigrated to Houston in 1853, were typical: "[To cure finger and nail abscesses] . . . take a fresh egg and open it on one end. Through this hole he inserts his finger and leaves it all night; that he may not forget the egg, he should wrap the whole hand with linen cloth securely so as not to damage the egg. In the morning, the egg is removed and the finger is healed."[77]

The most widely practiced method of preventing yellow fever and cholera was the removal of the entire household, including servants, from the area where an epidemic was expected. Popular destinations of fleeing Houstonians were inland resorts where they could take water cures, both internal and external, from natural mineral springs. Anglo-American settlers had learned from the Indians the medicinal effects of the pools and wells around Sour Lake, north of Beaumont in the Big Thicket. In 1847 Andrew Briscoe described "12 or 15 families camped about the lake—for all imaginable complaints."[78] The Sour Lake Springs Hotel, located in a grove of giant moss-hung live oaks near the lake, was a favorite resort of Houstonians until July 1902, when the Texas Company got its start by discovering oil there.[79] The resort generated the Sour Lake Medical Company in Houston, which manufactured medicated soaps, salves, and shampoos for use in the home. They were sold under the name of Dr. Mud, a black man who lived at the lake and was famous for concocting "cures" for the hotel's guests from muds, oil pitch, and mineral water.[80]

In July 1849 N. K. Kellum of Houston opened a resort at the White Sulphur Springs in Grimes County, seventy miles from Houston. Resemblance between this place and the West Virginia resort of the same name (now known as the Greenbrier) was probably intentional, for the latter was considered by its owners and patrons to be the social mecca of the antebellum South. Kellum's guests, like those at the West Virginia model, moved their families to the resort for months at a time, bringing children, servants, and horses. They could stay in the main building, rent separate houses, or purchase houses on the grounds. Messrs. Brown and Tarbox operated a stagecoach line directly between Houston and the Springs.[81]

By 1875 European research in microbiology had discounted theories that miasmas caused disease. Dr. Thomas Joel Boyles and Dr. Samuel Clark Red, two partners in the Houston Infirmary, were among those who stayed abreast of the latest scientific developments and introduced many of them to Houston. In 1879 and 1889 Dr. Boyles traveled to centers of medical research in Europe to update his knowledge.[82] Dr. Red was one of the chief proponents of window screens in Houston when the connection between mosquitoes and malaria was discovered. Nevertheless, cures were years away for most diseases, and the sickroom remained one of the pre–World War I homemaker's greatest concerns. On September 28, 1899, Bettie Palmer Hutcheson wrote to her husband from their summer home in Albionview, Tennessee: "It is perfectly fearful to live in this upset condition every year—last year I lived for four weeks after I went home, with my trunks packed ready to run away from yellow fever and the year before I spent two months here . . . I would rather have yellow fever than chase around the world this way . . . write me if it is safe for me to go home by Shreveport—is Texas quarantined against anyone passing through Jackson?"[83]

In both the city and the country, ethnic groups introduced new patterns of domestic life. By the 1850s farmers from many parts of Germany had fled political tyranny in Europe and established thriving communities in the north part of Harris County.[84] These isolated farming communities perpetuated German customs and traditions through the first half of the twentieth century. Residents continued to speak German in their homes, churches, schools, and gun clubs, and published German-language newspapers. They had to adapt their domestic lives to the local climate and geography, substituting cornbread for black bread in the absence of wheat, for example. Nonetheless, they maintained as much of their native culture as they could.[85]

Sausage-making was a social event at which neighbors gathered to help the family with their work (fig. 226). Beer, Lepküechen (a chocolate and citron Christmas cake), fruit pies, and pastries such as strudel were all favorite foods among Harris County's German families, who expanded their diets and created new recipes as a result of being able to plant two gardens a year in the new climate. Like Anglo-American settlers in both the country and the city, the Germans served dinner, the main meal of the day, at noon. Men came home from the fields or the office; those who could afford the time took naps before returning to work. Supper was a light meal served in the evening. Coffee, the favorite beverage, was served with pastries at midmorning and midafternoon in rural areas. Any time guests arrived, whether in the city or the country, food was offered. During the week German women held Kaffee Klatschen, or coffee conversations, at which they caught up on the latest news and did handwork.

On Sunday afternoon the coffee break was called lunch. Served to entire families of visiting relatives and friends, it might include meat, sandwiches, and cake, but never tea. Usually instrumental music and singing were part of the entertainment. To prepare for a Sunday of leisure with "no fire in the kitchen," many women spent Saturdays scrubbing their houses and cooking. On the third Sunday afternoon of the month many German families in northern Harris County gathered at one of the four "brother" gun clubs: Bear Creek, Spring Branch, White Oak, and Cypress. Target competitions were held for both men and women. Children participated in the dancing, which continued all evening. Homemade pies and cakes brought by the women and sandwiches and coffee were sold. Each June one of the clubs hosted the Big Feast to which they invited the members of the other three clubs and their families for competitions and dancing. The men cooked an all-beef stew in a large iron kettle, seasoning it with bay leaves gathered from the woods. Potatoes, sauerkraut, and prunes were also served.[86] Some German religious denominations, especially the Methodists, frowned on frivolity and dancing, however. For them Sundays were more solemn.

Most Germans were Lutherans, Catholics, or Methodists for whom religion and family were the cornerstones of life. They paced the progress of the year by the church calendar, and they celebrated each milestone with a festival that included all ages. They introduced the Easter Bunny and the Christmas tree to Texas, celebrating on Christmas Eve rather than on Christmas Day as the Anglo-Americans did. Candles were lit on a tree decorated with handmade ornaments, durable brass chains symbolizing German practicality, a few treasured glass ornaments from Germany, and an angel at the top (fig. 241). Family birthday parties were "the center and symbol of the Family Cult." [87] Known for their meticulous cleanliness, German women scoured their houses especially well for these celebrations.

Although German immigrants in Houston initially settled in predominantly German neighborhoods, they soon became amalgamated with the Anglo-Americans, Irish Catholics, Jews, French, and other groups that made up the city's diverse population. Their daily life followed the pattern of other Houstonians, but they kept their German culture alive in their homes, churches, civic organizations, and singing societies. The German Quartet Society was organized in 1847. Subsequent organizations included the Männerchor, the Liederkranz, and the Sängerbund. These clubs participated in annual statewide singing contests each May, which were held in Houston in 1885, 1894, 1902, and 1913.[88] On such occasions the singers' wives catered large feasts of German food from their homes. During World War I, the Sängerbund purchased the William P. Hamblen/ William E. Kendall house at 315 Milby Street for their headquarters.[89] Credited with introducing the waltz to Texas, the Germans taught all forms of dancing, imported musical instruments and sheet music, and furnished music for balls and parties. For example, in 1838 F. Lemky taught "music in its various branches" as well as German and French in his home.[90]

Religious worship in the home, as exemplified by the Methodist families of August, Conrad, and Charles Bering, who held private services in their parlors to read the Bible and pray before attending church on Sunday, was not confined to Methodists and Germans.[91] Throughout America domestic Bible-based religion promoted family unity and the notion of the home as a moral haven from the world of business and industry. The father read the Bible to the assembled family and led the prayers. The mother interpreted religion to the children and instructed them on moral issues.[92] Revivals, held in Houston as elsewhere in America, were designed to precipitate regeneration experiences (spiritual rebirth through the purging of one's sins) and reinforce domestic worship. Reaching out to the community, families such as those of Erastus Perkins and William A. Van Alstyne regularly held religious meetings in their homes, especially before Houston's churches were built.[93]

With the legalization of slavery by the Republic of Texas, many African Americans were brought to the area by slaveholding families from southern states who flocked to East and Southeast Texas after the battle of San Jacinto. Both prerevolutionary settlers and new immigrants from northern states found it economically expedient to adopt southern attitudes and the southern social system. Although some slaves were imported to Harris County directly from Africa, most were probably second- or third-generation native-born Americans brought to Texas from southern states. Available sources on slave life in Texas are sometimes contradictory and always sketchy, and few deal specifically with Harris County, which had no large plantations. As elsewhere in the South, wealthy households might have domestic staffs with specialized duties, including a personal servant for each member of the family. A separate group of agricultural laborers was required on farms and ranches. Less affluent households had fewer slaves, who were required to perform a greater variety of tasks. When their services were not needed by their owners, slaves were hired out. They were expected to work long hours and were always on call.[94]

The quality and quantity of food, clothing, medical attention, and housing of slaves were determined by the financial circumstance, whim, and conscience of their owners. The black man could not supply these things to his family in any significant way, although some supplemented their food rations with fish, wild game, and vegetables from their own small gardens. Some earned a little money selling vegetables they had raised or by doing extra work. With this they could buy a few more clothes. They also might make furniture for their cabins. The family unit, to the extent that it was allowed to exist among slaves, was the most stabilizing factor in their lives. Nevertheless, since the slave family was not recognized as a social unit under the law, it lived under the constant threat of being separated by sale when the owners needed funds. The lack of privacy and the communal way of life in many slave quarters created a pattern of domestic life quite different from that of white families.

The slave woman was primarily a fulltime laborer for her owner rather than a wife, mother, and homemaker. On a large plantation, the tasks of cooking, sewing, washing, and child care for the slave women were assigned to a few, relieving the rest from most of their own domestic chores except cleaning their quarters. However, this arrangement was probably rare in Harris County, where smaller staffs of slaves meant that each would have to perform her own domestic duties in her off hours. When only two or three slaves were on a staff, they all probably ate food prepared by the cook in the main kitchen, taking their meals either there or on the back porch. The typical slave's diet throughout the South was cornbread, a little meat, and "potlicker," a broth made from turnip greens, peas, beans, cabbage, and potatoes, or whatever combination of vegetables was available. Some slaves had their own tinware for meals and ate at tables. Others ate with wooden utensils out of a common trough or bowl. Household servants, skilled artisans, and foremen were usually supplied with better food, clothing, housing, and medical attention than field hands and other laborers received. One-room log buildings or barracks-like structures housed both urban and rural slaves. Like those of the earliest settlers, their beds often were bunks built into corners, using the walls for support in place of three of the legs. Sometimes a family was allowed the privacy of separate quarters, but it was not unusual for it to have to share space with unrelated slaves.

Owners determined the extent to which weddings, funerals, and baptisms were celebrated, and they supplied the finery and feasts that accompanied them. Baptisms involving complete submersion in one of the bayous were among the blacks' most important rituals (fig. 268). However, the Robert Lockart family preferred to have their slaves baptized from a ruby glass bowl in their house.[95] Preachers who conducted these ceremonies held the only positions of leadership that slaves were allowed to cultivate from their own ranks. They used white churches for their worship services or they worshipped outside. Typically slaves had Saturday afternoons off to wash their clothes and clean up for Sunday. Dances were held periodically on Saturday nights. In the rural areas blacks from surrounding farms and ranches were invited. In spite of the laws, some slave-owners allowed whiskey, wine, and brandy to be drunk at these parties, but others did not. Barbecues and games were often part of the festivities. Shooting, fighting, and gambling were strictly forbidden.

The biggest celebration of the year was Christmas. For some slaves it was the only time they received new clothes and shoes. Their festivities ranged from meager to elaborate, depending on the master's family. Most slaves were given a little money to spend at their discretion, plus candy, a hog, fresh beef or chickens, some eggnog, and a big dinner. Some were given their own Christmas trees decorated with popcorn, and perhaps individual gifts. Ex-slave Harriet Jones remembered that Christmas evening the slaves had a supper of wild turkey or chicken and special dishes on a long table in the yard. The rest of the night they spent in dancing while the white family watched. Some rural slaves had the week between Christmas and New Year's Day off to make up for the long work hours during the fall harvest.

A few free African Americans also resided in Harris County as early as 1836, but no record survives of their houses. Several in Houston owned land, including at least two women. In 1840 Ann Tucker purchased a lot and lived as a free black Houstonian until her death in 1846. Fanny McFarland was emancipated by her Texan owner in 1835. She lived in Houston from at least 1838 to 1866, engaged in a number of real estate transactions, and apparently was able to make a profit. Such free blacks lived between two worlds: forbidden to associate with slaves but excluded from white society. The republic passed contradictory laws, first granting and then revoking their right to stay in Texas. However, Harris County officials largely ignored the laws requiring free blacks to leave. The 1850 and 1860 censuses list seven and eight free blacks in Harris County, respectively; most were women and children.[96]

The Union blockade of Galveston Bay and the demands of the Civil War severely taxed the resources of Harris County residents, but the area was never invaded and its economy recovered within a few years. Houston's population began to grow again, swelled by southerners looking for a new start in life, a new wave of Germans fleeing from political oppression around 1870, and free African Americans looking for jobs. Existing neighborhoods expanded and new ones were created. As railroad yards concentrated in the northeastern sector of the city, residents of nearby Quality Hill and surrounding areas moved into new upper-income neighborhoods south of the business district. In the 1870s, following Reconstruction, very large houses suitable for lavish entertaining like the Van Alstyne house (figs. 44, 53) began to be built along Main Street. A few were built in the country as well, such as the Samuel Ezekiel Allen ranch house (ca. 1875) on Sims Bayou (fig. 27). As the economy strengthened and roads improved late in the century, many affluent people, influenced by the nationwide country house movement, purchased farms or ranches in rural Harris County or in adjacent counties for recreation. Some, like T. W. House's sugar plantation at Arcola, in Fort Bend County, were serious businesses. Others, like Judge James V. Meek's ranch at Katy, were more for pleasure. Judge Meek kept his pointers there but sent them to his family's plantation in Warsaw, Alabama, to be trained for hunting.[97]

North of Buffalo Bayou and east of downtown, in the area that became the Fifth Ward, one- and two-story houses on tracts of various sizes were interspersed with industrial sites, train stations, and warehouses. Former slaves from East Texas congregated in a grove of trees called a "brush arbor" along the north bank of the bayou where they built closely packed lean-tos and small frame houses. Known as "the Bottoms," this area was one of several such enclaves that developed as African Americans flocked to Houston from surrounding counties to find jobs.[98] Most Fifth Ward residents, both black and white, worked in the area. Mexican immigrants began to settle there in the 1880s, but did not establish significant communities until the Mexican Revolution in 1910. By that time, many of the original German families had prospered enough to move into more affluent neighborhoods. Mexican and newer European immigrants found employment in the railroad yards and moved into the vacant cottages or into new rental housing built in similar styles.[99]

Former slaves from plantations in Brazoria and Fort Bend counties settled on the south side of Buffalo Bayou where the Houston Coliseum now stands. The area was then known as "Baptist Hill." Others settled along Brays Bayou near present-day Bellaire. A group of black Canadians settled near present-day Westheimer Road south of River Oaks in an area called "Loving Canada." In contrast to the enclaves of newcomers, the majority of Houston's African Americans remained scattered throughout the city until the late 1880s, many living on the premises of their former owners or their current employers. Inspired by the Reverend Jack Yates, pastor of Antioch Baptist Church, some blacks began buying houses in the Fourth Ward soon after Emancipation.[100] By the 1890s leadership of Houston's black community was concentrated in two neighborhoods: Freedmen's Town, centered around San Felipe Road (now West Dallas Street) in the Fourth Ward, and the eastern portion of the Third Ward centered around Dowling Street. A thriving black business community was established by college-educated professionals. Houston was a popular place to settle among this group, many of whom built substantial houses alongside the community's smaller cottages and rows of shotgun houses. Legally enforced segregation meant that black neighborhoods were necessarily a mix of economic and social groups.[101]

Differences in domestic life between blacks and middle-class whites after Emancipation were primarily economic. Both groups had back-yard gardens, raised some livestock, cooked and did the laundry outdoors, used cisterns for their water supply, and used wood or coal stoves for heating. Blacks grew more of their own food and made more of their own clothing and furniture. The Good Hope Baptist Church in Freedmen's Town had a block vegetable garden to help supply that neighborhood. Blacks shopped at black-owned businesses, such as Robert L. Andrews's grocery store at 408 Milam, or at white-owned stores, where they had to use separate entrances. Lacking public facilities, blacks used their houses as meeting places for the same purposes as whites. The house of A. K. Kelley at 615 Hill Street in the Fifth Ward was the site of many functions. Churches organized at private residences included the United Mt. Vernon Methodist Church, founded under a brush arbor on ex-slave Rev. Emanuel Toby's acre of land in the Bottoms, and the Payne Chapel, African Methodist Episcopal Church, founded in 1886 in a house in the Fifth Ward on West Street, where many prominent blacks lived. Black social life, like that of whites, centered around parties in private homes and church functions.[102]

As the city's population grew, existing neighborhoods became more dense. Many people who had built houses in the center of city blocks and used the remainder of the property for agriculture moved the original house to one corner or to the side of the block and either sold off lots, built rent houses, or built houses for their children facing the other sides of the property (figs. 12, 16, 17, 36). In addition to providing neighborhood cohesiveness, this pattern of family compounds, like the practice of extended families living in the same house, preserved the bonds between generations and between collateral relatives as they interacted in one another's houses and gardens on a daily basis. Rural families and Houston families with country places divided properties similarly (fig. 252). Connections between relatives were strong, and family ties frequently paralleled those of business. It was not uncommon for men to marry the sisters or daughters of their business partners. For example, Benjamin A. Shepherd's three sons-in-law, A. P. Root, O. L. Cochran, and W. H. Palmer, were all officers and directors of Shepherd's First National Bank.[103]

Business partners who were related often lived near each other. Julius Cornelius Bering and Henry W. Cortes, brothers-in-law and partners in the Bering, Cortes Hardware Company, lived next door to each other at 1112 and 1118 Milam in the midst of a five-block-long neighborhood along Milam and Louisiana streets between Lamar and Leeland avenues nicknamed "Bering Settlement" because of the number of Bering relatives who lived there (fig. 103). Family ties among the Bering descendants resulting from this arrangement were so strong that, in 1889, fifteen female first cousins formed the Cousins Club at the house of Mrs. Alma M. Walker. This group met once a month in the house of one of the members for a spend-the-day party to keep up with family activities. They also made quilts for Mrs. De Pelchin's Orphans' Home, now DePelchin Faith Home. The club continued until about 1950.[104]

Although most business workers had separate offices in the business district by this time, some business activities were still attached to houses. Artisans and proprietors of small stores continued to live above or next to their shops, and professionals like doctors maintained offices in or adjacent to their residences. Dr. David Finney Stuart had a separate building in his front yard where he saw patients (fig. 233). His son, Dr. Joseph Stuart, lived in a house adjacent to the Houston Infirmary, the hospital where they both practiced. Dr. David Stuart's house was on the block diagonally across the intersection of Texas Avenue and San Jacinto Street from the home of his sister-in-law's parents, Dr. and Mrs. E. H. Blake, and only a few blocks from the home of another of his partners in the Houston Infirmary, Dr. Samuel Clark Red. Dr. Red's office was in a room on the first floor of his house at 817 Caroline Street, with a separate entrance for patients. This blending of business and social relationships around the domestic setting helped bring neighborhoods together.[105]

Schools also contributed to neighborhood development and cohesiveness. Small private schools in teachers' houses attracted children living nearby who could walk to school and walk home for lunch. The evolution of some neighborhoods and the development of new additions can be traced by the movements of such schools. Miss Mary B. Browne's Young Ladies School, founded in 1859, was the most prominent school of this type until it closed in the 1890s. Originally located at Caroline and Franklin on the edge of Quality Hill, it moved south to McKinney Avenue at Crawford Street when Quality Hill families began migrating south to escape the railroad yards during the last quarter of the century.[106] In 1896 Professor Christopher W. Welch opened his Houston Academy three blocks farther south, at the corner of Polk and Jackson, to accommodate neighborhood children when Miss Browne's closed (fig. 263). About the same time the Misses Waldo, who had been educated at Smith College and in Paris, opened a school in their house at 1213 Rusk Avenue at Caroline Street (fig. 51). The rapid development of the South End after the turn of the century is illustrated by Professor Welch's move to 2215 Caroline at Hadley in 1906 and the founding of Mrs. Margaret Kinkaid's school in her one-story cottage on San Jacinto at Elgin in 1904. Mrs. Kinkaid's school grew so fast that she raised her cottage and added a new first floor underneath. The family occupied the second floor while the school occupied the first. In less than a year the school invaded the second floor, and the family decided to move, leaving the entire house to the school.[107] Of all the private schools established around the turn of the century, only the Kinkaid School survives.

In 1885 a private school for African American children was opened in a house known as the Cooper Place, which was moved to the corner of Bell and San Jacinto on the edge of a fashionable white neighborhood (fig. 262). Jennie L. Peck and Florence Dysart, two white missionaries from the American Baptist Mission Women's Home Society of Chicago, founded the school with the help of the Reverend Jack Yates, who started a scholarship program among Houston's black churches to enable black children to attend.[108] The free public school system in Houston began with the conversion of Mrs. Zerviah Noble's private school into a public school, and it followed the pattern of private schools by locating permanent elementary school buildings in neighborhoods throughout the city (fig. 261).

Schools were among the public services that Harris County and Houston began to provide for their residents after the Civil War.[109] Provision of public services and improvements was sporadic, however. The city paved some streets, primarily in the business district, but mud continued to be a problem for many years. The sewer system was notoriously unsatisfactory well beyond 1916, when most sewage was still pouring directly into Buffalo Bayou—the main source of drinking water before 1891.[110] Franchised public services also arose. The Houston Gas Light Company began operations in 1868.[111] An editorial from 1875 expressed dissatisfaction with the way the company operated streetlights: "has not the "cow-boy" with his mustang pony, as much right to ride on the sidewalks as the lamplighter? We will venture the assertion that Houston is the only city on the face of the globe where a horse and the public sidewalks are used to light street lamps. Ladders are used everywhere else."[112] The Houston Electric Light and Power Company received its franchise in 1882. On December 13, the barroom of the second Capitol Hotel became the first place in Houston to be electrically lighted. In 1878 the city authorized a waterworks to supply piped water from Buffalo Bayou. In 1888 the Water Works Company began drilling wells to provide artesian water. In 1868 the Houston City Railway Company began operating mule-drawn cars over wooden tracks. The streetcars were converted to electric power in 1890 and continued in service until buses replaced them in 1941. Streetcars were extended to new suburbs such as the Houston Heights and Bellaire as they were developed, becoming, like most utilities, major factors in the expansion of the city. In 1911 the Galveston-Houston Electric Railway opened the Interurban between the two cities, which operated until 1936. Telephones arrived in 1879 through the Western Union Telegraph Company, but they were not extended to north Harris County until around 1915. Acceptance of utilities by the public and expansion across the city and county were gradual. Some portions of the city, such as the Fourth Ward, and most rural areas still lacked many or all utilities in the 1930s.[113]

The provision of city-sponsored utilities, accompanied by technological advances in household products and appliances and by easier access to ready-made goods, changed the urban domestic routine and eliminated the need for some of the traditional outbuildings. The rural life of the 1820s had concentrated on the *production* of the necessities of daily life. As more and more items were bought rather than made, domestic tasks began to emphasize home *maintenance*. The expansion of the railroad network to connect with midwestern lines during the last quarter of the nineteenth century made mass-produced appliances, building materials, household furnishings, durable goods, and clothing more available and more affordable. Indoor plumbing, gas water heaters, burglar and fire alarms, intercom systems, fire extinguishers, window screens, electric fans, cast-iron stoves, ice boxes, and sewing machines decreased the time and labor spent on household tasks while increasing domestic comfort and safety.[114] Artificial ice machines, probably introduced into Houston in 1870 by the Hutchins family, led to lower ice costs enabling more people to afford ice boxes.[115] New houses often included indoor kitchens by the late 1880s and indoor bathrooms were functional by around 1900. Basements lined with Portland cement or cinder block to keep out the moisture held large furnaces for central heating.[116]

Reflecting the consumerism that characterized late nineteenth-century American society, Houstonians responded to the availability of more and cheaper clothing, appliances, and household furnishings by complicating their lives with more material possessions—which in turn had to be cared for. During the 1880s and '90s, Constance Evershade lived in the Nichols-Rice-Cherry house on Courthouse Square with her parents, several siblings and their spouses, and her nieces and nephews. A day rarely passed when Constance, her mother, and her sisters were not sewing clothes for the family on their sewing machines, visiting dressmakers, or buying ready-made clothing and accessories from William L. Foley, Levy Brothers, Albert Hampe, shops in Mason's Arcade, and the Mistrot/Munn Department Store. Their more active social lives, made possible by improved utilities, transportation, and labor-saving devices, required a greater variety of clothes for different occasions and many outfits had several layers. They probably spent as much time sewing and shopping for clothing as pioneer women spent spinning, weaving, and hand-sewing to create the few simple garments they owned.[117]

More clothes added to the laundering and ironing: long, laborious chores that remained the same throughout the pre-World War I period. Most of the process took place in the back yard, in a separate wash house, or on a utility porch behind the kitchen after 1900. Water was hand-pumped from an underground cistern, pumped by a windmill, or flowed by gravity from a cistern on stilts next to the house. It was heated over a fire and sometimes softened with lye. Numerous kettles, pots, and tubs contained soap suds, rinse water, blueing, and starch. Clothes and linens were moved from one pot to another in an assembly line. Most clothes spent time in a "boiling bag," boiling in a copper or brass kettle of strong soap suds. (Iron kettles stained the clothes.) Rub boards were used to work on spots. White clothes were hung in the sun, colors in the shade. In bad weather, laundry was spread out on the porches. Wash sticks were used to move the clothes about in the kettles, preventing them from yellowing in spots. Articles to be stiffened when ironed were dipped in starch just before they were hung out. Several irons were required to smoothe one garment since one iron held its heat only for a brief time. Those not in use sat on the stove to stay hot. Probably the most widely used iron was the common flat iron, which came in various weights and sizes. It was called the "sad iron" (an English term meaning "solid iron"), surely an apt name since ironing next to a hot stove was one of the most unpleasant chores, especially during a Texas summer.[118]

Housecleaning, like washing and ironing, was a more consuming task than it had once been. In the frontier household, with most activities taking place outside and bare earth sometimes serving as a floor indoors, removal of dirt was not a major concern. The later, more sophisticated houses had more rooms and more furnishings that needed cleaning, while improved lighting in the house provided by gas or electricity revealed the dirt. The ritual of spring housecleaning arose to remove the buildup of smoke and soot caused by heating and lighting equipment and the dirt and dust from Houston streets that entered through open windows. Everything was taken outside to "air" and "sun," from the draperies to the mattresses and upholstered furniture. Dust was beaten out of the draperies, the upholstery fabric, and the wool rugs, which were hung on sturdy clotheslines for this purpose. Heavy wire paddlelike beaters were used on the rugs. The rugs and draperies then were moth-proofed and stored in the attic for the summer. Wool clothing and blankets, if not soiled, were always brushed or shaken out and aired on clotheslines before being stored for the summer in cedar-lined closets or in garment bags. Stained table and bed linens were dampened and spread on the grass overnight, then washed in hot suds. A combination of the dew, strong sunlight, and sometimes salt mixed with lemon juice usually removed the spots.

The ceilings, walls, and woodwork were washed and periodically repainted. All exposed wood on furniture and woodwork was lightly waxed. Wood floors were waxed and buffed to a patina, sometimes with improvised tools like a large brick wrapped in heavy wool and attached with a hinge to a pole handle. The alternative was to work on one's hands and knees. Those who could afford to do so placed custom-made linen slipcovers on upholstered furniture. Thin curtains, often of lace, and grass fabric rugs replaced the heavy draperies and wool rugs. Silver was stored away. Crystal and cut glass were displayed instead. The overall effect was light and airy. Since windows had to be kept open in warm weather, the dust from outside was more easily controlled in these sparsely appointed rooms. Outside shutters frequently were closed during the hottest part of the day to keep rooms cooler and to keep the sun from fading the furniture (figs. 215, 227). In the fall this process was repeated. The dust buildup was removed, exposed wood received another coat of wax, books were removed from shelves for dusting, and the heavy draperies and wool rugs came down from the attic. Men who specialized in heavy housecleaning moved from house to house twice a year performing this ritual.

During the rest of the year, housekeeping was still an onerous and unending task. The germ theory of disease became popular in the late 1890s, and microbes causing disease were thought to lurk in dust. Standards of cleanliness rose. The carpet sweeper, invented in the 1860s, helped keep rugs presentable, but hand beating was still necessary. Soot had to be removed from lamp chimneys, stoves, and fireplaces. Silver and brass had to be polished. Insects, rodents, and mildew had to be controlled. Back yards had to be swept. Housekeepers made their own cleaning solutions according to published recipes or family tradition. Among the substances most frequently used in Houston, either alone or in combination with others, were soda, lime, lemon juice, sulphur, borax, blueing (or indigo water), ammonia, vinegar, clay, and chalk. Lye was made by percolating hot water through wood ashes and lime and then combined with animal fat to make soap. Hard soap also contained quicklime, and fine white soap contained lard and salt.[119]

Since most Americans had access to the same manuals on domestic economy and the same hand-operated cleaning tools, the procedures they used for household chores were fairly uniform. Housekeeping in Harris County differed chiefly in regard to peculiarities of climate. Noting that "no complete treatise on the subject of cookery has been published in our latitude," the Ladies' Association of Houston's First Presbyterian Church published *The Texas Cookbook,* "the first enterprise of its kind in our State," in 1883. Their aim was to publish recipes and housekeeping techniques "suited to the requirements of our climate."[120] A saucer of quick lime was recommended to absorb dampness in a closet or other enclosed space. Red ants would avoid closets and drawers containing green sage or small bags of sulphur. Finely powdered borax sprinkled into crevices and around hot water pipes was a "cockroach destroyer" guaranteed not to fail. Mildew stains could be removed from fabric by dipping the cloth in buttermilk or by rubbing it with common brown soap and then with white chalk. In both cases the fabric was then laid on the grass in the sun. Pea-sized chopped potatoes brushed into carpets with brooms and then swept away removed all manner of debris from rugs. Straw matting was washed with coarse salt and water and then wiped dry. Cloths saturated with whiting or prepared chalk were used to clean windows and mirrors. A teacup of cornmeal heated on the stove in a dirty pot, and then rubbed around in it, left the pot perfectly clean.[121]

Surely the most disagreeable task was dealing with chamber pots, water closets, outhouses, and privies (outhouses with brick-lined vaults underneath to contain the waste). Some composted the waste and used it as garden fertilizer. In a practice dating back to medieval times, the Houston City Scavenger could be contracted to clean the privy vault or water closet of any house or yard and sprinkle lime or other disinfectants in the area. An 1878 or 1879 city ordinance made it "unlawful for the City Scavenger, or any other person, to empty, remove or carry away the contents of any privy vault or any other receptacle of human excrement at any time except during the hours of from 11 o'clock P.M. to 3 o'clock A.M."[122] Such contents had to be conveyed beyond the city limits. Until the late nineteenth century, very little trash was nonorganic. Most garbage was burned or buried in the back yard or left on the ground for the dogs and pigs. Tin cans were crushed and they disintegrated when buried. Bottles were reused for other purposes. In Houston, trash was thrown into ditches or gullies that meandered through the city, especially the Caroline Street gully.[123]

In most households the woman in charge juggled all the work, often with the assistance of other resident female members of her family. A middle-class family that could afford a couple of live-in servants might have a yardman who kept the grounds, looked after the chickens and horses, and did odd jobs; a maid who helped with housework, child care, and cooking; and perhaps a laundress or an ironing woman who came in once a week. In the grandest houses, household staffs differed little from those of antebellum days except that black servants were free. A housekeeper might be hired to oversee the others. The butler answered the door and the telephone, served meals and refreshments, ran errands, cared for the horses and carriages, and drove family members to and from their destinations. The nurse took complete charge of the children, accompanying them everywhere—even to parties with their mothers and on family vacations (figs. 38, 220, 221, 238, 269). She took babies on morning and afternoon strolls in the neighborhood, mended clothes, and did light laundry for the children while they took their naps. The cook planned and prepared three meals a day for both the family and the other servants.

Both upstairs and downstairs maids were probably needed to clean the largest houses. Frequent changes of clothing in the hot climate generated enormous amounts of laundry, requiring fulltime laundresses and ironing women who also dealt with frequent changes of bed, bath, and table linens. The gardener kept the grounds and grew the flowers and vegetables.[124]

Except when their duties required them to be in the formal rooms, servants stayed in the utilitarian sections of the house and circulated via the back stairway and the back and side doors. Children were expected to do the same. Only the owners and their guests used the front door. Female servants wore white or gray starched cotton uniforms with long white aprons and starched caps on a daily basis and black uniforms for company. Male servants wore starched white jackets and dark pants in the house, changing to black jackets and caps when chauffeuring (fig. 235). Typical servants' quarters, like slave barracks, were single rooms located on the second story of the stables (later the garage) or in a long, one-story building in the back yard (figs. 54, 213). Heated by individual fireplaces or small stoves, these rooms served both as bedrooms and as sitting rooms where servants entertained their friends. Until their rooms were equipped with piped water, servants pumped bath water from the main cistern and heated it on the laundry stove in the wash house where they washed and ironed their clothes in their free time. They ate their meals, provided by their employer, in the kitchen, on the back porch, or in the back yard of the main house. After hours and on their days off black servants changed to street clothes (often hand-me-downs from their employers) and participated in church and social activities in the black neighborhoods. White servants from the country probably visited in white working-class neighborhoods and returned to their rural homes infrequently (fig. 229).

As houses became more architecturally elaborate, with better furnishings, as more rooms were assigned to specific functions (such as ballrooms, billiard rooms, play rooms, solariums, conservatories, and butlers' pantries), and as women gained more discretionary time, life in Houston became more formal (figs. 216, 223, 224). From about 1870 on, elaborately engraved invitations were sent for various social occasions: picnics, hops, theater parties, balls, and even children's birthday parties. Socially prominent women received formal calls at home on specified days of the week. In between, engraved calling cards, delivered in person or by messenger, conveyed messages in code: "Turning the upper right hand corner of a card implies a call. Turning the upper left hand corner, congratulations. Turning the lower right corner, adieu. Turning the lower left corner, condolence. Turning the entire left end, a call on the family . . . ." Furthermore, "Persons who wish to gradually close an acquaintance respond to all calls paid them by persistent card leaving."[125]

By the 1890s, good manners had become an obsession with the gentry. The time was ripe for "the first Blue Book ever issued in the State of Texas."[126] Similar to New York's first social register, published in 1887, *The Houston/Galveston Blue Book, A Society Directory*, appeared in 1896. The book included sections listing Houston's and Galveston's elite, and it set forth the "Social Code." Assuming absolute authority, the "Social Code" dictated rules of conduct that indicated "perfect breeding." Above all, the code recognized the sanctity and privacy of the home as a retreat from public life and unwelcome acquaintances. The most prominent social, cultural, and religious organizations were listed with their current officers and members. Formal calling days were listed next to the names, addresses, and phone numbers. Discreet advertisements for expensive merchandise financed both the New York and Texas publications.[127]

The formality and extravagance of social life in Houston reached its apex between about 1890 and 1915. Houston's most elite social organization, the ZZ Social Club, was founded in 1868 in the house of Henry Sampson on Courthouse Square (figs. 23, 24). Its members had broken with the older KK Club, founded in 1865, over the KK's disapproval of waltzing. The membership in both clubs was male, but female relatives and friends were invited to their dances and soirées. In early years the KK Club frequently met in Edward Hopkins Cushing's house, Bohemia, (fig. 30), while the ZZ Club often met in the houses of Mrs. Erastus Perkins or Mrs. William Fulton, who chaperoned the gatherings (figs. 12, 217). The ZZ Club gradually absorbed the older KK membership. Spencer Hutchins led the ZZs and, by extension, Houston society from about 1886 until his death twenty years later (fig. 222). Under Hutchins's guidance, club events took on a new importance. In its heyday, the ZZ Club formally presented debutantes not only from Houston but also from Galveston, Austin, San Antonio, and other Texas cities. Although the ZZ Club's formal balls were not usually held in private houses, ancillary receptions and dinners honoring the debutantes were (fig. 219). The club's elaborate functions set the style for home entertaining among its social set.[128]

Second only to the ZZ Club in its reputation for elegant parties was the Houston Light Guard, a local volunteer militia organization formed on April 21, 1873. Many men were members of both groups, including Spencer Hutchins, and elite private parties, ZZ Club balls, and Houston Light Guards events were all attended by the same people. A valued benefit of Light Guard membership was the opportunity for men too young to have participated in the Civil War to obtain a military title which, during Reconstruction, distinguished patriotic southerners. Captain James A. Baker, who received his title in this way, was as synonymous with the Light Guards as Spencer Hutchins was with the ZZs.[129]

When dignitaries visited Houston, they were the houseguests of leading citizens who entertained lavishly. Thousands of southerners attended the fifth annual reunion of the United Confederate Veterans Association, held in Houston from May 22 to 24, 1895. The guest of honor at this event was Winnie Davis, youngest daughter of the late Jefferson Davis. She was the houseguest of Judge James Masterson in the former Van Alstyne house at 1216 Main Street (figs. 44, 53). Among the many large and elegant parties in her honor were receptions at the Mastersons' and "in the 'belle etage' of the new flats, corner of Texas Avenue and Travis Street" (Capitol Hotel Annex), the home of Mr. and Mrs. William Marsh Rice. Other important guests at the event, including the Texas governor and one of the state's U.S. senators who was the sole surviving member of Davis's cabinet, also stayed in private homes in the city and had dinners, receptions, luncheons, teas, and balls in their honor.[130]

Lavish home entertaining was not confined to special occasions for debutantes or distinguished visitors. Even an ordinary event could be the starting point for an extravagant display.

The birthday party given in the Van Alstyne-Masterson-Dickson house by Miss Belle Dickson about 1901 is a case in point. Billed as "a trip through Houston in ninety minutes," it featured decorations, refreshments, and music representing such Houston landmarks as Dawson's ice cream parlor, Sam Houston Park and zoo, Colby's Restaurant, Levy Brothers Department Store, and a carnival midway. Upon arrival, each costumed "tourist" received an itinerary for his or her trip, at the end of which dinner was served in the dining room, where the large oval dining table was surrounded by four smaller tables to accommodate all the guests. "White drawn work" tablecloths were laid over green satin. The centerpieces were calla lilies, narcissi, and hyacinths arranged in cut-glass vases between silver candelabra with green shades.[131]

Weddings and funerals continued to be home affairs, and could be very elaborate. Engagements were announced in imaginative ways at luncheons or dinners held in houses of the couple's closest friends and families. One creative touch was to extend long satin streamers from the floral centerpiece to each place at the dining table. When drawn from the flower arrangement, the other end of the ribbon revealed a cleverly disguised announcement (fig. 187). Weddings were carefully planned and staged events (figs. 254, 255, 256). At the wedding of Sallie Sewall to George F. Horton on November 17, 1906, in the Edward J. Sewall house at 614 San Jacinto Street, nine of the bride's friends joined the vocalist in the bridal chorus from *Lohengrin*. "The chorus was begun upstairs and sung as the party descended the steps carrying the ropes of chrysanthemums. The singers entered the drawing room and formed an aisle, the ropes of flowers defining it, and through this the bridal procession passed."[132]

Funeral customs were also complicated. Most people were born and died at home; just as doctors and midwives called to deliver babies, professional morticians came to the house to make burial preparations. Although morticians existed at an early date and caskets made by cabinetmakers were sold in furniture stores, some families had to prepare the bodies and construct the caskets themselves, as August Proetzel did for his children in the 1860s. The prepared or embalmed body was propped up on a couch or in its own bed and covered with a veil the texture of mosquito netting to keep the flies away. Friends and family sat up with the body all night until it was buried. Some families hired professional sitters. The bodies were placed in coffins before the funeral service, which usually took place the day following the death. Mourning rituals varied with economics. Ideally they included a black crepe ribbon or a spray of white flowers placed on the front door of the house and, where appropriate, the business. Sometimes mirrors in the deceased's house were draped in black. Death notices edged in black and giving the time and place of the funeral were posted on the door of the business, sometimes nailed to street posts, and delivered by hand or mail to friends. The post office delivered them free of charge.

Before the funeral, the principal mourners were secluded in the private sections of the house, while more distant relatives and close family friends ran the household and received callers bringing food or flowers. The funeral usually was conducted in the front parlor. Social, fraternal, patriotic, and military organizations to which the deceased had belonged often turned out en masse and in uniform for the funeral and the subsequent procession from the house to the cemetery. Participants in the procession draped their horses in mourning. African American funeral processions frequently included music. Horse-drawn hearses rented from livery stables or mule-drawn streetcars conveyed the casket. For a prescribed period, which depended on the person's relationship to the deceased, family members did not entertain or attend social festivities, except perhaps weddings. They communicated with friends through stationery and calling cards edged in black and received formal calls from friends who came attired in subdued colors.[133]

The unbending rigidity of the Social Code, the aging membership of the ZZ Club, and the death of Spencer Hutchins were all factors in the demise of Houston's "Elegant Era," as Hubert Roussel later termed the 1890s and early 1900s. The Thalian Club, organized on October 24, 1901, in the Van Alstyne-Masterson-Dickson house, superseded the ZZs and also presented the debutantes. Young, energetic, and socially ambitious, for a few years the Thalians maintained the standards for elegant entertaining set by the ZZs.[134] However, subtle changes were taking place as the social consciousness of the Progressive movement took hold in Houston. Spawned in the 1890s and culminating in the Progressive Party, an off-shoot of the Republican Party formed before the 1912 presidential elections, the Progressive movement promoted many political, economic, and social reforms relating to the health and welfare of the general population. The resulting social pragmatism, enhanced by a new emphasis on big business, hearkened back to the more democratic society that had characterized the city's antebellum white community.

Nowhere were the changes more perceptible than in *The Standard Blue Book of Texas Who's Who? Edition de Luxe of Houston*, published in 1907. In contrast to the small, primarily social *Blue Book* of 1896, this book had the appearance of a Chamber of Commerce publication. Over twice the size of the earlier work, it mostly promoted Houston's businesses. Photographs of prominent business leaders, their places of business, and some of the finer houses were interspersed with essays on the city's economic opportunities. The Social Code was replaced with the "Digest of the Latest Rules of Etiquette." Good manners were considered to be an expression of one's inner character rather than strict observance of arbitrary rules. The book pointed out that business success was one of the rewards of good manners. Indeed, the purpose of the book as stated in its introduction was to bring together "a happy combination of the social and poetic side of life intermingled with the prosaic conditions of commercialism and wealth." It was to serve as "a peerless and powerful advertising medium."[135] The social roster was slightly expanded and hard to find amid the advertisements and other commercial pages. Modern Houston was beginning to emerge.

The ultimate manifestation of this philosophy was the annual No-Tsu-Oh Carnival held each November from 1899 to 1915. Like cotton carnivals in Memphis and similar events in other cities, its purpose was commercial. According to an elaborately devised mythology, No-Tsu-Oh (Houston spelled backward) was the capital city of the Kingdom of Tekram (market) in the realm of Saxet (Texas). King Nottoc (cotton) emerged annually from the depths of the sea, or rather Buffalo Bayou, at the foot of Main Street to rule over his Court of Mirth. His identity was kept secret until the Coronation Ball, but his arrival opened the Gulf Coast Industrial Exposition featuring agricultural and horticultural products and items manufactured in Texas, along with a week of non-stop carnival activities. Early on, the Coronation Ball eclipsed the more sedate debutante balls as the social event of the year (figs. 271, 272, 273). The 1914 carnival, called the Deep Water Jubilee to celebrate the opening of the Ship Channel, included the first Woman's Department. It took up one-third of the exhibition building on Capitol Avenue. Five categories of exhibits relating to the home included art, needlework, domestic science, preserves and canned goods, and children's work. Lectures and lessons in domestic economy were major attractions. The last and most elaborate No-Tsu-Oh Carnival took place in 1915. The festival probably was discontinued because of the outbreak of World War I.[136]

The black population of Harris County had been included in the public activities of the predecessor to the No-Tsu-Oh, the Fruit, Flower, and Vegetable Show. However, servants were the only blacks included in the organized activities of No-Tsu-Oh. Searching for a new vehicle to promote their accomplishments in agriculture and industry, civic leader John A. Matthews suggested a parallel No-Tsu-Oh celebration for African Americans. With William Jones and Van H. McKinney, a black publisher, Matthews formed the De-Ro-Loc (colored) Carnival Association. On December 2, 1909, the first De-Ro-Loc opened with the arrival of King La-Yol-E-Civ-Res I (loyal service), who turned out to be the prominent black attorney M. H. Broyles. The subject of the king's address reflected his title: the loyal service of his race, as American citizens, to the United States. The annual carnival, which took place during the week following No-Tsu-Oh and shared many of its midway attractions, drew several thousand blacks from across the state each year through at least 1915. Two other themes reiterated each year in the king's annual address were the importance of home ownership and the importance of family values to the stability of the black community.[137]

Home ownership among blacks, which the Rev. Jack Yates had promoted since Emancipation, was also stressed in the social directory of the black community published in 1915. Entitled *The Red Book of Houston, a Compendium of Social, Professional, Religious, Educational and Industrial Interests of Houston's Colored Population*, it compared the statistics on the number of black-owned houses in Houston favorably with those in other U.S. cities. Photographs of a number of substantial houses were accompanied by biographical sketches of their owners. In addition to ministers and educators there were other black professionals such as A. J. Johnson, who lived at 319 Robin Street. A graduate of the Los Angeles Architecture School, he had been the contractor and builder for many black owned houses during the previous eight years. Organizations such as the Married Ladies' Social Club, founded in the house of Mary Crawford, and the Married Ladies' Progressive Club were listed. These organizations met in private houses to promote civic activities in the black community.[138]

The women who were freed from domestic tasks in the 1880s by modern conveniences and servants did not spend all their time in elaborate entertaining. Many turned their parlors into centers for adult education, cultural promotion, charitable activities, and forums for civic and domestic reform. Fund-raisers and war relief activities had been held in the home since before the Civil War. By the last quarter of the nineteenth century women had become aware of their own management skills and of the influence they could wield in organized groups. They also had learned to handle large sums of money. Desiring to keep up with the fast-changing world around them, and hoping to influence the changes, they formed study clubs to hone their minds.[139]

The club movement in Texas began with the Ladies' Reading Club, organized in Houston on April 5, 1885, by Adele Briscoe Looscan in the house of her mother, Mary Jane Harris Briscoe, at 620 Crawford Street. Subsequently, numerous similar organizations were founded in Houston and around the state. Civic improvement soon became as important to these groups as intellectual advancement. In 1895 the Ladies' Reading Club organized a citywide coalition of women's clubs to raise funds to establish the Houston Public Library. Out of this cooperative effort came a permanent organization called the City Federation of Women's Clubs, whose next civic triumph was the creation of Sam Houston Park. In an unprecedented action, Ladies' Reading Club members dared to lobby City Hall en masse on behalf of this, the city's first publicly owned park. In 1897 members of the City Federation of Clubs helped organize the State Federation of Women's Clubs, which in turn affiliated with the national organization, the General Federation of Women's Clubs. These organizations became primary vehicles of the Progressive movement, which profoundly affected the home as well as the community, both locally and nationally.[140]

The official periodical for the women's club movement in South Texas, published first in San Antonio and then in Houston, was known successively as the *Ladies Messenger* (1887–90) and the *Gulf Messenger* (1891–98). It was followed by the *Texas Magazine* (1909–1913). Through these magazines and national publications like the *Ladies' Home Journal*, Harris County women kept abreast of Progressive issues affecting women, children, education, health, recreation, and the home which were promoted by the new home economics movement (founded during the influential Woman's Congress at the Chicago World's Columbian Exposition in 1893) and the General Federation of Women's Clubs. These magazines encouraged their readers to install window screens, linoleum floors, electric stoves, white walls, enameled fixtures, and doors and woodwork without dust-catching carvings, moldings, or projections in order to keep their houses as sanitary as hospital operating rooms[141] (figs. 195, 206, 211). Reflecting these national concerns, the Ladies Reading Club worked for many reforms, including laws requiring the fencing of livestock, which until then roamed freely in the city. The Houston Pen Women established and maintained a playground and brought prominent public speakers, such as Horace McFarland, president of the American Civic Association, to Houston. They provided free concerts in Sam Houston Park and established official clean-up days with prizes for the cleanest yards.[142]

During the 1890s a new type of club, the patriotic organization that required proof of ancestry for membership, sprang up across the country to promote nationalism and to perpetuate through education the principles on which the nation was founded. The Philadelphia Centennial Exhibition in 1876 had stimulated interest in America's past and reinforced the Colonial Revival movement already underway. In Houston, Ella Hutchins Sydnor (a "Parisian") founded the Lady Washington Chapter of the Daughters of the American Revolution on November 14, 1899, in the

Western Parlor of the Capitol Hotel.[143] Texas's own version of this movement is the Daughters of the Republic of Texas, founded on November 6, 1891, in the house of Mary Jane Harris Briscoe.[144]

By the late 1880s, the woman's club movement had spawned numerous amateur groups that held musicales, plays, and poetry readings in private houses elaborately decorated for the occasions.[145] The Shakespeare Club once performed *As You Like It* in the gardens of the Emmanuel Raphael house at 1820 Rusk Avenue (fig. 21), using the large trees to represent the forest of Arden.[146] In April 1913, the Herbert Godwin house at 1112 Holman was transformed into a bower of "intoxicating" wisteria for a performance of Liza Lehman's musical version of Sarojini Naidu's poem, "The Golden Threshold."[147] Musical clubs such as the Treble Clef Club and the Women's Choral Club sang both for friends and for the public. Season subscriptions to their concerts also included performances by touring artists of national and international renown.[148] Visiting artists were houseguests of club members who introduced them to Houstonians at private luncheons, dinners, and garden parties. Lasting personal friendships developed between some hosts and their houseguests.[149] By 1915 the extensive list of imported performers moved visiting baritone Reinold Werrenrath to characterize Houston as suffering from "musical indigestion," since "your city isn't large enough to properly assimilate all the good things you have here during a season."[150]

The cultural fabric of modern Houston developed directly from the parlors of civic-minded women determined to transform some of these amateur groups into serious professional institutions. In 1900 women active in Houston study clubs met in the circular drawing room of Mrs. Robert S. Lovett (2017 Main Street at Gray Avenue) to found the Houston Public School Art League (shortened in 1913 to the Houston Art League) to cultivate the aesthetic tastes and artistic instincts of children by placing copies of great works of art in the public schools. Over the next twenty-three years, the organization brought lecturers, musicians, artists, and art exhibitions to the city. The nucleus of an art collection was formed from gifts including bronzes, statuary, and paintings donated by the descendants of John F. Dickson (figs. 175, 176, 177). These gifts were displayed in the C.S. House house at 1806 Main Street at Jefferson, which served as the Art League's first home (fig. 45). The Art League was the parent organization of the Museum of Fine Arts, Houston, organized in 1924.[151]

In the spring of 1913, leaders of the Women's Choral Club (including Miss Ima Hogg), the Treble Clef Club, and others met with Julian Paul Blitz, director of the Treble Clef Club, to plan the Houston Symphony with Blitz as the first conductor. Capitalizing on her volunteer experience as a president of the Women's Choral Club, Mrs. Edna Woolford Saunders became the professional impresaria of Houston's imported cultural entertainment from 1917 until her death in 1963. Houstonians who helped entertain the visiting artists in their homes later organized resident professional companies such as the Houston Ballet.[152]

Houston women also organized for charitable causes. They held social events to benefit temporary needs, such as relief for yellow fever victims, or for their new, permanent charities. Traditionally, relatives cared for the unfortunate at home. Beginning in the 1890s, however, charitable institutions such as Sheltering Arms, DePelchin Faith Home, Florence Crittenden Home for unwed mothers, the Houston Settlement Association, and the Emma R. Newsboys Home, or private institutions such as the Greenwood Sanatarium for Nervous and Mental Diseases offered alternatives for orphans, the elderly, the mentally ill, and the poor (figs. 266, 267). The creation of these institutions began to change the nature of the old multigenerational, extended family household.

New house types emerged in the twentieth century to accommodate the more streamlined functions of modern technology. Throughout Harris County houses dating from the 1820s on were still in use, having been updated to varying degrees over the years with utilities, attached kitchens, bathrooms, screened porches, and so forth. Remodeling often resulted in considerable overlapping of architectural styles within individual structures. Some older houses were turned into headquarters for civic and cultural organizations, boarding houses, funeral homes, or restaurants. It was in this state that many survived past World War I.

Most large two-story houses built after 1900 had upstairs screened porches for sleeping and downstairs screened porches that served as outdoor living rooms. Back porches behind kitchens, which by then were part of the house, were screened and the screens covered with painted wooden latticework. Called utility porches, they contained large wash tubs with scrub boards, hand-operated washing machines with wringers, mops, brooms, ironing boards, buckets, and other cleaning paraphernalia. Full bathrooms were included upstairs and half-baths (commodes and washbasins) were built downstairs, usually under the front staircase. Butlers' pantries had sinks for washing fine china and crystal and tall built-in storage cabinets with glass doors. Porte cocheres protected side entrances off the driveways. In houses built on high brick piers, the high porches under the porte cocheres had two sets of stairs: one at the end of the porch descending all the way to the ground and the other, with only two steps, intended for use when getting in and out of a carriage in the driveway. Small alcoves in the wall of the back stair hall downstairs were designed for telephones. Intercom or buzzer systems connected various rooms with the kitchen so the family could communicate with the servants. Dumb waiters were installed in very elaborate houses. Breakfast rooms were included in some new houses. Rooms planned as guest bedrooms, back parlors, third-floor storage, or basements might be turned into playrooms for the children. Large-scale entertaining was a main function for which these houses were built.[153]

In contrast, bungalows were built for economy and efficiency, bringing to fruition many ideas of nineteenth-century domestic reformers who sought to minimize housework and to free the homemaker to pursue jobs or activities in the community. They were one and one-half stories, usually without a front stairway or an entry hall. Their smaller number of rooms served multiple functions. Built-in cabinets, shelves, and seats around the walls reduced the amount of furniture needed. The lack of doors between the public rooms allowed them to be used together as one room for entertaining or used separately as libraries, living rooms, work rooms, or play rooms (figs. 203, 204). Life in bungalows was intended to be informal and uncomplicated; no servants were required for their upkeep. Associated with what was perceived to be a cleaner, healthier, outdoor lifestyle, they embodied principles of the Progressive movement advocated by Houston club women in their civic endeavors. These symbols of middle-class comfort were built throughout the city, especially in many of the new, planned subdivisions.

Another idea advocated by nineteenth-century domestic reformers and made possible by turn-of-the-century technology was the apartment house. In Houston the first apartment house was probably the three-story, twelve-unit Butler Flats, located at 1103 Rusk at Fannin. Designed by Olle J. Lorehn, it opened in 1899. Although by 1910 Houston had nineteen apartment houses, high-rise living has always been minimal. The seven-story Savoy Apartments, constructed by Daniel Ripley on Main at Pease in 1906, were considered the first high-rise units in the city. There were three apartments per floor, electric lights, steam heat, hot and cold water, cold storage, and "unsurpassed" plumbing and sewerage facilities, including a private water well. Each apartment had a dumb waiter in the kitchen for raising groceries and packages and for lowering garbage directly to the basement. Large refrigerators were built into kitchen alcoves. Freezing units on top of these refrigerators were connected to a system of pipes that circulated a brine solution throughout the building, probably with an ammonia compressor run by a gas or steam engine. Ice was made by lowering a metal container of water into the brine solution at the top of the refrigerator. This method of freezing had revolutionized the ice cream industry in 1902, so it is quite probable that it was installed when the Savoy was built. It continued in use there until the 1950s. Other attributes of the Savoy included large windows in every room, which provided cross-ventilation, bedrooms facing south to catch the Gulf breezes, and a twenty-four-hour elevator service. The Savoy, like many of the subsequent apartment buildings in Houston, had a rooftop terrace where each apartment dweller had a chair bearing his or her name.[154]

In 1910 J. O. Ross's Rossonian, designed by Sanguinet and Staats, opened at 913–919 Fannin at McKinney (fig. 106). Built of reinforced concrete, it too had seven stories and a basement. The roof garden was distinguished by pergolas in three corners. A gas company advertisement in 1911 declared that thirty gas ranges would keep the Rossonian apartments the most beautiful in the South—gas was cleaner to burn than the customary wood or coal.[155]

The last of the three major high-rise apartments built before World War I was the Beaconsfield, designed by Alonzo C. Pigg. Opened in 1911 at 1700 Main across from the Savoy, it was typical of early twentieth-century luxury apartments. Built of fireproof reinforced concrete faced with brick, it had eight stories and a basement. Two six-room apartments occupied each floor. Each of the three bedrooms in each apartment had a large private bath. All major rooms had outside exposures, and two screened balconies were attached to every apartment. Mahogany wainscoting and beams in the living and dining rooms, birch paneling, and oak flooring remain in the apartments today. Steam radiators, a centralized vacuum system, an icebox that held six hundred pounds of ice, and a wood-burning fireplace were features of all apartments. A private phone system connected the apartments with each other and with the main entrance. Today the Beaconsfield has been restored and the individual apartments have been sold as condominiums. It is the only apartment of its kind in Houston that retains its original architectural integrity.[156]

The apartment house was the logical outgrowth of the popular alternatives of the boarding house and the residential hotel. By this time many of the old household functions had been replaced nationally by manufactured goods, public services, and private or public institutions. Domestic reformers such as Charlotte Perkins Gilman advocated contracting for all household chores, including meals and child care, as outside services. Reflecting some of these ideas, the Rossonian included some kitchenless "bachelor" apartments; a cafe and a private dining room on the first floor provided meals.[157] For the small fraction of Houston's population who could afford it, cooking, washing, and ironing could be eliminated from the house by the early years of the twentieth century. In addition to the alternative of dining out at a restaurant, by 1902 the Big Casino Restaurant and Saloon would serve family meals "at your private home for 25 cents and upwards."[158] The Excelsior Steam Laundry on Texas Avenue opposite the Capitol Hotel, Burkhart's Laundry at 1702 Congress Avenue at Jackson, and the Through Throughout Model Laundry with dyeing and cleaning works at 1009 and 1011 Prairie Avenue relieved the homemaker of the burden of caring for fine fabrics and garments.[159]

For most people, however, domestic tasks continued as before. Although electricity was available to houses in 1884 and electric appliances soon thereafter, many families at all socioeconomic levels continued to use nineteenth-century appliances and housekeeping methods in Harris County well after World War I. One reason for this may have been a lack of confidence in the reliability of the new appliances or in the reliability of the electricity supply. Other possible factors were a natural reluctance to try something new and employers' concerns about retraining servants to use potentially dangerous appliances that did not necessarily offer extra convenience to the employer. The uneven adaptation of new technology is illustrated by the Heitmann houses. The Heitmann family owned a successful hardware company through which they had access to the most advanced technology and appliances on the world market. They also had the funds to furnish their houses as they pleased.

Frederick W. Heitmann purchased a house at 1116 Dallas Avenue at San Jacinto from a Mr. Sharp in 1866. In 1894 he sent the women in his family to Europe for two years while he remodeled the house. He added window screens, upstairs and downstairs porches, and electric lighting fixtures, and he converted closets upstairs and down to bathrooms with pressurized water. He added an attached kitchen, replacing the old detached structure, and bricked over the swept-earth back yard. He retained the original underground cistern, fed by enclosed gutters from the roof, and its pump; the chicken yard; the existing servants' quarters; coal grates in the fireplaces; the large heating stove in the entry hall that provided heat to the upper floors; and the two kitchen stoves (one wood and one gas). Although gas stoves were cooler for cooking in hot weather, cooks preferred wood stoves for baking. The porches were never screened because the extreme height of the ceilings and the full-length windows all around kept the house cool even in Houston's heat. As the sun moved around the house, the windows on the shady side were opened completely while those on the sunny side were opened only slightly at top and bottom to allow excellent cross-ventilation. The Heitmann house remained unchanged until it was demolished in the late 1930s.[160]

His son, Frederick A. Heitmann, built a house at Number One Longfellow Lane in Shadyside designed by William Ward Watkin and completed in 1924. Despite the advanced technology available for this new house, the laundry was still boiled in pots on a black pot-bellied wood stove in the wash house behind the garage. Mrs. Heitmann did not buy her first electric iron to replace the "sad irons" heated on the stove until the late 1920s. Cold running water was piped to the six servants' rooms over the garage, but the servants had to share a bathroom on the first floor and use the laundry stove to heat water and carry it to their rooms. Tall windows provided ventilation in a manner similar to those in the Dallas Avenue house. The rituals of spring and fall cleaning and the rotation of the heavy drapes, lace glass curtains, and wool rugs with lighter fabrics in summer continued. According to family sources, the house did have the first electric refrigerator (a Frigidaire) in Houston, however.[161]

Household routines—laundry, grocery shopping, and food preparation—changed little until the late 1920s. Milk, ice, and fuel continued to be delivered, and services like knife sharpening were offered door to door. The ice man, wearing a heavy leather vest, slung the ice over his shoulder with tongs to carry it inside. The Julius Cornelius Bering house, 1217 Holman at Caroline Avenue in the South End, built in 1912, boasted an enamel refrigerator constructed so that the ice could be replaced without the ice man's entering the house. The knife sharpener played a small musical instrument to signal his approach. He carried a large wheel over his shoulder which he would set up in the yard and use to sharpen the family's knives and scissors.[162]

The City Market continued to be the main source of fresh meat and fish. Clustered around the area were bakeries selling breads and pastries, specialty food stores, and grocery stores.[163] Across from the Market, at the corner of Congress Avenue and Milam Street, H. Henke founded a grocery store in 1873. Later known as Henke and Pillot, the company was a Houston landmark until it was bought by Kroger in 1956.[164] There and at small neighborhood grocery stores, fruits and vegetables were sold by the dozen. Flour, sugar, coffee, and other staples were measured by the pound from large barrels and then packaged. Eggs and live chickens were also available. Chickens could be killed and dressed on the spot or taken home and kept in the chicken yard until time for them to be cooked. The Heitmann family always bought two chickens because one might die of natural causes. Canned goods at Henke's store were stacked to the ceiling, requiring a tall ladder for the grocer to reach them. A few prepared foods like cornflakes were available by about 1905. Groceries selected at Henke's could be delivered by the store to the patrons' houses.[165] Families continued to keep milk cows, chickens, and horses even in the most exclusive neighborhoods, as photographs of Courtlandt Place in the 1920s and the restrictions of the River Oaks Corporation attest.[166]

The railroads made available Kansas City beef, and all but the most exotic and perishable luxury foods could be ordered and shipped from the East Coast or the Midwest.[167] The presentation of food became more elaborate as social functions became more formal and sophisticated. About 1901 Roene Masterson served the following menu at a women's luncheon, combining locally grown and imported products: strawberries with powdered sugar, cold chicken bouillon, fish croquettes with potatoes, broiled spring chicken with French peas and sweet pickle, mushroom and sweetbread patties served with a mint ice, Neufchâtel cheese in the shape of pink-tinted eggs covered with English walnuts and served with French dressing on lettuce leaves, ice cream in the shapes of pink roses and white carnations, and champagne and crème de menthe.[168] Ice cream molded into decorative shapes had been a popular luxury in Houston since before the Civil War. By the turn of the century, the Dawson-Wise Ice Cream Company seems to have been the most popular supplier. Ice cream cones were introduced at the World's Fair in St. Louis in 1904, where traveling Houstonians undoubtedly encountered them. Shortly thereafter, the Eden Park Say-So Cone Factory at 314 Dallas Avenue began manufacturing ice cream cones as well as ice cream. For years thereafter, ice cream cones in Houston were called "Say-Sos."[169]

Houston came into its own as a major urban market just after the turn of the century. Transportation and communication linked it more closely than ever to the rest of the world. Affluent Houstonians swarmed abroad, taking advantage of their new leisure to broaden their horizons by foreign study and travel. For example, in 1903 and 1904, following the tradition of her predecessors "the Parisians," Sallie Sewall spent two summers and a winter traveling and studying in Europe with chaperones. Her mother had died, and it was considered improper for her to live at home with her father and brothers with no other woman in the household. Through a voluminous correspondence with her father, she effectively ran the house at 614 San Jacinto Street from Paris, reminding her father when it was time to store winter clothing or do spring cleaning.[170]

As early as 1907, many Houstonians took their automobiles to Europe with them. Other popular destinations were Cuba, Mexico, Canada, and the east and west coasts. Groups of several families often traveled together, inviting the children of friends to accompany them on trips of several months' duration.[171] The Houston Trunk Factory, established in 1887, outfitted them for their journeys. By 1911 travel had become such a serious pursuit that the South End Travel Study Club was meeting twice monthly at the home of the president, Mrs. August L. Metcalf, at 402 Westmoreland.[172] Between trips, elaborate card parties featuring meticulously coordinated decorations and menus and expensive prizes such as crystal vases, hand-embroidered linens, gold jewelry and sterling silver were the main entertainment of affluent women.

Then as now, summers were scorching. Despite cross-ventilation created by high ceilings, large windows, and southern exposures, and even with heavy shutters to block out the sun, relief from the heat was sought primarily outside the house. Swimming in the nearest bayou or gully where one could float atop a large gourd was a fast way for Harris County residents to cool off. By the turn of the century, Houston boasted several amusement parks with large natatoriums (fig. 244). Picnics under the shade of large live oaks and magnolias, cooled by Gulf breezes, were popular with all Harris County residents throughout the period (figs. 2, 230). Iced-down watermelon and ice cream were appreciated (fig. 245). In Houston, Progressive ideals promoting a more active lifestyle in an outdoor setting influenced groups to organize bicycle clubs, yacht clubs, hunting and fishing clubs, and the Houston Golf Club (figs. 246, 264, 265). For the affluent, clubs offering sports entertainment became extensions of domestic life outside the house where families could meet with friends for casual meals or hold formal parties. Anyone who could afford to do so escaped to the seacoast, one of the bays, or an area lake. Transportation to these areas was down the bayous and across the bay by boat or overland by horseback, wagon, or stage. By 1897 railroads linked La Porte and the Morgan's Point/Bay Ridge area with the main line running from Houston through Seabrook, Kemah, and on to Galveston. The distance by train between downtown Houston and La Porte was twenty-three miles and took less than an hour. Trains ran frequently. The last train of the day spent the night at Seabrook and was ready to take commuters to work in Houston the next morning.[173]

The city of La Porte was founded by real estate developers from Iowa in 1892. Its advantages were advertised in the North with the hope that it would become a nationally famous seaside resort and shipping port. Subdivisions of both summer houses and permanent houses were platted. Agriculture provided for a year-round economy, and La Porte was surrounded by Satsuma orange and magnolia fig orchards. Ponderosa lemons, peaches, plums, pears, grapes, apples, and English walnuts were grown experimentally as well as vegetables and flowers.[174] One could take the train from Houston to La Porte in the late afternoon, spend the evening sailing, picnicking in Sylvan Grove park, or dining and dancing at the Sylvan Beach Hotel, and return by train later that night. Evening outings like this came to be known as "Moonlight Excursions."[175] "Who will ever forgo the delightful pleasure of a trip on the bay by moonlight? Nightly, one may see the sails like the wings of a bird of darkness skim the surface of the ocean, while aboard her is a merry company whose voices echo in laughter and song across the waters. . . ."[176]

By 1904 Sylvan Grove had become the Sylvan Beach Amusement Park. With the arrival of the automobile a shell road was constructed from Houston to La Porte and Seabrook. By July 1912 it looped back through Webster, where it connected with the main road between Houston and Galveston.[177] Eventually a branch of the road was built from Seabrook to Dickinson, where it also connected with the main road to Galveston. About 1910 a number of frame cottages were built at Sylvan Beach. The homesites were generally 50 feet wide and 125 feet deep, although some were larger. Artesian water, a septic sewerage system with mains laid in the alleys, electric lights, and telephone service, both local and long distance, were available. The boulevards and avenues were paved with cement and curbed. Four-foot-wide sidewalks lined the streets.[178]

The nationwide Country Place movement, locally manifested in bay houses, began for Houstonians in about 1890 when Mr. and Mrs. Henry Franklin Ring called a meeting of eleven other families in their home at 1510 Crawford Street. The group agreed to form a compound of summer houses near Morgan's Point. As the Bay Ridge Park Association, they purchased a forty-acre beach front tract where each family built a summer house (figs. 96–98, 247–50). Household procedures of permanent residents in the bay area must have resembled those of the summer residents as described by Mrs. Ring:

The first two or three years ice and food came down to Morgan's Point by boat, the cow furnished milk and butter, the Bay furnished crab and fish, and an occasional boat from Cedar Bayou, across the Bay, brought over melons, vegetables, fruit and chickens. How we enjoyed those first summers! No noise but that of the water and the birds. Later the town of

La Porte sprang up. Trains were within two miles of us and telephones were buzzing with plans. To a greater degree than any other settlement on the Bay, Bay Ridge Park remained quiet. All the activity was back of us. In front there was only water with constantly changing color, coolness and quiet.[179]

The property of the Bay Ridge Park Association with its homes and oak grove extended approximately two miles along the beach at the north end of Trinity Bay.

The homes were originally built to be sleeping cottages as all cooking and entertaining was done at a central clubhouse. The houses were designed to provide as much exposure as possible to the onshore breeze. They were characteristically one room deep, with an almost equal area of attached porch. More elaborate plans consisted of a narrow wing of service elements like bathrooms and kitchens extended from the living area to form a T shaped building.[180]

The constant breezes helped keep mosquitoes away, but many houses also had screens on the porches. The organization of the community around common dining and entertaining facilities resembled the facilities provided at nineteenth-century Methodist summer camp meeting grounds and Chautauqua gatherings across the country.

South of Red Bluff, where Clear Lake empties into Galveston Bay, Ritson Morriss built a house about 1830 on his Mexican land grant. His descendant, Oseola Morriss, married Judge John Grant Tod, Jr., in 1890. In 1900 Judge Tod founded a subdivision on part of the Morriss grant along the bayshore. Originally named Morrisstown, the beautifully wooded shoreline with summer houses facing the bay came to be known as Todville[181] (fig. 252). Nearby, Seabrook Sydnor founded the resort town of Seabrook the same year.[182]

Some families preferred the more secluded surroundings of one of the lakes or bayous for their retreats. John Henry Kirby's Camp Killcare was located on Middle Bayou (now Armand Bayou), four miles from Seabrook and one mile from Clear Lake. Kirby especially enjoyed gathering twenty-five to thirty influential businessmen for weekend house parties, where they swam and fished by day and hunted alligators by firelight at night.[183] Before the Civil War, C. E. Gregory purchased a 200-acre tract in the Ritson Morriss Survey on the north shore of Clear Lake. According to the local custom of naming houses for their owners, the property's house on the bluff overlooking the lake was known first as the Gregory Place and later as the Allen Place for the subsequent owner, Percy Allen. Visitors to the house wrote their signatures and the dates of their visits on "the doors, window frames, mantels and other smooth surfaces."[184] In 1907 Edward A. Peden purchased part of the tract, including the house, from Allen, his brother-in-law. It became Peden's summer home, Miramichi (figs. 134, 135, 160, 212). Although intended primarily as summer homes, Houstonians' bay area houses were visited year-round by the owners and their friends. Many, like Camp Killcare, were used as hunting lodges in the winter months. The Pedens often spent weekends and celebrated birthdays, Thanksgiving, New Year's, San Jacinto Day, and most other holidays except for Christmas at Miramichi.

Houston's summer social season was centered in these houses. Around the first of June each year, a mass exodus to the bay took place. Many Houston residences were closed and left in the care of a servant until September. The furniture was draped in cloth to keep off the dust. The chauffeur, the cook, and the housemaid accompanied the family to the bay, where they continued to perform their duties. The move was accomplished in several stages. A wagon was loaded with large items, such as extra furniture to supplement the permanent bay house furniture, and trunks. Saddle horses, carriages, and even cows had to be driven down individually. The men who summered at the bay with their families commuted to Houston daily by train or, after about 1910, by car. The daily household routine varied according to the location. In some areas, provisions were delivered to the door. Families in more secluded houses probably patronized the stores in neighboring communities. Some families bought groceries and staples in Houston each Saturday at Henke and Pillot and in the City Market.[185]

Neighboring summer residents called on one another at the bay as they did in the city (fig. 212). After the introduction of automobiles and shell roads, friends en route between Houston and Galveston stopped by for lunch or tea. Large groups came down to spend the day or several weeks. Bathing, "autoing," fishing, crabbing, sailing, and boating occupied the long summer days. Whist and other card and parlor games, dancing at Sylvan Beach, and moonlight sails filled the evenings. Lively boating parties launched from Miramichi engaged in treasure hunts around Clear Lake and Taylor Lake where, according to legend, henchmen of the pirate Jean Lafitte had settled in 1821.[186] Chaperoned house parties were held for the young people. Mrs. J. C. Hutcheson wrote in 1911: "Well darling, Palmer and I feel quite giddy and grand. We have just returned from a house party at Mr. Beverly Harris's at Bay Ridge.... He has great open porches screened in and had a row of cots on each porch—seven and eight cots on each. The men slept on one porch, the ladies on the other, and such laughing and screaming you never heard."[187]

Some Houstonians built summer houses in cooler climates where they entertained school friends from other parts of the country as well as friends from home.[188] While wealthy northerners during the same period built ostentatious and expansive "summer cottages" in fancy northern resort areas, most Houstonians preferred rustic summer houses comparable to those in Harris County. Near or far, these country places echoed the simpler life in the homesteads of Austin's Old Three Hundred, which the recreational houses had replaced along the rivers, bayous, and lakes that empty into Galveston Bay (see map 2).

Descendants of Austin's Old Three Hundred and of other early settlers still own portions of original Harris County land grants. For example, heirs of James Wyatt Oates, Sr., still live on Oates Road in a portion of Oates Prairie, a 640-acre tract in southeastern Harris County granted to Oates in 1841.[189] In 1974 the Texas Department of Agriculture began recognizing this continuity with the Family Land Heritage Program, registering farms and ranches that had been owned and operated continuously by the same families for one hundred years. In Harris

County these include the Lemm-Schmidt Ranch, the Strack family farms, the Peter Wunderlich farm, and the John Herman Telschow Ranch.[190] Each year this heritage becomes more tenuous as commercial and residential development continues to expand. Houston's world-renowned commercial architecture has supplanted many of its historic residential neighborhoods. "Progress" has replaced most of the pre-World War I houses with skyscrapers, oil refineries, and shopping centers. The only reminders of downtown Houston's domestic history are parking lots outlined with aging live oaks, an occasional dilapidated or restored house that somehow dodged the wrecking ball, and the reincarnated Kirby house.

During Harris County's first ninety years, the house changed from an all-purpose production center to a moral haven for the family from the outside world and finally to a center for civic improvement based on family values. By World War I, consumerism and mass production had simplified household tasks but complicated life by increasing the number of elaborate possessions to be maintained and encouraging a wide choice of lifestyles. Production processes, businesses, services, and cultural and civic activities were beginning to leave the home, but it was still the center of family and social life within the larger community, and the pattern of daily living retained many characteristics from earlier decades. As the composition of the family has changed, the concept of the multigenerational family home as the stabilizer and matrix of the community's social and cultural life has vanished along with such stereotypes as the self-sacrificing housewife. Geographic mobility has kept many from identifying with or remaining loyal to specific houses or neighborhoods. Proliferation of separate professional and social communities outside the home has destroyed the unofficial cohesiveness that was rooted in nineteenth-century domestic life. Harris County's pre-World War I houses and gardens were tangible symbols of the society and culture upon which its modern communities and institutions are built. Lost along with those houses and gardens is the historical perspective so important to a full understanding of the community and its people.

Notes

The following abbreviations for frequently cited sources have been used in the notes:

JLC: Junior League Component

HMRC: Houston Metropolitan Research Center

TLHD: Texas Local History Department

HCHS: Harris County Heritage Society

HPL: Houston Public Library

UH: University of Houston

WRC, FL, RU: Woodson Research Center, Fondren Library, Rice University

One publication changed its name several times during the years covered in this book: it was known variously as the Houston *Telegraph and Texas Register*, the *Telegraph and Texas Register*, and the *Houston Democratic Telegraph and Texas Register*, among other names.

INTRODUCTION

1. Margaret S. Henson, *The History of Baytown* (Baytown: Bay Area Heritage Society, 1986), 3–4; for the names of earliest settlers see "Gathered from Mrs. Hardin, formerly Mrs. Lynch," and "Furnished by William Pettus," in Charles Adams Gulick et al., eds., *The Papers of Mirabeau Buona-*

parte Lamar (Austin: Pemberton Press, 1968), vol. 4, Pt.1, 124–25, 224–27.

2. Margaret Swett Henson, "Hispanic Texas, 1519–1836," in Donald W. Whisenhunt, ed., *Texas: A Sesquicentennial Celebration* (Austin: Eakin Press, 1985), 34–48, gives a condensed overview of the Spanish period; "Jose de Evia," in Eldon Stephen Branda, ed., *The Handbook of Texas: A Sup-*

plement (Austin: Texas State Historical Association, 1976), vol. 3, 668.

3. Lawrence E. Aten, *Indians of the Upper Texas Coast* (New York: Academic Press, 1983), 104–139, 206–215.

4. Eugene C. Barker, *The Life of Stephen F. Austin: Founder of Texas, 1793–1836* (Austin: Univ. of Texas Press, 1969), 21, 23–39, 97–106, 121, 133.

5. Ibid., 109, 121–22, 140; Adele B. Looscan, "Harris County, 1822–1845," *Southwestern Historical Quarterly* 17 (Oct. 1914): 197 (cited hereafter SWHQ); Virginia H. Taylor, *The Spanish Archives of the General Land Office of Texas* (Austin: Lone Star Press, 1955), appendix, 151–258, lists all titles issued from which Harris County was abstracted.

6. Adele B. Looscan, "The Pioneer Harrises of Harris County, Texas," SWHQ 31 (April 1928): 365.

7. *Biographical Directory of the Texas Conventions and Congresses, 1832–1845* (Austin: Texas State Library, 1941), 21–22, 57, 142; Looscan, "Harris County," SWHQ 17:277; William Fairfax Gray, *From Virginia to Texas, 1835: Diary of Col. Wm. F. Gray* (Houston: Fletcher Young Publishing, 1965), 132, 134, 136. Cited hereafter Gray, *Diary.*

8. Gray, *Diary,* 134, 136, 144–51.

9. Dilue Rose Harris, "The Reminiscences of Mrs. Dilue Harris," SWHQ 4 (Jan. 1901): 162–66; Looscan, "Pioneer Harrises," 368–69; Henson, *History of Baytown,* 30–31.

10. Henson, *History of Baytown,* 29–31; Harris, "Reminiscences," 61–63, 67–69; Looscan, "Pioneer Harrises," 361; Lewis Birdsall Harris, "Journal of Lewis Birdsall Harris, 1836–1842," SWHQ 25 (July 1921): 137–40; Margaret Swett Henson, "What Happened to the Mexican Prisoners After San Jacinto," SWHQ 94 (Oct. 1990): 189–230.

11. Writers Program of the Works Projects Administration in the State of Texas, comp., *Houston: A History and Guide* (Houston: Anson Jones Press, 1942), 42–50.

12. Stanley Siegel, *A Political History of the Texas Republic: 1836–1845* (Austin: Univ. of Texas Press, 1956), 92–99, 112, 187, 189, 210–12; W.P.A., *Houston: A History and Guide,* 56–59.

13. Marilyn McAdams Sibley, *The Port of Houston: A History* (Austin: Univ. of Texas Press, 1968), 17, 19, 36–37, 56.

14. Max Freund, trans. and ed., *Gustav Dresel's Houston Journal: Adventures in North America and Texas, 1837–1841* (Austin: Univ. of Texas Press, 1954), introduction, xvii–xviii; Seventh Census, United States, 1850, Harris County, especially #578–599, #616–671, microfilm, Clayton Genealogical Library; *The Heritage of North Harris County* (n.p: North Harris County Branch, American Association of University Women, 1977), 58–62, 71–77.

15. David G. McComb, *Houston: The Bayou City* (Austin: Univ. of Texas Press, 1969), 52; Barker, *Life of Austin,* 207–25; William Ransom Hogan, *The Republic of Texas: A Social and Economic History* (Austin: Univ. of Texas Press, 1946), 21–24. Comparison of numbers of slaves in Harris, Brazoria, and Fort Bend counties from analysis of those counties in Gifford White, ed., *The 1840 Census of Republic of Texas* (Austin: Pemberton Press, 1966), 19–24, 42–48, 61–71. This "census" is from tax rolls.

16. *Texas Almanac,* 1857–1962; Terry G. Jordan, *Trails to Texas: Southern Roots of Western Cattle Ranching* (Lincoln, Neb.: Univ. of Nebraska Press, 1981), 72; Jesse A. Ziegler, *Wave of the Gulf: Ziegler's Scrapbook of the Texas Gulf Coast Country* (San Antonio: Naylor, 1938), 26, 29.

17. Walter P. Webb et al., eds. *The Handbook of Texas,* 2 vols. (Austin: Texas State Historical Association, 1952), vol. 1, 240, 779; McComb, *Houston,* 34–38.

18. McComb, *Houston,* 38–39; W.P.A., *Houston: History and Guide,* 72–79; Andrew Forest Muir, "William Marsh Rice and His Institute," ed. Sylvia Stallings Morris, *Rice University Studies* 58 (Spring 1972): 32, 36–38; Ziegler, *Wave of the Gulf,* 275, 300–303, 318.

19. Ziegler, *Wave of the Gulf,* 37; for battle of Galveston see Charles W. Hayes, *Galveston: History of the Island and the City* (Austin: Jenkins Garret Press, 1974), 549–79; "Richard W. 'Dick' Dowling," Webb et al., eds., *Handbook of Texas,* Vol. 1, 517.

20. McComb, *Houston,* 38–39, 73–77; *Houston:*

History and Guide, 72–79; Sibley, *Port of Houston,* 85–148.

21. For banking in the republic and early statehood see Margaret Swett Henson, *Samuel May Williams: Early Texas Entrepreneur* (College Station: Texas A & M Univ. Press, 1976), 138–48; William A. Kirkland, *Old Bank—New Bank: The First National Bank, Houston, 1866–1956* (Houston: Pacesetter Press, 1975), 1–48.

22. *Houston Daily Telegraph,* Sept. 19, 21, 25, 1875; David G. McComb, *Galveston: A History* (Austin: Univ. of Texas Press, 1986), 149.

23. John Edward Weems, *A Weekend in September* (College Station: Texas A & M Univ. Press, 1980, reprint of 1957 first edition), 80, 110–11, 157–59; *Houston: History and Guide,* 103–104.

24. Population figures from tables in *Texas Almanac, 1964–1965: The Encyclopedia of Texas. . .* (Dallas: *The Dallas Morning News,* 1964), 117–19, 123–25; McComb, *Houston,* 98–99, 109–110.

25. McComb, *Houston,* 113–17.

26. Ibid., 93–96.

27. Muir, "William Marsh Rice and His Institute," 67, 109–111.

CHAPTER 1

1. "J.C. Clopper's Journal-1828," *The Quarterly of the Texas State Historical Association* 12, no.1 (July 1909): 44–80; also Edward N. Clopper, *An American Family* (Huntington, VA: Standard Printing and Publishing, 1950), 176.

2. Information from observation of present undisturbed areas along Buffalo Bayou, from books by early travelers, and from consultation with horticulturist Doug Williams, Houston Arboretum and Nature Center, and John Koros, director, Mercer Arboretum.

3. Information from Don Gray, geologist; references: *Soil Survey of Harris County, Texas,* U.S Dept. of Agriculture Soil Conservation Service in cooperation with the Texas Agricultural Experiment Station and the Harris County Flood Control District, 1976; H.A. Bernard, C. F. Major, Jr., B.S. Parrott, R. J. LeBlanc Sr., *Recent Sediments of Southeast Texas* (Austin: Bureau of Economic Geology, Univ. of Texas), Guidebook No. 11, 19700; *Grasses of Texas* (College Station: Texas A&M Univ. Press, 1975), 2; George W. Bomar, *Texas Weather* (Austin: Univ. of Texas Press, 1983), 55.

4. Terry Jordan, *German Seed in Texas Soil* (Austin: Univ. of Texas Press, 1966), 28, illus. 4.

5. *A Visit to Texas in 1831* (Houston: Cordovan Press, 1975), 17.

6. Elizabeth Silverthorne, *Plantation Life in Texas* (College Station: Texas A & M Univ. Press, 1986), 176.

7. Mary Austin Holley, *Texas* (Austin: Texas State Historical Society, 1985), 50–51; rep. of original edition (Lexington, KY: J. Clarke, 1836). Wild peach is now known as cherry laurel.

8. *Visit to Texas,* 57.

9. Ibid., 20, 21.

10. Ibid., 118–20.

11. Elizabeth Silverthorne, *Ashbel Smith* (College Station: Texas A&M Univ. Press, 1982), 68.

12. Samuel Wood Geiser, *Naturalists of the Frontier* (Dallas: Southern Methodist Univ. Press, 1948), 55–65.

13. Ibid., 66. *Curtis' Botanical Magazine* was an English publication.

14. "Bill for Garden Seeds," Sayres & Nixon to Samuel May Williams, Samuel May Williams Papers, 23–0867, in Texas-Galveston history section, Rosenberg Library, Galveston, Texas.

15. *Telegraph and Texas Register,* Nov. 2, 1844, vol. 9, no. 45.

16. Edward N. Clopper, *An American Family,* 175. See also 130–31.

17. Ibid., 166, 256. The Cloppers had visited the 1812 battlefield below New Orleans while waiting for their ship to Texas and were astonished at the beautiful gardens around homes in the area, especially the orange trees planted as hedges. It is possible the seeds came from those gardens.

18. Ibid., 167, 179, 226.

19. Ibid., 156; "Clopper Correspondence, 1834–1838"; *The Quarterly of the Texas State Historical Association* 13, no. 2 (Oct. 1909): 2.

20. *Fragile Empires: The Texas Correspondence of Samuel Swartwout and James Morgan*

1836–1856 (Austin: Shoal Creek Publishers, 1978), 67.

21. John James Audubon, *Ornithological Biography*, xviii.

22. Ferdinand Roemer, *Texas*, trans. Oswald Mueller (San Antonio: Standard Printing, 1935), 53–54, 57, 58.

23. Elizabeth Silverthorne, *Ashbel Smith*, 66; Roemer, *Texas*, 60.

24. V. P. Hedrick, *A History of Horticulture in America to 1860* (Portland, OR: Timber Press, 1988), 12, 19. The southern Indians were good gardeners; a number of plants initially introduced by the Spanish and French in the seventeenth and eighteenth centuries found a place in Indian gardens along with their native staples of beans, corn, squash, and pumpkin. The peach tree, introduced by the Europeans, flourished in Indian orchards in Texas and the South long before Jamestown was founded.

25. Silverthorne, *Ashbel Smith*, 132, 180, 195.

26. Unpubl. letter, Mary Jane Briscoe to Andrew Briscoe, April 22, 1849, in possession of Dorothy Knox Howe Houghton, Houston, Texas.

27. Francis R. Lubbock, *Six Decades in Texas* (Austin: Ben C. Jones, 1900), 126.

28. *Morning Star*, June 18, 1839.

29. Gustav Dresel, *Houston Journal, Adventures in North America and Texas, 1837–1841*, trans. Max Freund (Austin: Univ. of Texas Press, 1954), 99.

30. *Morning Star*, Dec. 4, 1841; Ann Quin Wilson, *Native Houstonian* (Houston: Houston Baptist Univ. Press, 1982), 122. Mahan's garden appears on a map from Glenwood Cemetery records, ca. 1872.

31. Dr. S. O. Young, *True Stories of Old Houston and Houstonians* (Houston: Press of Premier, 1913), 3.

32. Knox Briscoe Howe Papers, JLC/HMRC/HPL.

33. *Houston Post*, Oct. 10, 1937.

34. *Houston Post*, Oct. 3, 1937, story about house being demolished.

35. Jordan, *German Seed*, 41; Ophia D. Smith, "A Trip to Texas in 1855," *Southwest Historical Quarterly* 59, no. 1 (July 1955): 29.

36. *Morning Star*, Jan. 7, 1840.

37. *Morning Star*, Jan. 26, 1843.

38. *Telegraph and Texas Register*, Sept. 6, 1843; Brent Elliott, *Victorian Gardens* (Portland, OR: Timber Press, 1986), 19.

39. Geiser, *Naturalists*, 133–39. Lindheimer eventually settled in New Braunfels, continuing his collecting, although in later years he became editor of the newspaper in that town.

40. Laura Shearn, "Houston Gardens Through the Years," *Houston Post* series of five weekly articles from Feb. 23, 1936, to March 22, 1936. *Houston Post*, Feb. 23, 1936.

41. *Telegraph and Texas Register*, Jan. 27, 1844.

42. *Telegraph and Texas Register*, July 31, 1844.

43. Clopper, *An American Family*, 272; *Civics for Houston*, Oct. 1928, 15. The founders had been joined in Houston by their whole family: their parents, Sally and Roland Allen; their brothers, Samuel, George, Henry Roland, and Harvey Halley Allen; and one sister, Jane Ann Allen. The Clopper correspondence mentioned that the Allens bought land on Sloop Point; this may have been the location of the plantation. It is interesting to note that one of George Allen's sons, Samuel Warner Allen, after his marriage to Frances Ione Spence, bought the E.S. Perkins place and raised his family there. The article in *Civics for Houston* is in error about the Allen family relationship.

44. Wilson, *Native Houstonian*, 36.

45. T. W. House Papers, JLC/HMRC/HPL.

46. Shearn, *Houston Post*, March 3, 1936.

47. Ellen Red, *Early Days on the Bayou, 1838–1890* (Waco: Texian Press, 1986), 113.

48. Young, *True Stories*, 66; John L. Davis, *Houston, A Historical Portrait* (Austin: Encino Press, 1983), 13; Red, *Early Days*, 115.

49. Red, *Early Days*, 83.

50. *Democratic Telegraph and Texas Register*, Nov. 23, 1848; David G. McComb, *Galveston, A History* (Austin: Univ. of Texas Press, 1986), 69; Clarence Pleasants, *Galveston, the Oleander City* (New York: Exposition Press, 1966), 15. In 1841 a Galveston ship captain, Joseph Osterman, brought an oleander bush from Jamaica to his sister, Isadore Dyer, who planted it in her garden. The beauty

and fragrance as well as the long summer bloom made this plant a favorite in both Galveston and Houston.

51. Frederick Law Olmsted, *A Journey Through Texas* (London: Sampson Low, 1857), 361.

52. *Tri-Weekly Telegraph*, April 16, 1862.

53. *Tri-Weekly Telegraph*, May 14, 1862.

54. Mrs. William H. Murray Papers, JLC/HMRC/HPL.

55. Ibid., newspaper clipping dated April 10, 1917.

56. *Houston Daily Post*, March 1, 1936.

57. *Houston Daily Post*, Aug. 17, 1911; Andrew Forest Muir, "William Marsh Rice and His Institute," ed. Sylvia Stallings Morris, *Rice University Studies* 58 (Spring 1972): 63.

58. *Houston Daily Post*, Aug. 27, 1911.

59. *Agricultural History* 31, no. 3 (1957), 40–48. Affleck Papers in possession of W. J. Bowen, Houston, Texas.

60. Letter from Claribel R. Barnett, librarian, U.S. Department of Agriculture, to T.D. Affleck, July 12, 1927. Includes copy of article for inclusion in the *Dictionary of American Biography*. Affleck Papers.

61. Barnett, *American Biography*. The move to Texas may have been influenced by the fact that Mrs. Affleck was the niece of Jane Long, "Mother of Texas."

62. Wilson, *Native Houstonians*, 65; Houston, *Telegraph Semi-Weekly*, April 25, 1855. A live oak that was in Stanley's garden still stands on Capitol and Bagby outside the Albert Thomas Convention Center.

63. *Tri-Weekly Telegraph*, May 4, 1855.

64. *Tri-Weekly Telegraph*, Dec. 7, 1859; *Daily Houston Telegraph*, early 1869.

65. Samuel Wood Geiser, *Horticulture and Horticulturists in Early Texas* (Dallas: Southern Methodist Univ. Press, 1945), 31.

66. Ibid., 41.

67. *Southwest Historical Quarterly* 4, no. 4 (April 1922): 267.

68. Geiser, *Early Horticulture*, 41.

69. Shearn, *Houston Post*, March 3, 1936.

70. Silverthorne, *Ashbel Smith*, 170, 177–78, 180, 195. He saw the Crystal Palace at the London Jubilee of 1851 and visited the Horticultural Hall at the Centennial Exposition in Philadelphia in 1876.

71. Harold L. Platt, *City Building in the New South* (Philadelphia: Temple Univ. Press, 1983), 38.

72. Ibid., 20, 24, 27, 29, 43.

73. *Houston City Directory*, 1866, 118.

74. Platt, *City Building*, 41–42, 56.

75. David G. McComb, *Houston: A History* (Austin: Univ. of Texas Press, 1969), 88; Platt, *City Building*, 38, 64, 67; *Houston Daily Telegraph*, July 22, 1876. The waterworks was organized in 1878, but private lines were not installed for several years.

76. *Industrial Advantages of Houston, Texas and Environs* (Houston: Akehurst Publishing, 1894), 107.

77. *Houston: A History and Guide*, Writers Program of the Work Projects Administration in the State of Texas, comp. (Houston: Anson Jones Press, 1942), 327–28.

78. *Daily Telegraph*, Oct. 26, 1871. Maresch files, vol. 38, no. 184.

79. *Houston City Directory*, 1877, 20.

80. *Houston City Directory*, 1882–83, 13.

81. *Daily Houston Telegraph*, May 19, 1870; April 28, 1870; May 28, 1870.

82. *Daily Houston Telegraph*, June 2, 1870. Excerpt from Report of the Committee to the Texas Legislature.

83. McComb, *Houston*, 44.

84. *Daily Telegraph*, May 13, 1871.

85. *Daily Telegraph*, Feb. 8, 1872.

86. *Daily Telegraph*, April 16, 1872.

87. *Daily Telegraph*, Oct. 27, 1871.

88. *Daily Telegraph*, May 16, 1873.

89. *Houston City Directory*, 1882–1883, 13; *Houston City Directory*, 1880–81, 49; Geiser, *Horticulture*, 21, 45, 90, 93. Meetings of the Texas Horticultural Society terminated in 1922.

90. McComb, *Houston*, 43.

91. *Houston Post*, March 20, 1928. Mr. J. J. Settegast birthday interview; *Houston Post*, March 1932; clippings in Settegast-Frost family papers in

possession of Mrs. W. H. Keenan; *Houston Style*, Jan. 1986, 84–85.

92. Shearn, *Houston Post*, March 1, 1936.

93. A. Whitaker, "Arcadia in Texas," *Houston Post*, Oct. 7, 1894.

94. *Houston Post*, Feb. 23, 1936.

95. Marguerite Johnston, *A Happy Worldly Abode: Christ Church Cathedral, 1839-1964* (Houston: Gulf Printing Company, 1964), 104.

96. Fannie Simpson Carter interview by Dorthy Knox Howe Houghton, Jan. 13, 1984. Fannie Simpson Carter Papers, JLC/HMRC/HPL; M. Christine Klim Doell, "Cottage Lawn" in *Gardens of the Gilded Age* (Syracuse, NY: Syracuse Univ. Press, 1986), 174–75.

97. Shearn, *Houston Post*, March 8, 1936.

98. *Houston Post*, 1904 clipping, Edmund Mc-Ashan Dupree Papers, JLC/HMRC/HPL; *History of Texas Together with a Biographical History of the Cities of Houston and Galveston* (Chicago: Lewis Publishing, 1895), 479–82, TLHD/HPL.

99. Shearn, *Houston Post*, March 1, 1936.

100. Frank J. Scott, *The Art of Beautifying Suburban Home Grounds* (New York: D. Appleton, 1870), 26, 51, 61.

101. Elliott, *Victorian Gardens*, 18, 133.

102. Shearn, *Houston Post*, March 8, 1936.

103. *Houston Post*, Aug. 19, 1923, "The Story of an Illustrious Houston Family"; notes from scrapbook of Ellen Hartung, granddaughter of T. W. House, Jr.

104. Ellen Hartung telephone interview by Sadie Gwin Blackburn, Sept. 25, 1990; handwritten diary by James Gaughan, gardener for the House family, unpaginated, TLHD/HPL.

105. Gaughan, diary.

106. Willie Hutcheson, "Houston's Old Homesteads," *Houston Daily Post*, Sept. 24, 1911.

107. Davis, *Houston*, 22.

108. Annual Message, O. T. Holt, Mayor of the City of Houston, and Annual Reports of City Officers for the Year Ending Dec. 31, 1902 (Houston: W. H. Coyle, 1903), 46, 49.

109. Ellen Red interview by Sadie Gwin Blackburn, 1990; William A. Kirkland, *Old Bank—New Bank: The First National Bank, Houston, 1866–1956* (Houston: Pacesetter Press, 1975), 49–50; Laura Bruce interview by Avon Smith Duson, 1989.

110. Hutcheson file, JLC/HMRC/HPL; Marilyn M. Sibley, *The Port of Houston* (Austin: Univ. of Texas Press, 1968), 117; Betty Bosworth Neuhaus interview by Sadie Gwin Blackburn, 1989.

111. Ellen Ross Hail interview by Dorothy Knox Howe Houghton, Aug. 5, 1985, J. O. Ross file, JLC/HMRC/HPL.

112. "Evolution of Main Street," *Houston Scrapbooks*, 27, 91. TLHD/HPL.

113. Ibid.

114. *Houston City Directory*, 1890–91, 68; Shearn, *Houston Post*, March 3, 1936; Shearn, *Houston Post*, March 8, 1936; *Minutes*, Glenwood Cemetery Association, 40.

115. Shearn, *Houston Post*, March 8, 1936.

116. *Industrial Advantages*, 91.

117. Julia Kutschbach Timmins, daughter of William and Mary Kutschbach, interview by Sadie Gwin Blackburn, 1987.

118. Robert A. Vines, *A Checklist of the Native and Naturalized Plants of Houston and Vicinity* (Spring Branch Independent School District, 1964), introduction.

119. Shearn, *Houston Post*, March 15, 1936.

120. *Houston Post*, Nov. 15, 1894.

121. *The Gulf Messenger* 11, no. 1 (Jan. 1898): 1–5.

122. Gaughan, diary.

123. Shearn, *Houston Post*, March 8, 1936.

124. *Houston City Directory, 1880–81, 49;* Lois Bute Porter and John Bute, grandchildren of James Bute, telephone interviews by Sadie Gwin Blackburn, 1989.

125. Sister M. Agatha, *The History of the Houston Heights, 1891–1918* (Houston: Premier Printing, 1956), 15–17.

126. Map of Houston Heights, Houston Subdivision Collection, RG#118, Item 35, TLHD/HPL.

127. Houston Heights file, JLC/HMRC/HPL.

128. Sister Agatha, *Heights*, 95–97.

129. *National Register of Historic Places* (Wash-

ington, DC: U.S. Dept. of the Interior, 1984), Nomination Form, Item #7, 1.

130. Platt, *City Building*, 132, 142–43.

131. Sibley, *Port of Houston*, 90, 111; Wilson, *Native Houstonian*, 104.

132. Platt, *City Building*, 161.

133. *Houston Architectural Survey* 6 (Southwest Center for Urban Research and Rice Univ. School of Architecture, 1980), 1270.

134. Norman T. Newton, *Design on the Land* (Cambridge, MA: Belknap Press of Harvard Univ. Press, 1971), 359, 367, 387.

135. Charles Platt, *Italian Gardens* (New York: Harper & Brothers, 1894), 6–7.

136. William Robinson, *The English Flower Garden* (New York: Amaryllis Press, 1984), 27–28, reprint (London: J. Murray, 1933); Reginald Blomfield, *The Formal Garden in England* (London: Macmillan, 1892), 19–20.

137. Newton, *Design*, 521–29. See also Mark A. Hewitt, *The Architect and the American Country House* (New Haven and London: Yale Univ. Press, 1990), 12.

138. Hewitt, *American Country House*, 153; quote from Peter Schmitt, *Back to Nature* (New York: Oxford Univ. Press, 1969).

139. Bay Ridge file, JLC/HMRC/HPL.

140. Charles C. Savage, *Architecture of the Private Streets of St. Louis* (Columbia: Univ. of Missouri Press, 1987), 3, 9–10.

141. Westmoreland file, JLC/HMRC/HPL.

142. Jennifer Lawrence, "Courtlandt Place: An Inner-city Success," *Texas Homes* (Jan. 1983): 23.

143. *Houston Chronicle*, July 22, 1902. Wilmer Waldo, second son of J. Waldo, had spent his formative years in St. Louis while his father was an official of the Missouri, Kansas and Texas Railroad. All five of the Waldo children were at school in the East when their father died in 1896. Waldo's familiarity with Julius Pitzman as engineer for the St. Louis Places may well have influenced Baldwin's choice of neighborhood layout.

144. Unpubl. research paper by Elaine Brady, "Courtlandt Place," 1983, 10. See also *Houston Chronicle*, Oct. 7, 1982.

145. U.S. Dept. of the Interior, Heritage Conservation and Recreation Service, *National Register of Historic Places Inventory—Nomination Form*, Section 7, Description, par. 3.

146. Unpubl. family history by Myrtle Seiders Cuthbertson, *Seiders Family History: 1700–Early 1900s*, undated, unnumbered pages.

147. *Progressive Houston* 3, no. 3 (July 1911).

148. *Houston Daily Post*, March 9, 1913, "Magnolia Park News" section.

149. Real estate promotion poster with map, photographs of improvements, deed restrictions, by Greater Houston Suburban Corporation, James L. Autry Papers, Box 13, file 574 A, WRC/FL/RU.

150. *The Red Book of Houston: A Compendium of Social, Professional, Religious, Educational and Industrial Interests of Houston's Colored Population* (Houston: Sotex Publishing, n. d.). Judging from statistics included, the date is ca. 1915.

151. *Houston Post*, March 30, 1913.

152. Letter, Joseph Henry Curtis to J.H. Kirby, Oct. 17, 1901, John Henry Kirby Collection, HMRC/HPL.

153. Letter, J. H. Curtis to Kirby, Nov. 30, 1901, John Henry Kirby Collection, HMRC/HPL.

154. At his own summer home in Seal Harbor, Maine, he terraced the hill on which his cottage stood and landscaped it entirely with native trees and shrubs; he named the place "Thuya," the botanic name for the evergreens most prevalent in the area.

155. *Houston Chronicle*, Feb. 21, 1937; *The Illustrated Book of Houston*, 1915.

156. *Pen and Sunlight Sketches of Greater Houston*, 86.

157. Labyrinths of tall hedges and mazes of low hedges were garden design features in the early eighteenth-century European gardens around manor houses wherein guests at large parties were amused by trying to find their way through the planted puzzles; such gardens also appeared around prestigious homes in the southern United States like Gunston Hall, VA.

158. Harris Masterson interview by Sadie Gwin Blackburn, 1988.

159. Geiser, *Horticulture*, 84; *LaPorte Chronicle*, Sept. 28, 1911.

160. Teas papers, page from *The Beacon* (Bellaire newspaper), Nov. 9, 1977, 14; *Outdoor Indiana*, Sept. 1977, 10–14.

161. Unidentified magazine article on Westmoreland Farms and Teas Nursery, Teas Papers, JLC/HMRC/HPL.

162. *Progressive Houston* 2, no. 2 (June 1910).

163. Mrs. Eiko Arai Harper, daughter of Saburo and Kyoko Arai, interview by Sadie Gwin Blackburn, 1939. Kyoko Arai was related to the Japanese royal family, according to John Teas. Kyoko was also a teacher in Ikebana flower-arranging in the early years of the twentieth century. The Japanese Nursery eventually did landscaping, and "their work on the grounds of the Houston City Hall, the Veterans Administration Building, and the City Zoo led to other contracts throughout Texas." From unpubl. excerpt from Tom Walls, *The Japanese Texans*.

164. Japanese Nursery catalog.

165. "Edward Dewson," vertical file, Architectural component, HMRC/HPL.

166. E. A. Peden, Miramichi Guest Book, 83; typed list on Peden Iron and Steel stationary entitled "List of Trees, Shrubs, Flowers, etc., planted by Edward Teas at Clear Lake place owned by E.A. Peden," enclosed in Miramichi Guest Book, WRC/FL/RU. Jasmine and cedar were included in the list of plants from Teas Nursery.

167. Peden, Guest Book, 133.

168. Staiti file, JLC/HMRC/HPL.

169. Newton, *Design*, 428.

170. Edward Dewson, "Planning the Southern Home," *The Southern Architectural Review* 1 no. 2 (Oct. 1910): 60.

171. Newton, *Design*, 351.

172. Leonard K. Eaton, *Landscape Artist in America: The Life and Work of Jens Jensen* (Chicago and London: Univ. of Chicago Press, 1964), 99, 111.

173. *Edwin Brewington Parker: A Memorial*, by his professional associates, 12ff. Parker became nationally and internationally known during World War I through his service on the War Industries Board as priorities commissioner, getting "the nation's industrial activities lined up behind its army and navy." Later, as chairman of the United States Liquidation Commission and the Mixed Claims Commission, he arbitrated settlements of all claims between the United States and the European countries until his death in 1923. His wife was an accomplished pianist and became the first president of the Houston Symphony Association, organized in 1913 to establish an orchestra in Houston. Hubert Roussel, *The Houston Symphony Orchestra, 1913–1971* (Austin and London: Univ. of Texas Press, 1972), 14, 20.

174. "Two Views of 'The Oaks'," *Houston Daily Post*, Oct. 17, 1912.

175. "Parker Home," *Houston Daily Post*, Sept. 5, 1909.

176. *Houston Daily Post*, Oct. 17, 1912.

177. *Houston Daily Post*, Sept. 5, 1909.

178. *Seiders Family History*.

179. *Houston Daily Post*, Oct. 17, 1912.

180. *New Encyclopedia of Texas*, 396–400; "Mrs. Sharp's Funeral Is Wednesday," Houston scrapbooks, TLHD/HPL; interviews in Sharp file, JLC/HMRC/HPL. Report of demolition, *Houston Chronicle*, Sept. 19, 1937.

181. Platt, *City Building*, 176, 186–88.

182. Muir, "William Marsh Rice," 11.

183. Stephen Fox, *The General Plan of the William M. Rice Institute and Its Architectural Development* (Houston: School of Architecture, Rice Univ., 1980), 18.

184. Ibid. Bertram Goodhue had spent a number of years developing various historical styles appropriate to the regions of his commissions; "the best known of these was the Gillespie house in Montecito, California of 1903, for which Goodhue also provided elaborate Persian-style gardens, inspired by a trip he and James Waldron Gillespie had made to Iran."

185. *Progressive Houston* 11, no. 2 (June 1910).

186. *Houston Architectural Survey* 6:1276.

187. Ibid.

188. Ibid.

189. *The Anglo-American Suburb*, ed. Robert A. M. Stern (New York: St. Martin's, n.d.), 52, ca. 1980, judging from the dates of his sources.

190. *Houston Architectural Survey* 6: 1279. "Because the City Council failed to establish the means for permanently financing the park system its support continued to be derived from annual appropriations from the city treasury. . . . This procedure obviously inhibited realizing staged plans for development, as the amount of annual appropriations could never be depended upon."

191. Archie Henderson, "City Planning in Houston, 1920–30," *The Houston Review* 9, no. 3 (1987): 107–136.

CHAPTER 2

1. Virginia and Lee McAlester, *A Field Guide to American Houses* (New York: Knopf, 1984), 94.

2. John Michael Vlach, "Afro-Americans," *America's Architectural Roots: Ethnic Groups that Built America* (Washington: The Preservation Press, 1987), 43.

3. Drury B. Alexander, "The Greek Revival Style in East Texas: Some Comparisons and Variations," *Texana II: Cultural Heritage of the Plantation South.* Conference proceedings Jefferson, Texas, June 4–6, 1981 (Austin: Historical Commission, 1982), 33.

4. *The Heritage of North Harris County* (North Harris County Branch, American Association of Univ. Women, 1977), 50–51.

5. John E. T. Milsap diary (1852–77), old ser. 1:62 TLHD/HPL.

6. Ferdinand Roemer, *Roemer's Texas*, trans. Oswald Mueller (San Antonio: Standard Printing, 1935), 55.

7. Terry Jordan, *Texas Log Buildings: A Folk Architecture* (Austin: Univ. of Texas Press, 1978), 83. "A puncheon is a short, thick board that reaches from the center of one sleeper [or joist] to the next. For this reason, the exact length of the puncheon is determined by the spacing of the sleepers, usually

two feet apart." Jordan's "Glossary of Log Construction in Texas" is a useful reference, 205–209.

8. Mudcats were brick- or cat-sized clumps enveloping moss, grass, straw, or horsehair which were flung into or plastered on the chimney frame and hardened. This type of chimney was common in Harris County as opposed to stone, brick, or wood chimneys used in other parts of Texas. James L. Glass has pointed out that the word "mudcat" could be a corruption of "mudcap"—to cover with a cap of mud.

9. "Reminiscences of Mrs. Dilue Harris 1833–1835," *Southwestern Historical Quarterly* 4, no. 3 (Jan. 1901): 86, 87, 103.

10. *Six Decades in Texas or Memoirs of Francis Richard Lubbock (Governor of Texas in War-Time, 1861–1863).* ed. C.W. Raines (Austin: Ben C. Jones, 1900), 53–54.

11. *J.C. Clopper's Journal,* trans. Gurner Grober, 13. Maresch Files, TLHD/HPL.

12. Harris, "Reminiscenses," 106.

13. Lewis Birdsall Harris, "Journal of Lewis Birdsall Harris, 1836–1842," *Southwestern Historical Quarterly* 25, no.3 (Jan. 1922): 185–86. Margaret S. Henson in her unpublished manuscript, "The Treatment of Mexican and Texas Prisoners of War, 1835–1837," has noted that Mexican prisoners were available from April 1836 to May 1837 to residents who would feed and house them.

14. Drury Blakely Alexander, *Texas Homes of the Nineteenth Century* (Austin: Univ. of Texas Press, 1979), 14.

15. Margaret S. Henson, *History of Baytown* (Houston: Bay Area Heritage Society, 1985). Called the "Old Place" by Heritage Society docents, this house was either intended as a dog-trot plan, but built fully enclosed, or modified by enclosing the central passage when the house was altered at some later date.

16. Vlach, 45.

17. *Roemer's Texas,* 57–58. Roemer does not give the planter's name.

18. *Morning Star,* Feb. 1, 1842. This article says that Judge Wyatt Hanks had a sawmill about one mile southwest of what was to become the Houston

townsite in 1828. See also *Texas Gazette,* n.d., Maresch Files, TLHD/HPL. "We take pleasure in announcing . . . that the entire machinery for the steam sawmill at Harrisburg has arrived in Trinity Bay form New Orleans. . . ." See also *Texas Gazette,* July 22, 1830: "The steam sawmill at Harrisburg of Messrs. Wison and Harris is in operation and works very well"; and *Texas Gazette,* July 31, 1830: "[A sloop] will leave tomorrow for Matamoras with cargo of plank from the [Harrisburg] sawmill."

19. Adele B. Looscan, "The Pioneer Harrises of Harris County, Texas," *Southwestern Historical Quarterly* 31, no. 4 (April 1928): 30.

20. *From Virginia to Texas, 1835: The Diary of Col. William Fairfax Gray* (Houston: Fletcher Publishing, 1965), 145. Gray says that Lorenzo de Zavala bought the property from Philip Singleton in the fall of 1835.

21. James Burke, Jr., *Burke's Texas Almanac* (Houston: privately published, 1879). C. Anson Jones wrote this description for a Centennial celebration. See also Adele B. Looscan, "Harris County 1822–1845," *Southwestern Historical Quarterly* 17 (Oct. 1914): 199.

22. S.M. Williams to C.C. Givens [the builder], April 28, 1830, and Oct. 21, 1830, Samuel May Williams Papers, Rosenberg Library, Galveston, Texas. See also Margaret S. Henson, *Samuel May Williams* (College Station: Texas A & M Univ. Press, 1976), 25. Henson quotes a letter dated Sept. 27, 1830, from Harris to Williams in which Harris also noted that flooring was to come on the next shipment [from New Orleans] and that his furnace was out of order. There was a brickyard at this time in San Felipe.

23. Lubbock, *Six Decades,* 54.

24. Doswell and Adams Ledger. 1837–38, HMRC/HPL.

25. Samuel A. Roberts to Mirabeau Lamar, Jan. 23, 1837, *The Papers of Mirabeau Buonaparte Lamar,* I: 534 and V: 130 (Austin: Texas State Library). "The schooner takes out the frame of a house for me 1½ story high 40 x 20 feet—Blair and Vedder have agreed to put it up. . . ."

26. Lubbock, *Six Decades,* 46.

27. Anonymous, "Houston in 1837," *Houston: A Nation's Capital 1837–1839,* ed. Andrew Forest Muir (Houston: S. Armstrong, 1985), 71.

28. Zachariah N. Morrell, "Tribulations of an Early Settler," *Houston: A Nation's Capital,* 102.

29. Francis R. Lubbock, "Early Days in Houston," *Houston: A Nation's Capital,* 27.

30. Mary Austin Holley, *the Texas Diary, 1835– 1838,* ed. J. P. Bryan (Austin: Univ. of Texas Press, 1965), 36.

31. Edwin A. Bonewitz Collection, typescript, 1957, HMRC/HPL.

32. Lubbock, *Six Decades,* 56. Lubbock says, "President Houston was occupying a small rough log cabin about twelve by sixteen feet, with probably a small shed attached. There was no fireplace—nothing but a small clay furnace in the room for him to get over and warm his fingers, Indian fashion."

33. Robert P. Boyce collection, handwritten book, 119, 124, HMRC/HPL.

34. Margaret Henson, "Robert P. Boyce: Nineteenth Century Houstonian," *Houston Review* 6, no.1 (1984): 25–39.

35. United States Census, Harris County, 1850 and 1860, microfilm, TLHD/HPL.

36. Willard B. Robinson, *Gone From Texas: Our Lost Architectural Heritage* (College Station: Texas A & M Univ. Press, 1981), 64.

37. *Evening Journal,* Houston, Texas, Nov. 13, 1884. The Briscoes moved to Houston from Harrisburg so that Judge Briscoe, then only twenty-seven years old, could assume his post as the first chief justice of Harrisburg County.

38. Gus Hamblett, "Anglo-American Architecture of the Texas Colonial Period," *Perspective* 11, no. 2: 14. Hamblett's article does not specifically discuss Harris County except to describe Harrisburg as "a little settlement near the site of the future Houston." See also Gus Hamblett, "The Plain Style: Some Sources for the Greek Revival in Texas," *Texas Architect* (May–June 1986): 60–69.

39. Reminiscences of Maggie Tod Milby as dictated to Rosa Tod Hamner, 1928. Rosa Tod Hamner Papers, JLC/HMRC/HPL.

40. Ray W. Irwin, *Daniel D. Tompkins, Gover-*

nor of New York and Vice President of the United States (New York: New York Historical Society, 1968), 57. "Tompkins and his family lived for a time at 349 Bowery . . . in an imposing three-story brick dwelling with marble mantels and fine woodwork. . . ." See also Looscan, "Pioneer Harrises," 369–70. Looscan states: "DeWitt Clinton Harris, who was in New York City in the interest of his mercantile business learned that the former home of Governor Tompkins was being razed to give room for commercial buildings, and the doors and windows were for sale. He bought and shipped them to Harrisburg for his mother's home. . . . At this time, the late forties, all fine carpentry was obtained from New York or Boston, and this opportune purchase was noted for its quality. The doors were heavy, handsomely paneled, and served admirably for the four large rooms and halls, downstairs. The windows fitted the openings in the same rooms. A simple devise for raising and lowering them consisted of wooden stops shaped like a bootjack, screwed to the casing at one side. The doorknobs were of brass and corresponded with the brass andirons in the large parlor fireplace."

41. Hamblett, "The Plain Style," 64.

42. Harvin C. Moore, AIA, "The Restoration of the Nichols-Rice House," *AIA Journal* (Jan. 1962): 28.

43. Frances Trollope, *Domestic Manners of the Americans* (1839, reprint, London: Century Publishing, 1984), 73.

44. Augustus Koch, *Birds Eye View of Houston, Texas,* 1873, shows dormers; Wood map, 1869, does not. TLHD/HPL.

45. William Kirkland Papers, JLC/HMRC/HPL.

46. "Progress Dooms City Landmark: Col. J.D. Andrews House Lavishly Furnished," *Houston Post,* Oct. 3, 1937.

47. Jesse Ziegler, *Wave of the Gulf* (San Antonio: privately published, 1938), 35–36. In addition to the Hutchins house, Ziegler discusses Quality Hill; see also Wille Hutcheson, "Houston's Old Homesteads," *Houston Daily Post,* Aug. 13, 1911; see also Ellen Douglas MacCorquodale, "County and City Buildings Mark Early Plan," *Civics For Houston,* Oct. 1928.

48. Wille Hutcheson, "Houston's Old Homesteads," *Houston Daily Post,* Oct. 1, 1911. This article discusses and illustrates the B.A. Shepherd house, a typical two-story, Greek Revival house with four, double-height square-cut columns, under a hipped roof. For information on the T.W. House house see Hutcheson, *Houston Daily Post,* July 23, 1911. See also "Colonel House's Birthplace Damaged by Fire," *Houston Chronicle,* Nov. 13, 1932; "Col. House's Home Dismantled at Smith and Capital," *Houston Post,* April 22, 1933; and "The Story of An Illustrious Houston Family," *Houston Post,* Aug. 19, 1923. For information on the Robert Lockart house see L.W. Duddlesten, "Old Lockhart [sic] Homestead Sold After 80 years for $55,000," *Houston Post,* April 10, 1927.

49. Jeff Lindemann, "Frosttown," *Deutsche Welt-U.S.A.* 7, no.2 (Sept. 1986): 6. Although the original pioneers in the Frost Town Community were Anglo-Americans who settled there in 1822, the area became known as Frost Town when Samuel Frost subdivided it into eight blocks in 1837. Frost Town is now wedged between the south bank of Buffalo Bayou and U.S. 59 on the west, north of Canal Street, once called German Street. German immigrants populated the general area loosely identified as Germantown.

50. Blanche Heitmann Strange, letter dated June 3, 1988, Blanche Heitmann Strange Papers, JLC/HMRC/HPL.

51. Ellen Robbins Red, *Early Days on the Bayou: 1838–1890: The Life and Letters of Horace Dickinson Taylor* (Waco: privately printed, 1986), 112–13.

52. William H. Pierson, Jr., *American Buildings and Their Architects* (New York: Anchor/Doubleday, 1976), 433–34. In discussing builders' handbooks, Pierson says: "The most important ones published in the United States were by Asher Benjamin of Greenfield, Massachusetts, and Minard Lafever of New York. Benjamin's earliest publication, which appeared in 1797, shows details in the Federal style, but in the sixth edition of his *American Builder's Companion,* published in 1827, some Greek details were included. In his later works Greek orders and Greek ornament prevail. Lafev-

er's first work was published in 1829." Hamblett, "The Plain Style," 61. Hamblett points out that "American carpenters enthusiastically received the new Benjamin handbooks, never referring to a 'Greek Revival' but rather to the 'New Plain style.'" Hamblett discusses the use of these handbooks in Texas.

53. *Democratic Telegraph and Texas Register,* Sept. 25, 1850. "Mr. J. Thompson has lately established in this city a window sash and blind manufactory on a very extensive scale. Most of the work is done by machinery, moved by two horses. These horses do the work of some dozen men. . . . Until recently large quantities of these articles were annually imported from the Eastern States, and thousands of dollars were sent out of the State to purchase them." See also William Keeton Turner, "The Early Texas Sash, Door and Blind Industry," *Perspective* 8, nos. 3–4 (1980): 1–8. Although Turner does not include Houston, his discussion of other Texas towns, particularly Galveston, is useful. This article contains much technical material.

54. Orson Squire Fowler, *A Home for All: or the Gravel Wall and Octagon Mode of Building, New Cheap, Convenient, Superior and Adapted to Rich or Poor* (New York: Fowler & West, 1854).

55. Peter Flagg Maxson, "The Octagon in Texas," *Perspective* 9 (Dec. 1980): 14–17.

56. Knox Briscoe Howe Papers, JLC/HMRC/HPL. Maurice Birdsall was the brother of Lewis Birdsall, Jane Birdsall Harris's father. Maurice's son was the attorney general of Texas, Judge John Birdsall. For information on L.J. Pilie see Bonewitz Collection, folder 1, HMRC/HPL.

57. United States Census, 1850, microfilm, TLHD/HPL.

58. RDP to EAP. Jan 19, 1858. Rosalie Sherman Cartwright Papers, JLC/HMRC/HPL. Two other letters mention the house: April 7, 1858, "I reckon you are now very much engaged about your new building" and July 17, 1858: "I hear from Reuben that you are nearly done your new building . . . we may yet occupy the room which you kindly mentioned." See also *Tri-Weekly Telegraph,* April 12, 1858: "Our friend Grainger has got the frame of Palmer's new residence up near the Academy, and a fine building it is." *Houston City Directory* (1866), xiii. C.J. Grainger advertised as "house builder." United States Census, 1850, lists Grainger as a 37 year-old "house carpenter." His country of origin was listed as England. See also Hutcheson, *Houston Daily Post,* Sept. 17, 1911.

59. "Henry Michael DeChaumes," *History of Texas, Together With a Biographical History of Houston and Galveston* (Chicago: Lewis Publishing, 1895), 515.

60. *Tri-Weekly Telegraph,* June 12, 1857: "Mr. DeChaume [s] is making bricks for the new Academy building which is to be a large handsome structure." See also *Capitols of Texas* (Texian Press, 1970), 126. "M. DeChaumes (who built as his home [in Austin] the A.B. Palm house) is architect and superintendent for the contractor."

61. *Tri-Weekly Telegraph,* June 12, 1857: "Mr. DeChaume [s], architect and builder will prepare designs, drafts and specifications for public and private edifices, machinery, etc. Orders from the County promptly attended to. Residence and office on Franklin Street."

62. *Morning Star,* Nov. 8, 1841.

63. "Wreckers Demolish Stately Ante-Bellum Schmidt Home," *Houston Press,* July 28, 1942.

64. *Democratic Telegraph and Texas Register,* Jan. 4, 1847.

65. Ibid., March 9, 1848.

66. *Morning Star,* Jan. 1, 1842. See also *Democratic Telegraph and Texas Register,* Feb. 18, 1846. "Cabinetware" was advertised by J.W. Kinney.

67. *Houston, A History and Guide* (Houston: Anson Jones Press, 1942), 287–88.

68. *Morning Star,* Dec. 25, 1841. The first mention of a tin roof in Houston was in this article: "the large and commodious fireproof store of Mr. Charles Power . . . which with its bright tin roof makes no inconsiderable show." See also *Democratic Telegraph and Texas Register,* Sept. 6, 1849: "There are several buildings in this city with tin roofs. . . ."

69. *Telegraph and Texas Register,* Dec. 31, 1845.

70. Ibid., Nov. 14, 1838.

71. Ibid., July 15, 1837.

72. *Democratic Telegraph and Texas Register,* Oct. 23, 1850.

73. *Telegraph and Texas Register,* Sept. 24, 1845.

74. *Weekly Telegraph,* Feb. 6, 1856.

75. *Morning Star,* May 15, 1841.

76. *Houston Republic,* May 29, 1858.

77. Newsclipping, Adele B. Looscan scrapbook, vol. 6, n.d., TLHD/HPL. Bonewitz quotes the Looscan scrapbook article and attributes it to the *Ladies Messenger,* 1888.

78. *Telegraph and Texas Register,* Dec. 30, 1837, 102–103.

79. *Morning Star,* May 22, 1839: "Engine House for first fire engine being erected. One-story building 18′ x 36′ with walls of brick 13″ thick . . . two rooms in the front 18′ x 15′ and back 18′ x 21′." *Morning Star,* July 23, 1839: "First brick house [building] now being erected on Franklin by Messrs. Allen."

80. Knox Briscoe Howe Papers, JLC/HMRC/HPL. Briscoe sold this house to Sidney Sherman about 1848.

81. Bonewitz Collection, typescript 1957, n.p. Bonewitz encloses this passage in quotes but does not cite the reference.

82. *Morning Star,* June 30, 1842. This article tells of the "large kiln of bricks, of an excellent quality, that have been made from the clay beds on this place," and of Kellum's new techniques that produce brick "as fine and durable as imported bricks."

83. Dr. E. N. Gray, "Dr. Recounts Stirring Scenes of Reconstruction Days in Houston: Memoirs of Dr. E. N. Gray," *Houston Chronicle,* March 4, 1934.

84. *Tri-Weekly Telegraph,* July 11, 1859.

85. *Houston City Directory,* 1870–71, 92–93.

86. Ibid., 1873, 4.

87. Hutcheson, *Houston Daily Post,* Oct. 8, 1911.

88. Ibid., Aug. 27, 1911.

89. Ibid., Sept. 24, 1911.

90. Beach Album, ms. 114–689, HMRC/HPL. Identification on the photograph reads, "Max Urwitz old home torn down for Stewart Building around 1906." *Houston City Directory,* 1899, identifies Max Urwitz as "physician and surgeon" with his office and home at 1104 Preston Ave. cor. of Fannin. This house is identified "H. Sampson" on the Wood map, 1989. It also appears on Koch, *Bird's Eye View,* 1873. *Houston City Directory,* 1866, identifies Henry Sampson as a general commission merchant with his residence at the corner of Fannin and Preston.

91. Florence Powers Stancliff Papers, JLC/HMRC/HPL.

92. Francita Stuart Koelsch Papers, JLC/HMRC/HPL.

93. Peter M. Rippe, "Harris County Heritage Society of Houston," *Antiques Magazine* (Sept. 1975): 495. The house was enlarged by Joseph F. Meyer, a subsequent owner, in 1876. It was moved to Sam Houston Park and restored in 1963.

94. "Dignified Mansion of Yesteryear Bows to Time as Workmen Dismantle Once Showplace of City," *Houston Post,* May 27, 1936. See also Bernice Keating, "Historic T.W. House Mansion in Louisiana Street Becomes Government Shelter for Transient Men," Houston Scrapbook, vol. 29. TLHD/HPL.

95. *Houston Daily Telegraph,* July 13, 1870.

96. Rippe, *Antiques,* 497–99. See also *Art Work of Houston* (1894) for the first published photograph of the Pillot house, TLHD/HPL. "Griffin Memorial House," Spring Creek County Historical Association, n.d., JLC/HMRC/HPL. The pamphlet includes a short biography of Eugene Pillot, who was born in France on February 10, 1820, and moved to Texas with his family, who settled on Willow Creek in 1837. Eugene Pillot was a carpenter and joiner, trades he learned in New York. He was said to have been one of the first builders in Harris County, but later he turned his attention to the timber business and farming. See also *Houston Chronicle,* August 26, 1984, which included another early photograph of the Pillot house. See also "Texas Builder and Lumberman Eugene Pillot," *Houston Chronicle,* Feb. 5, 1985.

97. For a discussion of Downing's architectural influence see Vincent J. Scully, Jr., *The Shingle Style and the Stick Style: Architectural Theory and Design from Downing to the Origins of Wright* (New Haven: Yale Univ. Press, 1971), rev. ed. Downing's most popular books were *A Treatise on the Theory and Practice of Landscape Gardening Adapted to North America* (1841); *Cottage Resid-*

ences (1842); *The Architecture of Country Houses* (1850); and *Victorian Cottage Residences* (1873), new ed. (New York: Dover Publications, 1981).

98. *Houston City Directory,* 1866, 1870–71, and 1877. An engraving of the Whitaker house was published on the Wood map, 1869, TLHD/HPL.

99. Ellen Douglas MacCorquodale, "County and City Buildings Mark Early Plan," *Civics for Houston* (Oct. 1928), 15.

100. *Houston City Directory,* 1877–78, first year listed. See also *History of Texas, Together with a Biographical Sketch of Houston and Galveston,* 566. Lucas came from England and settled in Houston in 1873, when he is listed in the *Houston City Directory* as a brickmason whose residence was on Montgomery Avenue. Therefore, this house was built between 1873 and 1877. Lucas's father was a builder in England, from whom he learned his trade. By 1877 James S. Lucas was listed as "contractor and builder." *Houston City Directory,* 1917, last year listed.

101. *Houston Daily Telegraph,* April 30, 1870.

102. *Houston City Directory,* 1877–78, 8.

103. Ibid., 10.

104. Ibid., 1882, xviii.

105. *The Age,* June 16, 1873.

106. *Houston City Directory,* 1880–81, 9.

107. Ibid., 1884, 11. See also *Houston City Directory,* 1877, 221. T. E. Byrne Marble Works was listed in the professional directory.

108. Ibid., 44.

109. Ibid., E. Brown advertised as a roof slater.

110. Ibid., 1880–81, 326. See also *Standard Blue Book,* 1907, 56.

111. Stephen Fox, "The Houston Buildings of N. J. Clayton," *The Houston Review* 9, no. 1: 3–4. This article is the most definitive study yet published on N. J. Clayton. See also Howard Barnstone, *The Galveston That Was* (New York: Macmillan, 1966). Clayton's first commission in Texas was the First Presbyterian Church designed by Memphis architects Jones and Baldwin. Today Clayton is best known for the Gresham house (Bishop's Palace) and the University of Texas Medical Department Building (Old Red), both in Galveston; St. Mary's Cathedral, Austin; and Sacred Heart Cathedral, Dallas.

112. Ibid., 8–9. "But from an architectural critic of the time its awkward vertical attenuation, asymmetric massing, and the aggressive, mannerist distortion of its conventional decorative detail likely would have earned the house the condescending designation of 'American Vernacular.'"

113. N. J. Clayton Collection, Rosenberg Library, Galveston, Texas.

114. *Houston Architectural Survey* (Southwest Center for Urban Research and Rice Univ. School of Architecture, 1980), 1:220.

115. *The Industries of Houston,* 1887, 75. See also *The Industrial Advantages of Houston, Texas and Environs* (Houston: Akehurst, 1894), 53. See also *Terre Haute City Directory,* 1874–75, 94; 1876, 127; 1877, 146. Heiner's work can be compared to Vrydaugh's, whose Opera House of 1889 (C. C. Oakey, *Terre Haute Illustrated,* H. R. Page Publisher, 1889) looks very similar to some of Heiner's early buildings like the Harris County jail. The author would like to thank Nancy Sherrill, genealogy librarian of the Vigo County Public Library, for information on Heiner's Indiana tenure. See also *Industrial Advantages,* 53. See advertisements in *Houston City Directory,* 1882–83, 16, 305; 1884, 47; 1890–91, 214. See also Eugene T. Heiner stationery, 1893 letterhead. George Fuermann City of Houston Collection; Special Collections, Univ. of Houston Libraries. See also Eugene T. Heiner obituary, *Houston Daily Post,* April 27, 1901: "Eugene Heiner, resident of Houston for 25 years . . . one of the best know architects in Texas . . . died in St. Joseph's Infirmary yesterday. . . ."

116. Kaufman and Runge (Stewart Title Building), ca. 1878; Leon and H. Blum Building (Tremont Hotel), 1879.

117. *Houston City Directory,* 1882, 16.

118. "Historical Records Scrapbook 1900–1924," Houston Museum of Fine Arts Archives.

119. Ibid. Annual Report by A. L. Guérard, President, Feb. 17, 1916.

120. Alfred C. Finn Collection, Architectural Component, HMRC/HPL.

121. *Houston City Directory,* 1882, 16.

122. *Houston Daily Post,* Feb. 21, 1884. "Dr. J. T. Blake to erect a house on Texas Ave., E. T. Hei-

ner, architect." See also *Houston City Directory,* 1884, 60.

123. *Houston City Directory,* 1882, 16. See also Francita Stuart Koelsch, "Dr. David Finney Stuart 1833–1909," typescript, Francita Stuart Koelsch Papers, JLC/HMRC/HPL. *Houston City Directory,* 1921, last year listed. Demolished for Keystone Building erected in 1922.

124. *History of Texas together with a Biographical History of the Cities of Houston and Galveston* (Chicago: Lewis Publishing, 1895), 509–510.

125. *Daily Mirror and American* (Manchester, NH), July 21, 1870. The author would like to thank Elizabeth Lessard, librarian of The Manchester Historic Association, for information provided on Dickey's New Hampshire tenure.

126. John B. Clarke, *Manchester: A Brief Record of its Past and a Picture of its Present* (Manchester: J. B. Clarke, 1875), 198–200. Dickey's designs for the First Baptist Church (1883) and Shearn Methodist–Episcopal Church (1883) in Houston, both of which have been demolished, were Victorian Gothic structures with tall spires much like those he designed in Manchester.

127. *Boston City Directory,* 1872. The author would like to thank Theresa D. Cederholm, curator of fine arts, Boston Public Library, for information concerning Dickey's Boston Tenure.

128. *Houston Daily Post,* May 11, 1884. Advertisement for Dickey & Simpson, *Galveston Daily News,* Jan. 1, 1887; Dickey & Helmich for H. & T. C. Passenger Depot, Houston, *Houston City Directory,* 1895; Dickey & Tempest, *Southern Architect* (April 1896); Dickey & Rue, *Houston City Directory,* 1900–1901 and *Picturesque Houston* (1900), 111. Advertisements for Dickey & Allen, *Houston City Directory,* 1904, with D. Anderson Dickey, his son.

129. *Houston Daily Post,* July 15, 1892. Dickey was elected president; A. Muller of Galveston, vice president; H. C. Holland of Houston, secretary; and Patrick S. Rabbitt of Galveston, treasurer. The Texas State Association of Architects was founded in 1886.

130. *New Orleans City Directory,* 1897–98.

Houston Daily Post, Feb. 26, 1899. Notice of Dickey's return to Houston. See also "A Building Fever," *Houston Daily Post,* Sept. 1, 1899. Lists houses designed by George Dickey: James I. Campbell, S. F. Carter, and Otto Witte. He also designed interior remodeling for the Texas National Bank (1899–1900); T. J. Broyles Building (1899); David N. Barry house (1900–1901); James E. McAshan house (1899); Christ Church rectory (1902); two houses for Allen Paul (1900–1901); and Houston City Hall and Market (1902–1904). *Houston City Directory,* 1906, was the last year that Dickey was listed.

131. "Old Ross Home, Huge Mansion of Gay Nineties Era, Is Being Razed," *Houston Chronicle,* Nov. 24, 1938. *Houston City Directory,* 1882–83, 15–16, lists J. W. Johnson house ($50,000) as having been constructed in the last two years; advertisement for George E. Dickey, Architect, ibid., xxiv, lists J. W. Johnson residence among recent projects.

132. The Waldo house was listed on George E. Dickey's 1901 letterhead. See also *Houston Architectural Survey* 4:844–49.

133. "Workmen Toil on Historic Ground," *Houston Post Dispatch,* Dec. 20, 1931. This article has a chronology of the design and dismantling of the J. Waldo house. See also *Houston Architectural Survey* 4:845; and *Houston Post,* July 30, 1964. Virginia Waldo interview with Dorothy Knox Howe Houghton, 1974.

134. Henry-Powell Hitchcock, *Architecture: Nineteenth and Twentieth Centuries* (Baltimore: Penguin Books, 1958), 255.

135. "Pavement Paragraphs," *Houston Daily Post,* Oct. 10, 1888: "The S. K. Dick house on Main Street is up to the second story." *Houston Daily Post,* Jan. 3, 1889: "S. K. Dick Mansion almost ready for occupancy." See also *Houston City Directory,* 1889–90; *Industrial Advantages,* 86; and "Another Landmark Passes," *Houston Post,* Sept. 9, 1923.

136. Michael A. Tomlan, "Introduction," *George G. Barber's Cottage Souvenir Number Two* (New York: American Life Series, 1982), 17. "William T. Comstock joined Amos J. Bicknell's firm in May 1877, became a partner in January 1879, and as-

sumed full control of the business in May 1881." Tomlan's introduction to this reprint of Barber's 1891 publication, which was the first volume to be marketed nationwide, is an excellent overview and critique of Barber's career.

137. Ibid, 5–7.

138. George F. Barber, *Cottage Souvenir No. 2* (Knoxville, TN: S. B. Newman, 1891), 6.

139. Margaret Culbertson interview with Barrie Scardino, Sept. 2, 1988. The author would like to thank Ms. Culbertson for her generosity in sharing her unpublished findings.

140. Sister M. Agatha, *The History of Houston Heights 1891–1918* (Houston: Premier Printing, 1956). See also Subdivision Collection. TLHD/HPL.

141. "How Will You Build?" *American Homes, A Journal Devoted to Planning, Building and Beautifying the Home* 4, no. 2 (Feb. 1898): 50. Quoted in Tomlan.

142. Palliser, Palliser and Company, "View of F. Egge's Cottage," *Palliser's Model Homes* (Bridgeport, CT, 1878), reprinted in Watkins Glen, N.Y.: American Life Foundation, 1978.

143. Robert W. Shoppell, *Shoppell's Modern Houses* (New York: 1887), reprinted in Rockville Centre, N.Y.: Antiquity Reprints, 1983.

144. Carrie Bergamini Coughlin Papers, JLC/HMRC/HPL. *Houston City Directory,* 1894, first year listed. *Houston City Directory,* 1929–30, last year listed.

145. "Two Deer on a Houston Balcony," *Houston Press,* Nov. 21, 1955. See also "The Mistrot-Segura Story in Louisiana and Texas by Mistrot Cartier," typescript, 1965, Mistrot Papers, JLC/HMRC/HPL.

146. George Fuermann, "Old DeGeorge Home: Monument to Past," *Houston Post,* Dec. 28, 1949. See also Marie de Mille Taylor, "The DeGeorge Family: Pioneers in the Growth of Houston," *Houston Post,* Sept. 4, 1949.

147. "Capt. T. D. Cobbs [sic] Residence," *Houston Illustrated* (1893), TLHD/HPL. *Houston City Directory,* 1887, first year listed. *Houston City Directory,* 1922, last year listed.

148. *Houston City Directory,* 1894, first year listed. *Houston City Directory,* 1927, last year listed.

149. This address, 2009 Live Oak, can be traced back only to the 1908 *Houston City Directory.* At that time it was the house of Jesse W. Wilson, a black railroad worker. The house appears to be older than that. In addition, houses in this neighborhood have been moved because of nearby freeway construction, making it difficult to tell if the house is even on its original site.

150. Knox Briscoe Howe Papers, JLC/HMRC/HPL. *Houston City Directory,* 1880, first year listed.

151. *Houston, A History and Guide,* 294–95. See also Rosa Tod Hamner Papers, JLC/HMRC/HPL.

152. Aurelia Hart Thacker Papers, JLC/HMRC/HPL.

153. B. C. Simpson Papers, JLC/HMRC/HPL.

154. Paula Johnson, "T Houses in Austin," *Perspective* 11, no. 1 (May 1982): 3.

155. Grace Noble Adkins Papers, JLC/HMRC/HPL.

156. *Sixth Ward Revitalization Plan* (Greater Houston Preservation Alliance, 1986). This study includes the architectural history of this neighborhood and is illustrated with current photographs.

157. German Heritage Society members, including Ann Lindemann, believe that this was a German folk symbol and have called it a *distel finke* (which means "little finch" in German).

158. *Houston City Directory,* 1904, first year listed. See also Peter L. Scardino interview with Barrie M. Scardino, Sept. 28, 1987, Lucy D'Amico Scardino Papers, JLC/HMRC/HPL.

159. Vlach, 43.

160. Merline Pitre, "Richard Allen: The Chequered Career of Houston's First Black State Legislator," *The Houston Review* 8, no. 2 (1986): 80.

161. *Houston Architectural Survey* 6: 1329–30.

162. *Houston City Directory,* 1910, 665.

163. "Dallas Architect, Designer of Odd Fellows' Temple, Wants Race Artisans to Get a Chance; He has Drawn Plans for Many Race Buildings," *Houston Informer,* Nov. 10, 1923. See also "Sidney Pittman" file, Architectural Component. HMRC/HPL.

164. *The Red Book of Houston* (Houston: Sotex Publishing, n.d.), 155, 158, 160. The contractors listed are J. H. Carter, Joseph H. Jackson, A. J.

Johnson, Ed. L. Longcope, Wm. Lumpkin, and S. M. Nelson.

165. Ibid., 109.

166. Ruth Arbuckle Russell Papers, JLC/HMRC/HPL.

167. Mr. and Mrs. James Lanier Britton, Jr., Papers, JLC/HMRC/HPL.

168. Charlotte Goss Lindsey Papers, JLC/HMRC/HPL.

169. Frank Lee Berry Papers, JLC/HMRC/HPL. See also *Houston City Directory,* 1884, 52. George E. Dickey advertisement refers to the Cotton house. "Famous Hutcheson Home, Landmark of City, Falls Before March of Business," *Houston Chronicle,* Aug. 1, 1927. See also Henrietta Hutcheson Schwartz Papers, JLC/HMRC/HPL, and Joseph Chappell Hutcheson Papers, JLC/HMRC/HPL.

170. *Houston Daily Post,* Oct. 9, 1889. "C. Lombardi's new building to commence construction soon on Rusk." *Houston City Directory,* 1890–91, first year listed. The Lombardi house was demolished ca. 1920 for the Kanawa Apartments. See also *Industrial Advantages of Houston* (1894), 10, for photograph; and *City of Houston* (1893), 82, for photograph.

171. "G. E. Dickey prepares plans for Charles Dillingham house at 1214 Rusk," *Houston Daily Post,* June 18, 1889. See also "Charles Dillingham issued permit for $7000 residence on Rusk Avenue," *Houston Daily Post,* Nov. 22, 1889. *Houston City Directory,* 1915, last year listed.

172. Mrs. Louis Letzerich Papers, JLC/HMRC/HPL. *Houston City Directory,* 1884, first year listed. *Houston City Directory,* 1929–30, last year listed.

173. *Houston City Directory,* 1892–93, first year listed. *Houston City Directory,* 1894, 6, lists A. P. Root house as having been constructed in the last twenty months. *Houston City Directory,* 1925, last year listed. *Houston Post,* Jan. 10, 1923: "City will start improving Root Memorial Square. . . . Root house to be moved." "Root Memorial Square to be Rededicated," Newsletter of the Park People (June–July 1987).

174. Scully, *Shingle Style,* 91–129.

175. *Houston City Directory,* 1901, first year

Kaiser house listed. Charles Louis Desel Papers, JLC/HMRC/HPL. *Houston City Directory,* 1904, first year Desel house listed. *Houston City Directory,* 1930, last year listed.

176. "Dignified Mansion of Yesteryear Bows to Time as Workmen Dismantle Once Showplace of City," *Houston Post,* May 27, 1936.

177. Randy Pace. National Register Nomination for the Benjamin Andrew Rogers house in Houston Heights, ca. 1987, JLC/HMRC/HPL. The Rev. Rogers was rector of Christ Church, where Tempest was a communicant and choir member. There he met and married Rogers's daughter, Susan. This relationship was probably the primary reason that Tempest was selected as supervising architect for the parish house (1892–93) and church (1894). The Tempests lived with the Rogers first at 609 Elgin and then in Houston Heights, where Rogers moved to found a new church. With their two children the Tempests moved to Mexico City in 1899, where he worked in the engineering department of the street railway company. They remained until February of 1902, when they returned to the Heights. At that time Tempest accepted a position in the engineering department of the Houston and Texas Central Railway Company. Tempest died on March 18, 1903, of tuberculosis at the age of thirty-eight and was buried in Hollywood Cemetery. See also *Houston Architectural Survey* 6:1361.

178. *Southern Architect* (Feb. 1893): 117. In "Building Notices," J. A. Tempest is named as the architect for the W. B. Chew house; $12,000 contract.

179. *Houston City Directory,* 1893–94, 6. "Erected in the last 20 months." J. W. Jones was listed at this address in 1877, but the appearance of this house is consistent with the 1893 date, indicating that Jones probably demolished his earlier house and built a new one at the same site.

180. *Houston City Directory,* 1900, first year listed.

181. *Houston City Directory,* 1902–1903, first year listed.

182. *Houston City Directory,* 1894, first year listed. *Houston City Directory,* 1920, last year listed.

183. *Houston City Directory,* 1902–1903, first year listed.

184. *The Standard Blue Book of Texas,* 1907–1908, 84. *Houston City Directory,* 1903–1904, first year listed. *Houston City Directory,* 1923–34, last year listed.

185. Helen Shofner Lorehn, "Biography of Olle Jonsson Lorehn (July 29, 1864–June 9, 1939), Architect and Engineer," typescript, 1985, Olle J. Lorehn Papers, LJC/HMRC/HPL. See also *Houston Architectural Survey* 1:68, 265; 4:883. Lorehn designed Houston's first skyscraper, the Binz Building, in 1895.

186. George E. Dickey's 1901 letterhead lists the Samuel Fain Carter house among his projects. Marge Crumbaker, "Mansion of Memories: Funeral For Proud Old House," *Houston Post,* Nov. 26, 1965.

187. "Two Fine Homes on South Main are Soon to be Demolished," *Houston Chronicle,* Sept. 19, 1937. Includes photograph; the two houses were the J. I. Campbell house (referred to as the M. T. Jones house after later owners) and the Dudley Sharpe house. See also "Wreckers Begin Razing Old Home of Mrs. M. T. Jones," *Houston Chronicle,* Oct. 12, 1937.

188. "Old Vince Place on Main torn down for Henry Fox Residence," *Houston Daily Post,* June 30, 1892.

189. *Houston Post,* Feb. 5, 1967.

190. Randy Pace (see note 175) writes that Tempest was originally chosen as architect for the new rectory and had begun plans, which were not completed before his death in 1902. George Dickey, who had been his partner, was then asked to complete the designs and supervise construction. Dickey is the architect of record.

191. Marguerite Johnson, *A Happy Wordly Abode: Christ Church Cathedral 1839/1864* (Houston: Cathedral Press, 1964), 141.

192. Hitchcock, 144.

193. Ibid., 232.

194. Tim Matthewson, "The Colonial Revival at the McFaddin-Ward House," presented at the symposium "American Homes in Transition," Mc-Faddin-Ward House Museum Conference, Oct. 30, 1987.

195. Susan Prendergast Schoelwer, "Curious Relics and Quaint Scenes: The Colonial Revival at Chicago's Great Fair," *The Colonial Revival in America,* ed. Alan Axelrod (New York: Norton, 1985), 191.

196. *Houston City Directory,* 1902, 517. *Houston City Directory,* 1912, last year Oliver was listed. See also *Souvenir of Houston, Texas* (1901–1902), 14, TLHD/HPL.

197. Laura Rice Neff Papers, JLC/HMRC/HPL.

198. *Houston Architectural Survey* 4:923–25.

199. *Houston Architectural Survey* 4:801–803.

200. Claude Hackney Papers, JLC/HMRC/HPL.

201. George F. Barber, Design no. 200, *Modern Dwellings* (1898), 202–203. The elevation, similar to the Hackney house, is signed Barber & Klutts, architects, Knoxville, Tenn. This design was captioned, "A most beautiful home of the Georgian type (Classic Colonial); Cost (handsomely Finished) $25,000 to $30,000."

202. *Houston City Directory,* 1908, first year Streetman house listed. A. C. Bering III Papers, JLC/HMRC/HPL. Both the Streetman and Bering houses were pictured in the *Standard Blue Book of Texas, 1907–1908* (Houston: privately published, 1907).

203. *The Insurance Maps of Houston, Texas* (New York: Sanborn Map Company, 1907), vol. 1.

204. Ibid., 49.

205. *Houston City Directory,* 1908–1909, 73.

206. *Standard Blue Book of Texas,* 1907–1908.

207. *The Red Book,* 106 (photograph), 153. See also "Dr. Covington Here 58 Years," *Houston Press,* July 24, 1961; *Houston Architectural Survey* 6:1410–13; and Dr. Benjamin J. Covington Collection, HMRC/HPL. Although the Covington house was listed in the National Register of Historic Places, it was demolished in 1980.

208. *Houston City Directory,* 1903–1904, first year listed. *Houston City Directory,* 1922, last year listed.

209. George Anna Lucas Papers, JLC/HMRC/HPL.

210. *Houston City Directory,* 1903, first year listed. *Houston City Directory,* 1922, last year listed.

211. *Houston Architectural Survey* 4:784–90.

212. Stephen Fox, "Sanguinet & Staats in Houston, 1903–1926," *Perspective* 12, no. 1 (Spring 1983): 2–11.

213. Ibid., 8.

214. *Houston City Directory,* 1916, first year listed. See also Augusta Sachs Usener Papers, JLC/HMRC/HPL.

215. William F. Stern, "The Lure of the Bungalow," *Cite* (Winter 1986): 8. Stern's article on the Houston bungalow is an excellent essay on the origins of the Bungalow style and its adaptation in Houston.

216. *Houston Architectural Survey* 4:852–54. See also George G. Barber, *Art in Architecture* (1902–1903), published in Tomlan, 16.

217. Katherine Cole Stevenson and H. Ward Jandl, *Houses By Mail: A Guide to Houses from Sears, Roebuck and Company* (Washington: Preservation Press, 1986), 19. Houston, Texas, is listed (p. 240) as a location to which design no. 126 was shipped. Described as "a popular, inexpensive and graceful bungalow," this model was sold between 1911 and 1913.

218. Crain Ready-Cut House Company, *Catalogue 6,* 1925, TLHD/HPL.

219. Stern, 8.

220. *Homes* (Houston: William A. Wilson, 1911–1912, published monthly), TLHD/HPL.

221. "What We Have Done for Others," *Homes* 2, no. 11 (May 1912): 6–7.

222. *Homes* (Feb. 1912): 6. See also Stern, 9; and Paul Hester and Peter Papademetriou, *La Arquitectura: Spanish Influences on Houston's Architecture* (Houston, Houston Public Library, 1979).

223. Fox, "Sanguinet & Staats," 7.

224. Ibid.

225. Ibid. See also *Houston Architectural Survey* 2:320; and Jay C. Henry, Judy Dooley, Patricia and Robert Cavanan, "Residential Design in Typical American Architecture: The Swiss Avenue District, 1905–1932," *Perspective* 9, no. 1 (1982):17. "We have coined the term 'Progressive' for such houses, which exhibit strict frontality, front verandas, and absence of historical detail. The term is obviously borrowed from the Progressive era in American politics, with which this period of history coincided. . . ." See also Fox, "Sanguinet & Staats," 7–8.

226. Hutcheson, "Two views of 'The Oaks.' The Beautiful Home of Mr. and Mrs. Edwin B. Parker," *Houston Post,* Oct. 27, 1912.

227. "Parker Home," *Houston Daily Post,* Sept. 5, 1909.

228. Fox, "Sanguinet & Staats," 8.

229. "Courtlandt Place: Title and development history, plan for private residential district, conflict with city, construction of homes, former residents of Courtlandt Place," typescript, April 8, 1976, 1. Courtlandt Place Papers, JLC/HMRC/HPL. The Courtlandt Improvement Company was incorporated on August 8, 1906, by A. L. Hamilton, T. A. Cargill, and Sterling Myer. The next 15.5 acres were divided into 26 lots and an esplanaded boulevard.

230. Henry et al., 17.

231. "Courtlandt Place Neighborhood Tour" (Houston: Rice Design Alliance and the Courtlandt Association, 1982).

232. Henry et al., 18.

233. *Houston Architectural Survey* 6:1363, 1387.

234. Ibid., 5:1126–39, 1180–91.

235. Barnstone, *Galveston,* 161. Located at 2424 Broadway, the Sealy house still stands. Barnstone said that it "may well be the last of the great romantic buildings stemming from the Richardson tradition." He continued to describe the house as a "free adaption of specific Italian precedents rather than a slavish copy such as those shortly to emerge in the great Neo-Renaissance, Georgian and Colonial revivals seen at the Chicago World's Fair of 1893."

236. Howard Barnstone, *The Architecture of John F. Staub* (Austin: Univ. of Texas Press, 1979). This is the definitive study of Staub's work.

237. Michael E. Wilson, *Alfred C. Finn: Builder of Houston* (Houston: Houston Public Library, 1983).

238. Stephen Fox, *The General Plan of the William M. Rice Institute and Its Architectural Development* (Houston: School of Architecture, Rice Univ., 1980), 9. See also *Houston Architectural Survey* 4:947.

239. Knox Briscoe Howe Papers, JLC/HMRC/HPL. Maurice Birdsall was Birdsall Briscoe's great-great-great uncle. See also Stephen Fox, "The Splendid Houses of Birdsall Briscoe," *Houston Home/Garden* (May 1981); James Charles Susman, "The Architecture of Birdsall Parmenas Briscoe" (M. Arch. thesis, Univ. of Texas, 1979), HMRC/HPL; and *Houston Architectural Survey* 3:519.

240. "E. L. Neville House," Courtlandt Place Papers, JLC/HMRC/HPL. The architect Charles L. Ligon is now in possession of the most complete collection of Briscoe's architectural drawings.

241. "Courtlandt Place Neighborhood Tour."

242. "Garrow House," Courtlandt Place Papers, JLC/HMRC/HPL. *Architectural Record,* July 1915, 170.

CHAPTER 3

1. Ferdinand Roemer, *Texas with Particular Reference to German Immigration and the Physical Appearance of the Country*, trans. Oswald Mueller (first published in English, 1935; Waco, TX: Texian Press, 1967), 65. Roemer was a geologist who traveled and researched in Texas between December 1845 and April 1847. His book was written in Bonn in 1849 (xi-xii).

2. Gustav Dressel, *Gustav Dressel's Houston Journal: Adventures in North America and Texas, 1837–1841*, trans. Max Freund (Austin: Univ. of Texas Press, 1944), 38.

3. An Inventory of Debts, Money, Merchandise, and property real and personal at Harrisburg and Neighborhood belonging [?] Estate of John R. Harris, Decd., 2nd October 1829, Adele B. Looscan Papers, Barker Texas History Center, Univ. of Texas, Austin. The "blue printed" ware listed in the inventory was probably transfer-decorated earthenware associated with Staffordshire, England, potteries from the 1820s throughout the nineteenth century.

From 1850 until as late as 1878 transfer-decorated wares made by Anthony Shaw in Burslem, England, commemorated the Mexican-American War with a series of patterns known as the "Texian Campaigne." Ellouise Parker Larsen, *American Historical Views on Staffordshire China*, 3d. ed. (New York: Dover Publications, 1975), 190–93. The lathe, saw, and glass knobs (probably drawer pulls) indicate that Harris was prepared to outfit a furniture maker.

4. Mary Austin Holley, "Letter XI, Bolivar, 1831," *Texas: Observations, Historical, Geographical and Descriptive* (Baltimore: Armstrong & Plaskitt, 1833), 123–25.

5. Deed from the State of Coahuila and Texas to Allen C. Reynolds, Harris County Deed Records, Houston, Texas, vol. B, 128–29, in S. F. Austin's Register of Families in Clifford White, *1830 Citizens of Texas* (Austin: Eakin Press, 1983), 39.

6. Roger Shatzel to Allen Reynolds, Oct. 23, 1832; and Inventory of the Estate of Allen C. Reynolds, April 28, 1837, Washington County Probate Records, Brenham, Texas. The author is grateful to Quenci Scott, a descendant of Allen C. Reynolds, for sharing her extensive research on him. According to the 1835–36 New York City directories, William and John Shatzel were grocers operating at 171 South Street.

7. Elizabeth Silverthorne, *Ashbel Smith of Texas: Pioneer, Patriot, Statesman, 1805–1886* (College Station: Texas A&M Univ. Press, 1982), 64, 66.

8. Roemer, 60.

9. No documented Harris County hide-seat chairs are known to have survived. For examples of this form made elsewhere in Texas, see *Early Texas Furniture and Decorative Arts* (San Antonio: Trinity Univ. Press for the San Antonio Museum Association, 1973), 4–11.

10. "Journal of Lewis Birdsall Harris, 1836–1842," *Southwestern Historical Quarterly* 25 (Oct. 1921): 139–40.

11. Probate of Jonathan B. Frost, Harris County Probate Records, vol. A, 228–30, 361–65, 385–86, Harris County, Texas.

12. Joseph Chambers Clopper, "J. C. Clopper's

Journal and Book of Memoranda for 1828," *Texas State Historical Association Quarterly* 13 (July 1909): 53.

13. Caroline von Hinueber, "Life of German Pioneers in Early Texas," *Texas State Historical Association Quarterly* 2 (Jan. 1899): 229.

14. By October 14, 1837, Jefferson Wright was in Houston advertising his services in the Houston *Telegraph and Texas Register* as a portrait painter (p. 3, col. 2). On December 24, 1837, Mary Austin Holley, accompanied by Sam Houston, visited "Wright's 'Gallery of National Portraits'" in the Capitol building. Wright painted at least two portraits of Sam Houston. Mary Austin Holley, *The Texas Diary 1835–1838*, ed. J. P. Bryan (Austin: Univ. of Texas Press, 1965), 36, 95. Ambrose Andrews also advertised in the *Telegraph and Texas Register* on October 28, 1837 (p. 3, col. 1), as a "PORTRAIT AND MINIATURE PAINTER." On May 5, 1841 (p. 3, col. 2), Andrews announced in the same newspaper that he was leaving Texas for a few months but, "having collected a considerable number of pictures that he has painted during his last three years residence in this City, he respectfully invites the ladies and gentlemen of Houston and its vicinity, to call and view them, before they are returned to their respective owners, which will be within a few days." Once returned, these portraits undoubtedly decorated the walls of Houston homes. Later itinerant artists like Thomas Flintoff (fig. 149) and Walter Sies Finnil (fig. 19) worked in the area. By 1873 photographs were also made in Houston. Williams' Gallery advertised "All classes of Photographic work done, and special attention to making Oil Portraits from any kind of old pictures of deceased parties, and warranted satisfactory in all cases." *Daily Telegraph*, Jan. 24, 1873, p. 5, col. 3.

15. *Telegraph and Texas Register*, Feb. 10, 1838, p. 3, col. 3.

16. Ibid., Jan. 3, 1844, p.1, col. 1, and p. 3, col. 5.

17. *Morning Star*, March 9, 1841, p. 3, col. 2, and *Democratic Telegraph and Texas Register*, Nov. 29, 1850, p. 3, col. 5. Later Chickering pianos were sold in the city "at the same price and of the same degree of excellence as at our Warehouses in Boston

[and] will be warranted as fully as if proceeding directly from our establishment in Boston," *Weekly Telegraph*, Feb. 20, 1856, p. 3, col. 7.

18. *Tri-Weekly Telegraph*, Jan. 1, 1858, p. 3. col. 7.

19. *Morning Star*, Dec. 8, 1840, p. 3, col. 2.

20. *Telegraph and Texas Register*, Jan. 13, 1838, p. 3, col. 3.

21. Ibid., Jan. 13, 1838, p. 3, col. 2.

22. Ibid., Nov. 25, 1837, p. 3, col. 3.

23. In addition to German Biedermeier influences on Texas-German furniture, a number of Texas furniture designs, particularly side chairs and pedestal-based center tables, were inspired by the Restoration style popular throughout the United States during this period.

24. Very little documented Houston-made furniture survives from this period. Occasionally a piece is described in detail as, for example, the rectangular one-drawer table appearing in an advertisement in the *Morning Star*, Aug. 27, 1842, p. 3, col. 3: "STRAYED OR STOLEN FROM THE CHURCH DURING the Extraordinary session of Congress, a small red TABLE, with turned legs, about 2 1/2 feet high, with a bulge in the legs 4 inches from the floor—top about 20 inches by 30, with a drawer and glass nub [knob?]—marked conspicuously in the underside. The owner would like the same to be returned to said Church without delay." The church mentioned was probably the First Presbyterian Church, which was completed by November 27, 1841, and was the only church building standing in Houston at that time. [Writers' Program of the Work Projects Administration, eds.], *Houston: A History and Guide* (Houston: Anson Jones Press, 1942), 58.

25. *Democratic Telegraph and Texas Register*, March 14, 1850, p. 3, col. 4.

26. Ibid., March 23, 1848, p. 4, col. 2, and Nov. 23, 1848, p. 3, col. 4. No James Sauters is listed in the 1850 Galveston census; Sauters is probably the same person as John A. Sauters, who is listed in the census as a merchant. See *United States Census for 1850*, Galveston, Texas, family no. 284.

27. William Prescott Webb, ed., *The Handbook of Texas*, 2 vols. (Austin: Texas State Historical As-

sociation, 1952), vol. 2, 705–706; *Telegraph and Texas Register*, March 6, 1844, p. 3, col. 1.

28. *Democratic Telegraph and Texas Register*, July 19, 1847, p. 4, col. 6, and July 26, 1847, p. 4, col. 6.

29. Ibid., July 13, 1848, p. 3, col. 4.

30. For example, Thomas Martin & Co. advertised that it might be found on Main Street at the "Sign of [the] Golden Coffee Pot." *Telegraph*, April 25, 1855, p. 4, col. 3.

31. Ibid., March 4, 1846, p. 3, col. 5.

32. See "A Checklist of Texas Cabinetmakers," in Lonn Taylor and David B. Warren, *Texas Furniture: The Cabinetmakers and Their Work 1840–1880* (Austin: Univ. of Texas Press, 1975), 273–330. Taylor and Warren compiled their list from references in Texas newspapers and from the United States census returns for the years 1850, 1860, and 1870. In addition to the Taylor and Warren list, Houstonians John and August Bering trained in Germany as cabinetmaker and apprentice, respectively, before migrating to Houston in 1846 and starting their lumberyard in 1854. "History of Bering Memorial United Methodist Church," Houston, Texas, April 11, 1948, Edna Earl Brazelton Taylor Papers, JLC/HMRC/HPL, 9–10. S. D. Staats advertised his trade in the *Morning Star*, March 30, 1843, p. 3, col. 2. A four-post bed and a cradle made in 1852 and attributed to August Proetzel (1817–85) belong to one of his descendants, and a walnut secretary said to have been made by Friedrich Usener in Houston in 1842 is in the Museum of American Architecture and Decorative Arts at Houston Baptist University. In addition, a late 1860s sideboard marked "Ed Brown Houston Tex" is in the collection of the Harris County Heritage Society. Brown, who is not listed in any Houston city directories, may have been the Edwin Brown listed by Taylor and Warren as working in Galveston (*Texas Furniture*, 282).

33. *Telegraph and Texas Register*, Dec. 2, 1837, p. 3, col. 1.

34. *Democratic Telegraph and Texas Register*, Aug. 19, 1846, p. 3, col. 4.

35. *Morning Star*, March 30, 1843, p. 3, col. 2.

36. *Tri-Weekly Telegraph*, Jan. 1, 1858, p. 3, col. 2.

37. Holley, *Texas*, 125. *Telegraph and Texas Register*, Sept. 22, 1838, p. 7, col. 2.

38. *Telegraph and Texas Register*, Jan. 21, 1846, p. 2, col. 4; Edward C. Hutcheson, *The Freedom Tree* (Waco, TX: Texian Press, 1870), 43.

39. Telegraph and Texas Register, June 7, 1843, p. 2, col. 5.

40. Lottman's improved mattresses were made of four different grades of moss designated by color and found in Harris and nearby Fort Bend and Brazoria counties—gray, dark gray, brown, and clear black—which cost from 50 cents to $6.00 per hundred pounds, after cleaning and ginning. Lottman Brothers to William H. Hamman, Calvert, Texas, Sept., 24, 1889, William Harrison Hamman Collection, Manuscript Administration Sheets, No. 6, WRC/RU.

41. *Houston Daily Post*, Oct. 27, 1895, p. 7, col. 4; interview by Katherine Howe with Enola LeBlanc, April 12, 1988. Mrs. LeBlanc (b. 1924) spent her early years on a plantation near New Iberia, Louisiana.

42. *Telegraph and Texas Register*, Nov., 14, 1838, p. 6, col. 4; *Tri-Weekly Telegraph*, May 4, 1855, p. 3, col. 5.

43. *Democratic Telegraph and Texas Register*, Oct. 23, 1850, p. 1, col. 3.

44. Snell advertised first as M. K. Snell and later as Snell & Moore. See *Morning Star*, Nov. 24, 1840, p. 3, col. 3, and Dec. 24, 1842, p. 1, col. 2. He was Houston's postmaster from 1843 to 1849.

45. *Telegraph*, April 25, 1855, p. 4, col. 4; *Weekly Telegraph*, Feb. 6, 1856, p. 3, col. 5.

46. *Democratic Telegraph and Texas Register*, Sept. 25, 1850, p. 2, col. 5, and Oct. 16, 1850, p. 3, col. 6. By 1855 Henry House was also manufacturing sashes and blinds in Houston. See *Tri-Weekly Telegraph*, June 29, 1855, p. 1, col. 5. Thompson was probably referring in his advertisement to what is known in the trade as red-heart cypress. Red-heart cypress was a highly regarded millwork wood indigenous to the area. It had several desirable properties for Houston: it was durable, and it was

rot and termite resistant. This wood has not been available in any quantity in Houston since the early 1950s; lesser variations known as yellow, swamp, and upland cypress have replaced it. The author is grateful to Bill Flanagan, manager of Allwoods-Schroeder (incorporated in Houston in 1935), for sharing this information. Telephone interview by Katherine Howe with Bill Flanagan, March 14, 1988.

47. Carpet Warerooms of J. D. Dameron and Company, *Tri-Weekly Telegraph*, Jan. 1, 1858, p. 3, col. 6.

48. *Tri-Weekly Telegraph*, Jan. 1, 1858, p. 1, col. 7.

49. Albro, Hoyt & Co. of New York City advertised its heavy, medium, and light floor cloths in the *Democratic Telegraph and Texas Register*, Feb. 8, 1849, p. 4, col. 5.

50. In 1851 Henry Sampson sold rope and grass mats and "Gowka [Ghurka?] matting." *Telegraph and Texas Register*, Nov. 7, 1851, p. 3, col. 2.

51. Henry Sampson & Co. advertised these wares in the *Telegraph*, April 25, 1855, p. 4, col. 4.

52. In what may have been one of the nation's first mail-order businesses, A. M. Gentry & Co.'s Express advertised "Merchants, Planters Mechanics and others by consigning their cotton, &c. or the cash through our Houston Office . . . can at all times have their supplies &c. purchased in the New Orleans market, and forwarded on by return Boat." *Telegraph and Texas Register*, Nov. 19, 1845, p. 3, col. 2.

53. "Valuable Property for Sale [W. W. Swain House]," *Morning Star*, Jan. 7, 1841, p. 3, col. 2.

54. Ophia D. Smith, "A Trip to Texas in 1855," *Southwestern Historical Quarterly* 59 (July 1955): 29. The reference is probably to the home of District Judge Constantine Whitehead Buckley (d. 1851).

55. Center tables first appeared in American interiors in the 1820s as a direct outgrowth of improved lighting and the need to put a table lamp in the middle of the room or to have a table in proximity to the gas or electric chandelier. *Morning Star*, Oct. 31, 1840, p. 1, col. 1, and Nov. 24, 1840, p. 1,

col. 1; *Democratic Telegraph and Texas Register*, Jan. 11, 1849, p. 3, col. 5.

56. M. H. Shepard & Co. and Messrs. Perkins & Randel were the manufacturers. See *Telegraph and Texas Register*, Jan. 3, 1844, p. 3, col. 1, and April 24, 1844, p. 2, cols. 4–5.

57. *Democratic Telegraph and Texas Register*, June 28, 1847, p. 3, col. 5.

58. The stoves were advertised in Houston by Peel & Dumble of Galveston in the W. A. Leonard, comp., *Houston City Directory for 1866* (Houston: Gray Strickland, 1866), xxxii. Kerosene stoves remained in use in more modest homes well into the twentieth century. Interview with Rosalie Taylor, June 17, 1988, by Katherine Howe. Taylor lived in the Fourth Ward from 1933.

59. *Tri-Weekly Telegraph*, Jan. 14, 1859, p. 2, col. 1; David G. McComb, *Houston: A History* (Austin: Univ. of Texas Press, 1981), 17. In 1871 the *Daily Telegraph* celebrated: "At last the Gaslight Company have received a quantity of coal, and last night the offices, counting rooms, and parlors of the city were treated to brilliant light again," Oct. 17, 1871, p. 5, col. 2.

60. These goods were offered by J. S. & J. B. Sydnor of Houston, E. A. Metcalf of Hempstead, and William Clarke. *Tri-Weekly Telegraph*, Feb. 23, 1863, p. 2, col. 4, and p. 1, col. 4; and March 9, 1863, p. 2, col. 6. The fact that all three advertisements appeared within two weeks of one another after a long hiatus causes one to suspect that a blockade runner had recently arrived in Houston or Galveston or that the goods had arrived overland from Matamoros, Mexico.

61. By 1867 New Orleans merchants were again advertising in Houston city directories. One of them was Charles Raymond of 51 Royal Street, who ran a bilingual advertisement for "Furniture of Every Style . . . Meubles de tous Genres." W. A. Leonard, comp., *Houston City Directory for 1867–68* (Houston: Gray, Smallwood, 1867), xxiv.

62. J. L. Mott Iron Works stoves from New York were sold in Houston by T. J. Riley. *Daily Houston Telegraph*, July 29, 1870, p. 6, col. 4.

63. Ibid., May 24, 1870, p. 1, col. 4.

64. The parties celebrating the marriage of Bessie May Kirby and James Schuyler Stewart on November 14, 1906, are probably the most elaborate example of this custom. There was even a special supplement to the *Southern Industrial and Lumber Review* (Dec. 10, 1906) covering the festivities.

65. By the late nineteenth century, Houstonians purchased at least some of their oriental rugs locally. As early as 1893, Ameen Semaan, a Syrian-born peddler, traveled to Houston to sell oriental rugs. At the time of his death in 1920, Semaan was a well-regarded Houston dealer in rugs and fine linens. Telephone interview with Frances Semaan Wilkins, July 1, 1988. Mrs. Wilkins is Ameen Semaan's daughter. Judging by surviving photographs, Houstonians favored large Persian rugs or smaller Caucasian area ones. The rugs were new in the period and of commercial, not special order, quality. The author is grateful to Daniel Walker, chair of the Islamic Department of the Metropolitan Museum of Art, for these observations.

66. Charles Locke Eastlake, *Hints on Household Taste* (1st ed., London: Longmans, Green, 1868; 1st U.S. ed., Boston: J. R. Osgood, 1872).

67. The inventory of the John D. Andrews house at 410 Austin Street in 1882 revealed that each of its five bedrooms contained these items plus a wash bowl and pitcher, a soap stand and "slop set," curtains, carpets, and rugs. See "Doswell & Adams Commission Merchant," unpublished ledger and record book, TLHD/HMRC/HPL. According to the ledger, J. Temple Doswell was an Andrews relative who lived with them temporarily.

68. *Mooney & Morrison's Directory of the City of Houston for 1877–78* (Houston: Mooney & Morrison, 1877), 218.

69. Berkey and Gay Company was a major manufacturer of Renaissance Revival furniture, which it distributed throughout the United States. Early in the twentieth century Stickley Brothers Co., Charles P. Limbert Co., and Lifetime, all of Grand Rapids, made and distributed Arts and Crafts furniture nationally.

70. Interview with Mrs. William H. Carter, Jr., by Dorothy Knox Howe Houghton, Jan. 13, 1984. Fannie Simpson Carter Papers, JLC/HMRC/HPL.

71. Donald C. Peirce, "Mitchell and Rammelsberg, Cincinnati Furniture Manufacturers, 1847–1881," ed. Ian M. G. Quimby, *Winterthur Portfolio 13* (Chicago: Univ. of Chicago, 1979), 218. The author is grateful to Patrick Butler, formerly curator of the Harris County Heritage Society, for calling the McFaddin-Ward house furniture to her attention.

72. Ward, Dewey & Co. at 29 Main Street advertised Texas state penitentiary furniture, mattresses, safes, and so forth in *Directory of the City of Houston for 1873* (title page missing), 33.

73. *Houston Daily Telegram*, Aug. 16, 1878, p. 1, col. 1; Richard St. John, *Longhorn Artist Wenzel Friedrich* (Wichita, KS.: Wichita State Univ., 1982), 12 pp.

74. The J. C. Hutcheson, T. W. House, John Henry Kirby, and R. C. Duff houses all had fur area rugs on their floors. The author is grateful to Conn Trussell, manager of the Neiman-Marcus Galleria fur salon in Houston, for identifying these furs by species.

75. See Edward Dewson, "Department of the Interior: The Special Functions of the Entrance Hall," *Southern Architectural Review* 1, no. 2 (1910): 67.

76. Harold L. Platt, *City Building in the New South: The Growth of Public Services in Houston, Texas, 1830–1910* (Philadelphia: Temple Univ. Press, 1983), 91–94. In 1889 the Houston Electric Light and Power Company bid for the contract to light the city's market house and police station. Part of the bid included "the rent of Gas meters and for any Gas that might be used during the failure of Electric Lights to burn." G. R. Vaughan to The Mayor and Board of Aldermen, Aug. 12, 1889, George Feurmann City of Houston Collection, Special Collections, Univ. of Houston Libraries.

77. Food safes have not yet been documented in Harris County, but their use here is highly probable, since they were made in Fayette County by Texas Germans as early as 1843 and they were also used by rural blacks near New Iberia, Louisiana, as late as the 1920s. See Taylor and Warren, 258–71, and interview with Enola LeBlanc, April 2, 1988.

78. Mrs. J. Milton Howe owned a complete dinner service acquired in 1901 bearing this mark.

79. For examples see *The American Artisan: The*

Hardware Record 16, no. 3 (July 13, 1903): 11–26. F. A. Heitmann Papers, JLC/HMRC/HPL.

80. Two letters, each from J. B. Collins to Joe Rice, Sept. 4, 1902. The Rice house was designed by S. A. Oliver & Co. in 1902. D. A. Crawford bid $23,028.30 to build it, exclusive of plumbing and heating. Laura Rice Neff Papers, JLC/HMRC/HPL.

81. Interview by Katherine Howe with Rosalie Taylor, June 16, 1988.

82. In 1924 F. A. Heitmann, president of his family's F. W. Heitmann Company, wrote an indignant letter to the E. T. Burrows Company of Portland, Maine. It seems that Burrows had provided some inferior screens for Heitmann's new William Ward Watkin–designed house in Shadyside. Heitmann wrote: "When I look back thirty years ago when I placed the first order with you for screens in the City of Houston . . . I had great difficulty having them installed in my house [at 1116 Dallas] because screens were unknown, some people thot [sic] unnecessary, others thot [sic] it extravagance; I had more fun out of the screens putting them in than anything." F. A. Heitmann to E. T. Burrows Company, Aug. 1, 1924; F. A. Heitmann Papers, JLC/HMRC/HPL. By 1897 Sears, Roebuck and Company was advertising wire-screen cloth, window-screen frames, and screen doors, which were "no longer considered luxuries but one of the necessities of modern life" in their catalog. See *1897 Sears Roebuck Catalogue* (reprint New York: Chelsea House, 1976), items 1100 through 1111, n.p. Houston's attitude toward screens seems to have been fairly typical. They do not seem to have been in general use in New England and Louisiana until the late nineteenth century. As late as 1912, Charles F. Lottman, Myers-Spalti Manufacturing Company, and Franklin Mosquito Bar Company, all local concerns, advertised themselves as mosquito net frame manufacturers. Their bed equipment continued to provide protection from mosquitoes in lieu of screens (Morrison & Fourmy Directory Co., *Directory of the City of Houston 1912* [Houston: Morrison & Fourmy, 1912], 832). The author is grateful to Richard Nylander, curator of collections at the Society for the Preservation of New England Antiquities, Boston, and H. Parrott Bacot, director of The Anglo-American Museum, Baton Rouge, for their counsel on this topic.

83. Interview by Katherine Howe with Rosalie Taylor, June 17, 1988. In the 1930s, Taylor lived in a four-room shotgun-style house at 1520 Arthur Street in the Fourth Ward. She remembers her family going next door to her grandparents' home to sleep on pallets in the entrance hall on hot summer nights and visiting with neighbors in the morning as they were rolling up their pallets.

84. The well-regarded New York firm Pottier and Stymus conferred with Narcissa Worsham Willis (Mrs. Robert Short Willis) on the interior of her house on Broadway in Galveston. Likewise, in 1914–15 Elsie de Wolf, New York's most fashionable decorator of the period, helped Willis's niece, Magnolia Willis Sealy, update The Open Gates, her McKim Mead and White-designed house also on Broadway. The author is grateful to Bradley Brooks, curator of the Willis-Moody Mansion, for sharing his research on the mansion. See also Jane and Rebecca Pinckard, *Lest We Forget: The Open Gates* (Houston: privately printed, 1988), 49–53.

85. Morrison and Fourmy Directory Co., comps. *Directory of the City of Houston, 1905–1906* (Houston: Morrison and Fourmy, 1905), 56; ibid., 1892, 299; *Men of Texas: A Collection of Portraits* (Houston: *Houston Post*, 1903), 244.

86. *Pen and Sunlight Sketches of Greater Houston* (Houston: ca. 1912), 117.

87. [George W. Sheldon], *Artistic Houses*, 2 vols. (New York: 1883; reprinted New York: Benjamin Blom, 1971).

88. *Morrison and Fourmy's General Directory of the City of Houston for 1880–81* (Houston: W. H. Coyle, 1880), 290.

89. "The Furnishings for the Rice Hotel," *Progressive Houston* 4, no. 4 (Aug. 1912): [8].

90. Catherine Lynn, *Wallpaper in America: From the Seventeenth Century to World War I* (New York: Norton, 1980), 417–18.

91. Ibid., 441–43; *Artistic Houses*, 24–26. A newspaper article specified that the dining room of the T. W. House, Jr., house was papered in Lincrusta Walton. See "'Houston Society,' a description of T. W. House home at Louisiana and McKin-

ney on a block of ground," *Galveston News*, n. d., n. p., as recorded in a scrapbook, Ellen House Howze Papers, JLC/HMRC/HLP.

92. *Morrison and Fourmy's General Directory of the City of Houston for 1880–81* (Houston: W. H. Coyle, 1880), n.p.

93. *Houston Daily Post*, Oct. 15, 1895, p. 6, col. 6.

94. Buie Harwood, "Charles Martin Meister, Decorative Painter in Texas," *Journal of Interior Design Education and Research* 7 (Fall 1981): 38–46. See also Harwood, *Decorative Painting in Texas 1840–1940* (College Station: Texas A&M Univ. Press, forthcoming). The author is grateful to Sarah Brooks Eihlers for calling Meisler's work to her attention and to Buie Harwood for sharing her research.

95. Recollection of F. A. Heitmann's daughter, Blanche Heitmann Strange, to Dorothy Knox Howe Houghton.

96. Many Houston houses continued to lack basic utilities. In the Fourth Ward, which had large black and Italian populations, as late as 1929 "less than one-half of the residents had an indoor water supply and only 18.9 percent of those polled had access to indoor toilets," as quoted in Kenneth A. Breisch, National Register of Historic Places Nomination Form for Freedmen's Town Historic District, Houston, Texas, National Register Department, Texas Historical Commission, Austin, Texas, 1984. At least two Fourth Ward families continued to use slop sets at night as late as the 1930s. As owners of a shared water closet, which was in a detached building in the back yard, they found slop sets more convenient than leaving their homes at night.

97. Edith Wharton and Ogden Codman, Jr., *The Decoration of Houses* (1902 ed., reprinted New York: Norton, 1978).

98. Ibid., introd., 2, 26, 28–29, 43–46, 69–71.

99. According to newspaper accounts of the wedding, Bessie May's gifts were equally extravagant. The groom gave the bride "a large and beautiful diamond in the conventional Tiffany setting," and his parents gave her "a solid silver tea service made by Tiffany." Mr. and Mrs. Kirby gave their daughter "a great chest of silver containing 1,100 pieces of [Tiffany and Company?] chrysanthemum pattern."

Unidentified newspaper accounts taken from an unpublished scrapbook, n.p., Bess Kirby Tooke Black Papers, JLC/HMRC/HPL.

100. Thorstein Veblen, *The Theory of the Leisure Class* (1st ed. 1899, New York: Macmillan, 1917), 68–101.

101. *Houston Daily Post*, April 5, 1914, 87.

102. Rookwood tiles were specified in the plans for the Autry house; see specifications for the work and materials to be used in the erection and completion of a two-story frame residence building on Courtlandt Place Street, Houston, Texas. For Judge J. L. Autry in accordance with the accompanying plans and details made for same by Sanguinet & Staats, Architects, Fort Worth, Houston, and San Antonio, Texas. James L. Autry Papers, Series 2, Box 28, WRC/FL/RU. The Autry house was built at 5 Courtlandt Place in 1912.

CHAPTER 4

1. An Inventory of Debts, money, merchandise, and property real and personal at Harrisburg and neighborhood belonging to the Estate of John R. Harris, Dec'd. Oct. 2, 1829, Adele B. Looscan Papers, Barker Texas History Center, Univ. of Texas at Austin.

2. Carmine Stahl, interview with Dorothy Knox Howe Houghton, Feb. 10, 1989.

3. Native food plants included corn, squash, beans, sunflower seeds, pokeweed, sassafras (for tea), and smilax roots (for root beer). Mulberries, dewberries, blackberries, elderberries, mayhaws, persimmons (for pie, pudding, and beer), and cherries (both black and choke) were found in the prairies and woods. Pecan trees grew especially well in the stream bottoms. Land cranes, swans, ducks, geese, passenger pigeons, quail, prairie chickens, snipes, plovers, rabbits, squirrels, wild turkeys, deer, and even bears were hunted for food and later for sport. Carmine Stahl, interview with Dorothy Macdonald Crocker, July 18, 1987; John A. Klein, *To You . . . My Legacy of Love* (Houston: privately printed, 1969), 7, 76, 78.

4. Dr. Ferdinand Roemer, *Texas with Particular Reference to German Immigrants and the Physical Appearances of the Country*, trans. Oswald Mueller (San Antonio: Standard Printing, 1935), 55–56.

5. *Telegraph and Texas Register*, Jan. 29, 1845.

6. "J.C. Clopper's Journal and Book of Memoranda for 1828," *Quarterly of the Texas State Historical Association* 13, no. 1 (July 1909): 59; *From Virginia to Texas, 1835, Diary of Col. Wm. F. Gray* (Houston: Gray, Dillaye & Co., 1909), reprinted by Fletcher Young Publishing (Houston: 1965), 144, 147; *Telegraph and Texas Register*, Sept. 9, 1837. Large deposits of salt known as salt domes date back to prehistoric periods when southeast Texas was under the sea. In the twentieth century domes became identified with the location of oil, which tended to pool around them.

7. "The Republic of Porkdom," *Star of the Republic Museum Notes*, ed. Ellen N. Murry, Fall 1986, 1.

8. Ruby O. Owens, "Good Ole Days to Remember" (unpubl. ms., 1980), 167, Ruby Oates Owens Papers, JLC/HMRC/HPL.

9. Ellen Garwood, "Early Texas Inns: A Study in Social Relationships," *Southwestern Historical Quarterly* 60, no. 2 (Oct. 1956): 225; Carmine Stahl, conversation with Houghton, Feb. 15, 1990.

10. Patricia Brady Schmidt, ed., *Nelly Custis Lewis's Housekeeping Book* (New Orleans: The Historic New Orleans Collection, 1982), 18–22; *MacKenzie's Five Thousand Recipes in All the Useful and Domestic Arts . . .* (Philadelphia: James Kay, Jun., and Pittsburg: John J. Kay, 1830); T. Webster and Mrs. Parkes, *An Encyclopedia of Domestic Economy: Comprising Subjects Connected with the Interests of Every Individual*, ed. D. M. Reese (New York: Harper and Brothers, 1855).

11. Carmine Stahl, interview with Dorothy Macdonald Crocker, July 18, 1987; C. A. Warner, "Texas and the Oil Industry," *Southwestern Historical Quarterly* 50, no. 1 (July 1946): 2; Elsa Detering Lottman, interview with Juliana Williams Itz, Nov. 7 and 9, 1984; Sidney Morse, *Household Discoveries: An Encyclopedia of Practical Recipes and Processes* (New York: The Success Company,

1908 and 1909), 324–26; Garwood, "Early Texas Inns," 232, 241.

12. Ophia D. Smith, "A Trip to Texas in 1855," *Southwestern Historical Quarterly* 59, no. 1 (July 1955): 27.

13. "Reminiscences of Cornelius C. Cox," *Southwestern Historical Quarterly* 6, no. 2 (Oct. 1902): 127.

14. Carmine Stahl, interview with Dorothy Macdonald Crocker, July 18, 1987.

15. Betty J. Mills, *Calico Chronicle: Texas Women and Their Fashions, 1835–1910* (Lubbock: Texas Tech Press, 1985), 157–62.

16. The author is indebted to Dorothy Justman for sharing information gleaned while translating a portion of the Henry Franklin Fisher Papers, Barker Texas History Center, Univ. of Texas at Austin.

17. "An Inventory of Debts," Looscan Papers.

18. *Telegraph and Texas Register* and *Morning Star*, various advertisements beginning in May 1837.

19. Rosa von Roeder Kleberg, "Some of My Early Experiences in Texas," *Southwestern Historical Quarterly* 1, no. 4 (April 1898): 298.

20. Advertisement by William Scott, *Texas Gazette*, San Felipe, June 19, 1830. See also *Gustav Dresel's Houston Journal: Adventures in North America and Texas, 1837–1841*, ed. and trans. Max Freund (Austin: Univ. of Texas Press, 1954), 77.

21. "Zavala, Lorenzo de," *Handbook of Texas*, vol. 2.

22. *Diary of Col. Wm. F. Gray*, 145.

23. Andrew Forest Muir, ed., *Texas in 1837* (Austin: Univ. of Texas Press, 1958), 17.

24. Frank W. Johnson, *A History of Texas and Texans* (Chicago: American Historical Society, 1914), vol. 1, 149; "Bradburn, Juan Davis," *Handbook of Texas*, vol. 2; Stephen F. Austin to Charles G. Sayer, Feb. 6, 1832, *Southwestern Historical Quarterly* 63, no. 3 (Jan. 1960): 454; Inventory of the Estate of William Scott, Harris County Probate Records A 321, E 133. The author is indebted to Dr. Margaret S. Henson for sharing her research on William Scott.

25. *Diary of Col. Wm. F. Gray*, 144, 146–48;

"McCormick, Arthur," *Handbook of Texas*, vol. 2.

26. "Harrisburg, Texas," and "Harris, Jane Birdsall," *Handbook of Texas*, vol. 1; *Diary of Col. Wm. F. Gray*, 161–67.

27. *Gustav Dresel's Houston Journal*, 33.

28. Greater Houston Preservation Alliance, *Sixth Ward/Sabine Historic District: Revitalization Study* (Houston: 1986), 11–13, 116–20.

29. Private libraries, or book collections, were important to many early Harris County households. The office with built-in bookcases and a separate entrance from the outside in the Kellum-Noble house (1847) and the study in the Christ Church rectory (1857) are early examples of the library/home office. Also Virginia Waldo interview with Houghton, Jan. 29, 1974.

30. *Gustav Dresel's Houston Journal*, 32.

31. Edward A. Palmer to Dr. Reuben D. Palmer, June 22, 1848, Rosalie Sherman Cartwright Papers, JLC/HMRC/HPL.

32. *The Diary of Millie Gray, 1832–1840* (Houston: Fletcher Young Publishing, 1967), 93, 123.

33. Events such as the wedding dinner for two hundred guests celebrating the marriage of William Marsh Rice and Margaret Bremond in 1850 (*Daily Telegraph and Texas Register*, July 4, 1850) set a tone for functions at the hotel, which was maintained through the mid-twentieth century, when dining and dancing on the Rice roof was considered the ultimate evening entertainment.

34. *Gustav Dresel's Houston Journal*, 89.

35. *Tri-Weekly Telegraph*, Feb. 14, 1859.

36. *Daily Houston Telegraph*, March 17, 1870; *Houston Post*, May 15, 1949.

37. Charles Thompson, telephone conversation with Houghton, July 18, 1989.

38. *Morning Star*, Oct. 30, 1841.

39. Edward Stiff, *The Texas Emigrant* (Cincinnati: George Conclin, 1840), 85. Beauchamp hauled and sold water for 75 cents per thirty-gallon barrel.

40. Advertisement, *Houston City Directory*, 1866, xii.

41. Joseph C. Jones, Jr., *America's Ice Men: An Illustrative History of the U.S. Natural Ice Industry, 1665–1925* (Humble, TX: Jobeco Books, 1984), 92–123; Dewey D. Hill and Elliott R. Hughes, *Ice Harvesting in Early America* (New Hartford, NY: New Hartford Historical Society, 1977), 23–25.

42. *Morning Star*, July 20, 1841.

43. *Democratic Telegraph and Texas Register*, May 16, 1851.

44. *Morning Star*, May 4, 1840, April 21, 1842, and May 7, 1842. Although ice cream was popular in colonial America, the first ice cream parlor in the South, the Exchange Coffee House in New Orleans, did not open until 1808. It used ice harvested from the Ohio River. Ralph Selitzer, *The Dairy Industry in America* (A Publication of Dairy and Ice Cream Field, 1976), 27–31.

45. Adele B. Looscan, "Harris County, 1822–1845," *Southwestern Historical Quarterly* 18, no. 2 (Oct. 1914): 201. The number and length of advertisements for imported clothing and fancy foods found in the earlier newspapers and continuing (except during the Civil War) throughout the pre–World War I period indicate a sustained market. Printed calicoes direct from Liverpool and London; Italian silks for dresses; birdseye and Russia diaper (figured fabric for table linens and hand towels); Irish linens; women's bonnets and caps, richly trimmed; silk gloves and mitts; silk pocket and neck handkerchiefs; and French cashmere were among the many luxury items imported through New York and New Orleans by the early 1840s. Advertisements, *Morning Star*, Dec. 15, 1840; *Telegraph and Texas Register*, May 5, 1841, Aug. 31, 1842, April 17, 1844, Feb. 4, 1846, and Dec. 7, 1846.

46. *Telegraph and Texas Register*, Feb. 4, 1846.

47. During the Civil War, most trade was diverted through Mexico to avoid the blockades. Thus, Hohenthal and Reichman advertised in 1862 "an elegant stock of imported goods just from France via Mexico. . . . The Ladies' shoes especially are the finest ever brought to this market." *Tri-Weekly Telegraph*, April 16, 1862.

48. Dr. Reuben D. Palmer to Edward A. Palmer, May 17, 1848, and June 19, 1848, Rosalie Sherman Cartwright Papers, JLC/HMRC/HPL; Andrew Briscoe to Mary Jane Harris Briscoe, April 26, 1849, private collection of Harris Milton Howe and Dorothy Knox Howe Houghton; Benjamin A. Shepherd, diary, Aug. 22, 23, and 24, 1881, July 31 and

Aug. 1, 1889, William A. Kirkland Papers, JLC/
HMRC/HPL.

49. C.L. Bethje to Wilhelm Quensell, Nov. 12,
1851, in E.E. Lackner, *From Tyranny to Texas: A
German Pioneers in Harris Co.* (San Antonio: Naylor, 1975), 33–34.

50. *Telegraph and Texas Register*, Oct. 15,
1845; *Democratic Telegraph and Texas Register*,
Feb. 15, 1849.

51. *Godey's Lady's Book* was advertised in the
Democratic Telegraph and Texas Register, Dec.
28, 1848, and June 14, 1849. The first mail order
catalogs were available throughout the United
States in the 1870s and were frequently advertised
in fashion magazines.

52. Mills, *Calico Chronicle*, 101.

53. Edward Albert Palmer to Reuben D. Palmer,
March 28, 1850, Rosalie Sherman Cartwright Papers, JLC/HMRC/HPL.

54. *Tri-Weekly Telegraph*, Jan. 1, 1858, and
Nov. 17, 1858.

55. Mills, *Calico Chronicle*, 83, 105.

56. E.B. Cushing, "Edward Hopkins Cushing: An
Appreciation by his Son," *Southwestern Historical
Quarterly* 25, no. 4 (April 1922): 267, 268.

57. Pearl Hendricks, "Houston By the
Bayou—100 Years Ago," 16, typescript, Pearl Hendricks Papers, Barker Texas History Center, Univ.
of Texas at Austin.

58. *Gustav Dresel's Houston Journal*, 141 n. 48;
Moritz Tiling, *History of the German Element in
Texas from 1820–1850 and Historical Sketches of
the German Texas Singers' League and Houston
Turnverein from 1853–1913* (Houston: 1913), 49.

59. Tiling, *History of the German Element in
Texas*, 163; Theodore G. Gish, "The Germans in
Houston," *Washington Cemetery Centennial Book*,
comp. Concerned Citizens for Washington Cemetery Care, Inc. (Houston: 1988), 9, 10.

60. *Telegraph and Texas Register*, May 29, 1844,
June 5 and 12, 1844, April 30, 1845, and May 7,
1845; *Democratic Telegraph and Texas Register*,
May 6, 1846, and Feb. 22, 1847.

61. *Tri-Weekly Telegraph*, May 30, 1862, and
April 4, 1862.

62. Invitation handbill, Special Collections, HPL;

Tri-Weekly Telegraph, Dec. 8, 1862, and Jan. 2,
1863.

63. "School at Harrisburg in 1854," unsigned article probably written by Adele Briscoe Looscan,
Adele B. Looscan Papers, HMRC/HPL; Klein, *Legacy of Love*, 10.

64. *Democratic Telegraph and Texas Register*,
Nov. 2, 1848. "School Notice," in *Telegraph and
Texas Register*, May 1, 1844, says: "board can be
had in highly respectable families in the city, at $10
per month—produce or other articles will be taken
in payment."

65. Adele Briscoe Looscan, "In Memorium" of
John Angier, unpubl., Adele Briscoe Looscan Papers, HMRC/HPL.

66. *Tri-Weekly Telegraph*, Sept. 15, 1862.

67. *Report of Harris County Schools for the
Year Ending August 31, 1914*, 6–11, Evelyn Matzke
Ramey Papers, JLC/HMRC/HPL.

68. Christ Church was built in 1847 on the half-
block bounded by Fannin, Texas, and San Jacinto.
The property was originally designated as the
School Reserve, and by 1840 the city operated a
two-story school building there known as the City
School. As Houston's first attempt at public education, the City School was short-lived, but the school
building remained on the property after the church
was built next to it. By 1846 the Rev. Charles Gillett, first rector of Christ Church, had opened the
first Houston Academy in the school building, but it
too was short-lived. Over the next sixty years other
schools advertised as "the Houston Academy" were
established. Principal among them was the one
financed by $20,000 in public subscriptions and
opened on the block bordered by Rusk, Capitol,
Caroline, and Austin on December 1, 1858, under
the direction of Dr. Ashbel Smith. The Houston
Academy for African American children promoted
by the Rev. Jack Yates existed from 1885 to 1921
(see fig. 262). From 1896 to 1921, Professor Christopher W. Welch operated a well-known private
school also called the Houston Academy (fig. 263).
Morning Star, Feb. 27, 1840; *Democratic Telegraph and Texas Register*, Sept. 2, 1846, and Feb.
10, 1848; *Weekly Telegraph*, Nov. 17, 1858.

69. *Catalogue of the Hartford Female Seminary*

1853–1854 (Hartford: Press of Case, Tiffany and Co., 1854). Blake was also listed in the catalog for 1856–57. Catalog information from Alexandra M. Schmidt, reference librarian, The Connecticut Historical Society.

70. William A. Kirkland, interview with Houghton and Francita Stuart Koelsch, ca. 1972. See also "Education in Houston," *Tri-Weekly Telegraph*, Feb. 4, 1857: "Almost always in the history of the city have parents been compelled to send their children abroad in order to secure for them an education sufficient to fit them for life."

71. "Ella Hutchins Sydnor," *The Gulf Messenger* 10, no. 1 (Jan. 1897): 32–33; Mrs. M. E. Bryan, "Belles and Beaux, Hostesses and Hosts of Other Days in Houston," *Houston Daily Post*, April 23, 1911; Marguerite Johnston, *A Happy Worldly Abode, Christ Church Cathedral, 1839/1964* (Houston: Cathedral Press, 1964), 94, 95, 107, 108.

72. William A. Kirkland, unpubl. memories of Woman's Choral Club and Treble Clef Club, William A. Kirkland Papers, JLC/HMRC/HPL; "Upward Step of Houston Symphony," *Musical America*, May 22, 1915, Cynthia Maddox Crane Papers, JLC/HMRC/HPL; Hubert Roussel, *The Houston Symphony Orchestra, 1913–1971* (Austin: Univ. of Texas Press, 1972), 14–22.

73. Richard Harrison Shryock, *The Development of Modern Medicine* (New York: Knopf, 1947), 273–303.

74. *Democratic Telegraph and Texas Register*, Aug. 3, 1848.

75. Ibid., Nov. 16, 1848.

76. Ibid., July 29, 1846, May 3, 1847, July 20, 1848, and July 12, 1849.

77. Christian Elias Quensell to Wilhelm Quensell, April 11, 1853, in Lackner, *From Tyranny to Texas*, 71.

78. Andrew Briscoe to Mary Jane Harris Briscoe, Aug. 6, 1847, private collection of Harris Milton Howe and Dorothy Knox Howe Houghton.

79. Margaret H. Foster, "Sour Lake," *The Gulf Messenger* 10, no. 5 (May 1897): 228–33.

80. Advertisement for Dr. Mud's Sour Lake Mineral Soap, Sour Lake Medical Company, Houston, Texas, in A.J. Peeler and Ingham S. Roberts, publishers, *The Standard Blue Book of Texas Who's Who? Edition De Luxe of Houston* (Houston: Who's Who Publishing, 1907), 154.

81. *Democratic Telegraph and Texas Register*, July 25, 1849; William Alexander MacCorkle, *The White Sulphur Springs* (New York: Neale Publishing, 1916), 395–407; "The White Sulphur Springs," *Harper's New Monthly Magazine* (Aug. 1878). Robert S. Conte, historian, The Greenbrier Museum and Archives, provided information about the West Virginia resort.

82. *Houston Post*, Aug. 14, 1913; George P. Red, *Medicine Man in Texas* (Houston: Standard Printing and Lithographing, 1930), 248–51, 255; "Houston Infirmary Sanitorium," *Souvenir Anniversary Edition, Houston Chronicle, Houston, Texas*, Oct. 1905, 91; information about Dr. Boyles from Frances Boyles Davis Wyllie Papers, JLC/HMRC/HPL.

83. Bettie Palmer Hutcheson to Joseph Chappell Hutcheson, Sept. 28, 1899, Betty Bosworth Neuhaus Papers, JLC/HMRC/HPL.

84. North Harris County Branch, American Association of University Women, *The Heritage of North Harris County* (Houston: 1977), 57–86.

85. The discussion of German domestic life is based on the author's conversations with Atha Dimon, Dorothy Justman, Lydia Kobs Peterson, Flora von Roeder, Ann Lindenmann, Ingeborg McCoy, Ann Schumacher Adkins, Blanche Heitmann Strange, Carolyn Frost Keenan, and Robert Renn, July 1989. See also Gish, *Washington Cemetery Centennial Book*, 3–15.

86. Atha Dimon, interview with Houghton, Sept. 9, 1985. For a listing of some other Harris County gun clubs, see *Houston City Directory, 1897–98*, 43.

87. Glen E. Lich, *The German Texans* (San Antonio: Univ. of Texas Institute of Texan Cultures, 1981), 174. See also pages 124–25, 159–66, 171–75, 180, 187.

88. Ann Lindenmann, "Houston Sängerbund," *Deutche Welt—U.S.A.*, Sept. 1986; Tiling, *History of the German Element in Texas*, 132, 153–59.

89. *Houston Scrapbooks: Homes, Hospitals, Hotels*, vol. 29, TLHD/HPL; Sidney Sherman Kendall Papers, JLC/HMRC/HPL.

90. Advertisement, *Telegraph and Texas Register*, Jan. 27, 1838.

91. Charles Thompson, telephone interview with Houghton, July 18, 1989.

92. Colleen McDannell, *The Christian Home in Victorian America, 1840–1900* (Bloomington: Indiana Univ. Press, 1986), 108–149.

93. Frances Trollope, *Domestic Manners of the Americans* (London: Century Publishing, 1984, orig. pub. 1839), 61–67; Catharine E. Beecher and Harriet Beecher Stowe, *The American Woman's Home or Principles of Domestic Science* (Hartford, CT: Stowe-Day Foundation, 1987, orig. pub. 1869), introduction, 4–5, 9–11; Rev. Charles Gillett, typescript of unpubl. journal, 1843–49, Christ Church Cathedral Papers, HMRC/HPL; Gish, *Washington Cemetery Centennial Book*, 13.

94. Documentation of slave life and culture in Harris County is found in several sources, including the Slave Censuses of 1850 and 1860. The Harris County Tax Records listed the owners' names, the number of slaves, and their total value for tax purposes. H. P. N. Gammel, comp., *The Laws of Texas, 1822–1897, Austin's Colonization Law and Contract . . .* , 10 vols. (Austin: The Gammel Co., 1898), and the Penal Code of the State of Texas include laws dealing specifically with slaves.

Houston City Council minutes and newspaper accounts of City Council proceedings record local ordinances. Harris County deed and probate records trace activities of free blacks in the county. *The Slave Narratives of Texas*, compiled by the Writers' Project of the W.P.A., is the best firsthand account of daily life under slavery in Texas. Unfortunately, few if any of the ex-slaves interviewed for this project were originally from Harris County. Private letters of slaveowners and letters and diaries of travelers who observed the institution of slavery provide insights found nowhere else.

Among the most important sources for the author's discussion of slave life are "An Act Concerning Slaves," *The Laws of Texas*, vol. 2, 345–46; "An Act to amend the sixth Section of an Act entitled 'An Act Concerning Slaves,' approved 5th February, 1840," *The Laws of Texas*, vol. 3, 870–72; "An Act prohibiting owners or employers of slaves from placing them in charge of farms or stock ranches, detached or removed from the home or place of residence of the owner or employer," *The Laws of Texas*, vol. 5, 484; Ronnie C. Tyler and Lawrence R. Murphy, *The Slave Narratives of Texas* (Austin: Encino Press, 1974), xxxiv-xxxvii, 19, 21, 22, 32–41, 70–79; and Kenneth M. Stampp, *The Peculiar Institution* (New York: Knopf, 1975), 59, 62, 63, 69, 71, 280, 290–91, 300–311, 337–40, 362–64.

95. Mrs. William H. Murray and Ellen Adele Sheldon, interview with Houghton and Francita Stuart Koelsch, April 3, 1974.

96. Andrew Forest Muir, "The Free Negro in Harris County, Texas," *Southwestern Historical Quarterly* 46, no. 3 (Jan. 1943): 214, 217–21, 227–35; Susan Jackson, "Slavery in Houston: The 1850's," *The Houston Review* 2, no. 2 (Summer 1980): 79, 82.

97. Virginia Meek Keenan, telephone conversation with Houghton, Aug. 25, 1986.

98. *Historical Pictoral: Souvenir Booklet, Texas Annual Conference, 200th Year History Methodist Church Bicentennial, 1784–1984*, courtesy of the United Mt. Vernon Methodist Church, Houston, Texas.

99. Thomas H. Kreneck, *Del Pueblo: A Pictorial History of Houston's Hispanic Community* (Houston: Houston International Univ., 1989), 28–30.

100. *Antioch Baptist Church Centennial: Houston, 1866–1966: 100 Years of Progress Spiritually, In Missionary Work, In Community Service* 1, Dr. Benjamin Jesse Covington Papers, HMRC/HPL.

101. *The Red Book of Houston: A Compendium of Social, Professional, Religious, Educational, and Industrial Interests of Houston's Colored Population* (Houston: Sotex Publishing, 1915), 108–111, 152–73.

102. *Historical Pictoral: Souvenir Booklet*. The author is indebted to Nia Dorian-Becnel and Patricia Smith Praether for sharing their oral history re-

search on Houston's African American community on which this discussion is based.

103. William A. Kirkland, *Old Bank—New Bank: The First National Bank, Houston, 1866–1956* (Houston: Pacesetter Press, 1975), 100–103.

104. "Pioneer Houston Builder Sees Unlimited Possibilities Ahead," *Houston Post Dispatch*, Feb. 9, 1930; "Cousins Club to Meet for 57th Year," unidentified newspaper clipping, 1946, Edna Earl Brazelton Woodard Taylor Papers, JLC/HMRC/HPL.

105. Ellen Robbins Red and Francita Stuart Koelsch, telephone conversations with Houghton, July 1989.

106. *Houston Post Dispatch*, Jan. 23, 1927; *Houston Post*, Aug. 27, 1886.

107. Susan Hillebrandt Santangelo, *Kinkaid and Houston: 75 Years* (Houston: Gulf Publishing, 1981), 13–16.

108. *Efforts of Jack Yates* (Houston: Texas Southern Univ. Press, 1985), 42, 44; Martha Whiting, telephone conversation with Houghton, Feb. 2, 1986; *Antioch Baptist Church Centennial*, 2.

109. Edwin A. Bonewitz, "To a Fellow Student of History," unpubl. comments, Dec. 31, 1964, Edwin A. Bonewitz Collection, HMRC/HPL.

110. McComb, *Houston: A History*, 55, 89–91.

11I. Ibid., 17.

112. *Houston Daily Telegraph*, Aug. 27, 1875.

113. Writers' Program of the Work Projects Administration in the State of Texas, comp., *Houston: A History and Guide* (Houston: Anson Jones Press, 1942), 226; McComb, *Houston: A History*, 30, 73–75, 88, 89, 95, 125; Lydia Kobs Peterson, telephone interview with Houghton, July 1989.

114. Advertisements, *Daily Houston Telegraph*, beginning Sept. 28, 1869. See also advertisements in the *Texas Almanac*, 1870–1914, Houston city directories, the 1896 *Blue Book*, and the 1907 *Blue Book*.

115. *Daily Houston Telegraph*, March 17, 1870. Three artificial ice companies were operating in San Antonio by 1867, and an ice manufacturing company opened in Waco in 1869. Census statistics on the total number of ice plants in the U.S. from 1869 to 1909 show Texas as having significantly more than any other state. By 1878 Messrs. Leigh, Hutchins and Company, members of the family that owned the Hutchins house, were also the sole proprietors of the Pictet system for the state of Texas. Presumably they were franchised distributors of the equipment and would have used it in their hotel. The Pictet system, patented in the U.S. in 1869, used the volatilization of anhydrous sulphurous oxide as the cooling principle. The system could be driven directly by a steam engine or by a belt from shafting powered by a waterwheel. *The Pictet Artificial Ice System*, pamphlet, Messrs. Leigh, Hutchins & Co., Houston, Texas, 1878, TLHD/HPL.

116. Although central heating was not enjoyed by American working-class families until after World War I, large coal- or oil-burning furnaces were installed routinely in waterproofed basements in upper-middle-class houses in Houston and elsewhere around 1900. Portland cement was manufactured by J. A. Courtney in the Fifth Ward by 1873. In 1916 the Texas Portland Cement Company began operation in Houston. *Houston Daily Telegraph*, May 15, 1873; McComb, *Houston: A History*, 81; Thomas J. Schlereth, "Conduct and Conduits: Home Utilities in Victorian America, 1876–1915," lecture, McFaddin-Ward house museum conference on "Life at Home, 1890–1930," Beaumont, Texas, Nov. 18, 1989.

117. Constance Evershade, diary, various entries 1885–1900, Marjorie S. Werlein Papers, JLC/HMRC/HPL. See also Ruth Schwartz Cowan, *More Work for Mother: The Ironies of Household Technology from the Open Hearth to the Microwave* (New York: Basic Books, 1983), 73–75, 77, 78, 99–101.

118. Witold Rybczynski, *Home: A Short History of an Idea* (New York: Penguin Books, 1987, orig. pub. 1986), 141; Catharine E. Beecher, *A Treatise on Domestic Economy For the Use of Young Ladies at Home and at School* (New York: Source Book Press, 1970, orig. pub. 1841), 308–311, 318–19; Elsa Detering Lottman, interview with Juliana Williams Itz, Sept. 10, 1986; Blanche Heitmann Strange, conversation with Houghton, June 5, 1989. The discussion of housecleaning is also taken from these sources and from Dorothy Howe Dupree, conversation with Houghton, Oct. 1987.

119. Rybczynski, *Home*, 141, 142, 149; Ladies' Association of the First Presbyterian Church, ed., *The Texas Cookbook: A Thorough Treatise on the Art of Cookery* (Houston: 1883); Catharine E. Beecher, *A Treatise on Domestic Economy*, 318, 319.

120. *The Texas Cookbook*, preface.

121. Ibid., 174–78, 185.

122. "City ordinance creating the office of City Scavenger and defining the duties thereof," 1878 or 1879, in the George Fuermann City of Houston Collection, Special Collections, Univ. of Houston Libraries.

123. Dr. Ron Brown, conversation with Houghton, June 1988; Rybczynski, *Home*, 92, 128–30; Ann Leighton, *American Gardens of the Nineteenth Century* (Amherst: Univ. of Massachusetts Press, 1987), 98.

124. Blanche Heitmann Strange, interview with Houghton, June 5, 1989.

125. J.R. Wheat, publisher, *The Houston Blue Book: A Society Directory 1896* (Houston: Cumming and Sons, 1896), 143; *The Standard Blue Book of Texas Who's Who? Edition De Luxe of Houston* (Houston: Who's Who Publishing, 1907), 116.

126. 1896 *Blue Book*, introduction, vi. The publisher noted that Blue Books had "been copyrighted for San Antonio, Austin, Waco, and other cities," to be published when the necessary data were available.

127. Ibid., 140–42, and various advertisements.

128. Hubert Roussel, "Houston's Elegant Era," *Houston Press*, May 27 and 28, 1934, and June 1, 1934; Mrs. M. E. Bryan, "Belles and Beaux, Hostesses and Hosts of Other Days in Houston," *Houston Daily Post*, April 23, 1911. Bruce A. Olson, "The Houston Light Guards: A Case Study of the Texas Militia, 1873–1903" (M.A. Thesis, Univ. of Houston, 1985), 243.

129. Bruce A. Olson, "The Houston Light Guards: A Study of Houston's Post-Reconstruction Militia and its Membership, 1873–1903," *The Houston Review* 7, no. 3 (1985): 111–42; "The Houston Light Guard," *The Gulf Messenger* 8, no. 11 (Nov. 1895): 889–98; "Houston Light Guard Celebrates Its 70th Year of Military Service," *Art Gravure Magazine* in the *Houston Chronicle*, April 25, 1943.

130. William Bledsoe Philpott, ed., *The Sponsor Souvenir Album and History of the United Confederate Veterans Reunion, 1895* (Houston: Sponsor Souvenir Company, 1895), 14, 23–30.

131. Unidentified newspaper clipping, ca. 1901, Dickson Papers, JLC/HMRC/HPL.

132. Unidentified newspaper clipping, Nov. 1906, George F. Horton Papers, JLC/HMRC/HPL.

133. Norman Lewis and John Morrow, Sr., interview with Houghton, April 17, 1986; Juliana Williams Itz Papers, JLC/HMRC/HPL; Edward E. Williams, "A Fourth of July in Spring," *Texas Magazine* in the *Houston Chronicle*, July 3, 1988, 7; Dorothy Howe Dupree, interview with Houghton, June 1988; Mrs. J. C. Hutcheson to Rosalie Hutcheson, Nov. 20, 1908, Betty Bosworth Neuhaus Papers, JLC/HMRC/HPL; Martha V. Pike and Janice Gray Armstrong, *A Time to Mourn: Expressions of Grief in Nineteenth Century America* (Stony Brook, NY: The Museums at Stony Brook, 1980), 91–105; Patricia Smith Praether, interview with Houghton, July 24, 1987; *Houston City Directory 1867–1868*, 126; funeral notices in pre-1915 Houston newspapers.

When funeral homes began building chapels in conjunction with their facilities during the 1920s, the tradition of home funerals began to wane. The turning point was 1928, when Settegast-Kopf held 90 funerals in private homes, 85 in their funeral chapel, and 38 in churches. After that year, the number of funerals in their chapel exceeded those in homes and continued to increase over the years. Of course, some funerals were held in churches, but statistically those were in the minority. "History and Trend of Livery Stables and Funeral Homes in Houston, 1890–1956," unpubl. statistics, courtesy of Norman Lewis and John Morrow, Sr.

134. Paul G. Taylor, "Rivalry With Z.Z. Organization in Entertainment of Bygone Debs Evoked Magnificent Affairs," *Houston Post*, Oct. 25, 1938; Roussel, "Houston's Elegant Era."

135. 1907 *Blue Book*, iii.

136. No-Tsu-Oh grew out of the Fruit, Flower and Vegetable Show, which began in 1895 or 1896 to

promote Harris County's leadership in agriculture and horticulture. After about three years, a greater variety of entertainment was needed to attract visitors and focus attention on the event. Thus, the No-Tsu-Oh Carnival Association was organized. 1907 *Blue Book*, 63–68; Clarence C. Coyle, "His Majesty, King Nottoc," *The Texas Magazine* 7, no. 1 (Nov. 1912): 51–54; *Progressive Houston*, Carnival Editions, Nov. 1909, 1910, 1911, and 1912; *Houston Daily Post*, Nov. 8, 1914.

137. *Houston Chronicle*, Nov. 16, 1913; *Houston Daily Post*, Nov. 16, 1913; ibid., Dec. 3 and 4, 1909; ibid., Dec. 10, 1911; John E. T. Milsaps, unpubl. diary, Nov. 15, 1910, John Milsaps Collection, HMRC/HPL.

138. *The Red Book of Houston*.

139. Anne Firor Scott, *The Southern Lady: From Pedestal to Politics, 1830–1930* (Chicago: Univ. of Chicago Press, 1970), 138, 144, 147–56; *Houston City Directory, 1897–98*, 50; "Chautauqua Movement," *Encyclopedia Americana*, 1956 ed. The Chautauqua Study Club of Houston was organized in October 1909, with Miss Ima Hogg as the first secretary. Jean Rainwater, conversation with Houghton, Jan. 22, 1989.

For most women in America, volunteer work in the community beyond the home began with church-related activities such as fairs held by Christ Church in the 1840s. Women sharpened their managerial and organizational skills while running family businesses when the men were away during the Civil War. The next step usually was involvement in the Women's Christian Temperance Union, founded in 1874, where many women gained their first experience in public speaking on a civic issue. The final step was the formation of women's study clubs. In Houston the last two steps were reversed. The Ladies Reading Club was organized in 1885. The Houston Branch of the WCTU was organized in 1894, by which time numerous women's clubs were actively involved in Houston's civic affairs.

140. The Ladies' Reading Club met weekly for the first seven years in the parlor of Adele Looscan's sister, Jessie Briscoe Howe, at 918 Austin Street (fig. 48). Mrs. Roland Ring, *Highlights of the History of the Ladies' Reading Club, 1885–1960* (Feb.

1983), 1–14, courtesy of Grace Kentner; Adele Briscoe Looscan, "Ladies' Reading Club of Houston, Texas," typed ms., printed in the *Houston Post* about 1904, Adele B. Looscan Collection, HMRC/HPL; "Excerpt from Address of Mrs. M. Looscan: Ladies' Reading Club Tenth Anniversary, 1895," unpubl. ms., Adele B. Looscan Collection, HMRC/HPL; *Houston Post*, April 21, 1936; unidentified newspaper clippings, Mrs. Roland Ring Papers, JLC/HMRC/HPL.

141. Clifford Edward Clark, Jr., *The American Family Home, 1800–1960* (Chapel Hill: Univ. of North Carolina Press, 1986), 156–62; Dolores Hayden, *The Grand Domestic Revolution: A History of Feminist Designs for American Homes, Neighborhoods and Cities* (Cambridge, MA: MIT Press, 1981), 186.

142. Ring, *Highlights*, 19–21; *Houston Post*, April 21, 1936.

143. One of the five original D.A.R. chapters in Texas, it is now the largest in the United States. It met in members' houses until recent years, when it became too large. *History of the Texas Society, National Society, Daughters of the American Revolution, Commemorating the Bi-Centennial Era in Texas, Nineteen Hundred Twenty-Nine Through Nineteen Hundred Seventy-Four* (Texas Society Daughters of the American Revolution, 1975), 118–20; Claire McElroy, telephone conversation with Houghton, June 27, 1988.

144. "Minutes of the First State Meeting of the Daughters of the Republic of Texas," Lampassas, Texas, April 20, 1892, 12–13.

145. Theater, opera, and ballet in Houston date back to 1838, when Henri Corri and John Carlos imported musical and dramatic productions from New Orleans and elsewhere. By 1840 the Houston Dramatic Association and the Thespian Society were holding amateur performances and donating the proceeds to charity. The Houston Literary, Musical and Dramatic Club (organized 1866) and the Pickwick Club (organized 1874) entertained Houstonians between visits from professional stars such as Jenny Lind, Lillie Langtry, Otis Skinner, Maurice Barrymore, Sarah Bernhardt, Ignace Paderewski, Lionel Barrymore, and Oscar Wilde. *Gustav Dre-*

sel's *Houston Journal*, 147; Middy Randerson, "Stage Struck," *Houston Post*, May 10, 1987; *Telegraph and Texas Register*, June 19, 1844; *Morning Star*, July 7, 1840; ibid., Jan. 28, 1843; *Houston City Directory 1867–68*, 123; *Houston City Directory 1877–78*, 45; *Houston City Directory 1880–81*, 48.

146. Wille Hutcheson, "Houston's Old Homesteads," *Houston Daily Post*, Aug. 27, 1911.

147. Arthur Saft, "Mrs. Godwin's Musical One of Rare Joy," unidentified newspaper, April 6, 1913, Lila Godwin Moore Papers, JLC/HMRC/HPL.

148. *Houston Daily Post*, Jan. 9, 1916.

149. Cynthia Maddox Crane Papers, JLC/HMRC/HPL.

150. *Houston Daily Post*, March 19, 1916.

151. Scrapbook entitled *Historical Records of Houston Public School Art League/Houston Art League, 1900–1924*, various entries, Museum of Fine Arts, Houston archives.

152. David H. Kaplan, "The Lady in the Green Room," *Performing Arts Magazine* (May 1980): 8; "Upward Step of Houston Symphony," *Musical America*, May 22, 1915. Preceding the Society for the Performing Arts, Saunders brought many famous artists to Houston, including the Ballet Russe de Monte Carlo for an annual engagement during Christmas week beginning in 1936. In 1955, when the Ballet Russe could no longer come, the Houstonians who for years had entertained the visiting dancers in their houses organized the Houston Ballet Foundation in the home of Mr. and Mrs. McClelland Wallace. Dorothy Knox Howe Houghton, "The Monte Carlo Connection and the Beginning of Houston Ballet," *Ballet Guild News* 5, no. 2 (Summer 1983).

153. This description is based on Houghton's memories of her childhood home at 1112 Elgin Avenue at San Jacinto Street, built ca. 1905 by the Rev. Wm. Hayne Leavell, bought ca. 1909 by the author's grandfather, Joseph Milton Howe, and demolished in 1959.

154. Southwest Center for Urban Research and the School of Architecture, Rice Univ., *Houston Architectural Survey* 2(Houston: 1980): 428; *Houston Post*, July 20, 1985; *Houston Daily Post*, March 11, 1906; Mary Alice Elgin, conversation with Houghton, June 12, 1987; Selitzer, *The Dairy Industry in America*, 235.

155. *Houston Daily Post*, Oct. 2, 1910; *Illustrated City Book of Houston Containing Annual Message of Ben Campbell, Mayor of the City of Houston, With Reports of All Departments of the City and An Analysis of the City By the Chamber of Commerce* (Houston: 1915), 57; *Southern Architectural Review* 1 (Sept. 1910): 29, 31, 33, 35; *Houston Daily Post*, Feb. 12, 1911.

156. *Houston Daily Post*, Feb. 12 and Oct. 1, 1911; *Houston Post*, May 28, 1950; *Houston Chronicle*, May 28, 1950; *Houston Post*, Sept. 3, 1961; *Houston Architectural Survey* 1:141.

157. Charlotte Perkins Gilman, Catharine Beecher's great-niece, advocated removing domestic work and child care from the home in her 1898 book, *Women and Economics*. Although her ideas were not generally accepted, they had an influence on apartment design. Hayden, *Domestic Revolution*, 183–85; *Southern Architectural Review* 1 (Sept. 1910): 31, 35.

158. *Houston City Directory, 1902–1903*, 25.

159. Advertisements, 1907 *Blue Book*, 136, 142; advertisements, Charles F. Morse, publisher, *The City of Houston and Harris County, Texas*, World's Columbian Exposition Souvenir (Houston: Post Engraving, 1893).

160. Blanche Heitmann Strange, conversation with Houghton, June 7, 1989; Robert Renn, conversation with Houghton, July 28, 1989. Marion Frost Keenan, conversation with Houghton, Aug. 1, 1990.

161. Blanche Heitmann Strange, conversation with Houghton, June 7, 1989.

162. Mary Alice Elgin, conversation with Houghton, June 12, 1987; "The Residence of J. C. Bering," *The Book of Houston* (Houston: Paget Printing, 1915), 63.

163. Advertisements, 1907 *Blue Book*, 145, 154.

164. *The Industrial Advantages of the City of Houston, Texas, and Environs* (Houston: Akehurst Publishing, 1894), 115.

165. Blanche Heitmann Strange, conversation with Houghton, June 7, 1989; Mary Alice Elgin, conversation with Houghton, June 12, 1987; Robert

Cummins Stuart, conversation with Francita Stuart Koelsch, 1976.

166. *Reservations, Restrictions and Covenants in River Oaks Addition*, 6, courtesy River Oaks Property Owners Association.

167. Advertisement, 1896 *Blue Book*, 120.

168. Unidentified newspaper clipping, Dickson Papers, JLC/HMRC/HPL.

169. Selitzer, *The Dairy Industry*, 241; William A. Kirkland, interview with Houghton, Sept. 29, 1983.

170. Unpublished letters of Sallie Sewall to Edward J. Sewall, June 1903–Sept. 1905, George F. Horton III Papers, JLC/HMRC/HPL. The Sewall correspondence is rare documentation of the itineraries, curricula, and daily life of the relatively large number of Houstonians traveling and studying abroad before World War I. During part of her stay, Sallie was accompanied by Houstonians Edith Paine, Ione Roberts, and Bettie Taliaferro. Another friend, Mary Kidd, was studying in Florence. The girls frequently met other Houstonians in their travels.

171. Bettie Palmer Hutcheson to Rosalie Hutcheson, April 29, 1907, and April 6, 1910, Betty Bosworth Neuhaus Papers, JLC/HMRC/HPL; *Houston Daily Post*, June 12, 1910.

172. *Houston City Directory, 1912*, 49.

173. *Houston City Directory, 1895–96*, 21; *Houston City Directory, 1897–98*, 8; Bernhardt Wall, "Texas Coast Resorts: I. La Porte, The City of Groves," *The Gulf Messenger* 8, no. 7 (July 1895): 854; Klein, *Legacy of Love*, 79; Charles Dow Milby, interview with Houghton, Oct. 27, 1986.

174. *Houston Daily Post*, Jan. 1, 1895; *La Porte Chronicle and Herald*, Sept. 28, 1911.

175. Gordon Black, "Sylvan Beach: Houston's Playground 1892–1943," *The Houston Review* 10, no. 1 (1988): 35–39; *Houston Daily Post*, Jan. 1, 1895; "First Moonlight Excursion to Sylvan Beach," advertising flyer, George Fuermann City of Houston Collection, Special Collections, Univ. of Houston Libraries; Wall, "Texas Coast Resorts." By 1895 the Houston newspapers reported the existence of four hotels and several boarding houses at La Porte. The elegant Sylvan Hotel (later the Sylvan Beach Hotel) opened in 1893 adjacent to the park. It was a large three-story structure with four-story cupolas on three corners. Galleries surrounded it on all sides and all floors. From the observatory, sixty feet above the ground, Galveston was clearly visible across the bay. Damaged by the 1900 hurricane, the hotel was purchased by the Catholic diocese in 1901 and converted to St. Mary's Seminary. Also in 1895, two blocks of lots were set aside on the south bluff of the shore at La Porte as the site for assembly buildings of the state Chautauqua Association, which apparently were never built.

176. Wall, "Texas Coast Resorts," 854.

177. Miramichi Guest Book, Edward A. Peden entry, July 15, 1912, Edward Andrew Peden Collection, WRC/RU/FL.

178. *La Porte Chronicle and Herald*, Sept. 28, 1911; Black, "Sylvan Beach: Houston's Playground 1892–1943."

179. Mrs. Roland Ring, Sr., unpubl. notes written in 1893, Mrs. Roland Ring, Sr., Papers, JLC/HMRC/HPL.

180. Gordon Wittenberg, "Morgan's Point: Once Bustling Bay Ridge Survives," *Cite* (Aug. 1982): 16.

181. "John Grant Tod, Jr.," and "Todville, Texas," *The Handbook of Texas*, vol. 3; James Glass, *A Replica Chart of the Galveston-Houston Area Circa 1836* (Houston: James Glass, 1986); Charles Dow Milby, interview with Houghton, Oct, 27, 1986.

182. "Seabrook, Texas," *The Handbook of Texas*, vol. 2.

183. John Henry Kirby to Judge Nelson Phillips, the Hon. S.B. Cooper, Jr., J.A. Mooney, Judge R.L. Batts, and the Hon. Louis J. Wortham, July 26, 1915, John Henry Kirby Papers, HMRC/HPL.

184. Miramichi Guest Book, Edward A. Peden entry, p. 43.

185. Charles Dow Milby, interview with Houghton, Oct. 27, 1986; Mary Alice Elgin, interview with Houghton, June 12, 1987.

186. Miramichi Guest Book, various entries.

187. Mrs. J. C. Hutcheson to Rosalie Hutcheson, July 3, 1911, Betty Bosworth Neuhaus Papers, JLC/HMRC/HPL.

188. Among them were the Hutchesons' retreat, Stonecliffe, on Signal Mountain at Albionview, near

Chattanooga, Tennessee; the Kirbys' house at Saranac Lake, New York; John M. Dorrance's house, The Willows, in Easton, Maryland; and Captain James Baker's house at Bass Rocks in Gloucester, Massachusetts. A few Houstonians traveled to those destinations by private railcar.

189. Jacinto City is located on another portion of the Oates tract. Ruby Oates Owens Papers, JLC/HMRC/HPL.

190. *Texas Family Land Heritage Registry* (Austin: Texas Dept. of Agriculture), vol. 2 (1975), vol. 4 (1977–78), vol. 6 (1980), vol. 8 (1982), and vol. 9 (1983).

List of Illustrations and Credits

1. S. D. and R. Wilson house, Rosenberg Library, Galveston, Texas
2. Buffalo Bayou at Magnolia Park, Estelle Garrow Perlitz Papers; JLC/HMRC/HPL
3. Log cabin,s33mudcat chimney, Marmion Scrapbook; TLHD/HPL
4. Log house, board and batten addition, Marmion Scrapbook; TLHD/HPL
5. J. Morgan plantation, Mr. and Mrs. James Lanier Britton, Jr., Papers; JLC/HMRC/HPL
6. A. Smith house, Baytown Historical Museum
7. F. R. Lubbock Ranch house, *Six Decades in Texas;* TLHD/HPL
8. J. B. Harris–J. G. Tod house, Rosa Tod Hamner Papers; JLC/HMRC/HPL
9. Jane B. Harris house, Collection of Harris Milton Howe and Dorothy Knox Howe Houghton
10. A. Briscoe house, Collection of Harris Milton Howe and Dorothy Knox Howe Houghton
11. Charlotte B. Allen house, George Fuermann City of Houston Collection; Special Collections, UH
12. E. Perkins house, Wood Map, 1869; TLHD/HPL
13. G. Allen plantation, Texas Memorial Museum, Austin, Texas

14. T. W. House, Sr., house, Ellen House Howze Papers; JLC/HMRC/HPL

15. W. J. Hutchins house, *Standard Blue Book*; TLHD/HPL

16. E. A. Palmer house, Edward C. Hutcheson Papers; JLC/HMRC/HPL

17. H. M. DeChaumes house, Mrs. Daniel Bayless Papers; JLC/HMRC/HPL

18. Houston street scene, 1856, William Rubey, Jr., Papers; JLC/HMRC/HPL

19. R. Lockart house, Collection of William H. Murray

20. C. Ennis house, Henrietta Cargill Adkins Papers; JLC/HMRC/HPL

21. E. Raphael house, *Houston as a Setting of the Jewel: The Rice Institute*; TLHD/HPL

22. Judge J. A. Baker house, Alice Baker Meyers Papers; JLC/HMRC/HPL

23. Houston street scene, 1860s; HMRC/HPL

24. H. Sampson house; HMRC/HPL

25. W. Powars house, front, Florence Powars Stancliff Papers; JLC/HMRC/HPL

26. W. Powars house, rear, Florence Powars Stancliff Papers; JLC/HMRC/HPL

27. S. E. Allen Ranch house, Francita Stuart Koelsch Papers; JLC/HMRC/HPL

28. E. Pillot house, *Art Work of Houston*, 1904; TLHD/HPL

29. Title page, *Affleck's Southern Rural Almanac, 1860,* New Year's Creek Settlers Association, 1986 reproduction

30. E. H. Cushing house, *Civics for Houston* (Oct. 1928, 15); TLHD/HPL

31. A. Whitaker house, Wood Map, 1869; TLHD/HPL

32. J. S. Lucas house, George Anna Lucas Burke Papers; JLC/HMRC/HPL

33. W. J. Settegast house, Marion Settegast Frost Keenan Papers; JLC/HMRC/HPL

34. Christ Church rectory, 1857, Christ Church Collection; HMRC/HPL

35. B. C. Simpson house (Youngs Avenue), Fannie Simpson Carter Papers; JLC/HMRC/HPL

36. B. C. Simpson house (Main Street), Fannie Simpson Carter Papers; JLC/HMRC/HPL

37. Swept yard, unidentified house, Richard C. Noble Papers, JLC/HMRC/HPL

38. J. M. Frost house, Vernon Frost Papers; JLC/HMRC/HPL

39. S. M. McAshan house, Edmund McAshan Dupree Papers and Mary McAshan Adams Papers; JLC/HMRC/HPL

40. W. D. Cleveland house, William A. Kirkland Papers; JLC/HMRC/HPL

41. T. W. House, Jr., house, *Houston Post* (3/1/1936); TLHD/HPL

42. J. T. D. Wilson house, Mrs. Alfred Neal Dargan Papers; JLC/HMRC/HPL

43. J. T. D. Wilson house, entrance, *Standard Blue Book*; TLHD/HPL

44. A. A. Van Alstyne–J. F. Dickson house, Exxon Corp.

45. C. S. House house, *Art Work of Houston*, 1894; TLHD/HPL

46. H. F. Smith house, *Art Work of Houston*, 1904; TLHD/HPL

47. E. A. Peden house, Cora Conner Spear Papers; JLC/HMRC/HPL

48. M. G. Howe house, Knox Briscoe Howe Papers; JLC/HMRC/HPL

49. A. P. Root house, Cora Conner Spear Papers; JLC/HMRC/HPL

50. J. C. Hutcheson house, Edward Chappell Hutcheson Papers; JLC/HMRC/HPL

51. J. P. Waldo house, *Art Work of Houston*, 1894; TLHD/HPL

52. Main Street scene, 1890s; HMRC/HPL

53. A. A. Van Alstyne–J. F. Dickson garden, Louise Dickson Adams Papers; JLC/HMRC/HPL

54. J. W. Johnson–O. W. Ross house, Ellen Burnett Ross Hail Papers; JLC/HMRC/HPL

55. T. H. Scanlan house, *Art Work of Houston*, 1894; TLHD/HPL

56. S. K. Dick–Capt. J. A. Baker house, *Art Work of Houston*, 1894; TLHD/HPL

57. A. Bergamini–S. P. Coughlin house, Carrie Bergamini Coughlin Papers; JLC/HMRC/HPL

58. G. A. Mistrot house, *Art Work of Houston*, 1904; TLHD/HPL

59. M. DeGeorge house, T. C. Guseman Papers; JLC/HMRC/HPL

60. T. D. Cobb house, *Standard Blue Book*; TLHD/HPL

61. H. W. Wood house, *Art Work of Houston*, 1894; TLHD/HPL

62. Cottage on Live Oak, photo by Barrie Scardino, 1985

63. Kutschbach Florist farm, Juliana Williams Itz Papers; JLC/HMRC/HPL

64. J. J. Atkinson garden, John F. Sullivan Papers; JLC/HMRC/HPL

65. T. W. House, Jr., house after 1890, Ellen House Howze Papers; JLC/HMRC/HPL

66. T. W. House, Jr., gardens, 1898, *Houston Post* 3/15/1936; TLHD/HPL

67. J. F. Crosby–J. Bute house, *Art Work of Houston*, 1894; TLHD/HPL

68. C. H. Milby house, Rosa Tod Hamner Papers; JLC/HMRC/HPL

69. Reed Singleton house, Aurelia Hart Thacker Papers; JLC/HMRC/HPL

70. Bird porch brackets, photo by Barrie Scardino, 1983

71. Shotgun houses, photo by Paul Hester, 1985

72. Annie L. Hagen house, *Red Book of Houston*; TLHD/HPL

73. H. M. Curtin house, Ruth Arbuckle Russell Papers; JLC/HMRC/HPL

74. Houston Heights, plat map; TLHD/HPL

75. Houston Heights, esplanade; TLHD/HPL

76. D. D. Cooley house, *Art Work of Houston*, 1894; TLHD/HPL

77. N. L. Mills house, *Art Work of Houston*, 1894; TLHD/HPL

78. Egge's cottage, *Palliser's Late Victorian Architecture*; FL/RU

79. J. M. Cotton house, Frank Lee Berry, Jr., Papers; JLC/HMRC/HPL

80. C. M. Lombardi house, *Art Work of Houston*, 1894; TLHD/HPL

81. C. Dillingham house, Charles Dillingham Papers; JLC/HMRC/HPL

82. W. H. Palmer house, Mrs. Louis Letzerich Papers; JLC/HMRC/HPL

83. L. M. Kaiser house, *Art Work of Houston*, 1904; TLHD/HPL

84. W. B. Chew house, *Art Work of Houston*, 1894; TLHD/HPL

85. L. B. Menefee house, *Art Work of Houston*, 1904; TLHD/HPL

86. J. M. Rockwell house, *Art Work of Houston*, 1904; TLHD/HPL

87. H. Waddell house, *Art Work of Houston*, 1904; TLHD/HPL

88. J. E. Lester house, Earl L. Lester, Sr., Papers; JLC/HMRC/HPL

89. S. F. Carter house, *Art Work of Houston*, 1904; TLHD/HPL

90. J. I. Campbell–M. T. Jones house, *Art Work of Houston*, 1904; TLHD/HPL

91. H. S. Fox house, *Art Work of Houston*, 1904; TLHD/HPL

92. A. M. Levy house, Leopold Meyer Collection; HMRC/HPL

93. Magnolia Park map (detail), Palmer Hutcheson, Jr., Papers; JLC/HMRC/HPL

94. J. T. Brady house, Lennie Estelle Hunt Papers; JLC/HMRC/HPL

95. City Park (Sam Houston Park); HMRC/HPL

96. Bay Ridge gazebo, Harry S. Filson Papers; JLC/HMRC/HPL

97. J. T. Scott bay house, Martha Scott Moore Papers; JLC/HMRC/HPL

98. H. S. Filson bay house, Harry S. Filson Papers; JLC/HMRC/HPL

99. Courtlandt Place gates, *The City Book of Houston*, 1915; TLHD/HPL

100. J. W. Link–T. P. Lee house, *Houston as a Setting of the Jewel: The Rice Institute*; TLHD/HPL

101. Magnolia Park Addition; HMRC/HPL

102. Park Place advertisement, James L. Autry Papers; WRC/FL/RU

103. Houston street scene, ca. 1910, Edna Earl Brazelton Taylor Papers and August Charles Bering III Papers; JLC/HMRC/HPL

104. W. E. Miller house, *Red Book of Houston*; TLHD/HPL

105. B. J. Covington house, *Red Book of Houston*; TLHD/HPL

106. The Rossonian, A. C. Finn Collection; Architectural Component, HMRC/HPL

107. J. S. Rice house, Laura Rice Neff Papers; JLC/HMRC/HPL

108. E. R. Richardson house, *Art Work of Houston*, 1904; TLHD/HPL

109. W. R. Nash house, photo by Paul Hester, 1980, for *Houston Architectural Survey*

110. T. L. Hackney–J. J. Sweeney house, Claude Hackney Papers, JLC/HMRC/HPL

111. Barber plan, *Modern Dwellings*; Architecture Library, UH

112. Sanborn map, shotgun row, Sanborn Insurance Maps, vol. 1, 8; TLHD/HPL

113. Sanborn map, Main Street, Sanborn Insurance Maps, vol. 1, 55; TLHD/HPL

114. A. T. Lucas house, George Anna Lucas Burke Papers; JLC/HMRC/HPL

115. L. C. Luckel house, *Art Work of Houston*, 1904; TLHD/HPL

116. W. A. Cooke bungalow, photo by Paul Hester, 1988

117. W. S. Wall house, HCHS

118. J. H. Kirby house and gardens, Bess Kirby Tooke Black Papers; JLC/HMRC/HPL

119. J. H. Kirby side garden, Bess Kirby Tooke Black Papers; JLC/HMRC/HPL

120. J. H. Kirby fountain and lily pond, Bess Kirby Tooke Black Papers; JLC/HMRC/HPL

121. J. H. Kirby pergola, Bess Kirby Tooke Black Papers; JLC/HMRC/HPL

122. J. H. Kirby greenhouse, Bess Kirby Tooke Black Papers; JLC/HMRC/HPL

123. J. H. Kirby natatorium, Bess Kirby Tooke Black Papers; JLC/HMRC/HPL

124. J. H. Kirby house, Mirror Lake, Bess Kirby Tooke Black Papers; JLC/HMRC/HPL

125. R. C. Duff house, Cynthia Maddox Crane Papers; JLC/HMRC/HPL

126. R. C. Duff garden, Cynthia Maddox Crane Papers; JLC/HMRC/HPL

127. R. C. Duff Psyche garden, Cynthia Maddox Crane Papers; JLC/HMRC/HPL

128. H. Masterson maze garden, Chaille Cage Thompson Papers; JLC/HMRC/HPL

129. H. Masterson gardens, Chaille Cage Thompson Papers; JLC/HMRC/HPL

130. E. L. Neville house, Mrs. Louis Letzerich Papers; JLC/HMRC/HPL

131. E. L. Neville house, first-floor plan, Courtlandt Place Papers; JLC/HMRC/HPL

132. E. L. Neville house, second-floor plan, Courtlandt Place Papers; JLC/HMRC/HPL

133. J. W. Garrow house, John Wanroy Garrow, Jr., Papers; JLC/HMRC/HPL

134. E. A. Peden lake house, Cora Conner Spear Papers; JLC/HMRC/HPL

135. E. A. Peden lake house, Cora Conner Spear Papers; JLC/HMRC/HPL

136. H. T. Staiti house and gardens, Litterest–Dixon Collection; HCHS

137. H. T. Staiti landscape plan, A. C. Finn Collection; Architectural Component, HMRC/HPL

138. H. T. Staiti garden, Litterest–Dixon Collection; HCHS

139. E. B. Parker–J. A. Baker house, *Houston as a Setting of the Jewel: The Rice Institute*; TLHD/HPL

140. E. B. Parker–J. A. Baker house, *Houston as a Setting of the Jewel: The Rice Institute*; TLHD/HPL

141. E. B. Parker–J. A. Baker house, *Houston as a Setting of the Jewel: The Rice Institute*; TLHD/HPL

142. W. B. Sharp house, entrance, Dudley Sharp Papers; JLC/HMRC/HPL

143. W. B. Sharp lawn, Dudley Sharp Papers; JLC/HMRC/HPL

144. W. B. Sharp garden, pittisporum, Dudley Sharp Papers; JLC/HMRC/HPL

145. W. B. Sharp porch, Dudley Sharp Papers; JLC/HMRC/HPL

190. B. M. Kirby bedroom, second view, Bess Kirby Tooke Black Papers; JLC/HMRC/HPL

191. J. H. Kirby bathroom, Bess Kirby Tooke Black Papers; JLC/HMRC/HPL

192. J. H. Kirby bathroom, Bess Kirby Tooke Black Papers; JLC/HMRC/HPL

193. W. B. Sharp dining room, Dudley Sharp Papers; JLC/HMRC/HPL

194. W. B. Sharp butler's pantry, Dudley Sharp Papers; JLC/HMRC/HPL

195. W. B. Sharp kitchen, Dudley Sharp Papers; JLC/HMRC/HPL

196. J. P. Carter house, *Southern Architectural Review;* TLHD/HPL

197. J. P. Carter hall, *Southern Architectural Review;* TLHD/HPL

198. J. P. Carter dining room, *Southern Architectural Review;* TLHD/HPL

199. R. C. Duff entrance hall, Cynthia Maddox Crane Papers; JLC/HMRC/HPL

200. Carter's Grove entrance hall, Colonial Williamsburg Foundation

201. R. C. Duff library, Cynthia Maddox Crane Papers; JLC/HMRC/HPL

202. F. E. Ward house, *Homes* 2, no. 9:7; TLHD/HPL

203. F. E. Ward living room, *Homes* 2, no. 9:7; TLHD/HPL

204. F. E. Ward den, *Homes* 2, no. 9:7; TLHD/HPL

205. G. G. Heyne house, *Homes* 2, no. 12:6; TLHD/HPL

206. G. G. Heyne kitchen, *Homes* 2, no. 12:7; TLHD/HPL

207. H. T. Staiti dining room, Leonore Averill Papers; JLC/HMRC/HPL

208. J. S. Boyles house, Frances Boyles Davis Wyllie Papers; JLC/HMRC/HPL

209. Christmas, 1912, Frances Boyles Davis Wyllie Papers; JLC/HMRC/HPL

210. G. W. Roff house, *Homes* 2, no. 11:7; TLHD/HPL

211. G. W. Roff bathroom, *Homes* 2, no. 11:7; TLHD/HPL

212. E. A. Peden front porch, Cora Conner Root Papers; JLC/HMRC/HPL

213. J. H. Kirby stables, Bess Kirby Tooke Black Papers; JLC/HMRC/HPL

214. A. T. Lucas house, second-floor porch, George Anna Lucas Burke Papers; JLC/HMRC/HPL

215. R. A. Giraud parlor, Giraud Family Papers; JLC/HMRC/HPL

216. J. H. Kirby billiard room, Bess Kirby Tooke Black Papers; JLC/HMRC/HPL

217. William Fulton house, Mary Alice Elgin Papers, JLC/HMRC/HPL

218. B. F. Weems house, Carrington Weems Papers; JLC/HMRC/HPL

219. P. K. Ewing house, J. Kittredge Vinson Papers: JLC/HMRC/HPL

220. Birthday party, front porch, J. Kittredge Vinson Papers, Jane Cochran Coleman Peck Papers, and Robert Renn Papers; JLC/HMRC/HPL

221. Birthday party, back yard, J. Kittredge Vinson Papers, Jane Cochran Coleman Peck Papers, and Robert Renn Papers; JLC/HMRC/HPL

222. S. Hutchins and Mary Root, Cora Conner Spear Papers; JLC/HMRC/HPL

223. J. H. Kirby ballroom, Bess Kirby Tooke Black Papers; JLC/HMRC/HPL

224. J. H. Kirby natatorium, Bess Kirby Tooke Black Papers; JLC/HMRC/HPL

225. Butchering hogs, Thornwell Kleb Papers; JLC/HMRC/HPL

226. Making sausage, Thornwell Kleb Papers; JLC/HMRC/HPL

227. O. J. F. Berry rolling dough, Frank Lee Berry, Jr., Papers; JLC/HMRC/HPL

228. O. J. F. Berry feeding chickens, Frank Lee Berry, Jr., Papers; JLC/HMRC/HPL

229. Auntie Jordan with cow, Frank Lee Berry, Jr., Papers; JLC/HMRC/HPL

230. Horse in fenced lot, Earl L. Lester, Sr., Papers; JLC/HMRC/HPL

231. Holsmith and Isensee Grocery, Gertrude Ackerly Papers; JLC/HMRC/HPL

232. Nick D'Amico Grocery, Lucy D'Amico Scardino Papers; JLC/HMRC/HPL

233. D. F. Stuart house, Daisy Sturgis Hendrickson Papers; JLC/HMRC/HPL

234. K. B. Howe on moving day, Knox Briscoe Howe Papers; JLC/HMRC/HPL

235. A. P. Root dining room, Cora Conner Spear Papers; JLC/HMRC/HPL

236. T. W. House, Jr., sitting room, Ellen House Howze Papers; JLC/HMRC/HPL

237. Mrs. Westheimer in sitting room, Jacolyn Alexander Papers; JLC/HMRC/HPL

238. Lucy Collins with babies, Ellen House Howze Papers; JLC/HMRC/HPL

239. Roberta Westcott, goat cart, Lynne Beach Reynaud Papers; JLC/HMRC/HPL

240. M. G. Hester in playhouse, Maud Gray Hester Norris Papers; JLC/HMRC/HPL

241. Christmas, 1911, Carrie Bergamini Coughlin Papers; JLC/HMRC/HPL

242. J. W. Link–T. P. Lee house, Thomas Peter Lee, Jr., Papers; JLC/HMRC/HPL

243. J. E. Lester back yard, Earl L. Lester, Sr., Papers; JLC/HMRC/HPL

244. Bismark Park natatorium, Elaine Finrock Roberts Papers; JLC/HMRC/HPL

245. Beatty's truck farm, Imogene Kennedy Plank Papers; JLC/HMRC/HPL

246. M. Floeck–C. S. Longcope house, George Fuermann City of Houston Collection; Special Collections, UH

247. H. F. Ring bay house, Mrs. Roland Ring., Sr., Papers; JLC/HMRC/HPL

248. R. D. Gribble bay house, Risdon D. Gribble Papers; JLC/HMRC/HPL

249. D. E. Kennedy bay house, Jeanne McElvouge Papers; JLC/HMRC/HPL

250. Children on stile at bay, Flora Streetman Lawhon Papers; JLC/HMRC/HPL

251. Horse-drawn lawnmower, Cora Conner Spear Papers; JLC/HMRC/HPL

252. J. G. Tod bay house, Charles Dow Milby Papers; JLC/IIMRC/HPL

253. Cora Root Peden crabbing at bay, Cora Conner Spear Papers; JLC/HMRC/HPL

254. W. G. Sears–H. E. Detering entry, Sears McGee Papers; JLC/HMRC/HPL

255. W. G. Sears–H. E. Detering parlor, Sears McGee Papers; JLC/HMRC/HPL

256. W. H. Palmer dining room, Mrs. Louis Letzerich Papers; JLC/HMRC/IIPL

257. Mrs. J. J. Atkinson, Easter lilies, John F. Sullivan Papers; JLC/HMRC/HPL

258. August Jantz house, wisteria, August Jantz Papers; JLC/HMRC/HPL

259. A. C. Bering, Sr., house, daisies, Jo Ann Bering Sellingsloh Papers and August Charles Bering III Papers; JLC/HMRC/HPL

260. S. K. McIlhenny house, Ray Watkin Hoagland Papers; JLC/HMRC/HPL

261. N. K. Kellum–Z. K. Noble house; HCHS

262. The Rev. Yates's Houston Academy, Rev. Jack Yates Family and Antioch Baptist Church Collection; HMRC/HPL

263. Prof. Welch's Houston Academy, William A. Kirkland Papers; JLC/HMRC/IIPL

264. Houston Golf Club, Peggy Golding Hamill Papers; JLC/HMRC/HPL

265. Clear Creek Fishing Club, William A. Kirkland Papers; JLC/HMRC/HPL

266. Greenwood Sanitarium, Dr. James Greenwood Papers; JLC/HMRC/HPL

267. Emma R. News Boys Home, Elaine Finrock Roberts Papers; JLC/HMRC/HPL

268. Baptism in Buffalo Bayou, George Fuermann City of Houston Collection; Special Collections, UH

269. Christ Church May Fete, Lila Godwin Moore Papers; JLC/HMRC/HPL

270. Christ Church rectory, 1902, *Art Work of Houston*, 1904; TLHD/HPL

271. King Nottoc, No-Tsu-Oh, 1907, Robert Renn Papers; JLC/HMRC/HPL

272. No-Tsu-Oh flower parade, 1915, Elaine Finrock Roberts Papers; JLC/HMRC/HPL

273. Decorated doll carriage, Jane Cochran Coleman Peck Papers; JLC/HMRC/HPL

274. M. Yates Jones and P. V. Yates in decorated carriage, Rev. Jack Yates and Antioch Baptist Church Collection; HMRC/HPL

275. G. M. Harris house, Red Bluff, Collection of Glenn Emile Seureau

Index

About the Authors

Dorothy Knox Howe Houghton is a descendant of Jane Birdsall and John Richardson Harris, the family for whom Harris County is named. She is a graduate of Bryn Mawr College and holds a Master's degree from the University of Texas at Austin. She is a member of the Junior League of Houston and is active in numerous other civic and cultural groups.

Barrie Scardino is an architectural historian and has written and lectured extensively on preservation and local history. She received a B.A. from Duke University and a Master's degree from the University of Southern California. In addition to belonging to the Junior League of Houston, she is active in professional and civic organizations and she owns Preservation Services, a consulting firm.

Sadie Gwin Blackburn, a descendant of Harvey H. Allen, brother of the Allen family that founded Houston, graduated from the University of Texas and received an M.A. from Rice University. Active for many years in a variety of Houston cultural and civic groups, including the Junior League, she was national president of the Garden Club of America from 1989 to 1991.

Katherine Howe is presently the Curator of Decorative Arts at The Museum of Fine Arts, Houston. She has published books and articles and has lectured on nineteenth-century American interiors, furniture, and silver. She is a graduate of Connecticut College and holds a Master's degree from the Cooperstown Program at SUNY, Oneonta. In addition to numerous professional societies, she belongs to the Junior League of Houston.

Margaret Henson earned a Ph.D. in history at the University of Houston and was an associate professor of history at the University of Houston, Clear Lake, until her retirement. She has published extensively on Texas history, and two of her books have won awards: *Samuel May Williams, Early Texas Entrepreneur* and *A Pictorial History of Chambers County*.